EACH STEP I TAKE

Visit Amazon.com for other Christian autobiographies.

Photo by Dean Eades.

ISBN: 1490949348
ISBN 13: 9781490949345

Library of Congress Cataloging-in-Publication Data
Each Step I Take / W. Elmo Mercer
ISBN: 1490949348

Printed in the United States of America.

"EACH STEP I TAKE"

THE AUTOBIOGRAPHY OF

W. ELMO MERCER

EACH STEP I TAKE

(W. Elmo Mercer)

Verse One

Each step I take my Savior goes before me, and with His loving hand He leads the way.

And with each breath I whisper "I adore Thee;" Oh, what joy to walk with Him each day!

CHORUS

Each step I take I know that He will guide me; to higher ground He ever leads me on.

Until someday the last step will be taken, each step I take just leads me closer home.

Verse Two

At times I feel my faith begin to waver, when up ahead I see a chasm wide;

It's then I turn and look up to my Savior: I am strong when He is by my side.

Verse Three

I trust in God no matter come what may, for life eternal is in His hand;

He holds the key that opens up the way that will lead me to the Promised Land.

DEDICATION

To my wife, Marcia

Who fills my daily life with her love,

And who became my favorite proofreader

Foreword

I have said to artists for years, "Much of our success in life comes from simply showing up. Be dependable. Day by day, week by week, year by year just keep showing up and doing what you do." And if ever there was a perfect example of this principle, it is Elmo Mercer.

Elmo has been a constant, faithful presence in the music publishing industry for as long as I can remember. He has been a cheerleader for so many artists, including Gloria and myself. He arranged many of our early songs for choirs and included them in numerous songbooks he published over the years. He had a special way of making our music accessible to church choirs who did not possess professional singers with a three-octave range. He kept them simple and singable.

Not only did he successfully arrange existing songs, he also wrote a number of his own songs. Those two very different skills – editing and writing – do not often go hand-in-hand, but Elmo has done both tasks equally well for decades.

People who have successful careers are not always as successful as fathers and husbands, but I am pleased to point out that Elmo has remained a devoted family man throughout his years in the music business. I commend and applaud him for keeping that balance.

I am glad this music industry veteran has seen fit to document his life through this book and I believe anyone who loves him and loves gospel music will find the story of his life to be as enjoyable, accessible and unpretentious as he is. I hope you will see from his story just how far consistency can take you in life.
Bill Gaither

Preface by WEM

I saw a video clip one time at a church that left a lasting impression on me.

The speaker drew about a 30% grade line across the blackboard and said, "This represents the plan and blessings God chose for your life. Ok, let's say for a time you were right on target...then you faltered. And even though you got back on track, you were now below where you **could** have been." Think about that for a while – happens to all of us, I guess.

That brings to mind another thought of my being led through heaven and I see a big door with my name on it. Upon asking God He told me that inside that room were all the blessings in life He had for me... but I never asked for them. The Bible says something like "we have not because we ask not." Oh, my!

My parents recognized my musical ability as God-given and helped develop it. Through the years along the way I was tempted with opportunities to use those gifts in more prominent and lucrative venues. I look back with gratitude to God for closing those doors while opening others for me. As I tell my story I try to do so as humbly as I can. I sincerely want any and all glory to go to my Lord and Savior Jesus Christ.

I do not understand God's patience with me, nor His forgiveness, mercy, love and grace. Yet He extends them to me on a daily basis. There are times in my life I wish I could remove from memory; there are other times I cherish and think about often. How I look forward to the glories of Heaven! And you know, each step I take just leads me closer home.

And so, I sat down and wrote about my earthly trip from Big Creek Community to my Heavenly Home. I hope I remembered correctly the things about which I wrote. If not, I apologize.

Anyway, I hope you enjoy reading about it.

W. Elmo Mercer

PART ONE
The Early Years in Louisiana

MY BIRTH DAY

A mocking bird, perched on the east side of the old dug well, turned her ear toward a piercing sound, one altogether new to her. It increased in volume and became quite frantic. This was certainly a sound she would never try to imitate! Enduring it for only a few moments longer she flew off beyond the woodpile.

That sound was, of course, **me**, having just arrived in the world! It was 6 a.m., February 15, 1932. It had been raining heavily all night. My Daddy had gotten there only a short time before, bringing with him a doctor by the name of Donaldson, who lived in Dry Prong four or five miles to the west. The doctor's car got stuck on the muddy road that linked Dry Prong with Pollock and they just left it and rushed on in Daddy's Model T, hoping they would get there before I did.

Little did I know that I made my debut in a troubled world, in Big Creek community of Grant Parish, LA. I was born in a three-room log house, set on solid pine blocks: the very same house my Daddy had been born in on December 24, 1896. "Aunt" Sarah Smith (no relation) had come to be with Mama.

Afterwards, for years she bragged that she pinned the first diaper on me. Years later, Mama's brother married her daughter.

Mama found out later that at the exact time I was born, one of her sisters passed away! And thus was my humble beginning. Not sure if I was planned, it being during the Great Depression, but I **know** I was loved.

DADDY'S FAMILY TREE

My family has been traced back twelve generations to Scotland. I am talking about MY Daddy, MY Grandpa, etc. I didn't just write to New York or Salt Lake City and get a history of the Mercer name. William, James and Joseph were passed down as men's names. For instance: my Daddy's Daddy was named William Eli; Daddy was named William Fred; I was named William Elmo. I am told Daddy and Mama named me Elmo after a dear friend, but the woods were full of guys named "Elmo" in north central Louisiana back then.

Two of my distant cousins are buried in Big Creek cemetery, having been killed in the Civil War. Marcia has two cousins buried in Vicksburg National Cemetery, also killed in the Civil War. At a church not far from our hometown of Winnfield, LA, there are a dozen graves in a straight line where Union soldiers are buried. One of my great (perhaps to the 4th power) grandpa's nephew, admittedly another limb on the family tree, founded Mercer University, now located in Macon, Georgia. Also another such "great", with the help of a second man, started the first Baptist church ever in the southeast part of Louisiana, known as the Florida parishes. Originally Florida extended to the Mississippi River!

Grandpa Eli Mercer married Annie Ward and they had thirteen children. Daddy said that every Monday morning "Grannie" would line them up and give them a dose of castor oil. I'm sure the school teacher appreciated that. Why didn't she do it on a Saturday? I was fourteen when Grannie passed away. Grandpa had died years before; I remember he had a big western-type handlebar mustache. I don't know their ages when they died.

Daddy and his siblings were playing around the house one day when he happened to find a wooden box. He couldn't get the thing open so he got the double-bit ax, saying "I WILL get you open if it kills me." And it almost did! The box exploded when the ax hit it. The ax went flying through the air, and Daddy dove under the house to the chimney foundation and stayed there for hours. Come to find out, it was a brand new box of gun powder! He never told us if he was disciplined for doing that.

I won't go into detail about all those Mercer children, but the youngest, named Moses became a Baptist preacher. When my brother, sister and I were growing up in Winnfield, Daddy did not have a car, so we really didn't know a lot of our aunts, uncles and cousins. Many of them stayed there in Grant Parish.

Daddy did have a Model T as I mentioned when I was born at Big Creek. Sometimes it was hard to start. If a man wasn't careful, the crank would jerk backwards when the motor started, and could break his arm. One time, I am told, Daddy was trying to crank the old car, when it suddenly started, lurched forward, knocking him down. It straddled him and chugged off down a stump-filled incline. He managed to catch up and corral the contraption. And if it wouldn't climb up a hill on the dirt road, you would let it roll back down, get out, pick the front end up and turn it around, then BACK up the hill. It usually worked every time.

MAMA'S FAMILY TREE

Mama was born July 22, 1900 as Lottie Bell Johnson, in the red clay, piney woods hills of Jackson Parish in north central Louisiana. Everyone called her "Johnnie". Her Daddy was John Daniel Morgan Johnson, and her Mama was a Stuart. Mama had three sisters and one brother, and two older half-sisters.

One of Mama's half-sisters was Aunt Delia (pronounced *Dee-ly*). She and her family lived in Jena, LA, about forty miles east of Winnfield. The whole family was very talented musically. One day we all sat on their front porch and listened to them play and sing. They had an upright bass, a guitar, a fiddle, and maybe more. Her other half-sister was Aunt Mary. She and her husband had no children and lived several places in north central Louisiana. Both Delia and Mary were quite a bit older than Mama. As a kid I went to see Aunt Allie, her names was Alabama. She and her husband had no children. She gave me a big slice of coconut cake, and I dropped it on the kitchen floor. Looking up at her I pleaded, "Can you wash it?"

For some reason Mama had to drop out of high school, but came back to finish in 1921 at Verda High School in Grant parish. Once she took me to a high school reunion (must have ridden with somebody), and she had me to play a selection on the piano for everyone. I think I played "The Yellow Rose of Texas", by ear I'm sure. Mama taught school for a couple of years. I don't know how she and Daddy met, but on October 25, 1924 they were married in the Methodist parsonage in Winnfield.

THE MERCER CHILDREN

Daddy was working in the shop of the Tremont and Gulf Railroad, located on the southeast side of Winnfield, the parish seat of Winn parish. They lived in a white frame house at the northwest corner of Pineville and Maple streets. I don't know when it was built, but it is still there, having been well maintained through the decades. Across the street from it was the "Long Mansion." Earl K. and Huey P. Long were raised there. The house has been gone for decades and a city park was built at that location, honoring Earl. A bigger-than-life-size bronze statue of him stands there. One night many years ago, Marcia and I (with Bill and Kellye asleep in the back seat) passed there about 2 o'clock in the morning, having left Nashville around 4 p.m. We were on our way to Mammaw and Pappaw Fletcher's house and it was raining. Someone had hoisted a big pasteboard box up over Earl's head, clearly visible under a light and through the raindrops.

My brother Earl was born September 7, 1925, and my sister Gertrude was born April 14, 1927 in the house I described above.

In July 1946, Ronnie made his entrance into our Mercer family. I'll explain that later.

LIVING IN BIG CREEK COMMUNITY

Well, Daddy got laid off from his job at the T&G Railroad in Winnfield as the depression worsened, and moved the family back to his old home place. He plowed the 40 acre cotton field with Princess, his horse. I guess we lived for a year off what he got for that cotton. He would pick up other work whenever he could find it. I think I remember we kids loving to slip off out in the field to the cotton house to play in it.

Naturally, I don't remember all that much about the place where we lived when I was born. My grandpa had built it probably in the 1870s. It was indeed a three-room log house thus qualifying me to run for governor of Louisiana. It set on about two feet high pine blocks. It had a narrow front porch on it with a railing about waist high. I'm told that Earl leaned out to look up at a star Gertrude was trying to show him, and flipped right over the railing. He saw stars alright.

Grandpa Mercer was known to be the best mud and stick chimney builder in those parts. He got red dirt and mixed in either horse hair or hog's hair, then added some water and put sticks in just the right places. The house collapsed decades later but that chimney still stood tall. On either side a platform was built on which firewood was stacked. There were no screens on the windows, just wood shutters. The logs for the house had been split and the smooth side turned inward, the round side outward. The mud and hair mixture was packed between them as insulation. The roof was made of long, split wooden boards.

Mama was known to have nightmares occasionally. She'd start out with a vibrato low moan, getting louder and more frantic. Daddy was awakened one night and for some reason he thought the house was on fire. He ran to the chimney, bent over and looked up. There happened to be a full moon positioned right over the opening in the chimney. A fire did break out in the kitchen one time but little damage was done.

We had coal oil lamps, but during the cold months would just let the fireplace provide light. We usually went to bed early. I do remember the fluffy feather beds. Mama would set a flat iron or bricks in front of the fireplace and heat them then wrap them in a cloth and place them under the covers at the foot of the beds. In warmer months we would have to sleep under mosquito nets. A pot was placed under the bed, if needed.

One day we kids were playing in the yard and spied a big black snake coiled around a limb on an oak tree just above our heads. Mama came out with a pistol and shot that sucker. Our yard was mostly dirt and fun to play in. We'd make roads for our stick cars and trucks. There was a big split-wood pile, probably some pine knots, too, outside our yard on the way down to the "Pluto Hole." Mama kept milk, butter, whatever, in the spring that was there, and I guess she didn't want me wandering off and falling in it. I never got a glimpse of ol' Pluto but I did believe in him, like I did Santa Claus.

Daddy was "big" on picket fences. He built them all over the place. Out back was the outhouse. They grew a dandy vegetable garden. We had a cow and some chickens, but I don't think we raised hogs. Grandpa had some goats like a lot of other folks did back then. Daddy's horse was black and shiny. He rode her to work when he could find it....anywhere.

The barn and lot were out in front of the house. When I was about a month old, a tornado (called cyclones back then) hit our place. It split the barn in half and the boards kept hitting the wood-shingled roof of our house. They said the log house was lifted up in front by the winds, but thank the good Lord it stayed together and set back down on the pine blocks, although several inches from where it had been. Daddy had the family huddled in the far corner, and for a moment Mama thought she had smothered me. It must have been a terrifying experience. Fences and trees were blown down. Mama had a turkey on a nest of eggs in a coop about fifteen feet from a Chinaberry tree. Winds tore that tree up and never ruffled the canvass over the coop. Neighbors as far as three miles away brought back some of our stuff.

Our house was a good quarter mile from a dirt road. I've told people I was born "nine miles from a dirt road." Earl would mount Princess from the front porch and Gertrude and I would walk with him to the mail box. One day coming back, a limb knocked him off and he couldn't mount up again, so the three of us trudged back home, with Earl leading Princess. It was funny to Gertrude and me, but Earl didn't laugh. In that area there had been some erosion; to me as a kid, the red and yellow "canyons" were huge. We enjoyed playing there also. Actually to us, the entire 40 acres seemed big but later as an adult it all looked rather small.

Remember, this is the place Grandpa built and started his family. Later they went across the ravine and built a larger plank house. I think I can remember walking from our place to theirs: down the hill into the wooded area, crossing the plank bridge over the branch (southern for little stream) that undoubtedly came from the Pluto spring, then up the hill to Granny and Grandpa's house.

A Billy goat that Grandpa had seemed to look forward to scaring the daylights out of us kids. He probably meant no harm and may have just wanted us to play with him. One day Gertrude went over there and came back with a newspaper (where Grandpa got it I don't know). The goat advanced menacingly but before he lowered his head, Gertrude rolled up the paper, shook it at him and read him his rights. Whenever he took another step toward her, she dropped the paper Mama had sent her for, and screamed all the way home: down the hill, over the branch and up the hill through a picket fence to safety!

Like other men in the community, Grandpa would slaughter certain livestock when the weather turned cold enough. Neighbors would even share. Someone had hogs because we had hams to hang in the smokehouse above a smoldering fire to "cure" it so we'd have meat during the winter. Earl and Gertrude told me when goats were slaughtered it looked and smelled awful. Goat meat is good when prepared right, I've been told.

In those days, livestock roamed free, picking up lots of ticks, etc. Once a year they would be rounded up and run through a dipping vat with some solution supposed to kill the critters. It was on the south side of the Dry Prong to Pollock dirt road, not far from where we lived. I remember going there when that was done.

The only church in the community was Big Creek Baptist, located just off the main road. There was a big cemetery behind it. Over the years many of my relatives have been buried there, including a first cousin's wife and newborn child. Mama said she would put me on a quilt with the other babies during the services. Two small creeks ran through the area. Of course one was called Big Creek, though it actually was not. The other was Dyson and it was so cold, year round. I am told that Mama took us three kids to one of those creeks for a cooling dip in a swimming hole one hot afternoon. We had just gotten out and started the long walk back home, when a big limb from a tree came crashing down...right where we had been! I guess the Angel of the Lord was holding that limb up, wishing we'd hurry up and get out.

Daddy would get to work sometimes for the CCC, Roosevelt's Civilian Conservation Corp, setting out pine seedlings. Forests are a *renewable* resource. He would ride Princess wherever there was work and sometimes would be gone a week or more. I remember one night we kids were playing on the floor by the front door, after dark, when a *store-bought* loaf of bread glided across to us. Daddy was home, and he brought real "light" bread. Those men were paid one dollar per day for their work, and this was in the mid-thirties. He would also try to raise a cotton crop.

Those years must have been awful to live through. It was said you could buy an acre of land or a 25-lb sack of flour for a *quarter*...but no one *had* a quarter. One day Daddy went to the smokehouse to get a piece of meat and it was all gone. He and Mama thought they knew who had taken it.

Bill and Lena Wallace lived further down the dirt road from our mail box. The road curved around and there was a trail from our house to theirs. Both of them were practically toothless, poor as a church mouse (or is it a computer mouse now days?). Ol' Bill could tell some tall tales. Sometimes he was known to outright lie. Case in point: One day the rural mail carrier came by and Bill began telling him to watch out, that he had seen a crazy man out in the woods. Well, the mail carrier, knowing Bill, said, "Why Bill, I reckon I just saw him, over near the Smith place." Bill swallowed hook, line and sinker and hollered, "(beep) Lena's gone over there a-viztin'!" He ran in the house, got his shotgun and headed over to bring Lena home safely.

I'm told our family was at Bill and Lena's house one day for a visit. Bill waited till Earl looked at him and emitted a toothless snarl, meaning to make him laugh. Instead Earl fainted, cold as a wedge. Out of one of the creeks (I hope it wasn't Dyson or Big Creek) Bill had somehow gotten a big, and I mean BIG, turtle. He actually stood on the turtle's back, and it walked with him on it.

Daddy somehow got hold of a battery-operated radio. It had a rounded top and sat on a table. We could not listen to it during the week, but on Saturday nights the neighbors would come over to listen to the Grand Ole Opry from Nashville, Tennessee. I had no idea, of course, that in less than twenty-five years I would be working across the street from that famous Ryman Auditorium, as music editor of one of the largest church and gospel music publishers and recording companies in the nation.

The same Dr. Donaldson that brought me into the world comes to mind once again. Back in those days diphtheria and other diseases were quite rampant. Mama and Daddy took me to him, in Dry Prong, to get a shot. To distract me, Mama said, "Oh, look out the window there at that pretty little pony, isn't he so cute?" POP! It's a wonder I hadn't grown up hating horses: instead Marcia and I later owned seven of them, plus 86 head of Black Angus cattle!

THE MOVE TO "TOWN"

News came that the T&G Railroad wanted Daddy to come back to work for them. That meant we would be moving to "town." I don't remember how we got there; we didn't have much to move. But for a while we lived in "the Nance house". I suppose a Mr. Nance owned it. It was a monstrous old wood structure on Tremont Street, near the railroad track.

We did not have any plumbing or electricity. I recall one of Daddy's sisters from Bossier City and her son, Jackie, came to visit. He was fortunate to possess a metal toy truck. It had headlights that were powered by a battery, and this was in 1937! We kids went off in a dark room and drove it around. I imagined I was told to just watch them! That was really neat and we had great fun...until the battery ran down.

I couldn't get over the fact that the road (street) ran right in front of the house, just outside the fence! Not a quarter mile away like down at Big Creek. We were located between two settlements of black people. To the east was the Red Quarters: all houses were painted red. To our west across South King Street was the T&G Quarters. The houses were set only about four feet apart and were called "shotgun" houses. They were built only one room wide and had a couple of other rooms behind that. It was said a person could stand in front of it and shoot a shotgun hitting everything in the house! Back then, we all played together: games like "Kick the can," "Hide and seek," or some such game.

This was in the 40s and it was not until 1954 that President Eisenhower and Congress instituted what was called desegregation. I remember in the early 50s I was in our post office and saw one of those black friends who was in the military. His Mama simply called him "Brother," so I said, "Hey, brother!"

Folks in the lobby were shocked as we shook hands. Across the street from where we lived was a little house that was not a part of the Red Quarters where a black family lived. They had a bunch of children older than me. We heard a lot of yelling one day and looked out to see a lanky boy up in a big Chinaberry tree, while his Mama threw old shoes up at him, calling him all kinds of names.

We ate a lot of cornbread, cooked in a round skillet. Mama set a freshly cooked pone on the pulled-down wood stove oven door. I was at the table and was trying to see how far I could lean backward, trying to balance on the two back legs of my chair. I went a little too far and fell over; the top of the chair glancing off the oven door with the cornbread sitting on it. That pone of cornbread popped up in the air, turned a flip and landed on the floor end-ways. It made a circle then plopped down. I think I blamed Gertrude, to no avail.

There were two empty lots between us and the Skains' house. One day Mama took me with her to visit Mrs. Skains. While they talked I played in the sand under (yet another) Chinaberry tree. I took about a six inch piece of one inch steel pipe that I found lying around to make my roads, then it miraculously became my truck. I took it with me when we left so I could play with it in our yard. Apparently I immediately began making roads in our front yard when Mama asked me where I got that piece of pipe. I told her at Mrs. Skains' house. She marched me back over there and made me apologize for stealing that object. Her wisdom worked! I don't recall stealing another thing.... well, maybe a grape in the grocery store.

THE NEW BARN

Somehow Daddy was able to purchase the four lots in the middle of the block between Tremont and King Streets. About halfway between he built a barn. Our family moved into that barn and lived there during the winter months of 1938. The feed room had a wood floor in it and somehow Earl and I got to sleep in a bed in there. The whole barn had a tin roof and we loved to lay in bed listening to it rain. The three stalls provided the other two bedrooms and kitchen. Green grass grew under the wood stove. Across the front of the barn was a walled-in hallway connecting it all. Later the siding was removed and it became a sheltered space for chickens and cows. The hens built nests up in the attic space. We got a dog but Daddy caught him climbing the ladder! He was an egg-suckin' dog. Daddy sent him on his way down the road.

One day a woman came to visit Mama and I wanted to impress her with my young talent by pretending to read a book. After she left Mama pointed out to me that I held the book upside down. Now why didn't I notice that? It was quite an experience living in that barn. Since then if someone yelled, "Close the door, were you born in a barn?" I could truthfully say, "No, but I used to live in one!" People can't believe that, but it was an experience I'm glad I had.

A LESSON LEARNED...WELL

I can't remember how old I was, but surely old enough to have known better. I got peeved at Mama about something, and in my frustration to reveal to her just how I felt, I blurted out, "You old...duck!" Whoa, that was a big mistake! Mama got a pasteboard box and set me down in it in the middle of the living room floor. She strutted and quacked in circles around me. That's all she did, but I guarantee you her point was made, and I never called her a duck again!

When I was six, we all walked several blocks to Aunt Allie's house. Uncle Wiley was a big tall man; I'm not sure what he did for a living. Earl, Gertrude and I were playing out in the yard, running here and there. I ran out of a shed just as the wind blew the door shut. There was a nail driven through the door near its edge about knee high to me and it hit me just above my left knee, causing a big gash. I was carried quickly to the doctor. He put seven stitches in my leg and the scar is still visible. So I was out of the running business for a while. Along about then I had to have my tonsils removed also.

MY FIRST DAY AT SCHOOL

Having been born February 15, 1932, I turned six years old in 1938, so I was six and a half before I even started to first grade in the fall. We had to walk to school, of course, and this incident stands out in my memory. We lived over a mile from the school. We were poor, but most people were back then. I lived on the right side of the tracks, though, because there *were* no houses on the other side.

Mama didn't want to take her three children up the busy US-167 (Lafayette Street) that had no sidewalks. She made the decision to walk up the T&G tracks! Well, there were no sidewalks there either. On our way that morning a big locomotive chugged down the track, headed straight for us. I made my own quick decision, forget the rest of the family. I jumped into the ditch that was filled with slimy, oily, green muck. My shoes and socks were never quite the same. As the train got about even with us, it let off a snort of steam. This was natural, I guess, although bad timing. Still, I bet the engineer had to suppress a laugh. He must not have known that my Daddy worked for that railroad, too!

The school building that awaited me was intimidating. It was old, and ugly too, made of red brick- probably built right after the Civil War! The basement was half underground where the boilers were, then three floors. And the auditorium was on top! Not many handicapped folks made it up there. The kids would go up there to eat their lunches. Mama put mine in a syrup bucket: likely a peanut butter sandwich. After eating, sometimes the Carpenter sisters would sing for us. I was not a blooming musician as yet....let me rephrase that: I had not yet begun to bloom as a musical-type person. I don't know how many grades were in that old building, so I don't remember where Earl and Gertrude were. There may have been two such buildings.

The janitor, to us kids at least, was frightening. He just looked mean. But not only were the boilers down there, so were the restrooms and the stench was awful! We would dare each other to run in one door and out the other side. It was scary. I don't remember any playground equipment but there must have been some. The teacher told us whenever we heard the bell to head for our classroom on the double. It was not all that inviting, either. We were having fun at recess one day when I heard the bell. Since I was already a model student (not), I dashed for the door on the east side. There was a terrace around that end of the building, head-high to me. As I rounded the corner, some kid who was lying in wait, stuck his leg out and tripped me. I made a perfect three-point landing, my nose taking the brunt of the fall. I never knew who did it and would like to think he meant to do that to some other kid and not me.

MY ELEMENTARY TEACHERS

My first grade teacher was Miss Edith Ann Long. She claimed to be kin to Earl and Huey, but all the Longs around there made that claim. There was no kindergarten back then, but I imagine Mama had made me acquainted with the alphabet and numbers: remember, she had been a school teacher. I don't have any outstanding recollections of my first grade, except when that kid tripped me.

Mrs. Lucille Dyess, a widow, was my second grade teacher. One of my best friends was Roy Jones. Our friendship has lasted through the decades and I'll have much more to say about him later. Around that time a troupe from the Grand Ole Opry came to town, put up a huge tent near "Uncle Earl's Pea Patch Farm" on the Horseshoe Road and announced show times. It was Roy Acuff, Minnie Pearl and Bill Monroe. We had listened to them on the radio and here they were in person... in Winnfield! I reckon we went to it.

My first girlfriend was Earlene Melton, a blonde. I don't know if I shared this with Mama or not, and yet she may have been the one who gave me two suckers. I shyly gave Earlene one. Not long after that, I dropped mine in the dirt then watched longingly as Earlene licked on hers. There used to be a very old man that stumbled along on one crutch on the street east of the school. He was balding and had a long, scraggly beard. People called him Major Boze, so he must have been an old soldier.

In the fall of 1940 when I started third grade, we moved into a fabulous (at the time) new yellowish-white two story brick building built just north of the old ones. And during that summer, *Colonel* Dwight D. Eisenhower had his "field office" for US Army maneuvers in OUR school. Apparently the U.S. government was starting to prepare for WWII. Plus, I believe I am correct in saying, (General) Patton and his tanks were also in those maneuvers. Camp Polk was located west of Alexandria.

Winnfield's population then might have been 4,000. Soldiers were supposed to "eat off the land" but the streets were filled with them. Mama saw an opportunity to give the boys a helping hand and also make some money. She had every chicken on the yard killed and made chicken salad sandwiches and wrapped them in napkins. Earl and I pedaled them up and down Lafayette Street in shoeboxes selling them for fifteen cents.

I cannot recall the name of my third grade teacher! In fourth grade, I had Miss Gertrude Payne. Years later she married a local man named Shorty Bowen. I don't remember much about that grade. In June I was reading my Sunday school lesson one Saturday morning. Everyone else in our family was saved except me. I came under conviction, told Earl and we walked the mile up to First Baptist Church. Bro. H. H. McBride was in his office! I knelt by a "straight chair" and prayed the sinner's prayer. I was nine years old and made public my profession of faith at First Baptist church the next morning. But I was not baptized until November. Then on December 7th the Japanese bombed Pearl Harbor and the U.S. entered the already-raging Second World War...not only in Europe, but now in the Pacific.

That year I somehow convinced Mama I needed cowboy boots, so we ordered them out of the Sears and Roebuck catalog. The day they arrived I tried them on...too small, Mama said. I braced myself against one door facing, put the new boot against the other one and struggled, but that didn't work. We had to return them. We must have gone to Milam's department store because I did get my cowboy boots.

SCHOOL DISCIPLINE

Miss Ruth Wood was my fifth grade teacher, and I loved her... even though she paddled me *twice* in about 15 **seconds**! First, I will tell you that my "new" girlfriend (I did not share suckers with her) was a pretty, brown-haired, brown-eyed girl named Johnette Allardyce! [Control yourself] I just knew we were meant for each other: I, too, had dark brown hair and brown eyes; we were the same height and weight and get this: we had the same birthday! Dear Lord, how many coincidences did I need to see the possibilities!

One day Miss Wood had to leave the room for a few minutes and instructed us to behave while she was gone. We waited perhaps ten seconds, then erupted into spitballs, shrieks, antics to impress the girls, etc. Upon her return, she assumed I was the instigator (guess I already had a reputation back then). To make a point, I became the example as I was called to the front of the room. She spanked my bottom with a paddle! I was appalled and embarrassed to know that Johnette had witnessed my disgrace. The wheels of my mind were spinning as I headed down the aisle to my seat at the back of the room. All eyes were on me. What could I possibly do to redeem myself, at least in Johnette's eyes – to heck with the rest of the kids. I recalled seeing Mama test her flat iron to see if it was hot by licking her fingers and smacking the iron. That's it!!!

So, making sure everyone saw me, I licked the inside of my right hand then slapped my bottom and went "Zssssttt". Miss Wood's eyes had apparently followed me as well. She called me back up for a *second* paddling! Drat it...horrors...egads! I meekly slinked back to my seat in total defeat and shame. And you know, I never knew what happened to Johnette. The family moved away soon after that. She probably decided she didn't want a jailbird for a boyfriend...shoot, she never really liked my cowboy boots anyhow.

My sixth grade teacher was Miss Goodman, fresh out of college, I reckon and she was pretty. Another sixth grade teacher was Miss Teddlie, who lived with her parents on Lafayette Street just east of the "overhead" bridge. Her father had both legs amputated and sat on the porch in a wheel chair. We'd always wave at each other when I passed by. The third sixth grade teacher was Miss Slack (why were they all called "Miss"?) and she was feared by most students. She walked with a stiff leg and was said to be tough and strict in class.

Miss Goodman lived on Center Street not far from where my friend Eddie Ray Brock lived. We rode our bikes to school together. One day we waited for her car to come down the street. We had our bikes parked with the kickstand holding them up. We waved at Miss Goodman, getting her attention, then broke and ran for our bikes, leaping astraddle of them like the cowboys in the movies got on their horses, then took off behind her to the school house. This acrobatic move did not help our grades, however.

It was in the sixth grade that some teacher on the playground one day noticed my fallen arches. I mean, my foot would suction to the ground (or floor) it was so flat. Mama and Daddy got me Dr. Scholls' steel arch supports with leather on top to wear in my shoes. Every few months I had to go to Milam's department store where Mr. Harper Terrill would put them in a vice, take a small hammer and beat them back up some more. I will have more to say about my flat feet later.

WASH POTS AND DOCTORS

We had a big black cast iron wash pot. Well water was poured in it to over half full, then a wood fire built under it. Monday was wash day, and a black woman named Georgie from the T&G Quarters came to do the job... for 50 cents! She would stand by the wash pot, enduring the heat, prodding the clothes with a long stick. Some of them needed to be rubbed on a wash board in a tub. After that they were placed in a tub of cold water to rinse them. They would be rung out then hung on the clothes lines for the sun to dry them.

One day Mama gave her a big "mess" of string-beans (green) out of the garden to take home. She said, "Laud, Mizrez Mercer, if'n I dies tonight, I'll be full o' beans! God bless you." This is the truth...she did die that night! Surely it was from some other cause. I remember we went over to her house several nights later to the wake to pay our respects. I guess Mama did the washing after that.

There were two doctors in town named Dr. Faith and Dr. Fittz. It was said "if you didn't have Faith you would get Fittz." Somehow I got what was called "proud flesh" in one of my big toes...I might have been 6 or 7. I could hardly walk much at all. Mama carried me on her back most of the way from our house to Dr. Faith's house on Center Street...after dark, about five blocks. (Or was it Dr. Fittz?)

In addition to Dr. Faith and Dr. Fittz, another medical doctor in town was Dr. John Moseley. He had a clinic on Abel Street one block north of the Bank of Winnfield. His nurse was Carrie McLeod, everyone loved her. In 1942 Marcia's brother, Leslie Bernard, was born there. Also Daddy was there for a while, after his accident at the T&G shop. He was standing on a short log, oiling places on a locomotive. At first they were powered by fires built with wood or pine knots that heated the water in the boiler to make steam which ran the engine. They later converted to coal, then oil. Anyway, the log he was standing on rolled and he fell backwards on the concrete floor on his tailbone. At our house a couple of days later he went into convulsions. I remember Mama kneeling by his bed, saying, "Please don't leave me and the kids!" At the clinic Dr. Moseley said Daddy actually died, and he and Carrie brought him back, an amazing accomplishment in the early 40s.

The General Hospital was founded by Dr. Moseley. Dr. George Rogers joined him. He later delivered our son Bill, 17 minutes till 11 p.m. December 31, 1957....he was a 77 minute income tax deduction! PTL! And prior to that, in the fall of 1957 while Marcia was being checked out in Dr. Rogers' office, I composed "The Way That He Loves" while sitting in the waiting room! Dr. Moseley lived on US-84 west of town and Dr. Rogers lived across Country Club road from him. "Mama Bell" Moseley (Dr. John's mother) lived on West Court street a block north of General Hospital. She was a faithful member of our church choir. A few years later on Dr. Roy Martin built a 2-story brick hospital on West Main Street that was operational several years.

OUR KING STREET NEIGHBORS

Just to the north of our house at 405 South King Street, lived a German family: Mr. and Mrs. Herman Pelz and their mentally challenged son Leon, perhaps in his 30s. Herman worked for the T&G. His wife became quite ill and stayed in bed most of the time. Leon wore overalls that were never buttoned on the side, the tail of his shirt usually sticking out, and only one strap over his shoulder. He would be working out in their garden, adjoining ours, hoeing and expel a loud amount of gas. He would exclaim, "(bleep) them beans!"

One day Mr. Horace Hicks, the T&G section "fo'man" who lived in a yellow house right by the tracks, was driving to town. He stopped and offered Leon a ride. Leon said, "No thank ye, Cap, I'm in a hurry!" Leon would walk to town two or three times a day, and we lived a mile from town center. Leon took a liking to my sister Gertrude. One day he called her out to the 5' white picket fence between our houses. He reached over to hand her an orange that he had apparently sucked on: it had a little hole in the top and was sunk in a bit here and there. He said, "Here, Missy, see if you can get any more 'good' outta this!"

When Leon's Mother died, Mama was asked by the neighbors to tell him. He flippantly said, "Well, somebody better call the avalanche!" Back then the ambulance and hearse was usually the same vehicle. Leon was sent off to the Louisiana Asylum in Pineville, located on US-167 across from Lake Beulow, just before you cross the O. K. Allen Bridge over Red River. When Herman died, our family went down to tell him (Daddy had bought a new 1956 Ford but I think we went in our car). We took him outdoors and sat at a picnic table. An orderly went with us because we didn't know how he might react. Mama said, "Leon, I've got some bad news to tell you. Your

Daddy has died." He just sat there a few seconds, then shook his head and looked out in space and said, "Now I wonder why that ol' man didn't tell me he was goin' to do that!"

Directly across from the Pelz house was where Mr. and Mrs. "Hawk" Shaw lived. Mama would take chickens she wanted killed to Mrs. Shaw, so she could prepare them for us to eat. She did not hesitate to wring their necks. After Hawk died, she married a German man named "Blackie" Jourdan. Now he was a character! Then after Mrs. Shaw died, Blackie married Mama's first cousin, a 72-year-old spinster! They lived in a red brick house on the southwest quadrant of Maple and Pineville streets, due south of the house Earl and Gertrude were born in. The Nazarene church had once stood there. Blackie lived to the ripe old age of 104, I was told. Years before he had bought a new Ford from the local dealership. In a day or two he discovered the extra tire was "a doughnut"...one of the small ones. He took it back up, opened the glass front door and yelled, "Hey, Buck! You know what you can do with this!" and rolled the tire toward him!

The Dawson family was next coming south down King Street. About the only thing I remember about them is that Mrs. Dawson had to hide the castor oil from her son, Sammy. He was about my age. I just cannot imagine that! I never really liked karo syrup! Mama gave us castor oil this way: Get a table spoon, fill it half full of cold, slimy castor oil then fill the other half with hot coffee! Gag! That's why I don't drink coffee today. Marcia doesn't drink it either, and then wonders why her day never gets started. But think of the money we've saved over the years! A few years ago I had to have a lower GI test done. The instructions called for two ounces of castor oil the night before coming for the test, and hopefully the way would be made clear for all concerned. Marcia couldn't find it in the stores. A druggist told her they had to keep it in the back where they worked – if they put it out on the shelves, people would steal it! Have mercy! Imagine being sent to jail for stealing castor oil!

The Clyde Jones family lived directly across from our house. They went to Laurel Heights Baptist church and I will talk more about it later. He delivered butane gas to rural locations. Next house was where Mr. and Mrs. Box lived. To our south, across from our playground, Mr. and Mrs. Charlie Taylor lived. I don't know what he did for a living, but he had a little dark brown jackass in his lot that would bray on the half hour. You could set your watch by him.

The block to our north toward Lafayette Street was not developed when I was a kid. A brush arbor was built and a revival held for several weeks. Out of that grew the First Pentecostal Church of Winnfield. On down the other side of the street was where Mr. and Mrs. Al Dowden lived. What a precious couple! When Marcia and I married, he gave us a typing desk and an end table he made for us. South King Street was dirt and every now and then a road machine would grade it. You could bet a gulley washer would occur afterwards and ditches would be washed in the road. We'd be walking to church and Daddy would say they ought to make the mayor come and lay down in those ditches to make the road smoother for cars to travel on (and he didn't even have a car then).

Do you remember the move (true story) about the Sullivan brothers, who during WWII were put on the SAME ship that was sunk and all five of them perished? Winnfield had the Harrell family…five brothers in the military during WWII. Thank the Lord they all came home safely. I remember going by the Harrell house and seeing the five stars displayed in the windows.

GROWING UP ON KING STREET

One Saturday while we lived on South King Street, a couple of young men came through the front gate of Daddy's hip-high picket fence. They wore white shirts and ties and carried satchels. Daddy answered their knock and they introduced themselves as "missionaries." Daddy listened for a few seconds, then said, "Good day!" (I wonder if Paul Harvey got that from Daddy) and shut the door. I peeped out the window and after they went out the gate, they shook the dust off their feet. That IS Biblical, right?

Daddy and Mama bought a big floor model radio. Two men brought it from the truck but as they came through the gate, one lost his grip and dropped it. Knobs flew everywhere. They put them back on and brought it in the house and assured us the set was fine. And I guess it was, for many years afterward.

Mama and Daddy set out some peach and plum trees. I don't remember Daddy ever spankin' me, but Mama used switches off those peach trees. I was appointed to go out and get them, and I learned quickly not to bring a puny one to her. She would switch me and if I cried she'd say, "Swallow it!" and I managed to hush so she would stop. It wasn't long till the orchard didn't look quite as good as it once did.

Earl got a little phonograph; it had a crank to wind it up, plus a "well" in which extra needles were kept. It played 78rpm vinyl records. The three of us kids would sit out on the grass in the orchard and listen and sing along with the likes of Jimmy Rogers, Bill Monroe, Roy Acuff, Elton Britt, Gene Autry, Tex Ritter, etc. We would also go down near the T&G tracks and cut long-stemmed cattails. We would soak them in kerosene (15 cents a gallon then), stick one in the ground and strike a match to it. They would burn at least 20 minutes, so we played in the side yard a many a night by cattail light.

I saw my first snow when I was in the second grade; actually it had a lot of freezing rain in it, too. I thought how utterly cool (pun intended) it would be to ride Earl's bike on that substance. NOT! I promptly slipped all over the place and after a few bad wrecks I gave up, hoping Earl didn't learn about my idea.

I liked to go crawfishing in the "bar pits" along the tracks connecting the T&G with the L&A (Louisiana and Arkansas, I guess). I would take a piece of fatback and attach it to a string. I'd cut me a stick by the pond, attach the string and I was in business. When I caught as many as I wanted, I'd carry them home in a "handle or foot tub". With a hammer I'd knock them in the head, cut off their meaty tails and peal them. Mama would fry them in a skillet. I'd eat them with a cold biscuit. Maybe I was a distant cousin to a Cajun after all!

Daddy went hunting for squirrels along the south side of the T&G tracks that went through the swamp of Port Lou and Dugdemona (more bayous than rivers). One track went to a lumber company in Rochelle, the other up to a paper mill in West Monroe. Daddy didn't have a dog that treed squirrels, so he took me sometimes...that didn't come out right, did it? We would get up long before daylight and walk down the railroad tracks. Usually it would be foggy and even chilly. Leaving the tracks we would slip quietly through the woods, swiping spider webs off our faces as dew dripped from the leaves down on us. We usually got our feet and pants legs wet, too. Daddy could hear squirrels chattering and most of the time we'd get a few. Mama would know how to prepare them, but I didn't like helping Daddy skin them.

Gertrude and I would team up when mowing the yard. All we had was a rotary blade push mower, and we would walk side by side. Now that I think of it, where was Earl? Daddy had erected his famous picket fences all over the property. They were topped at a 45 degree angle, then two backed up together. That looked nice, spaced an inch apart and painted white. The one in front was about hip high and set back from the dirt road called South King Street perhaps four feet. This required mowing both outside and inside the fence. The "front yard" extended across the two lots on King Street, the vacant one being our playground. A five foot picket fence separated the two. For some reason the fences were not put up between us and the Charlie Taylors to our south.

Daddy bought six pecan trees, about the size of what we called "bean poles." He spaced four across the two front lots, then one behind the house and another on the back of our playground. The two lots on Tremont Street served as the cow pasture and had no trees on it. He hired a black man name "Wash" to dig 4x4 holes to plant them in; I don't know how deep they were dug. Over time they grew to be huge trees bearing lots of pecans. The house has been gone a very long time, but the trees still stand tall.

Around Christmas-time one year, Mama took us kids "to town" just as it turned dark. Looking from the intersection of Pineville and East Main Street, there were lots of cars heading away from us and their red tail lights looked pretty. Mama exclaimed, "Oh, look at all those Christmas lights; aren't they pretty!" She was trying to make the long walk exciting. We kids looked at each other and thought, "Po' ol' Mama." I do remember that Winnfield put out decorations at Christmas-time that were unique and pretty.

Now, every meal at our house was serious business – no fun and games. You came to the table to eat. One night we kids got so tickled about something that Daddy told us to hush up and eat. Gertrude was to my left as we sat on a bench and Daddy was at the end of the table to my right. I couldn't hold it in any longer and cackled out. I mean lightning fast, Daddy backhanded me upside the head. The back of my head ricocheted off an upright 2x4, (the inside of the house had not been sealed), followed by a cry that sounded like my own. I don't remember if I got to finish my supper or not. I reckon Daddy had had a bad day at the shop.

As nice as our new four room house was at 405 South King Street, we still used a wood cook stove for a while. It was set crossways between two walls, thereby creating a triangular space behind it. That's where the #3 washtub was placed, so we three kids could take a bath, especially on a Saturday night. Water was heated in the reservoir on the side of the stove, then dipped and poured into the tub. Earl, then Gertrude got to go before I did. Mama was in a Shreveport hospital a hundred miles away for several days. Daddy was working at the T&G shop and trying to hold the family together till she got back home. Well, when my time came to hit the tub, I announced to him that I had no intentions of getting into that cold and soapy water. I'm sure his patience was about gone and he whopped me upside my head (again) and it bounced off the door facing. Oh, friends, I saw the most beautiful stars: all sizes and colors. I wondered if they were the same stars I had seen at the supper table. Anyhow, I dived into that tub!

The entire time we kids were growing up in Winnfield, Daddy didn't have a car. They would hire a Mr. Lee Bolton (who later married one of Mama's sisters) to drive us when and where we needed to go. I recall two such trips. One was made to Alexandria, 48 miles south of Winnfield, down US-167, then a gravel road. Now it is a divided 4-lane. We had three flats on the round trip. He would have to take the tire off the rim, put a "hot patch" on the inner tube then he would put the tire back on the rim and hand-pump it back up. It took all day to make the trip. The other trip was made to Winnsboro in the Louisiana Delta west of the Mississippi River where Mama's parents were buried in the Liddieville cemetery nearby. On that trip Lee's brakes failed! He had to downshift to finally come to a stop. The road was also gravel and dusty with narrow bridges, too.

One Sunday at Tullos Baptist church, 20 miles east on US-84, the choir loft and baptismal pool blew up, about ten minutes after the service. It was blamed on a gas leak. Tullos was surrounded by oil wells.

Earl "won" a bicycle by collecting "Blue Horse" labels from school supplies. I don't know how many he sent in. When I was in high school I managed to collect the unbelievable number of 3,300 labels, and sent them in. I won a bike, too! But who knows but what I might have won if I'd sent in only 800, or 900…?

Gertrude could never seem to get the hang of riding a bicycle. I imagine Earl would cringe (pray, maybe?) when she would try to ride it. She would take off in a straight line in our backyard and invariably head for yet another of Daddy's infamous picket fences. They separated the house and side playground from the garden, the chicken yard and the fruit orchard. Forget about riding *through* the gate. Her legs would shoot out sideways, followed by a scream, then the season-ending crash into said fence. I think she finally gave up her aspirations to win the bike riding event in the Olympics.

Sometime later, Daddy got enough money to seal the inside of the house, with vertical twelve inch "paneling" and in several pastel colors. Now that I think about it, it may have been Johns-Manville that was associated with causing cancer later. It was like shiplap: the sides would link together and were stapled to the studs with a staple *gun*...a new invention in those days. Daddy rented one from Harrell Builders Supply and all went well till the gun jammed. He was working with it, trying to solve the problem, and shot himself in the knee! Ouch!

Gertrude and I were playing in the side yard one day, and she lay down flat on her back on the grass. She pulled both knees up to her chin and told me to lean back on her shoes. Innocent like I was (then), I did. Immediately I was catapulted into the air, and landed flat on my back. It knocked the breath out of me. Mama appeared about then and wondered why I was writhing on the ground making unintelligible noises! Gertrude just shrugged, like, "Aw, you know how he acts sometimes, Mama!"

Mama and Daddy were not home one day so we three kids got to "horsin' around." Earl shook up a bottle of Ginger Ale and proceeded to chase Gertrude and me through the house, spraying us. He shook it again and for some ungodly reason stuck it in his mouth! Ginger Ale shot out both his nostrils like a mad horse. That scared all of us! Then the thought occurred to us – we needed to clean up all traces of our fun and games.

Along about that time our family went to New Orleans on the train! Apparently the various railroads would give passes to men who worked FOR a railroad. We rode the L&A passenger train called "The Flying Crow." This may be hard to believe, but there was NO railroad bridge across the Mississippi River. A big barge had rails on it and it took a couple of trips to get the train to the east side! Daddy hired a cab driver to show us around town. Daddy's big comment back then was to say, "Absolutely." Jackson Square and the buildings around it were fascinating, including the French Quarter. Another time Earl took me with him to New Orleans. He woke me up before daylight so I could look down out the window to see the men emptying the garbage bin. There wasn't anything in Big Creek community that even came close to that!

Our toilet was called a sanitary privy. A concrete "cube" was buried in the ground much like a septic tank of today. Between it and the chicken house was a big red cherry tree. They were about the size of marbles, and a bit tangy. It took two cups of sugar to make one pie! I always dreaded the first mouthful but after that I would eat my fill. It seemed the most luscious ones would grow in the top middle part of the tree, out of my reach from the ground. Being the promising young intelligent boy that I was, I lugged about a 2x12 board to the area that actually reached both roofs. Hey, where there's a will, there's a way, right? Somehow I got up on the roof of the chicken house and slowly made my way on all-fours out to the middle of that tree. I grinned, rubbed my hands together and said to those cherries, "I gotchu now!"

The Herman Pelz family on our north side had a tall mulberry tree in their yard. I would climb up in it and eat all I wanted. Behind the houses across the street from us was Albert Kemp's Stave Mill. {After Daddy left the railroad job he worked a while for Mr. Kemp. Then he was foreman for a team of men that cut the right-of-way for an electric transfer high line from Winnfield to somewhere in east Texas}. Anyhow, the Oak staves were stacked in squares about five feet high to dry out. There was a black cherry tree amongst all that. I liked to eat them because they gave me a "buzz." Sometimes I had trouble getting back home.

It was said that perhaps 80% of the jobs in Winn parish were derived from forest products. The Tremont Lumber Company later moved to East Winnfield, now called Joyce. (Hey, it used to be called Gorhamtown)! On the horseshoe road, past Uncle Earl Long's Pea Patch Farm north of town was the Thomas Lumber Company. On the south side of Winnfield was the Mansfield Lumber Company. Later a paneling plant was built in the southeast part of town along US-167. Out on the Atlanta road (LA-34) they built a Louisiana Forest Festival facility along with the fairgrounds. Uncle Earl's Hog Dog Trials is still held out there. The Winnfield High School general reunions are held there as well on the fourth weekend in June with well over 300 attending. We go regularly and look forward to seeing "old friends" again.

One hot summer afternoon the Mansfield Lumber Company caught fire. Gertrude and I sat on a stack of staves looking west a half mile and watched it burn. You should have seen the flames and smoke. The updrafts lifted pieces of tin roofing up into the air. Eventually the hot cinders reached us and we had to retreat from our "box" seats.

Mama and Daddy always had a vegetable garden, a fruit orchard, also a few chickens and one to four cows. Gertrude's and my job was to keep the calf away from the cow while Mama or Daddy milked. They were always frisky and would grind our toes into the ground or mud. Many times the calf would forget about "mama" for a little while and would run about in the lot, with the singular purpose of throwing us off his/ her tail. I was usually the one thrown off…maybe Gertrude tripped me? Mama even had poke sallet growing in rows in the garden, so we didn't have to go out in nearby pastures and search for it. It is said to be poison and must be parboiled: pour the first water off and boil again with fresh water. Some mix it with other greens. But Mama prepared it in a skillet with eggs and onions. It is tangy and I guess you have to create a liking for it. Ok, so it looked like something the cat threw up, but it was/is delicious!

We had a pretty good snow one winter and Mama's brother, Uncle Morgan, was visiting us. Blackbirds were everywhere. He and Daddy took an old door and propped it up with a stick and sprinkled some chops (corn) under it. A rope was attached to the stick that reached to the place where the two of them hid out of sight. When that area filled with blackbirds, the rope was yanked and the door fell and killed a bunch of them. Blackbird stew or pie was pretty good eatin' back in those days. Yet another snowy time I went with Daddy across the tracks where the oil storage bin for the T&G engines was. We could hear the hundreds of blackbirds chirping. Daddy shot his 12-gauge shotgun one time and we gathered over two dozen birds!

Our water came from a new drilled well, slightly uphill from the toilet. [You may find this hard to believe, but I remember our textbooks in school had a diagram showing that the well should be dug uphill from the toilet!] A cylindrical tin bucket was let down by a rope on a pulley, filled, then pulled back up. Gertrude was pulling it up one hot day and told Earl to look and see if it was nearing the top…it was, and busted him in the forehead. In the summertime we would draw enough water to half-fill a #3 washtub, then let the sun warm it; we would take our baths later in the day.

I rode my bike all over the place, and would go from home "to town" three or four times a day, a two-mile round trip. Mrs. Felix Mercer (he was Daddy's cousin) was a clerk at the post office. [Her daughter was named Patty. She married Jim Hutchens, a career army man who retired a general. They live in the D. C. area]. Some folks would order little chicks and when they came in the chirping could be heard a block away! I came out of the post office one day (I still remember our box number was 963). I noticed a lot of adults were standing around talking. My bike was parked by the waist-high hedge with the kick-stand down. I ran to the concrete abutment at the end of the multiple steps, yelling like a wild Indian, leaped over the hedge and landed astraddle of the bike, just like I'd done for Miss Goodman. Only thing, this didn't work as well. When my bottom hit the seat, the back tire blew out! People saw me alright and burst out laughing. I slunk away, pushing my disabled bike toward

405 South King Street, a mile away. That surely had not turned out the way I thought it would. Hollywood would just have to wait. Gene and Roy breathed a sigh of relief.

One day I got the bright idea that I wanted to smoke cigarettes. I rode my bike uptown to a store and selected a pack of Camels, or maybe Lucky Strikes. It cost 19 cents, and I don't know where I got the money! The clerk should not have sold it to me. I rode my bike past our house and across the T&G tracks to the west of US-167 where big logs were stock-piled. I sat on the ground by myself and leaned back on a big pine log and smoked me one. I'd hold my hand out to see the cigarette between my fingers. Man, I had arrived! I smoked SIX, one right behind the other! Then I headed home. Well, Daddy had told me to pick up cow piles in the pasture just about every day. I had made a two wheel cart with a five gallon bucket attached to it with a stick for a handle. I pulled it over the two lots on Tremont Street and would empty the contents in the corner of the lot so it would dry out for use on next year's garden.

Out in the pasture picking up the cow manure I got to coughing really bad. I suddenly thought, "Oh, Lord, I've got TB. Now Mama and Daddy will know what I've done." I took the pack with fourteen still in it and buried it in the 55-gallon barrel where Daddy burned trash in the back yard. And that was my smoking experience. I still don't know if Mama and Daddy ever knew anything about it.

Along about then, we got a little white Spitz dog that I named Wally. Where that name came from, I don't know. His curly hair was about seven inches long, and his tail curled over his back. You should have seen the house I built for him. I could even crawl through the front door, before I got too big. It had a front porch with columns (2x4s). Wally liked to jump up and set on the porch roof. It had a chimney (2x6 with a 2x4 above it, painted like bricks). Wally and I both loved that house. It set under the pecan tree in the back yard between the tree and the orchard.

EARL'S VIVID IMAGINATION

While we lived in the barn that winter, Daddy and "Ol' Man Noah" (he didn't know we kids called him that) built a four room house, facing South King Street. Our address was 405. He was a short, powerful man with bushy eyebrows and quite deaf. He had to saw the lumber and sills with a hand saw back in those days. His right arm and biceps were considerably bigger than the left. Perhaps 30 feet behind the house the sanitary privy was built. It was a "one-holer" with a tin roof. We made good use of every Sears catalog, too. [No corn cobs, please].

My brother Earl had a very vivid imagination. Back then we would listen to KWKH radio in Shreveport. I remember the Sunshine Boys – I think it was the Shelton brothers; the Bailes Brothers; Kitty Wells with Johnny and Jack, etc. [Kitty lived not too far from us when we lived in Parkwood Estates in Nashville; I believe she was 92 when she died in 2011]. Earl invented him a band, and called them *The Atlanta Boys.* I don't know where he came up with that name. They were unique in that they rode their horses to their personal appearances. They were stabled in a lot at the corner of Lafayette and South King streets.

His imaginary radio station was WINN: the parish we lived in was Winn parish, hence the county seat being called Winnfield, with two "n's" – the only one in the nation. He would sit in the toilet and do his broadcasts. The Atlanta Boys' theme song went like this (I wish you coulda heard him sing it):

"Hear our song as we ride along, we're just some happy, rovin' cowboys – herdin' the dark clouds outta the sky, keepin' the heavens blue."

Then he would break into some instrumental music. Gertrude wrote a poem and thumb-tacked it on the inside of the door: ***"If you in the toilet sing, you may hear the doorbell ring!"*** But Earl was on a mission! The two sponsors of the broadcast were (1) A company that sold a salve you would rub on your chest when you had congestion or a cold, and (2) a famous oil company. Earl wrote all the commercials, too. Now, keep in mind: this was all in his imagination.

His second invention was ***The Hamilton Newscast.*** Here again, I have no idea where he got the name Hamilton. Winnfield had two competing weekly newspapers and Earl always had a yearning to be a journalist. He even came up with the town characters, relating them to us.

Mama was *Pink Spillers,* the town mayor; Earl was *George Stokes;* I was his brother, *Harry Stokes;* Gertrude was *Dorothy Stokes,* our sister. Daddy wasn't involved in this apparently. I don't remember what Stokes Brothers' business was, but it seems like they had a lot of "irons in the fire." Earl would take a blank 8-1/2 x 11 sheet of paper and fold it in half, making a 4-page newspaper with headlines and 3 columns along with ads here and there. He typed it on our old L. C. Smith typewriter. I think it came out weekly. Earl would pay us a penny to read it, but get this: he would give us a test to see if we really had read it, before he paid up.

Life was never dull at 405 South King Street.

LON, THE BARBER

Mr. Lon Anderson was my barber when I was growing up in Winnfield. His shop was in his house at the west side of the "overhead" bridge. Cost for a kid was ten cents. He'd run 'em through so fast, the new-fangled electric razor would almost become too hot to touch my neck. An ol' boy came in one day and his shock of hair was slicked down. Lon said, "Buddy, you want an oil change or a haircut?"

Lon was an unusual character. He had a peg (wooden) leg, to start with, also a false eye and false teeth. He needed a wig, too. By the time he took all that stuff off, plus his eye glasses, there wasn't much left to put in the bed. He said for years he fussed at his wife for shoving his shoes under the middle of the bed. Then he discovered that when he put his walking stick under the bed, HE was the one pushing his shoes. His son's name was Carmen and he married the daughter of "Pa-Mac" McBride. In 1957 we built our first house on Marcia's Daddy's garden plot (we bought it from him) and it was right across the road from the McBride house. Pa-Mac said when I sneezed, our whole roof lifted up off the house four-and-a-half feet! I'll admit I enjoy a good sneeze, especially when I'm outdoors!

Lon and his wife moved from town out on a road that went north off US-84 a couple of miles west of town. He built a modest house during WWII. In 1950 Marcia's family bought and moved in that house! Lon built a nicer one a little further down that road. He and Pa-Mac loved to try to out-do each other when it came to telling tall tales. Some of them would end up in the weekly newspaper, too. For example:

Pa-Mac said, "Lon, I went fishin' t' other day, over b' 'at big dead tree whur Sandy Creek runs in th' lake. I thought I'd caught me a big one, but when hit cleared th' water, you know whut it wuz? A dadgum lantern, like on th' back of a caboose, and git this: hit was still a-burnin'!"

Lon drawled, "Now I didn't set in to tellin' no tall tales t'day but dadgummit you got me started now. I wuz out in 'at same area not long ago an' I managed t' pull in a ol' catfish 'at was sooo big, th' level of 'at lake went down two feet!"

Pa-Mac raised his forefinger in Lon's face and said, "Aw now, c'mon, podner. Tell ya what I'll do. I'll blow out th' light in my lantern if you'll put a foot o' water back in 'at lake!"

THE START OF MY MUSIC CAREER

Mama and Daddy were paying fifty cents for each thirty minutes of piano lessons for Gertrude to take from Mrs. W. R. Horton, a faithful member of First Baptist church. The Hortons lived on West Main Street, about a mile and a half from where we lived. The big old house had a veranda around the front and side that was attached to a kind of round tower reaching above the roof.

The doorbell had to be pushed in and released to make the ringing sound. Big Creek community houses had nothing like that, for sure!

I would walk with Gertrude the three mile round trip from our house. During her lesson I would either sit on the front porch swing or go out in the back yard. One day her son was home and he showed me a duck that was pecking around. He whistled some and it paid him no mind, but when he started whistling "Dixie" that duck's head would come up, he would flap his wings and strut all over that yard. Well, I told that story every now and then in our concerts across the USA, in connection with my having taken piano lessons for two years from Mrs. Horton. One night we were at a church in Pontiac, Michigan and I told it. When I got through, no one laughed like they usually did. Then it hit me! If I'd had that duck strutting to the tune of "Yankee Doodle" they likely would have laughed.

Often at home I would go to the piano (a monstrous old upright they'd bought so Gertrude could practice) and play from her music instruction book. Mama and Daddy noticed...Say, do you think this kid might have some talent, too? So when I was in the fourth grade they had Mrs. Horton start teaching me. I was pretty good at playing what she put in front of me. She would pop the back of my hands if I didn't hold them up off the keyboard. Oh how I hated practicing finger exercises. I just wanted to play songs. I would hear something and figure out quickly how to play it on the piano. That's called "playing by ear." She didn't like that. I played in her piano recital that first year and told Mama and Daddy I'd never be in another. And I wasn't. 'Course I just took lessons for one more year – that was in the fifth grade. Now I know I should have practiced those finger exercises. About all I do is run in octaves UP the keyboard (or up or down with my left hand). I seem to have a mental block about running down it like most pianists can do. BTW, decades later when Marcia and I were traveling the nation in church music evangelism, a newspaper article said I'd had two years of piano lessons when I was in the fifth grade! Say, what?

Mrs. Horton moved her teaching place to a house across the wide street from the new elementary school building where I was then in fifth grade. My time was 7:30 a.m. Can you believe that? Often I would come in the side room where she taught before she would come in, and I'd light the natural gas heater, in cold weather. With my luck it's a wonder I didn't blow us all up!

Earl got a $10 "Gene Autry" guitar that must have had a book of instructions, and in no time he was playing fairly well. I must have asked him to teach me some chords, so he did, perhaps a half dozen. It was no time before I was singing and playing country songs. I would sit out on the front steps of our house and pick and sing. I did songs like Roy Acuff's "A jewel here on earth, a jewel in heaven" (a tear jerker) and Elton Britt's "There's a star-spangled banner waving somewhere," (a WWII song). Somehow I got a steel apparatus that fit around my neck and held a harmonica. I'd sing a verse then blow a verse. Mrs. Jones and Mrs. Box, across the street, who had been sitting on their front porches, would get up quickly and go in their house and shut the door. Some folks just couldn't recognize talent.

So I changed venues. I took my entire unique act...to school! I'd start in Miss Wood's room, and she would tell me to go play in Miss Teddlie's room, and she'd tell me to.... Well, you get the picture. The thought never occurred to me that they were likely thinking, "I gotta get this kid outta my room before I start climbin' the walls!" For a while Daddy rented our front bedroom to a man who later lived in the Star Hotel up town. I went there a time or two and he taught me more chords. I could play "Under the Double Eagle" like a pro...*I* thought so anyway.

A juke joint down on US-167 a half mile from our house was called *Green Garden.* It may have been a drive-in, I don't remember. Inside was a juke box that was filled with great country hits, like: "Bouquet of Roses," sung by Eddy Arnold; "Lovesick Blues," sung by Hank Williams (Sr), etc. I'd take my guitar down there and play along with the juke box. I guarantee Mama and Daddy didn't know about it. One night when I was there, business was very slow. A man there started tossing quarters out on the floor in front of me. He would take a sip from a brown paper sack every now and then! I went home with $1.75 that night, and that was more than Aunt Allie paid me to mow her yard! Hey, was a career opening up for me, I wondered? I imagine God was quite amused, knowing His plan for my life.

Just to increase my "worth," I got a **fiddle**: I guess Mama and Daddy did, anyway it cost $17.50. The dadgum thing didn't have any frets on it like a guitar. My "Listen to the Mocking Bird" sounded like he was choking on a worm! In my opinion, folks who play the violin have to be very talented! I moved on to the **mandolin.** Earl and I would ride down the highway with me plunking away. I played chords with no problem, but I just couldn't pick out a melody. Did you know a mandolin and a violin can be tuned the same way, and either bowed or picked? That's really something!

At Winnfield's First Baptist church I began playing piano in the "Intermediate" department, probably after my second year of piano lessons when I was eleven or twelve. Later, when I was thirteen, I was chosen to be pianist for the new Laurel Heights Baptist church, and I'll tell more about that later. When I was fifteen, a tent revival was held out at East Winnfield and a man named George Hughes and his wife were musicians for it. I rode my bike out there, about a five mile roundtrip so he could teach me more about playing the piano. He had been saved out of the entertainment world and was very talented. I owe a lot to him. Years later, Earl told me about a young man who was a student at New Orleans Seminary. The man said when he got his degree in music he was going to go out on the Earl (or Huey?) Long bridge over the Mississippi River and throw all those textbooks in it. I know he must have been a joy to work with, whatever church was fortunate enough to have him. I would love to have had all those books!

WINNFIELD BUSINESSES

I want to describe the town we grew up in. There were several drugstores: Shirley Jackson, Sam Brian, John Emerson, Branch, and Dick Porter. Dick's was not a pharmacy. His store had the black and white square tiles and soda fountain, and it was directly across from First Baptist church. Dick played the violin and sometimes he and Mrs. Stinson (organist for decades) played offertories at church. I remember one Sunday he played "Humoresque," and did some of it staccato! Later John Emerson's brother Joe started his own drug store a couple of blocks away. I went to school with John's children: Sammy was in my class and became a doctor; James became a pharmacist I believe. They had a sister named Mercedes! (MUR-sa-DEEZ). An executive at the Carey Salt Mine just west of town was named Cameron and I went to school with his son who was named Wheelock!

The Lone Star Café was on Main Street across from the Bank of Winnfield where I later worked for nine years. It was a popular hangout for Winnfield's cronies. A waitress there was named Mary and she married a man whose last name was Christmas. Houston Gates operated the Men's Clothing store between the Lone Star and Morgan & Lindsey, a five and dime store. He also led singing at First Baptist church. On the corner was Max Thieme Chevrolet. U. B. Carpenter's department store was on the south side of Main just east of the bank. "Brandy" Hammond worked there and taught me how to properly tie a tie. Branch Drugs was south of the bank on Able Street across from the courthouse. Marcia worked there her senior year, making $3.75 per DAY. On my break I would go over and sit on a barstool talking with her. Around the corner on Court Street was Russell Tullos' Dry Goods store. He and Marcia's Daddy were close friends. On down the block was a pool hall. One day Mr. E. L. McGuffey, who led singing at Laurel Heights Church saw Marcia's Daddy come out of the pool hall, and he proceeded to chastise him for setting a bad example. Her Daddy said, "Mac, I went in there 'cause I had to use the bathroom!"

There were several grocery stores in town. Milam's sold groceries, dry goods as well as clothes and shoes. It was across the Rock Island railroad tracks east of the main part of town. I remember Mama buying a "brick" of chili, kept in Milams' cold meat display case. It was greasy, but so good. In addition to the Chevrolet place there was E. J. Byrnes Ford, Clyde Taylor's Studebaker/Pontiac, and Winnfield Buick/Oldsmobile. And Winnfield's First Federal was very successful for many years, but failed when all the other Savings and Loans did. Their mascot was a little rubber man about 4 inches high named Winnie-the-First.

The courthouse was of course, the focal point in town. Being the parish seat, we had both sheriff department (in the courthouse) and city police (by the City Hall). On the south side of the court square was the Venus movie theatre, run by Jerry Lacefield. He would purposely misspell something in the movie title that had everyone looking daily to see what it was. That was right clever of him. One day I went in back of it to the trash barrel and found a ticket that was not torn much at all. I held it between my thumb and forefinger firmly, had it torn again and enjoyed the movie...I did that only once, though, just to see if I could. Saturdays were something. Usually a double feature, it also had previews of coming attractions, a news reel, a cartoon, a weekly serial plus advertisements of local interest. I believe I got in for nine or ten cents. Behind the Venus was the jailhouse and you really didn't want to go there. Our church "ministered" there a time or two and I couldn't wait to get out of there.

On the east side of the square was Bill Heard's hardware store. You could buy anything from horse collars to caskets there. Bill was a brother to Joe R. Heard, owner/president of the Bank of Winnfield where I worked later. Next to that was a Ben Franklin store.

There were several hotels in Winnfield in the 1940s. The biggest and finest was called the Winnfield Hotel, made famous by Huey P. Long and his brother Earl K. Long. It had three floors and must have really been something back in those days. It was located on Main Street across Laurel Street from First Baptist church. It had a front porch (an alcove) with rocking chairs on it. I think I went in the lobby only once. Many legendary figures, most of them political, came there for meetings, lodging and dining. It was placed on the Historic Landmarks Registry, but the entire back wall finally succumbed to gravity and fell away. It was torn down and is now a paved parking lot for First Baptist church.

I have mentioned the Star Hotel already, and west across Front Street from it was the Davis Hotel. Marcia's brother-in-law Bartlett Kennedy lived there before he and Johnnie married. He worked for the US Forestry for 38 years after two years in the army during WWII. Then down by the L&A railroad on South Jones Street was the Imperial Hotel. On east Main Street was the Clewis Hotel. It outlasted all the others and is now a Bed and Breakfast.

One day I came up with what I thought could become a bicycle fad across the nation and make me both rich and famous. The welding underneath my bike basket had come loose from its two supports that went down to the front wheel axle. I got a wrench and loosened the nuts and bent the supports forward to bumper height which was horizontal with the ground. I tightened the nuts and proceeded to ride around, showing my friends that I had the only bike in town with a *front bumper.* [Decades later Gallagher rode his bike on a TV program while holding a car door, remember that?]

Now, don't get ahead of me, ok? A few days later I was happily riding (well, speeding) southward in front of our house on the grassy area between the hip-high picket fence and the dirt King Street. In "the twinkling of an eye" the bumper dropped and dug deep into the ground, causing the bike to buck upward. I went sailing over the handlebars into Charlie Taylor's hedge, to my left just beyond the end of the pointed picket fence, thank the Lord! Being somewhat shook up, I went into our house, my tears mixing with the dirt and sweat on my face. Gertrude wanted to know what in the world had happened and when I told her I'd had a wreck on my bike, what does she do? Check me for bruises, console me? Noooo, she dashed madly outside to see if the dadgum bike was damaged! Aw...we were such a close, loving, caring family. She later joined the Cadet Nurse Corp toward the end of WWII.

Mama had a Mimosa tree in the chicken yard and those old blooms kept falling off, strangling the chickens till finally they learned to leave them alone. One day I was playing on top of the barn we had lived in that winter. I lost my balance and slid off the front side of it, making a slight dip in the tin roof. Amazingly, I lived to see another sunrise. I reckon Daddy didn't notice the dip. Near our house was a very sharp curve where US-167 turned west and became East Lafayette Street. There was a huge tree on the north side of the curve that bore many scars where cars/trucks had run into it, heading into town.

On the south side, the inside of the curve, was "Cowboy" Powers gas station. I'd get a 6-1/2 ounce bottle of coke there when I had a nickel. He sold kerosene for 14 cents a gallon, I think it was. The old gas pump had a handle on it that was used to put gas in the glass top which had red lines circling around it to tell how much was there. It seems like gasoline was about the same price as the kerosene.

Mr. and Mrs. John Steen's house was on the northeast corner of South King and Lafayette Street. He was a brakeman on T&G trains and drove a big blue Nash automobile. He would pack it with folks going to and from church. He said the Lord provided him with that car and he was using it for His glory. We rode with him some, but I'd rather walk. That was my "quiet time" with the Lord when I would talk with Him about any problems, especially walking home Sunday night after church. Mr. Steen always had a big smile and was one of the finest Christian men I've ever known.

About 3 a.m. one morning, fire broke out in the T&G quarters to our west. Before it was put out, thirteen shotgun houses had burned. Daddy and I dressed and went over there. Suddenly shots rang out and everyone took cover. They said it was likely guns or ammunition in one of the houses. I can still see in my mind's eye this elderly black man seated safely at a distance, as I heard him say, "Well...I guess I won't git m' coffee dis mawnin'!" That was so sad.

One hot summer day, some teenage boys were racing recklessly through the Red quarters in an old jalopy. A big pine tree put a stop to that. A friend of Earl's, who lived about three blocks away on Center Street, was injured. In 1937 when we moved to Winnfield from Big Creek community, there was a wooden bridge on US-167 that went over the railroad tracks that connected the Rock Island to the L&A. It went up sharply, leveled off maybe ten yards then went down just as steeply. It was replaced with a concrete bridge with longer ramps that also went over Front Street, with the sidewalks going down on the east side of it. We called it the "overhead bridge." At the west end of the bridge, Laurel Street began going north. It came off Lafayette Street steeply. I would ride my bike up there, put on my steel skates and attempt to go down it standing upright. I would always "bust my setter." Remember those old skates? You carried a key on a string around your neck that was used to tighten clamps down on your shoes.

Winnfield actually had a skating rink back in the late 40s. One night Jerre McBride and I were skating with a lot of our teenage friends. Jerre told me to squat down on my skates and he proceeded to pick up speed as we headed down toward the other end. I had the sick feeling there was no way we'd make the 180 degree turn, so when we were at maybe 90 degrees,

I went back on my behind and skidded into the outer wood wall – there was no inner wall. My feet literally went *through* the wall and there I sat like Paul and Silas in stocks in the jail! I would assume that Jerre crashed into the wall as well! We skated many a time to the music of Owen Bradley on the organ, and another organist, I can't remember his name. One song was "You can't be true, dear."

Chickens...now I had trouble with chickens. Don't get me wrong, I love them fried, roasted or baked. Maybe I just brought the feeling on myself. For instance, one day Mama had thrown some chops (corn) out for them to eat. I had a slingshot (we had another name for it) and proceeded to shoot little rocks among them. Well, unfortunately for one hen – and me – a rock hit her upside the head. She began to twirl around like a pretty ballerina in an awkward dance. I guess Mama saw me do it. She came out and said, "What is wrong with that hen yonder?" I doubt I confessed, but she made me get the ax and chop its head off so we could eat it for supper. I don't remember if I ate any of it but I wondered why Mama would smile when I looked at her. Maybe Daddy never found out.

Louisiana is noted for its politics: an understatement what with the likes of Earl K. and Huey P. Long, both born and raised in our hometown of Winnfield. Recently a lawyer friend from Ashland City gave me a thick book simply titled "Huey Long." It took a while for me to read it. For decades amazing events occurred in Louisiana a lot like those in Chicago and New York. Can you spell "gangsters"? Every article had numerous footnotes to verify the facts.

Also back in the late 1800s a gang of robbers called *The West Clan* began operating in Winn parish. They would rob and sometimes murder travelers passing through. In the 20s and 30s just about any- and everything happened. Enter *Bonnie and Clyde*, who were ambushed on a lonely country road about 40 miles northwest of Winnfield. A marble monument is/was placed at the very spot, but people have chipped on it to where most of the wording can hardly be read any more. Election results often took days to be determined. One day an elderly man in town got so upset...apparently his candidate wasn't doing so well...that he *kicked in* the front of his big floor model radio, ruining it for future election broadcasts!

It must have been around 1943 to 1945 I would go with my friend Eddie Ray Brock to Gum Springs. We'd ride in the trunk, holding the lid up, of their Hudson Teraplane automobile. It was a great swimming place, built in the 30s by the Civilian Conservation Corp, about 9 miles west on US-84 toward Natchitoches. That is where I learned to float and swim. It would become dark after we got there.

Bombers from Barksdale AFB in Bossier City, LA, perhaps 90 miles northwest of Gum Springs, would do practice bombing runs on a range just north of the highway. They would drop flares, later we would hear the bombs explode. Also practice bombing was done on Winnfield's "overhead bridge", but they used sacks of flour! In Grant parish between US-167 and US-165 a large tract of land was used for maneuvers and I am told there are still unexploded shells all over that area!

Sunday was a day of rest. "Blue Laws" kept every business closed except for one gas station and one drug store. We went to church morning and night. We were forbidden to shoot the .22 rifle, and forget about going to the "picture show." So, Mama and we kids would take long walks. One afternoon we were on the L&A railroad tracks when we heard a train coming. Mama said, "Let's run and get under the trestle, quick!" I didn't know about that, but we did all get under it up at one end. The ground shook and we kids became terrified. About that time the engine rushed over us and we felt the heat from the firebox. Whew! Perhaps it was on another such walk, that we spotted a big owl sitting on the limb of a pine tree not far off the tracks. I picked up a rock and threw it at him, thinking to make him fly. It hit him right in the face and he dropped, dead. I felt so bad. I never dreamed I would hit him!

In a small town like Winnfield, perhaps 4,000 residents, when a church was having a revival meeting, a lot of us teenagers would attend. I remember going to one at the Nazarene church. A man played the accordion and sang solos. He stuttered so badly he could hardly call out the page numbers, but he could sing beautifully. During an altar call, the pastor came up the aisle to me and asked, "Son, have you been sanctified?" I don't remember what my answer was. I believed that at the moment of salvation God sent his Holy Spirit to live in me and set me apart for His service. There would be "fillings" later on in my Christian walk. I don't recall attending the Methodist church services, but remember Mama and Daddy were married in the Winnfield parsonage. Nor do I recall going to the Episcopal Church or the Catholic Church, except to play for Johnnie and

Bart's wedding back on October 2, 1958, four years to the day after ours.

When I was nine years old I was reading my Sunday school lesson on Saturday. Gertrude had reminded me I was the only one in our family that was not saved yet! Something in that lesson convicted me and Earl took me up to see Bro McBride. He was in the church office! After talking a while I knelt by a straight chair and asked Jesus to forgive my sins and come into my heart as Savior and King of my life. I made it public in the morning service. This was in June but I was not baptized until November!

Mama and Daddy let me have a .22 rifle, can you believe it? I was probably twelve or so. It was a single shot. I would walk along the T&G tracks, sometimes shooting at some target, like a limb or tin can. The T&G had a reservoir of water for their locomotives and it was enclosed by a wire fence. I shot some big moccasins there. One day I was shocked to see about a three-foot alligator floating out in it. I nailed him! That afternoon Daddy came home from work and said a man there was complaining about somebody shooting his alligator in the reservoir. Do you think I kept my mouth shut?

One of my neighborhood friends was Bobby Mixon. We went to Laurel Heights Baptist Church together. We rode our bikes everywhere. One day we rode down US-167 south about three miles to where Cedar Creek went under it. We got down the bank and walked upstream perhaps 40 yards. Suddenly, snakes began coming at us from all directions, climbing over limbs, out of holes, the water, etc. One, we thought, was a coral snake.

Bobby had a .22 rifle that was smaller than mine. We literally shot our way out of there and never went back.

After that experience we came up with an idea that evolved into a plan. We were going to ride our bikes THROUGH Cedar Creek. We'd never heard of anyone doing that, perhaps we'd go down in the Guinness World Book of Records! Bobby went first but didn't make it to the other side. I reckon the water might have been six inches or so deep, and maybe eight feet across. I got on the highway, built up speed, flew down the embankment and into the creek. I MADE IT! And nothing ever happened. In fact, most people thought we were stupid or crazy for trying such a fool thing anyway.

It must have been the early 40s, maybe even during World War II there were a lot of "hobos" around, probably still results of the Great Depression. One camp was between the L&A tracks and the spur joining it to the T&G tracks. We could see their camp fires and hear them singing, especially in the wintertime. They would come to our back door sometimes, asking if there was any job they could do in exchange for something to eat. Mama or Daddy, if he was home, would let them chop up some firewood then Mama would give them a sandwich or a plate of food. Times were still hard, but the bustle of WWII got the country up and going again.

THE CREOSOTE PLANT

Before my tenth birthday, Mama and Daddy added a built-in porch across the back of our 4-room house, full of windows.

We even had a bed or two in it, and often listened to the radio out there. It was cooler. They also added two bedrooms to the south side of the house, with closets in between which were needed. But the best thing: the trusty old outhouse was torn down and a bathroom installed between the back bed room and the glassed-in porch. We were uptown now!

Mama got a secretarial job at the American Creosote Works in south Winnfield, during WWII. She walked to work, rain or shine, a good mile or so one way. She was paid $25 per week. That was good compared to some ladies who worked in stores for $15 or even $12 per week. She liked her job and they liked her. She said some trucks would bring in pine poles 125 feet long. All the run-off from the plant's chemicals was simply dumped in a little creek that flowed into Dugdemona Creek and eventually into the Mississippi River. I read the area where the Creosote Plant was situated is the worst polluted spot in the USA. It would take $300 million to clean up. In June of 2012 we purposely drove by there. Nothing has been done. Through the trees and bushes we could see the old office building was about to fall down.

After we moved to Winnfield, Mama didn't know about that creek. We walked down there and enjoyed playing on the sandy banks like we did in Big Creek or Dyson Creek. But shortly after getting home we began to turn red like we had been blistered! We never did that again. During the school year, we kids would be at school while Mama worked at the Creosote Plant. But in the summer, we were left at home. Lots of times, Mama would bake cornbread, and at lunch time, Gertrude and

I would crumble some up in a pan, pour buttermilk on it, stir it up, then Gertrude would take her spoon and draw a line across the middle. We'd go to eating our half. We might have had a raw onion out of the garden, but I doubt there was any meat. I still love a glass of bread and milk every now and then.

I used to ride my bike all the way home from school to eat lunch (over a mile). There was a nice lunchroom at school, added onto the south side of the elementary school. I remember when I ate lunch at school one day that a tray of milk (half-pint in cardboard) was left close to some of us boys. I think I drank eight of them myself. Anyhow, one day I had eaten lunch at home and decided to wheel by to see Mama at work. Then I took a dirt road back in the general direction of school, but I passed a pine thicket. We used to love to play *Tarzan,* swaying back and forth on a tree then leaping out to land in another. I got off my bike and climbed one. Alas, no time to play, I had to get back for 4th period. I climbed higher, swayed a little then dropped my feet bending it toward the ground. Horrors! It didn't even get me low enough to turn loose and drop. So I wrapped my legs around it and moved up higher, when it suddenly snapped off and I landed flat of my back. It's a wonder I didn't break *something!* I finally made it back to school…late, and I had to go by the office. I wrote my reason for being late: "ate with a coming appetite." That meant I got hungrier the more I ate (that's me, alright!) Would you believe the lady in the office laughed and approved it!

Winnfield had the T&G railroad, the L&A railroad and the Rock Island railroad. The latter ran to El Dorado, Arkansas, perhaps a hundred miles due north. It served a paper mill, later a container mill, in Hodge between Winnfield and Ruston (Louisiana Tech is in Ruston). We always knew when the wind was coming out of the north, because you could smell that paper mill. There must have been some reason for the train to go on up to El Dorado.

They also operated a passenger train...I guess you could call it. A small engine pulled one car. Everyone called it *The Doodlebug.* I remember riding it twice in one day, when Mama took us three kids to visit her cousin. We went perhaps 40 miles north to a little town called Quitman, got off, and walked along US-167 through a swampy area, up a long hill, in the hot sun, then a half mile or so down a dirt road. We got to stay there perhaps three hours; then we made the long walk back to the station at Quitman. But another time we rode it all the way up to El Dorado. We had a two hour layover so we walked around "the big city." I recall the black people on the train would wave and yell at others along the way...they were a happy bunch.

At times the rainfall would be such that the dyke over Port Lou and Dugdemona would go underwater. Did I tell you that it got its name from the roaming gangs of robbers who would bury their booty along its banks in the area south of Winnfield known as the Pardon hills. It was slang for "dug de money." I am serious! In winter time, if we were lucky to get a good snow deep enough, Mama would have us carefully gather up some in a pan and she would make "snow ice cream." I was in the second grade before I ever saw snow. Then in 1959 we got a twelve inch snow.

EARL'S ACCIDENT

When Earl was a senior in high school, Miss Mary Riser, owner and publisher of the weekly Winn Parish Enterprise newspaper, hired him to be sports writer. Back then Winnfield had a men's fast-pitch softball league. I can still remember some of the players – Robert Lee Dunn, Mike Tinnerillo and Bill Postel. Earl took me with him one night and I sat with him in the "press box" right behind the umpire. There was a wire fence stretched across the space. I watched as the pitcher wound up and fired the ball in, the batter foul- tipped it right back and it went through the wire and hit me square on the knee cap. I reckon I yelled.

Miss Riser sent Earl down to the T&G railroad office, which was in the huge shop building across the tracks from South King Street. He was to interview Mr. John Corley about something. New railcar wheels had been delivered earlier, but must have been set up too straight. Earl was standing on the outside wooden platform waiting, when the one on the end for some reason tipped over and fell on him, knocking him down. The "lip" of that wheel caught the second one and it collapsed over on him as well. It took several men to lift one wheel off him: they weighed 750 pounds each.

Earl's left leg was broken, or crushed so badly that the surgeon had to wrap a silver "band" around the bone, held in place by seven screws. He was put in a cast from his armpits to his ankles, to lie in bed for SIX MONTHS! He would lay there and cry, saying it was hot and it itched. He got so discouraged because he had to miss that entire year of school, causing him to graduate only one year ahead of Gertrude.

When he got out of the cast, he literally had to learn to walk all over again. He was on crutches a while. He wanted to get outside so badly, and one Sunday afternoon we all walked down to the railroad tracks. I don't know why, but he tried to cross a narrow bridge (2 or 3 crossties) on his crutches, lost his balance and fell down in the ditch. He was salutatorian of his class and Gertrude was valedictorian of her class. I came in 10th out of 65! Gertrude's husband Dan said he was 10th in his class. I asked how many were in it, he said eleven!

Earl left for Louisiana College to study for the ministry. The next year Gertrude left for college studying to become a cadet nurse. I did some work for Miss Riser at the newspaper office. I kept up with the ads placed in the paper, and also rode my bike around town collecting subscriptions. They were $3 per year! She let me keep one dollar of each one. On one Saturday I made $18. I bought myself a cream-colored table model ARVIN radio that I kept for many years, even after Marcia and I married.

I would lie in bed and listen to the Grand Ole Opry. {Later in Nashville I met a lot of those people I had listened to}. The Friday Night Opry used to be held in the National Life building southwest of the capitol, on the second floor. WSM broadcasted it of course. We got to talk with lots of the Opry members, including Jim Reeves. He once played AA baseball for the Alexandria Aces. He was an announcer on the Louisiana Hayride in Shreveport (KWKH), where many individuals and groups got their start, including Elvis. Some artist didn't show up and Jim talked the director into letting him go on stage and sing while picking a guitar. A talent scout was in the audience so you know what happened. East of Carthage, TX on US-79 is a memorial for Jim that has a life-size statue of him. Very interesting.

Saturday night I would listen to the Grand Ole Opry. Randy's Record Shop sponsored some of it. I even ordered some 78 rpm records from him, in Gallatin, TN. Red Foley would sing about "Old Shep", a dog and I'd just about cry every time. Some western-style group (probably Pee Wee King and the Golden West Cowboys) would sing "Cool Water" and I'd have to get up, go in the kitchen and get a drink. I would listen to Dr. J. Harold Smith broadcasting from a 150,000 watt station in Mexico. About ten years later I was finance chairman of a Winn Parish Crusade he led, held at the rodeo arena off the Atlanta road. {Johnny Cash and the Tennessee Two also came to that rodeo arena in the early 50s}. About twenty years later we had J. Harold at Park Avenue (where I was pianist over 38 years) for a revival. One night about one hundred responded to the invitation.

He came to our Winnfield home several times. But in Nashville one day I boarded a plane and there sat J. Harold. He was on his way to bring the address at the first commencement at Jerry Fallwell's Liberty University in Lynchburg, Virginia. Jack Price was Bob Harrington's music man for several years. He and I did six choral books together, the first selling over 500,000 copies. Jack told me if I ever got on a plane and saw him, not to yell, "Hi, Jack!"

EARL AT LOUISIANA COLLEGE

While Earl was going to Louisiana College in Pineville, the only Baptist college in the state, he would go out with a team of students to do street ministry. Some Sundays he would be assigned to "fill a church pulpit somewhere." I visited him there on campus. This was in the mid-40s and rules were quite different. The male students could use the swimming pool on a certain day of the week; the females another. It was located right behind the only men's dorm! A canvass covered that part of the pool fence. There were two female dorms on the campus.

The men's dorm was named after a Dr. Godbold, a former president. It had three floors, stairs, and the bath rooms and showers were at each end of the halls. Sometimes the one phone in the building, placed at the stairwell on the second floor, would ring 40 or 50 times. Finally, some boy who could stand it no longer would run answer it saying, "Godbold, who in the **hall** do you want???"

A terribly destructive hail storm occurred one time. Marcia remembers it, as they were living in Pineville then. She said jagged pieces of ice fell from the sky. A "preacher boy" at L. C. had a convertible and it was torn to shreds. It may have been the same young man who owned thirteen cars in a calendar year. He kept trading and ended up with a nice car.

A whiskey still was discovered in a remote corner of the campus! Somebody said, "Aw, that's just some preacher boy tryin' to work his way through college."

EARL'S MINISTRY

The first church where Earl was pastor was Mars Hill Baptist in the southwest corner of Winn parish. A lot of Marcia's relatives are buried there, including her parents. Her Daddy lost his three older brothers in a 42-day period; they are buried in adjoining plots. I went to Mars Hill a lot, played piano for their afternoon "singings". Everyone enjoyed the "dinners-on-the-ground" as they were called. Windows were raised as there was no air conditioning. Insects would fly in and out – dirt dobber "houses" dotted the upper walls and ceilings. People used fans furnished by some funeral home, and if you weren't careful the boards on the bench seat would pinch! One old fellow directed "When the roll is called up yonder" and when he'd sing, "I'll be there," his arm would come down with his forefinger pointing DOWN! I never will forget that.

A revival was held at a country church called New Salem where Earl was later pastor; the railroad crossing said Crews, and it was just up US-71 north of Montgomery, Louisiana. [I pause here to say, PLEASE don't pronounce it *Louise-e-ana.* It was NOT named after Louise. It was named in honor of Louis and Anna of France. Please say *Louie-z-ana,* or, as the locals say *Lose-e-ana.* This ends our "southern English" lesson].

During that revival we stayed in the Arrington family home in Montgomery, with toilet out back. I was about fourteen, I guess. Earl had his 1938 Chevrolet, so mid-week we decided to go take a bath in a creek east of town on the way to Hargis community. It had high banks and we slid down them to the cold water. We splashed around to get wet then soaped up, but wondered aloud how we would get back up the bank. Then Earl spied a moccasin swimming up the creek toward us. Next thing we knew we were standing up on the bank looking down at him.

Earl became pastor of a quarter-time church in a community called Rhinehart, east of Jena. The other Sundays the members met for Sunday school only. We ate Sunday lunch at the Richardson's house then sat out on their front porch a while. Their little dog strolled along the edge, yawned and lay down...the wrong way...he fell off the porch. All we heard was "Umphhh!" Earl conducted the funeral of a baby that was only a few days old and I went with him. It was a long way out in the country and no funeral home was involved. Men dug the grave and covered the small white casket while the Mother stood out under a pine tree smoking a cigarette. Earl and I had gone over to a place called Nebo one day and on the way back he let me drive a couple of miles. That was more fun than playing the guitar at school!

LAUREL HEIGHTS CHURCH

Our entire family was very active at First Baptist Church in Winnfield. Mama enjoyed being a part of the Women's Missionary Union until she overheard a remark about her dress made by an affluent lady. She dropped out of church. Soon Earl, then Gertrude left home for Louisiana College.

In 1945 our church started a mission in Laurel Heights, a southwest community of Winnfield. Daddy and I went out there to help. Someone must have carried us. We met in the James family house for quite a while. Somehow the members were able to get a loan and start construction on a small building, complete with a steeple. I remember sitting on kegs or boxes during Sunday school, before the concrete slab was poured. They were constituted as Laurel Heights Baptist Church and I was made pianist when I was thirteen years old.

Mr. E. L. McGuffey, an insurance salesman and collector was the song leader. At first he had to pick from a list of songs I could play. I tried to master two songs a week. I guess later on I got good enough in my playing that I began "tearing up" the keyboard. One Sunday night Bro. Mac said, "I'm going to ask our pianist if he would just play the song as it is written, please!" That embarrassed me somewhat and I don't recall if I did tone it down or not. Lord, forgive me!

There were some great saints of God in that church. I can't name them all, but I remember folks like Bro. and Mrs. Sam Fox, Mr. and Mrs. Clyde Jones (our neighbors), and even Judge Cass Moss, who thought he was "the head of the church." There was Marcia's Uncle Murphy Worsham who was church treasurer. He was famous for sleeping through every sermon. It was jokingly said he had slept with all the women in the church! Marcia's family attended also, but she was almost five years younger than me. There were two families in the church named Curry. Dennis either had trouble with dentures or had a speech impediment – he would pray, "Heavenly Masture, we thank you for our pasture." We had a gospel quartet that went down to Roy Brady's house in Verda and cut a 78rpm record. Roy's wife Hazel was S. Q. Fletcher's sister, Marcia's aunt. I remember the vinyl had to be swept to the center out of the way as the record was cut.

The Elton Mixon family were faithful members. Their son Bobby was a close friend of mine. Nedra was a close friend of Marcia's. In later years she lived in Dumas, TX. On one of our western trips, Marcia and I stopped on I-40 east of Amarillo to eat and saw a bus "First Baptist Church of Dumas, TX". Wearing name tags they were easy to spot. We asked a lady if Nedra Napp was in the group and she said 'yes, that several others were eating next door.' We went in, saw her at a table and I wish you could have seen her face when our eyes met. She dropped her fork and bounded toward us! Another of Marcia's close friends was Thelma Bright who came from a family of thirteen children, I believe. Marcia would occasionally spend the night there; she said that family was well organized and well behaved. Mr. Charley Bright worked two jobs.

Marcia's sister Johnnie and I "ran around" together with a couple of other teens from Laurel Heights. The four of us would spend Sunday afternoons together, after having "dinner" at one of our houses. They were Johnnie, Louise Austin, Bobby Mixon and me. From the time I finished high school till Marcia and I married in October of 1954, I did date a lot of girls. Marcia later said

I dated just about everyone in town. I begged to disagree: "I never dated Deweylene Stringer!" Marcia's reply was, "only because she's black!"

Bro. E. M. Bounds was a good friend of many in and around Winnfield. One night he preached at a church near Monroe and asked me to make the trip with him. On the way home he was tired and sleepy, so he asked me if I could drive on home. I jumped at the chance. My window was down, the moon was full, and I enjoyed driving SR-34 as I hummed a tune or two. I was truly in hog heaven...breaking the law, too!

The first pastor of Laurel Heights was Bro. Henry Mott. He was a friend of Earl's, as well as my and Marcia's parents. He started preaching at about 35 and attended Acadia Academy, located in South Louisiana. It was founded and run by Bro. V. K. (Vern) Fletcher, a distant relative of Marcia's Daddy. Its sole purpose was to help prepare men who late in life wanted to preach. Earl and I had been in revivals with Henry. He was known to drink three cups of coffee before breakfast and sometimes a dozen a day as he visited in people's homes.

He told of the time he was invited to preach a "trial sermon" at a church, in view of a call to become pastor. After the song service the spokesman said, "We're happy to have Bro. Henry Mott with us today and I'll ask him now to come on up and *take charge of the service.*" Henry said his bifocals misjudged the height of the platform. He hung his toe on it and sprawled flat on his all-fours. He thought, "That did it!" When he got up he commented, "Well, any old cow could have done that!"

The little church did call him. I was glad they did because he really *fell for the church.* (Sorry, but that's a true story).

Laurel Heights had several pastors, including Henry's son, Waynon. The church erected an all-purpose building and also a big new sanctuary. Marcia and I did a revival and a couple of concerts there through the years. Marcia's parents observed their 50th wedding anniversary there, too.

I have to tell you this: You know what a Benzedrine inhaler is, right? It will flat open up your sinuses. Daddy got a head cold and I guess Mama told him to use the inhaler. He did…just a wee bit too much. He couldn't walk a straight line come Sunday morning, but he was happy! Mama forbade him going to Laurel Heights that morning. A day or so after, Bro. Mott saw Mama somewhere and asked about Bro. Fred's absence the past Sunday. She hung her head, hesitated just a moment then said, "Oh, Bro. Mott…he was drunk!" I assume she went on to explain. I'm telling you, Mama was a character. You may see a little of her in me, you reckon?

"PUT 'ER IN HIGH, JUDGE"

During those "Laurel Heights years" I would accompany Judge Cass Moss down LA-34 perhaps thirty miles to Union Hill Baptist church, near Montgomery. [On a hill next to it was Union Hill Methodist church]. Mr. Roy Moore was the song leader and he also had to choose from my list of songs that I could play. The old hymn, "The kingdom is coming" gave me a fit…my rhythm sounded like a three-legged donkey. I hated sharps and most of the time would play them in flats...like if the song was in 3 sharps (A) I would easily play it in flats (Ab); all you did was alter the accidentals. And most of the time they were "accidentals" for me.

Judge Moss had a big green Studebaker *President.* He would drive in low or second gear on the gravel road until finally I would say, "Judge, I believe she'll take *high* now." Gravel would pile up in the center and every now and then the under carriage of the car would loudly scatter it. His sister, Mrs. Ruby Hanks (a widow) often went with us. She introduced me to Bible Memory Association. One summer I memorized 250 verses from the book of John. I received several prizes along the way – a book, a wall plaque, a box of *Precious Promises* cards (read one a day) and the last prize was a thick Scholfield Bible with many references. You could also attend a "Bible Memory Camp" located south of Minden, LA on old SR-7. But I was such a Mama's boy I didn't want to be gone for a week!

When I was fourteen, Mama sent me over to Marthaville, LA to play piano in a revival at a country church. She had met this sweet old lady while they were in a Shreveport hospital. Late Thursday night the lady's son came home drunk and loud. The next morning I told her I had to be back home that day so they took me to the bus station in Many (pronounced *"Man-e")* LA for the ride home to Mama.

While at Laurel Heights, I was "sweet" on Luella Curry, Dennis' niece. Her family lived on the street behind the church. She had a brother and two sisters. We have done concerts where the two sisters came to hear us. Many years later, during our traveling concert years, we went to Luella's church in Ozona, TX, only to find she and husband Huey Ingram had moved west to Odessa. On one of our visits to FBC, San Angelo, TX, my friend Jerre McBride (pastor there for 31 years) had Huey and Luella come up for supper one night.

Marcia tells the story about being on the Laurel Heights church bus one night coming back to Winnfield on US-167. {Daddy and I, after 3 years there had moved our membership back to First Baptist where I became pianist}. They had probably been to "M" night somewhere: "Mobilization" Night was held monthly on Monday nights at neighboring churches. The church that had the most members attending got to display the "champion banner" in their sanctuary till the meeting next month! Now in 2012 lots of churches don't even have Sunday night OR Wednesday night services! "Mobilization" has faded in the past, I guess.

Mrs. Joyce Rigdon, whose husband "Rig" helped the high school football coach, had all the youth singing, "He Lives," to the top of their lungs, when a cow stepped out in front of the bus. There was no stock law back then. WHAM! This happened around Big Creek Bridge south of Dry Prong. HE lives but the cow did not! She doesn't remember how they all eventually got back to Winnfield that night.

THE ADOPTION

When I was fourteen, in early August of 1946, Gertrude came home from her nursing job at an Alexandria hospital all excited about a baby boy who had been born and was going to be put up for adoption. She said he was the cutest little thing! For years, Mama and Daddy had wanted another girl; that would have made two boys and two girls. It had not happened...but another boy?

It had to be in God's plan, because they went down there (I don't know about transportation, we had no car) and brought him home in a woven basket, when he was TEN DAYS old. We were given his birthdate as July 29th, but Gertrude told us it could have been the 28th or 30th. We sat in the glassed-in back porch and tossed boy names around trying to decide what to name him. After a while we all agreed on *James Ronald Mercer,* destined to be called Ronnie. I was no longer the baby in the family!

When he got old enough, I would put a pillow in the basket of my OWN Blue Horse bicycle and ride him all over our end of town. We could go down to the Louisiana Highway Barn by the T&G tracks on US-167 and watch the trains switch around, blowing the whistle every time it had to cross the highway. He especially laughed when the brakeman, Mr. John Steen, would turn cartwheels on top of the boxcars.

One evening I was riding Ronnie down the highway south of those tracks when up ahead I saw a big water melon rind. I pointed it out to him and told him I was going to smash it on the concrete. That was a mistake. It slipped as the front tire went over it and we both tumbled out on the pavement. Neither of us was hurt, though I think he cried some, probably scared him. The little "rat fink" told Mama, though, when we got back home and I got a stern reprimand. Still today he will remind me of that incident.

Ronnie was more like a *grandson* to Mama and Daddy, and in my opinion, he *got away with murder!* One day Daddy took off his belt and proceeded to spank him, but Ronnie timed it just right and it was like jumping rope. I don't think Daddy landed two good licks! One Christmas season, I bought him a little train set from Western Auto on Main Street, owned and operated by Mr. Burden. His daughter, Betty Lee, was in my class at school. Christmas Eve night after Ronnie had been put to bed I attempted to assemble it and discovered that a piece of track was missing. I phoned Mr. Burden at his home and told him my little brother would surely be disappointed. He said for me to meet him at the store. I rode my bike taking the train set with me – and he swapped me a new one. That was certainly a kind thing for him to do.

MY HIGH SCHOOL TEACHERS

Mrs. Zelma Frazier (widow) was a beloved teacher in Winnfield high school. She taught history – ancient world and American. We dwelt on the Civil War for so long we had barely started riding with Teddy Roosevelt when the school year ended. She had a way of bringing it all alive to us. She must have taught for decades. Many years after she retired, Marcia and I went by her big, columned house on Maple Street to see her. We talked for perhaps thirty minutes then I stood and said:

"Well, I guess we'd better be….." "No, you don't have to go either. Sit down." "Yes ma'am, we need…." "I said SIT DOWN!" My rump hit the chair.

Mr. W. J. Austin taught math and science. I ended up taking biology in my senior year. It was either that or home-economics. I'd compliment him on his ties, laugh at his jokes, and didn't really do much class work, but I passed. That was the 1949-50 school year. When Marcia and I married October 2, 1954, we rented the bottom of his garage apartment for two years, as we had promised him. The rent was $25 per month, plus $1.50 for water! It was located about 100 feet north of that sharp curve I've mentioned earlier.

Several different people rented the upstairs apartment while we were there. The first thing they would do was mop the floor, and it would drip all down on us. The Winn parish sheriff moved in above us. One night we woke up to hear someone out in the street calling him. We didn't know if it was friend or foe. The head of our iron bedstead was against the front window and we hoped he knew the sheriff lived UPSTAIRS!

Mrs. Naomi Crawford was the home-economics teacher, and she taught my sister Gertrude…and Marcia. After school was dismissed one afternoon, another boy and I had a fistfight behind the building. Tensions had been building for some time. We fought all around the fenced-in gravesite of former governor O. K. Allen who was a cousin of the Longs. One of us got a busted lip and the other a black eye. Thank God, Mrs. Crawford heard the commotion, came out and stopped the fight. Later in my yearbook she wrote: "Three lovely Mercer children have been my students…" Well, Earl and I were not her students, and she had apparently forgotten all about the fist fight. After all, it was the end of another wonderful school year!

Floyd "Poochie" Smith and I got into a fight in class as the teacher came in. It was more of a mouthing-off, shoving match, I guess. That six weeks I got a "D" and had some explaining to do when I got home. Another time a friend of mine needed help on an English test. He sat to my right at the back of the classroom, when my answer sheet somehow fell off my desk. As he slowly picked it up he found the answers he needed. When I got my grade for that six weeks, Miss Perdue said, "I'm lowering your grade to a 'B', Elmo, and I believe you know why." Ok, so I had more explaining for that one. Floyd was later elected mayor of Pineville, LA, across the Red river from Alexandria. He attended a high school reunion several years ago. He is now deceased.

In chemistry class one day, the teacher was delayed and a couple of boys (names withheld) started shaking and pouring stuff from bottles in the sink. Suddenly the mess exploded, and gooey spider web-looking stuff hung from the ceiling. I <u>was</u> innocent of that escapade...I got under a desk! My friend Bobby Gassiott brought a camera to school. A picture was made as he pretended to leap from the second floor window in our English classroom. Then we went down and out to the front steps, perhaps ten of them. He sprawled himself out like he had landed there and another picture was snapped.

In those days, there was no Middle School or Junior High, which was a good thing because there was no building for it. When we entered the seventh grade, we were moved across the street to the high school building. We were on our way now. My principal since the first grade was Mr. W. D. Walker. He was promoted to high school principal therefore I had the SAME Principal all twelve years. Another interesting item is that my class of 1950 was the first one to have to go twelve years. My sister and brother, and Marcia's sister Johnnie only went eleven years back then. I don't know who to "thank" for that.

Mrs. Nettles (a widow) was my seventh grade teacher. She was a lovely lady and her students loved her. She taught there for many years and later after we were married, Marcia and I went by to visit her. My senior year some of us started a morning devotional about fifteen minutes before school began. We'd usually sing achorus, read a scripture verse and pray for the school day, etc. That would not be allowed today.

MEANWHILE, BACK AT FBC

Dr. B. C. Land was Winnfield's First Baptist Church pastor when we moved back to Winnfield. When Earl and Gertrude made professions of faith, Dr. Land baptized them. Before my voice changed, I would sit with Gertrude in church and sing alto with her. During the sermon I'd point to one title in the hymnal, then to another, usually making a silly sentence. Did you ever do that? It must have been around 1940 that Dr. Land and Houston Gates reportedly had a foot race across the Dugdemona Bridge north of town on US-167. It was longer than a football field! I don't know who won.

Bro. H. H. McBride followed Dr. Land as FBC pastor. He and "Mrs. Mac" had an older son we never knew; a daughter named Dorothy, then Jerold (Jerre) my close friend. He was in my graduating class because he took summer school. Oh, my, the things we got into! And we were the pastor's son and the church pianist. The church property was not locked up at night. Our "gang" liked to play in it at night. The sanctuary had a balcony around three sides of it, with only two rows of theatre seats. We'd play Hide and Seek, sometimes walking around with candles: it's a wonder we didn't burn the place to the ground. It had four floors, then two rooms (cupolas, so to speak) on the roof of the 4th floor. The youth met up there for Training Union for a while, then were moved down to the 4th floor.

One New Year's Night we (probably Bobby Gassiott, Jerre and I) were up on the roof of the 4th floor, up to no good. We had water balloons and tossed them down on people passing by on the sidewalk in front of the church. Suddenly someone whispered loudly, "Get over here quick!" We went to the side where Laurel Street ran between the church and the Winnfield Hotel. (Some folks should have pulled their shades down).

We looked down to see a man get out of a big black car and head for the side door on the first floor of our church. We were famous for "praying in the new year at midnight." We fired a barrage of water balloons and too late discovered it was Winn parish Sheriff Robinson. I want you to know that by the time that side door opened, we boys had gone down three flights of stairs and were sitting on the back row, bowed in prayer with angelic faces...and heaving chests.

Another night we were playing downstairs in that very fellowship hall when we heard the outside door of the education building open. It was Ethel McKeithen, our Youth Director, dropping by her office for some reason. I think it was Bobby who tried to hide quickly and fell over a natural gas space heater. Blue flame shot across the floor. Miss McKeithen left the premises...and we did, too.

In daylight, playing in the educational building, just for fun we would climb up through the shaft to the big fans mounted on the roof of the second floor. What if someone had turned those fans on when one of us was climbing through the blades! At age sixteen, Jerre and I came to the conclusion we were too grown up to attend Vacation Bible School any more. We went up the street to Morgan and Lindsey 5 and 10 cent store and bought cap pistols with plenty of ammo. We rode our bikes through the downstairs hallway of the educational building, playing Cowboys and Indians. We landed in a bit of trouble that day, too.

Bro. Mac had a black 1949 (I think) Packard. Yet, in those days, it had no air conditioning, no power anything and a stick shift. After church one Sunday night, several of us boys piled in, with Jerre driving. We headed out US-84 west toward the Winn Rock Company (a huge hole) and the Carey Salt Company (with an 800 foot deep shaft). Jerre turned around and floored it back toward town. Richard Drewett was in the back seat and saw the speedometer. He said, "Wow! Eighty-five!" Jerre smugly looked back and said, "Wait'll I put 'er in *high*!" Each gear had an overdrive! He slipped the shift into high and we flew over the hill. Then he put it into neutral and cut off the engine and said, "We're savin' gas, boys!" NOT!

I rode the elevator three different times going down in the salt mine. Marcia's Daddy worked on the surface in a tall building. I remember one time an underground river broke through the wall down in the mine. A Mr. Camp rode some kind of conveyance way back in an area and rescued a lot of workers.

In the late 40s we did have a great bunch of youth. On Sunday afternoons at 3 o'clock we'd go to some shut-in's home for a time of singing, praying and a short devotional. The church bought a portable "pump" organ and I lugged that 75 pound monster around, in and out of a car trunk. The Men's Brotherhood would go to a shut-in's home on Tuesday nights, and I would play that same pump organ. Oh, those great old saints of God had such an influence on my life! How I loved to hear them pray. Their names and faces come to mind, but I will not attempt to name them. They have long since gone to their heavenly home.

One Tuesday night we were at the Machen's home out on West Court Street (US-167 north). The quartet sang, "I Need the Prayers of Those I Love," and a lady living there (sister, cousin) cut loose to shoutin' – like to have scared me to death. I believe if I had pumped those pedals harder and faster I could have flown right outta there, even over Kansas!

Bro. McBride was a student of Bible end-time prophecy, and he had big charts that he set up on the floor in front of the pulpit. I think back now, that so many prophecies have been fulfilled SINCE that time! He also had missionaries come to speak. Miss Josephine Harris was one. She had a lot of artifacts for us to look at, including a big long snake skin. The church's janitor was named "Shorty." I don't know if anyone knew his real name. He and his wife would sit in the balcony on the east side of the church. Sometimes he couldn't help but say, "Amen."

We had a lot of great revivals, too. I remember the famous evangelist Gypsy Smith came one time; also Dr. J. Harold Smith from Ft. Smith, Arkansas. At the beginning of one revival, the youth listed six names of our friends that we wanted to see saved. By Wednesday night three of them had been. I believe it was in 1949 that we went to someone's house to see a TV...we had never seen one. The screen was "snowy" and at times we thought we could see someone walking!

THE LITTLE BROWN CHURCH

In the summers of 1946, 1948 and 1949 I believe it was, Earl and I did mission work in the Atchafalaya River Basin for the LA Baptist Convention. The big brown boat looked somewhat like Noah's Ark. It was called "The Little Brown Church on the Water." The area is located between Baton Rouge and Lafayette, deep in the heart of Cajun country. It's actually more like an ocean with occasional land areas. A few oil or gas wells are scattered around.

The boat was powered by two big engines on a small barge attached to the back. A French man and his wife were caretakers. The kitchen and their room and bath were at the back also. Toward the front was the auditorium that seated a hundred or more. Upstairs were a couple of bedrooms and a bath where Earl and I stayed. At night tug boats with barges would pass us (anchored to a land area) and would shine a spotlight into our room. On one day the lily pads would float one direction and the next the currents would bring them back the other way! The first time we anchored on Bayou Chene (pronounced "Shane").

I was in my teens then and enjoyed all this so very much. I played guitar in the services and sang such songs as "Where Will You Spend Eternity?" The people came by motorboats from all over the place. We had some difficulty understanding what they were saying! In the mornings we had Vacation Bible School for the children. I made a bookshelf with dachshunds on the front of the shelves out of lumber and plywood. We still have it here in our home!

You could hear the motorboats coming bringing the kids to VBS. Being the upcoming young composer that I was, I wrote a little song (not an original tune, however) and the lyrics went like this: ***"Well, early in the mornin', 'bout a quarter to five, you can hear the motorboats a-clickin' out the jive to the Bayou Chene Boogie, the Bayou Chene Boogie, Well, the Bayou Chene Boogie makes you really come alive!"***

You can imagine the humidity on a hot summer afternoon when Earl and I went across the gangplank into the woods. We gathered enough moss to make a "long-haired wig" for me, and

I rolled up my pants legs. Earl put his arm around me, giving the impression I was his girlfriend. I guess Bro. Pete Eiselstein made the picture. (See further explanation below about Pete).

The people lived in houseboats. There was a narrow porch, like eighteen inches, around them. They said their kids learned to swim before they learned to walk! A gallon jug was strapped to their backs in the event they fell overboard...that's how they learned to swim...and there were alligators all over the place! The unwritten law was, when you passed a houseboat, you'd better slow down. If you rattled the dishes in that houseboat you might get shot at!

We had to go on the other side of Bayou Plaquemine one day, in a pirogue (pronounced *P-row*). It is a flat, narrow boat, like a skiff. I was scared it would tip over. Not only were there alligators, but big long Gar fish, turtles and snakes. At Bayou Plaquemine a little Cajun boy asked Earl, "Broder Mercer, which is de best – de Ford or de Chevrolet?" Earl gave him a diplomatic answer.

The couple in charge of the Little Brown Church ministry was Pete Eiselstein and his wife. He had a 19-foot boat with two inboard motors and it would fly. One time he took Earl and me riding around the vicinity. We sat 'way in the back of the boat. He slowly turned into a close area and looked back and said, "Y'all comin'?" Earl and I would put down some fishing lines on the boat, mainly for crab and we caught some, too. Some were huge, big enough to fill the bottom of a foot tub. A boat delivering mail to those remote areas would come once or twice a week. There was a 12-year-old girl there who said she had never seen a car! And this was 18 miles west of the state capitol in Baton Rouge. That ministry was later discontinued by LA Baptists, but I'm thankful we got to participate in it. We were at Bayou Chene, Bayou Plaquemine and Six-Mile Lake north of Morgan City.

OTHER PASTORATES

Another church where Earl was pastor (during seminary days) was in the SE part of Louisiana, near Hammond. It was named Zion Hill and that was the first parsonage Betty and Earl lived in. It was a four room frame house with a toilet out back. The church also built new outdoor toilets. Betty was in the house getting ready for church when she overheard a girl passing by ask another one, "Have you been to the new *statehouse* yet?" I visited them around Christmas and the church was singing carols. On "The First Noel" in the chorus Earl shocked us all by going up a little too high. We all had a good laugh at his expense!

He also was pastor at a church named Colyell, between Hammond and Baton Rouge. It was a huge country church, running several hundred in Sunday school and services. One night after a revival service just about everyone had left. The evangelist and Earl were talking under some trees in front of the church when Earl said, "Oh, I almost forgot to turn the lights off." I volunteered to do it. I had to stand on the back of a pew to reach the power box handle and just as I yanked it down, the pew fell forward. Several of them started going down like dominoes and I was riding the tide on top of them.

It created quite a commotion. I just wish the whole church could have seen my Oscar-winning performance.

There was a 94 year old man in that community that still rode his horse. He came by one day and told Earl he was upset because his 74 year old son had not attended his birthday party. He claimed he was sick! In a town west of Hammond called Baptist (of all things) there lived an old preacher by the name of T. T. Edwards. He and Earl were close friends. Earl said Bro. Edwards would be preaching away and would take out his comb and run it through the three hairs on top of his head several times. He would refer to somebody as "an ol' bird." One night he was preaching away and quoted God as saying something. He got distracted for a while, and finally said, "Yes sir, God was the very ol' bird that said that!"

I was visiting Earl and Betty in New Orleans when he told me to go with him to a cemetery. As you know the city is about 9 feet below sea level and people cannot be buried underground. He showed me an above-ground brick grave that was breaking apart. You could see the skeleton (if you stayed there long enough). We loved to ride the trolley cars. The city's boulevards are beautiful with large oaks and stately houses. For a dime you could ride the ferry back and forth across the Mississippi River, both there and in Baton Rouge.

Then Earl was pastor at Twelfth Street Baptist church in Lake Charles for over ten years. It began as a mission of Trinity Baptist church. Earl said when Trinity's new pastor drove into town for the first time in a red convertible with the top down it raised a few eyebrows. While Earl was pastor, the church built a two-story educational building. Some members did a lot of the work to save on costs. One man slipped and fell on his back and left his two shoe prints on the wall. Another deacon was dozing in the morning service and his wife elbowed him. Earl was preaching away but happened to see the wife nudge him again and he elbowed her right back. Earl said it was all he could do to keep from laughing out loud!

The government closed the Air Base at Lake Charles, and Earl lost a third of his congregation. Marcia and I later discovered that two of our friends in Okeechobee, FL had been stationed there but didn't know each other then – Red Larson and Lewis Smith. Twelfth Street Baptist doesn't exist anymore. On a trip through Lake Charles a few years ago, we had trouble finding it, but I finally recognized the two-story educational building. In the late 40s Earl took me to Immanuel Baptist Church in Alexandria. I think the state convention was going on. A fiery young minister brought a message to thrill and encourage everyone. His name was W. A. Criswell, who later became pastor of First Baptist in Dallas for decades.

In the summer of 1949 I went with Earl and Betty to the Southern Baptist Convention, held in Oklahoma City. Earl bought a brand new Kaiser automobile. Sunday morning we attended a mission where American Indians worshiped. I will always remember they had me to play piano while they sang, "What a Friend We Have in Jesus" in their native tongue. When the official picture of the convention was to be made in the auditorium, Earl had the idea for us to go up in the balcony.

We had no trouble finding ourselves in the picture – we were the only ones up there.

I remember rushing along the streets trying to find a place to eat a quick lunch (dinner for us). In passing I heard a man tell another one going the opposite direction: "It's because all these (bleep) Baptists are in town and…" The closing service was held in a huge football stadium. They announced that 28,000 people were present and that was more than I had ever seen at one time…seven times more than Winnfield's population. The song director had us sing "Revive Us Again". When we got to the chorus, one side would sing the word "Hallelujah!" and the other would sing, "Thine the glory," etc. I believe we were sitting down on the playing field. I just stood there as though I was watching a tennis match. It was to me a "foretaste of glory divine."

TROUBLE IN THE ALLEY

The parsonage was situated on the southwest corner of the block the church was on, just north of the Post Office. Behind it was the American Café on Main Street. Winn parish was "dry" but some folks knew where to find a strong drink. The McBrides had a huge Chow dog, aptly named King. His chain ran up and down the clothesline in their back yard, adjacent to the alley. At times, especially at night, some guy who'd had too much to drink, would go down that alley, only to discover old King. And he did not look favorably on their being near his domain, especially in that condition. But…that's the very reason that King was put there.

One night, all was well, sleep was being enjoyed, when suddenly a terrible loud commotion erupted. King had caught him another one red-handed! Bro. Mac, in the upstairs bedroom, literally tore up the bed sheet, plus ripped off a bad toenail, trying to get up and pull King off the guy.

Mr. B. L. Anderson even got in a situation with King one afternoon. He was a pillar in our church, but spoke with difficulty (some said due to smoking). He owned an insurance agency at the corner of Main and Laurel, diagonally across from the church. He went to take a shortcut down the alley one afternoon. Mrs. Mac just happened to look out and see him. She ran to the back door and yelled, "Mr. Anderson, you'd better not go down that alley, King's liable to get you!" He replied, "Aw, that dawg...won't bother...me!" But he did. She watched with mixed emotions as he tore off a piece of tar paper (*) big enough to wrap around his tattered pants' seat, and made his way on to his office. (*) The new education building was under construction.

FREE DELIVERY

As I have mentioned, my two very best friends when growing up were Jerre McBride and Bobby Gassiott. I don't know who (?) came up with this plan, but one night we went over to the back of Branch Drugs and got a big dark brown jug, maybe two or three gallons. We went back to the church kitchen and filled it almost to the brim with water, then generously sprinkled black pepper on top.

Very carefully, we carried it across the street from the Winnfield Hotel to the house Mr. and Mrs. Hasson Morris had moved to. Then we went back to the church office where I dialed his number and in my deepest voice told him I was a salesman for Hadicol (*). I said he had been selected to receive a trial shipment and we had left a sample jug on his front porch. Then the three of us dashed to the hotel's concave porch.

(*) Hadicol was a cure-all drink conjured up by Dudley J. LeBlanc; it was sweeping the south at that time.

We sat in the rocking chairs and soon the front door opened and we heard him yell, "Ruby, there IS a jug on our porch!" He stepped out, picked it up, unscrewed the lid and took a big whiff. His reaction was one for the record books. Today it would have been posted on youTube. It would have made a great cartoon for the movies down at the Venus. He sneezed violently, threw the jug onto the hedge and ran back inside his house. We boys rocked wildly trying to keep from blowing our cover by hee-hawing and arousing the city police. Then we headed home…another night's work completed…

"RUN, RUN!"

We three were playing once again in the new educational building one night, and didn't know Bro. Mac was in his office. I guess we made a noise, and we heard him running toward us. He might have thought it was a burglar or something, because the church was not locked at night! Again, he MAY have known it was us and intended to teach us a lesson…which he did!

We scrambled out a window and took off running, clearing about a four foot hedge that ran between the church and Walker's cleaners. We thought that would be the barricade that would save us. Wrong! Hearing his footsteps, we looked back and he was coming right on. He'd leapt over it, too! I crossed Main Street and slid under Fannie's Flower Shop's delivery van. I don't remember where Jerre went, but he didn't want his Daddy to catch him, that's for sure.

Bro. Mac caught up with Bobby and drew back a fist. Bobby shouted, "Don't hit me, it's me, Bobby Gassiott, don't hit me!" You know, I don't remember us ever playing in the church any more after that.

BOOSTING T. U. ATTENDANCE

I got to where I could play just about any song I heard. My peers and I would meet in the sanctuary before Training Union on Sunday night, and I would entertain them on the Hammond organ. I set up that folding pump organ to my right, pumping it with my right foot. My left foot got the bass pedals on the organ and my hands played on both manuals. It also had chimes and an echo box up in the balcony.

I would play pop songs like "Twilight Time" just like The Three Sons, I thought. Other titles were "Autumn Leaves," "Music, Music, Music," "Cruising Down the River," "Third Man Theme," "Goodnight, Irene," "In the Mood," and a bunch of others. The gang would often sing along. I looked back one time and was horrified to see a little Dean boy walking that narrow plank on top of the balcony like a tight rope artist! Had he fallen, it would have killed him for sure. Anyhow, I feel like I helped boost T. U. attendance. My close friend, Gail Tarver would bring with her a friend, Annette Taylor who lived in Florida. She always had the darkest tan, and came to visit her grandmother Taylor who lived next door to the Tarver family. Her grandfather was a barber and often cut Huey P. Long's hair! Gail and I dated some while I worked at the bank in the early 50s.

I remember one Sunday afternoon at church when we were all assembled around the organ, news was brought by a friend that Larry Kennedy and some friends out "joy-riding" had run off the dyke east of town on US-84, landing in flood waters. It seems like the Kennedys had a Kaiser or Fraser automobile. One old boy began frantically swimming for higher ground only to discover he was in about two feet of water!

Another time, Jerre, Bobby and I got the bright idea of laying a hymnal on the blade of a ceiling fan hanging down from the ceiling of the balcony. One of us would go back to the electric box in the left vestibule and touch the switch to the power, making the fan start turning. The idea was to see how fast the fan could go before the book went sailing across the room. Instead, the *blade* came off and flew across the room, hitting a door facing just as one of our friends (a girl) walked through. We had not counted on something like that, and it scared us good! It notched the door facing! Needless to say we never did that again, either.

Mr. Walker owned the Cleaners on the west side of the church. He would sit in his office at night and drink. We would phone him and hang up, or knock on the front door, to make him mad. He would cuss. I guess we'll answer for that meanness someday. I don't know where I would have gotten a nickel, but some Sundays between Sunday school and church, we boys would run to the American Café (between the cleaners and Buchanan's grocery) and get a Grapette or an Orange Crush. We would flip the coin in the air, then flop it on our forearm and call it. The one who lost paid for the drink. I reckon I bragged one day to Mama that Bobby had to buy my drink and when she found out what we did, said that was gambling, and not do it again.

B. B. McKINNEY

Mr. Tom McKinney lived about three blocks from our South King street house, up on the north side of Lafayette Street. He was a brother of the famous hymn writer, B. B. McKinney, who was with the Baptist Sunday School Board (now Lifeway) in Nashville for many years. Tom had a beautiful tenor voice and was in demand to lead singing in revivals, as well as sing solos. Gertrude (and then I) played for him on many occasions. I remember Gertrude played for a revival at some country church and her gift for doing so was a brand new pair of underwear!

Bro. Tom, as well as Roy Miller, had their own shape note Broadman hymnals, kept in the choir room at First Baptist church. Houston Gates was the song leader at First Baptist. He would come in after Sunday school and say, "Well, what do you want to do as a choir special this morning?" But I do remember us working up some choir music on special occasions. Houston would sit in one of the big chairs on the platform, and during the offering, the big heavy wooden plate would be passed through the choir loft. Well, all those faithful folks had already put their offering envelope in Sunday school. When the empty plate came back to Houston, I've seen him sit there and fan with it. He would stand out on the sidewalk when he had no customers and drink a coke. I went to his house one time on Maple Street. They had about two dozen cats! He had perhaps fifty suits in his closet!

I got side-tracked. Let's go back to the McKinney family. I was privileged to attend their family reunion once, just south of Minden, LA. I heard B. B. tell how he got the idea for some of his compositions; here are two of them: 1) Growing up he noticed that every evening at dusk his Mother would "come up missing." One day he followed her from a distance and she walked out in the pasture to a grove of plum trees, where she knelt and prayed; he returned home. Later he wrote his song, "In the Secret Place of Prayer." 2) He and his wife had apparently not been "home" in several years and he was having trouble finding the road to old Bistenau Church. He stopped his car and said to a black man walking along the road, "I'm trying to get to old Bistenua Church, but this old road here is the only one I can find." The man replied, "The old road is the only road." And B. B. wrote his beautiful song by that name.

He certainly wrote a lot of songs we sing like, "Breathe on Me," "The Nail-scarred Hand," "Speak to my Heart," "God Give us Christian Homes," "Send a Great Revival," "Take up thy

Cross," "I am Satisfied with Jesus," and on and on we could go. He was called to his heavenly reward much too soon for all of us – I think he was in his fifties. It was my privilege to accompany him as he sang solos at First Baptist in Winnfield, while visiting his brother Tom. His widow used to phone me at the Benson Company in the 60s and we'd talk awhile. They said she drove a VW bug and when she entered the First Baptist Church parking lot downtown, folks got out of her way. She lived to be at least 92. First Baptist downtown is currently in a 20-year expansion plan. It will be across the street from the new convention center, a fantastic facility covering about six blocks and includes an Omni Hotel.

BAPTIZING IN DUGDEMONA

Here's an interesting, TRUE story about a baptizing Bro. H. H. McBride, pastor at FBC in Winnfield, *almost did* in Dugdemona Creek, where it goes under US-167 about four miles north of town. I was not there, but the complete story was told to me by Bro. Mac himself a few years ago when Marcia and I saw them in San Angelo, TX. Their son Jerre was pastor at FBC there for 31 years, and Bro. and Mrs. Mac had retired in that beautiful city. They passed away there, and Jerre's wife also passed away while living there. Here's the story:

"Big Brother" Long (or was it "Little Brother?" – doesn't matter I guess) had been saved in a meeting that Bro. Mac had preached at the Tannehill church, a small community just north of the creek. On a Sunday afternoon folks gathered on the creek bank to observe with glee his baptism. The water was much clearer then that it is now. After singing a hymn, Bro. Mac and Big Brother waded out in the water, and as Bro. Mac raised his hand and started speaking the appropriate words Big Brother spied a moccasin snake twisting toward the intruders of his domain.

Big Brother shouted, "(Bleep), preacher! There's a snake! Let's git outta here!" He exited the creek rather quickly and undignified. As he did so, he pushed off from Bro. Mac, who went backwards into water over his head. A month or so afterwards, someone told Bro. Mac that Big Brother had not been back to church services. Bro. Mac went to talk with him. Big Brother told him he really didn't remember what happened that day, but somebody told him he had yelled a "cuss" word and he was just too ashamed to go back to church. Bro. Mac convinced him that he should.

DRUG PROBLEMS IN TOWN

We became aware of illicit drugs in Winnfield when I was in high school. I'm sure they could have been there prior to that, however, and this was in the 40s. I will not name anyone, of course, but will tell of one outstanding instance. Bro. Mac stood up for "his church kids."

One day a suspected dealer was driving on Laurel Street between the church and the Winnfield Hotel. Bro. Mac flagged him down and confronted him about his activity. A heated argument ensued and before he knew it, Bro. Mac slugged him through the open driver's window. The man bounced off the passenger door and took off promptly to the police station. When the case came up, the judge fined him one dollar, then paid the fine for him! Some residents said if the truth came out about the drug problem it would "blow the lid" off Winnfield." At least that is the way it was told to me.

Even a high school teacher was involved. I was glad to see him become a one-year-teacher, for personal reasons. I guess I was bored in whatever class he was teaching and did something he didn't like. He said, "Alright, Mercer, git up here." As I stood up I managed to slip the text book in the seat of my pants, but he didn't see me do it. He said to grab my ankles and he hit me a good lick with his paddle that left him vibrating like some character in a cartoon. Everyone laughed, but he was not a happy camper. He yanked the book out and told me to bend over again, and he sho' 'nuff set my posterior on fire.

Bobby Gassiott was on the Tiger football team. Mama let me ride with the Gassiotts in their Dodge car to a game in Mansfield, south of Shreveport. On the way back I was squeezed in the back seat between Bobby and another player named Chan Hambleton. Their body odor liked to have "got" me! Yet another time, Mama let me ride the bus with the football players for a game in Bastrop, north of Monroe.

Several of us boys at Winnfield High School formed a group we called the WPLA, which stood for "The Winnfield Professional Loafers Association." What did we do? **Nothing...** And we were good at it, too. We were often seen on campus jammed close behind each other walking in step like a centipede. It was fun and funny. We even got our picture put in the school yearbook! Bobby Gassiott could wiggle his big ears and he kept us amused in dull classes. I don't know how he could do that.

Eula's "Tiger" Inn was situated across the street just north of the high school. It was a little one room shack. Her last name was Ezell, I believe, and she operated it for 30 years! Just about any time of the day kids would go over there for cokes, cookies, and other stuff, like cigarettes I imagine. The fourth weekend in June is when the general reunion of WHS is held and usually well over 300 attend. The class celebrating their 50th anniversary is in charge of the program – actually all activities (including food) for the 2-day event. The 2013 class built a replica of Eula's!

Moving on – there was a preacher from Oklahoma who came to Winnfield, bringing his campaign against the evils of strong drink. Bro. Mac had him speak at our church. His name was Sam Morris, and he published a newspaper called *The Voice of Temperance.* After the service…and I don't know how this happened…but Daddy got him to come home with us for "dinner." Only thing, Mama may not have known about it. But she whipped up a good meal and fixed her special combination of home-made lemonade "spiked" with ginger ale. Ol' Sam smacked his lips and, frankly, I don't recall how many glasses he drank!

For offertory one Sunday (Mary Nell Beck on the Hammond organ and I on the grand piano) we played "In the Garden." As we got near the end, "None other...has ever..." TOIOIOINNNGGGG! A treble string broke and popped against the raised lid like a rifle shot. It even woke up Bro. Milam who had already settled down for a good nap. [One Sunday he did go to sleep standing during the invitation and leaning against a column supporting the balcony. Bro. Mac called on him to dismiss in prayer! Mrs. Milam elbowed him and told him to pray and he laid a good one on us]. Another time I was "gettin' with it" on a foot-stompin' evangelistic song, ran up the keyboard and a piece of ivory flew off the keyboard out into the congregation!

I entered a jingle contest for Charcoal Gum: can you imagine chewing gum that tasted and looked like a piece of charcoal? The brand didn't last long. My jingle won me a carton of the stuff. I don't remember exactly what I wrote but it went something like this: *"Charcoal gum is good to chew...Makes your false teeth look like new."*

PLAYING HOOKY

Roger Melton and I were good friends. One day at school Roger decided to take a ride on Jenna Faye Whatley's motor scooter – a big bulky contraption. Apparently she rode it to school from her house out on US-84 west. He talked me into going with him. I shouldn't have!

We were enjoying a good ride through town when he turned east on Maple Street. Roger thought it would be great fun to ride the thing on the sidewalk. Then, suddenly he turned down a short but steep driveway back to the street. Loose gravel was our downfall, literally. Legs, arms, elbows, heads went everywhere! He was wearing Jenna Faye's athletic (letter) jacket and tore the elbow badly. Thank the Lord, the scooter started - we got back on and went straight to Walker's cleaners, next to the First Baptist Church, where it was repaired.

I just about "majored" in *playing hooky.* I rode my bike to and from school, sometimes grabbing onto a long pole hanging off the back of a truck heading for the creosote plant. My guardian angel must have been horrified while undoubtedly protecting me! I imagine he requested a transfer many times!

I never was good at any kind of athletics. My flat feet were the problem. I was recruited by teachers to type for them, sometimes cutting stencils of their tests and running them off on the mimeograph machine. They trusted me not to give them to my friends, which I did not. Our sophomore class was the first allowed to take "commerce" or typing. Miss Lois Edwin Rogers was the teacher. In six weeks I took a ten minute typing test and made 100 words per minute...but I'd made ten errors so that lowered me to 90 wpm. Still not bad! Keep in mind this was not an electric typewriter either! Probably an old Underwood or L. C .Smith.

Our football coach was Emmit Cope. Because of my extreme flat feet I had a doctor's excuse from PE class. I typed the thesis for his Master's Degree...with all the margins, footnotes, ibids, etc. One day he had nothing for me to do so I said I'd go by the office and see if any teachers had work for me. Well, I went BY the office alright and right out the front door where I leaped on my trusty Blue Horse bike and took off. Then I heard a shrill whistle and knew I was caught. Coach Cope and the football team came around the side of the building on their way two blocks east to the football field for practice. I sheepishly waited for him to approach me. He said, "Now, Mercer, that's the first typewriter I ever saw with wheels on it." Pointing at the school, he added, "Get yourself back in there!"

The assistant coach was a young man named Bill Davis. Both men later went to other schools and moved up in their school positions. Bill Davis and his wife have attended our high school reunions.

EARLY ROAD TRIPS

I guess the first vacation trip our family got to make was in 1949. Earl and Betty, in their car, took Mama, Daddy, Ronnie (3 years old) and me to Hot Springs, Arkansas, 225 miles north of Winnfield. The Ouachita Mountains in that vicinity are the first mountains I ever saw, about 1500 feet in elevation. From West Mountain you can look down on Central Avenue. We heard singing apparently coming from a rescue mission. Years later Rev. Rex Humbard told me his Mother operated a rescue mission at Hot Springs along about then. By the way, Rex and wife Maude Aimee recorded on a Benson label; and years later I went to his *Cathedral of Tomorrow* in Akron, OH with Bob Harrington, Jack Price and Steve Adams.

Across the way was Hot Springs Mountain. There was a Navy Hospital located up there, along with a tall observation tower. Down on Central Avenue were all the historic bathhouses. There is a HOT water fountain on the sidewalk that you can drink from – it is 142 degrees and it won't scald your mouth. But if you re-heated the water to that temperature and take a drink it would burn you! Go figure.

There was a place called "Happy Hollow" on Fountain Street just east of the huge Arrington Hotel. You could drink all you wanted and have no adverse effects. Believe it or not, I drank eight "horseshoe glasses" and it never bothered me. You didn't even feel full. We also visited the Alligator Farm and the horse racing track south of town. There are three beautiful lakes in the vicinity – Catherine, Hamilton and Ouachita.

FAREWELL TO WHS

Jerre and I came up with a plan to bid farewell to good ol' Winnfield High School on the last day we seniors were required to attend. We gave a maid a quarter to let us use, very briefly, a 55-gallon steel barrel that trash was dumped in as they cleaned the building. Returning from lunch after all students were in their 4th period classes, we went to "work."

We positioned that barrel with almost half of the bottom hanging out over the top step. I stout string was attached to a handle and run down the stairway and back up. Miss Perdue's English classroom had a front and back door. Jerre went in the front apologizing for being late to class, as I slipped in the back door and sat down at a desk. I held the string in my hand.

Jerry looked back my way with a slight nod of his head. I gently pulled on the string and threw it out in the hallway. KA-LAM-BAM! The barrel bounced down the steel steps, somehow made the turn at the landing and rolled down onto the first floor very near the door to the school office. Our plan worked to perfection! The school was in an uproar. Students on our floor rushed to the doors wondering what had happened. Mr. Donald Turner, across the hallway from where I was sitting, rubbed his chin and with a smile said, "Well, I have no idea what happened, but I imagine Elmo had something to do with it!"

OUR TRIP TO MEXICO

The biggest trip was when Earl and Betty took our family to Mexico. We crossed the border at Del Rio, TX. Along the highway headed for Monterey we saw a flock of sheep with their shepherd, his dog and a little burro. We spent the night further down in the town of Saltillo. The meat at supper was tough and Mama said, "I wonder if it's that little burro we saw back up the road!" Our "motel" room was rustic and during the night I heard a screeching whistle on a train...not like the one Andrew Jenkins blew on the T&G engine. It was unnerving, making me realize we were in a *foreign* country! But by going on this trip I missed my high school graduation exercises. When we got home I went to the school board and picked up my diploma.

Between Winnfield and Natchitoches on US-84 by the bridge that crosses the Red River are the Grandicore Bluffs. That is pronounced *Gran-d-ko.* Earl took us over there for the day and we had a great time exploring the hills and ravines. It is now a Louisiana state commemorative area. Mama excused herself and disappeared over a forested hill. After a couple of minutes we heard a surprised yell. Mama had bent down and grabbed hold of a weed or bush for support, and it had come out of the ground, sending her "heels over head" down the ravine. When we left the area Earl pulled out onto the highway just as Daddy went to drink from a half-gallon glass jug of water. When Earl shifted gears from low to second the water sloshed and almost drowned Daddy. He just looked over at Earl and said, "Well, son!"

In June of 1947 I had played piano for Earl and Betty's wedding at First Baptist Church in Epps, LA, in the northeast part of the state. Her father, Bro. Dewey Rockett, was pastor there and performed the ceremony. It was the first of hundreds of weddings I've played for over the decades. One big wedding I played for was in Bowling Green, KY in 1970 (I believe it was). Duane Allen, the lead singer of the Oak Ridge Boys, who were then recording gospel songs on a Benson label. He married Nora Lee Stuart, the Benson receptionist at our Fourth Avenue offices in the Benson Printing Company building. She and her two sisters were known as the Stuart Sisters and sang on gospel music programs. Later she, along with Carol Snow and two men were the back-up singers on the Grand Ole Opry for years.

Moving ahead to 1953, in my new red and white 4-door Chevy, I took Mama, Daddy, Ronnie, plus Uncle Morgan and Aunt Lorraine on a trip up the Blue Ridge Parkway in North Carolina. We did not go on up into Virginia. It is such a beautiful drive, no trucks allowed, with numerous pullouts for distant views. We enjoyed Mt. Mitchell, the highest point east of the Mississippi River. We took the beautiful drive up Grandfather Mountain, believed to be the oldest mountain range in the US. We went to Linville Falls and Gorge, Blowing Rock, etc. Apparently, Daddy didn't have much confidence in my driving the mountainous road, and he told me, "Be careful, son. If you was to run over a corncob it could throw us off the mountain!" Uncle Morgan got such a kick out of that! About the time Daddy said it we came out of a tunnel. Water was pouring down on the highway and hit the windshield. Daddy threw up his hands in self-defense!

It was on that return trip that we came by Nashville, and spent the night in the Mercury Motel on Lafayette Street. Next day I met Mr. John T. Benson, Jr. for the first time. [I had been a staff writer since March 1951].

MY COLLEGE EXPERIENCE

In view of my going to college I began checking into different ones. I even thought about Ouachita Baptist College in Arkadelphia, AR, not many miles south of Hot Springs – also Oklahoma Baptist College. I had my mind set on becoming a commerce (typing) teacher in high school. Then came the idea to attend Louisiana Tech at Ruston, 48 miles north of Winnfield. The First Baptist Church there invited me to come play their organ on a Sunday morning as they were needing one. I wore a robe with the biggest sleeves I'd ever seen. I could hold both arms out beside me and look like a big bat! I was told to hit a chime eleven times and that signaled the service would begin. God had other plans for me, however.

It was probably the school year 1949-50, my senior year, when Ralph Young came to First Baptist Church in Winnfield to lead singing in a revival. He was from southern Mississippi. Little did I know that was the start of a lifelong friendship. He had a red Ford coupe, so Jerre and I liked to ride with him, it didn't matter to us where we went. Of course, I was pianist for the meeting.

Ralph told me later that he saw the talent God had given me. He encouraged me not only to keep composing gospel songs and hymns but to see if I could join some evangelist and tour the country. Of course that never occurred to me. Perhaps God *did* want me to do that, *but I didn't.* Ralph entered the preaching ministry later and was pastor at FBC in Escatawpa, MS for 28 years. He had other pastorates in Fulton, AL and Moss Point, MS. He had Marcia and me to come sing at all three places. He was such an inspiration to me! Ralph never married. He and his Mother lived together until she passed away. He had a little dog named "Mister" that loved to ride a tricycle. Ralph passed away in the early 2000s.

When I finished WHS in May 1950 I had decided to go to Louisiana College in Pineville like Earl and Gertrude had. So I left home that fall for that purpose. Marcia's distant cousin, Bullard Jones, agreed to let me be his roommate...a senior and a freshman. Like a good Baptist, I immediately moved my church membership to First Baptist in Pineville where most LC students went. Yet that wasn't really necessary because I planned to go home every weekend! I just attended Wednesday night prayer meeting there. I rode with Edward Smith who lived up in the Sikes LA area. By the way, the Pineville church was built exactly like the one in Winnfield. I guess they used the same blueprints.

One Sunday night while I was enrolled at LC, and home for the weekend, after the service at FBC was finished, several of us headed out north of town to a farm "they" knew had a field of sugar cane just waiting to be thinned out. I never stole a watermelon in my life, and this is the only time I "procured" a few stalks of sugar cane. We helped the girls over the fence and proceeded to harvest some. But a hound dog cut loose to baying at us. Soon we heard the screen door slam and a man hollered, "You boys git outta my cane patch," followed by a shotgun blast (into the air I hoped).

Hey, the girls were on their own getting back over that fence. The pickup truck took off, with the cane in the back blowing in the wind. The car I was in was close behind. We stopped up the road somewhere and enjoyed some sugar cane. I got home just in time for Edward to pick me up going back to college. Edward did become an outstanding preacher and pastor.

My college "career" didn't last nearly as long as Earl and Gertrude's. Actually, it was only 3 and ½ weeks! I had become a rebellious teenager. I did not take any courses in Bible or music.

On a test in one of my courses, I thought I had done quite well. But when the grades were posted on the classroom door, there was a "D" by my name! I couldn't find a job on or off campus. Earl usually preached somewhere on Sundays. Gertrude became a nurse at an Alexandria hospital. I knew Mama and Daddy couldn't afford tuition. So we discussed this while I was home and it was decided for me to just come back home and attend the Huey Long Memorial Trade School, which I did.

Before my final departure, I left my "mark", or reputation on the L. C. campus. One night I went into the main administration building where the big practice pipe organ was located. I turned the contraption on, opened a window and blasted out Tommy Dorsey's "Boogie Woogie!" I turned it off, left, and cut through the bushes and shadows to make my way back to my room in Godbold Hall. Next day that was the talk of the campus. I just smiled. At breakfast one morning in the dining hall, not many showed up; but plates of eggs, toast, sausages, jelly were set on the table(s). Well, I asked around the rectangular tables (seating eight) and nobody wanted any of it. I guess they just ate dry cereal. Well, you know what eventually happened!

Edward Smith brought me back home with what little belongings I had down there. I had bought me a cap with the letters "LC" on it. First Baptist in Pineville returned my letter to the Winnfield church in good standing (they didn't know about the sugar cane heist). Later I received a bill from the college for $105 to cover the three and a half weeks I spent there...I guess that included the eggs, too.

Well, a few months later, on March 27, 1951, I signed my first writer's contract with John T. Benson Publishing Company in Nashville. F. D. "Pete" Borland, led singing in a revival at FBC Winnfield and I showed him some of my original songs. As God would have it, he was compiling a songbook for youth called "Singing Joy" for Benson, and he took five of my songs to show to Mr. John T. He took all five of them (pretty good percentage, right?). That's how I was introduced to Benson. As time went on, I continued to meet my songwriting obligation to the Benson Company: to write 26 songs a year. That was one every two weeks...no sweat. This somewhat soothed my conscious about not going into full-time Christian work.

SITTIN' SIDEWAYS

Bro. McBride moved on to another pastorate, and the First Baptist Church at Winnfield began the search for a new pastor. The church voted to call Dr. W. L. Holcomb of Mississippi, and he was there many years. He assisted my brother, Earl, in our marriage ceremony in October 1954. I'll cover that story later.

A revival meeting would sometimes go on for two weeks back in those days. Some said you couldn't get saved except during the August revival! It was quite evident that an evangelist was sitting sideways in the pulpit chair one night, with his hip raised a bit. We wondered if he had gas! Well, we found out what had happened. He was staying down at Mercer's Goat Castle Motel, built by a third cousin to Daddy during WWII, and frankly, it had some construction flaws. As he went to take a quick shower, he laid his lighted cigarette (are you kidding me?) on the edge of the lavatory. Upon stepping out, he toweled off his upper body and then bent forward to dry his legs. CONTACT! His posterior came in direct contact with the fiery end of the cigarette. [God has a sense of humor, you know]. He lunged forward still in a crouched position and it was said that his head busted through the wallboard! So, he sat sideways! His head looked okay to me.

MY FIRST FULL-TIME JOB

I immediately enrolled at the Huey P. Long Memorial Trade (Vocational) School in Winnfield, located then at the corner of West Lafayette and South Jones Streets. I finished their two year typing course in three months. I took shorthand, using "the latest technology": a wire recorder! When that thing jammed, you had problems. I made 175 wpm. I also took a bookkeeping course with all the debits and credits, and learned how to use a calculator which did come in handy.

Then I got a job with Alvin Hahn Insurance, also known as General Finance Company on north Abel Street. He was the husband of a high school teacher, Sadie Hahn, who was a character herself! His mother was a Russian Jew, his father was a German Jew (or vice-versa). They had two daughters: Suzanne, was the oldest (she later married John Astin who starred in the "Addams Family" TV program. They later divorced). The younger daughter was Abigail, who has attended our general high school reunions in June.

Mr. Hahn was quite a man-about-town. He would park his Mercury automobile somewhere then walk around talking with folks, finally coming back to the office. Sometimes he would send me out looking for his car, not remembering where he had parked it! Mrs. Lessie Lee Cockerham worked there. She later married Marcia's Uncle Clifford, a brother to her mother. They lived around the curve on the same road the Fletcher house was on. He passed away a few years later. Also Mary Lou Shelton from Calvin worked there, too. I remember folks coming in to pay their notes on refrigerators, washing machines, cars, etc. They would pull money out of several pockets till they came up with enough.

GOD GETS MY ATTENTION

When I got the full-time job at Alvin Hahn's, I had to switch to night classes at the Trade School. [By the way, several years later Marcia took some classes there, too]. On the evening of February 18, 1951 while riding my bike to the school, I was hit by a pulpwood truck whose driver "cut the corner" at Lafayette and Bevill Streets, at the west end of the overhead bridge. My left thigh was broken, likely by the left handle bar that was broken as well.

I do not remember this, of course, but they said I landed on the hood then slid off on the ground, the dual back wheels stopping about six inches from crushing my skull. Had the truck been loaded I would surely have gone through the windshield. I do remember in the ambulance, I pleaded for them to "break the news *easy* to Mama," because of Earl's traumatic injury about ten years before.

I lay flat on my back in the Winnfield General Hospital for two weeks, with traction on my left leg: the heavy weights pulled me to the foot of the bed. Two nurses would occasionally come in my room – one would lift the weights while the other pulled me back toward the head of the bed. My leg swelled to twice its usual size. So, while lying there, looking up at the ceiling (no TV then), I began to do some thinking. God had gotten my attention in a violent way, but had spared my life as well. You could say I came to my senses, repented and asked God to help me get my life back in His will.

And you know, the Bible says God chastens HIS children when they stray, to bring them back to HIM *because He loves them.* This has happened several times in my life, I regret to say. But that just reinforces the FACT that I AM His child...that I am passed from death unto life! Such assurance is beyond our understanding, yet we know our blessed Savior died ONCE for ALL. Praise His holy name!

After two weeks or so, a nurse and a black orderly came to get me up so I could try out my new crutches! Why, I hadn't even been operated on yet! The weights were disconnected and when my foot hit the cold floor, I slumped and passed out. The nurse grabbed onto me, but the orderly moaned, "Lawdy me, he's gone!" and headed out the door. The nurse ordered him back to help her get me back on the bed. *Why couldn't they have laid them by me on the bed to see if they were the right length?*

Dr. John McElwee was my doctor. I needed surgery. He called a surgeon friend of his in Monroe to come down and do the operation. I believe his name was Dr. Altenberg. That type surgery cost $500 back then and he did it for only $150, and it lasted 3 or 4 hours. During WWII the Germans invented a new way to treat broken bones. Remember ten years earlier, Earl was put in a body cast for six *months.* I don't know the full procedure but a long incision was made on the front of my thigh, then they went into the hip and drove a steel pin down through the bone. I was up walking with a cane in no time. The first day I returned to work at Hahn's, he dictated 34 letters to me (I took them in shorthand) to send to people who were delinquent in their note payments. They all began with, "For your information and guidance..."

Three months after my surgery I took the afternoon off and went to the hospital where Dr. McElwee, cranked the pin back out. The thing went from the hip to just above the knee, maybe fifteen inches long...it looked like a towel rack! It was coming right along when it stopped. I am telling the truth – the doctor got a hammer and somehow was able to hit (not tap) the apparatus that was twisting the pin out. I feel certain I left my finger prints under that steel table. A nurse put a pillow over my head and sat on it, probably thinking Mama would hear me screaming a mile away! It's a wonder I wasn't suffocated! After a few minutes of that torture, I walked out of the hospital twirling my walking cane, and went back to work the next morning.

THE BANK OF WINNFIELD

A former schoolmate of Earl's, Bob Baker, worked at the Bank of Winnfield and Trust Company, the only bank in the parish. He said I might be able to go to work there. I began to give that serious thought. Several weeks later the opportunity presented itself and I told Mr. Hahn what I was going to do. He said he would match what the bank offered if I would just stay on with him. I told him my mind was made up.

My first duty there was running a Burroughs-Sensimatic-200 bookkeeping machine, posting deposits and checks to customer accounts. I caught on to that quickly and enjoyed it. After a few days, and this was in November 1951, all staff had left but the owner/president Mr. Joe Heard and me. As he was leaving he paid me for about three days' work...in silver dollars. I thanked him and dropped them in my pants pocket and they almost fell to my ankles. I tightened my belt. A man at our church, Fletcher Melton, asked me to be on the lookout for a 1907 silver dollar...that was his birth year. Those coins were still in circulation quite a bit, and almost a year later I found one.

My fellow workers were Mr. Heard's two sons, Robert (the older) and Richard. They were both sergeants during WWII and chased Field Marshall Rommel all over North Africa and up into Italy! Then there was Bob Baker, Marvin Carraway,

G. W. Jones and Jim Russell. Joyce Rigdon and Louise Frazier rounded out the employees. A black and white TV set was mounted at the front corner above and between the heavy glass front doors: one opened on Main, the other on Abel Street. Before we opened we would watch the Jack Parr show; and after we closed, the serial, "The Edge of Night" came on.

Robert, a bachelor, loved to fish. A friend of his, Carmen Anderson (son of Lon, the barber) arrived one morning before the blinds were raised (they hung about two feet from the floor), and the doors opened. He stood so his long string of about ten big crappie could be seen by Robert from where he stood getting his window ready for business. He started salivating! Carmen knew he would. He walked in to Rob's window when the doors were opened by one of us, and said, "Robert, you'll think I'm lyin', but I caught all these from the time I lit a cigarette till I flipped it away!" Robert was sick that he had to stay and work till at least 2 p.m. when we closed.

Richard was married with two sons until another one came along. Their ages were twelve, six and the baby. He said he and his wife "misbehaved" every six years! Robert got the nick name "Po' Rob" from talking to a little black boy who came to his window at the bank. He said, "Son, what's your name?" The boy simply replied, "They just calls me Po' Rob."

We were like a big family at the bank. We all got along so well. Sometimes we'd play practical jokes on each other, mostly on Bob Baker who took it all good-naturedly. One particular morning, he had gone back to the men's restroom, down a narrow hallway. (Mr. Heard had not come in yet). I lit and threw a firecracker that landed just outside the men's room door. The noise was loud! A few minutes later Bob came out, smiled and said, "Thanks, fellers, I needed that this morning!"

THE CAMP HOUSE PARTY

The Heard brothers had a camp house on Saline Lake, eighteen miles west on the north side of US-84. Saline had trees in it and was an excellent place for fishing. One night, they gave a party for bank employees and their spouses. Rob had me go with him ahead of time and we got in his flat-nosed boat with a small gas engine on the back. He knew where mayhaws could be found. Mayhaws are like plums and a lot of the time they are found in areas where water abounds.

We were scooping them up with nets and dumping them in a #3 washtub in the boat. He decided to bump a tree to make them fall and told me to hold on. BUMP! Then he yelled, "Be still, be still!" as he eased back away from the tree. I looked up and saw a huge hornet's nest hanging from a limb, and they were buzzing all around. They were mad...and we were scared!

We moved to another area and he thought I could do better if I got out in the water, so over the side I went. I stumbled over a log (I guess it was) and briefly went under the surface. Soon we left and went to the camp. I reckon I carried other clothes to put on for the party. Rob took the mayhaws out to a homemade still. He said they would pour off the mash and wild hogs that ate it would go staggering off through the woods! Someone asked Rob where he found all the mayhaws and he said, "Over at Alligator Slough." I almost fainted! When you opened the door to enter the bathroom, your eyes fell on a life-size cardboard cutout of Marilyn Monroe like she'd just gotten up from the john. People would jump back and say, "Oh, excuse me!"

At the bank, I got two weeks paid vacation plus we observed about a dozen (paid) holidays each year. At Christmas we would receive bonuses, usually a month's salary. We closed for Robert E. Lee's birthday, Jefferson Davis' birthday, Confederate Memorial Day, etc., but stayed open for Lincoln's birthday. Southern sentiment was still alive and well in the 50s in Winnfield, LA.

After we married, and Marcia got the secretarial job at the LA Welfare Department, we thought we had the world by the tail. Mr. John T. Benson tried to get us to move to Nashville in 1956 but I (we) didn't want to. Why, our combined salaries were over $9,000 per year! Our awesome Heavenly Father is so very patient and loving. He continued to work His will in our lives and *we didn't even know it back then!*

NATCHITOCHES, LOUISIANA

A famous sports caster on NFL football games one time commented that a player who had just run for a touchdown was a graduate of Northwest Louisiana State located in *Natch-e-toe-chis.* That was so funny. It is pronounced *Nack-uh-tush.* This lovely city is the oldest city in the state. Folklore says an Indian chief had two sons. One was named Natchitoches, the other named Nacogdoches, said to be the oldest town in Texas. If I am wrong, I apologize.

Natchitoches is 33 miles west of Winnfield and the beautiful and peaceful Cane River flows through it. Some say it used to be the channel for the Red river as it is noted for changing course when it takes a notion. The Civil War movie "Horse Soldiers" was shot along the Cane River east of downtown. We drove over there one day. It starred John Wayne and William Holden. In the story, they had to vacate their position and field hospital fast. The last man to leave rode his horse frantically across a plank bridge which was blowing up in sections right behind him! You don't shoot a scene like that but once. And down US-71 south of Clarence there was a little white wooden church up on a hill. You may recall the scenes in the church service when the black choir was singing. Now they have a new brick sanctuary.

"Steel Magnolias" was also filmed in downtown Natchitoches. A sign in the front yard of an antebellum home tells about that. Front Street on the west side of the river has French ironwork on two and three story buildings for several blocks. When we lived there we would go over the first Friday night in December to watch their fireworks on both sides of the river. Marcia's brother, Bernard attended Northwestern State there for a couple of semesters, then joined the Navy. He got his college degree while he served 27 years. In the spring of 2013 we drove through town and found the city still does the fireworks, now a tradition.

IT HAPPENED AT THE BANK

Mr. George Brown (not his real name) drove a Studebaker and lived on Maple Street. He was so germ-conscious. It was said that if he picked up someone in his car, he flipped open the glove compartment and had them wash their hands in rubbing alcohol. One day he came in the bank to go to his safety deposit box. He paused, as usual at the steel door to come behind the counters to get to the outer vault, and put on his white gloves.

Waiting a few minutes for him to open his box, I told my fellow employees to "watch this." I grabbed the key to the inner vault and as I passed Mr. Brown I cheerfully said, "Good morning, Mr...uh...ah, ah, ca-CHOO! Excuse me, sir, I'm afraid I'm catching a cold this morning." As I put the key in the vault door, I heard Mr. Brown slam his box shut. He practically *ran* out of the building, the guys said. [Hey, I was just building my reputation, ok?]

A local logging contractor came to see Mr. Heard one day to finance the purchase of a new *power saw.* Mr. Heard thought he said *parasol,* and exclaimed loud enough for us to hear, "What? You want me to loan you two hundred dollars to buy a parasol?" We tried to control ourselves. They finally came to an understanding!

We learned not to ask Mrs. Perkins (not her real name) how she felt "today." She would take time to alphabetize her ailments for us. Finally the teller would get to wait on her. Another lady came in every now and then. It was told that she once wheeled into a gas station and said, "Jeff and I are going on vacation. Please put some fresh air in the tires!" I am serious. Winnfield had some characters living there.

A high society-type lady came to Bob's window and loudly said, "Good morning, Robert. Would you change this *hundred dollar bill* for me, please?" "Yes ma'am, I'll be glad to. How would you like it?" "Oh, *four twenty-fives* will be alright." "Uh...how 'bout I give you *five twenties?*" "Oh, that will be just fine, Robert." An elderly lady would come in and the teller would ask her how she was feeling and she'd say, "Well, just *sorta." What the heck did that mean?* A Mr. Horace Peters would walk around downtown carrying his little dog in the crook of his arm licking an ice cream cone. Joe Bevill ran for alderman one time and got very few votes. The next day he walked around town with toy (I hope they were) twin pistols on his hips. He said a fellow with no more friends in town than he had should never go out on the street unarmed!

One of Po' Rob's cronies came to his teller window. Rob asked him how he was doing and he replied, "Not too good, Rob. Last night I eat some turnip greens and they *went down on me!"* Again, what did that mean? On the day the new 1955 Chevrolet hit the showroom, before 9 a.m. some of us walked across the street and down the block to Max Thieme's dealership to view them. I was not all that impressed (I had a 1953 Buick) and on the way back I commented, "Why I've seen prettier grills on gas space heaters!"

My first car was a pale green 1950 Chevrolet Styleline. It was a "demonstrator" that A. G. Kimball drove, a salesman at Max Thieme. I put a squirrel tail on the radio antenna, mud flaps behind all tires, chrome rain guards over the four windows and ordered off for turn signals for $8.95. I got a mechanic to install them on the steering column. I put a knob on the steering wheel for quick turns. I parked it right outside the bank, we all did. Most customers walked to the bank anyway. Then in 1953 I bought a brand new red and white 4-door Chevy, but in about six months traded it for a 1953 Buick...the last of the straight 8s. I had just gotten it when Marcia and I started dating. Bless her heart, she married a banker, but little did we know God's plans!

The bank was open Mon-Fri 9 a.m. to 2 p.m. and on Saturday 9 a.m. to noon. I soon was working teller's windows also. Sometimes we left shortly after closing. Later I was moved over to the Loan department and I was once again taking payments for appliances, cars/trucks, even houses. Merchants would come in on Friday mornings and make a weekend loan of several thousand dollars in order to cash payroll checks at their stores. On Monday they brought in those checks as a deposit and paid off that short loan. You will NOT believe this – the fee was $1 per thousand borrowed!

{Before we left for work one morning Marcia said we would have breaded beef cutlets (?) for supper. I got home and had time to prepare them before going back to town to pick her up at 5 p.m. As I was dipping one back and forth between flour and a "beat-up" egg, suddenly something EXPLODED and yellow stuff blew all over the place! What in the world? I finally remembered we had set a frozen can of orange juice on the countertop but forgot to make it up for breakfast. It had ruptured! Then I had to clean up the mess!}

Mr. Joe Heard died in 1955. He was a respected man and had certainly been a blessing to my life. Back in those days, people *sat up with the dead* (like Ray Stevens' song says). My time was four to six a.m. and I think G. W. Jones was with me. It was a big funeral in Winnfield. We man at the bank were pallbearers. Robert and Richard took over operations. Years later Richard's son became bank president to the present.

Many times during a work day I would get an idea for a new song. I'd turn over a blank counter check and start writing notes and words so I would remember it. "Whatcha doin', Mercer?" "Writin' a new song." Laughter and some comments about my future would follow, all in good nature.

The bank was examined annually by both state and federal bank examiners. We all dreaded that. About the time they were expected we would glance occasionally toward the glass front doors. Finally below the venetian blinds we would see men with big briefcases standing there. Reluctantly we would open the wooden side door and welcome them inside. Yeah, right! It took several days for them to complete their work, and we always had to dig back into files and boxes, silently praying we could find items they wanted to review.

Sometimes after the 2 p.m. closing time, when teller's windows would be "balanced", there would be a discrepancy. We all would descend on that window to help find where the error or mix-up was. And I can tell you the sweetest, most welcome three words to hear someone shout was "Here it is!" I definitely remember the day my and Jim Russell's window was short a thousand dollars!

All of us searched. Jim and I went over transactions we'd made. That was a Friday when local merchants made their weekend loans. When I began thinking about bill denominations I had given to a merchant in East Winnfield (now Joyce), Tuley Wells, it became clear to me that I had actually given him a thousand dollars too much! The bank cashier, Po' Rob, had me to call Tuley and thank the Lord, he had not had occasion to get into any of that money yet. He counted it and sure enough, said he had a thousand more than he was supposed to have! I went with Rob about three miles out there (near the spot where the tent revival was that I rode my bike out to) to pick up the money. I said, "Thank you, Lord!" and was so relieved.

COURTIN'

After church one Sunday night I volunteered to drive Marcia Fletcher home, just off US-84 west of town. Joe Hassell seemed to be with her. We said goodnight to her and made sure she got in the front door and drove off. I thought it strange Joe didn't walk her to the door, but come to find out they were NOT dating. He said they used to live across the street from each other and were just good friends. Hmmm. Ideas began to swirl in my head. Johnnie's little sister had suddenly grown up!

I was a man of action. No grass grew under my tires! In a day or two I called and asked her if I could take her to a church youth party and she accepted! JOY! I didn't know but Branch later called her to work and she tried to get her Mama to call me. She refused, so Marcia phoned the bad news. I went on to the party and later she walked in after getting off work. I sidled up to her and said, "You wanta pick up where we left off?" What a line, huh? Obviously we did!

That was on the 8th of January, 1954. An old fiddle tune is named that, plus it is the anniversary of the Battle of New Orleans that Stonewall Jackson fought three weeks after the Civil War Armistice was signed! News traveled slowly in those days. Branch Drugs was right next to the Bank, on the Abel Street side. She worked there during the summer, too. Naturally, on my break-time I would go over for a cherry coke, sit on the stool at the counter and talk with her. We would go to church, to the movies, to parties, whatever…but most of our "courting" was done in her living room! About that time Patty Page was a favorite singer, and I especially liked, "Cross over the Bridge." Sitting there on the couch, Marcia threatened to throw me out in the middle of the floor! *{Egads! What did I do?}* Anyhow, I hooted at the idea. Next thing I know I am laid out flat on my back, looking up at a smiling face! **Note to self** - this girl has skills I knew nothing about. Watch her. I did!

[Marcia told me that when she was a child, she and some other kids (likely cousins) were playing Hide-and-Seek. It was night time and the adults were talking in the living room. When the door was closed the rest of the house was quite dark. A kid was counting and Marcia leaped up on the countertop and stood quietly against the upper cabinets. The "seeker" was roaming and looking everywhere. Suddenly, Marcia began to lose her balance (leaning forward) and had to take a step toward the stovetop. Her foot went right into a pot of white beans! Her parents wondered why she didn't eat any of them...she loved white beans! About forty years later she told them about the incident and her Daddy, smiling, threatened to still whip her!]

Her Daddy had a little squirrel dog named Trixie. She loved to "tree" squirrels, 'possums, or whatever. We would be sitting on the couch talking and we'd hear her barking down in the woods somewhere. Knowing she would bark all night, I would get her Daddy's gun (he was working the night shift at the Carey Salt Company) and along with her 12-year-old brother, Bernard, we'd take a flashlight and go to where she was. One night she treed three times. I thought, "This dog is interfering with my love life. What can be done? I mean like NOW!

We heard the door knob rattle between the front bedroom and the living room where we sat one night. Come to find out, Bernard had been peeping through the keyhole at us, dropped off to sleep and hit his head against the knob. We didn't know we were that dull! The view wasn't worth a black eye!

I was one who liked to plan my schedule in advance, and I always had a number of dates lined up – church, movies, parties, etc. After a few weeks, one night we stopped in her front yard. She was sitting by me (bench seat in the '53 Buick). Somehow I led up to the point where I asked her if she would marry me! And she said, ***"YES!"***

Apparently she had been talking with the Lord, and her Mama about *us!* You won't believe this: When she said yes,

I tilted her face to me and *kissed her for the FIRST time!* Ok, maybe I was a slow leak! On March 23, 1954, I presented her with her engagement ring. She was the envy of her high school girlfriends! [I sold my Webcor tape recorder to help pay for the engagement ring, the best one Paul's Jewelers had! Mama had been taping Sunday night radio programs of "Gunsmoke" for me to listen to later.

MARCIA'S GRADUATION

Marcia's high school graduation ceremony was held at night. Afterward two other couples piled in the back seat of my '53 Buick and we drove 24 miles north to a drive-in at Jonesboro. We sat in the car and ate hamburgers! Hey, we knew how to celebrate, didn't we!

One couple was Kathryn Prescott and Roy Jones, who both lived in the Pleasant Hill community off US-84 east of Winnfield. The other couple was Evie Sue Austin and A. L. Shirley, who both lived in the Tannehill community off US-167 north of town. They both married in December following our October wedding.

After more than 25 years, Kathryn passed away; and A. L. also died. In a year or so Evie Sue and Roy began dating and soon they were married. We thought that was so neat! Marcia and I have enjoyed staying in their home many times, especially during the WHS general reunions.

OUR WEDDING

On Saturday night, October 2, 1954, we were married in Marcia's living room. My brother, Earl, assisted by our pastor, Dr. W. L. Holcomb, performed the *short* ceremony – twelve minutes! That included two songs, "Always," and "Because", sung by Tom Marshall, who worked for the US Forestry. Earl's wife, Betty, played that now famous pump organ from our church.

When Earl, Dr. Holcomb, and my best man Gerald Buckley (Youth Minister at FBC) walked out of that front bedroom, I thought, "OK, boy, this is it!" Sweat was running down my back, even though it was October 2nd and I assure you there was no fire in the fireplace. Marcia's sister, Johnnie, was her bridesmaid. A few close relatives were present.

After the cake was cut and other "festivities" concluded, we left. It had been planned that Gerald would depart the house earlier to go to a designated meeting place. We bid everyone goodbye and got into Earl's car. My Buick was parked at a friend of Mama's in Jonesboro. I just knew the Buick would be "molested" if left available.

Three or four cars followed behind us. When Earl went up on the "overhead" bridge, he suddenly stopped by the stairwell on the east side. Marcia and I leaped out, ran down the steps and jumped in Gerald's Olds. As we took off north on Front Street the others were left up on the bridge, blowing their car horns in frustration. Earl went back to pick up Betty. He is lucky they hadn't formed a lynch party!

Well, that was the longest 24 mile trip I've ever experienced! Gerald was in a talking mood, with gesturing hands and no attention to his speed. Finally the swap was made and we thanked him, then headed north on US-167...another 25 miles to Ruston, LA. We were on our own at last...for the rest of our lives! We turned on US-80 and pulled up to the Lincoln Courts.

I cut the motor off and sat there a few seconds. Then it hit me: I've got to go in and get a room. Later, I discovered I was still wearing my dadgum flower, whatever it's called. I may as well have gone in with a big sign saying "Just married!" The guy carried our luggage in the room: I can't remember if I tipped him or not, probably didn't know I was supposed to! I do remember he shook my hand and as he was closing the door said, "Good luck!"

Next morning we headed for Hot Springs, AR, some 200 miles north up SR-7, a scenic highway. OK, I can see you smiling. Our honeymoon was in "hot springs". We stayed at the Aubuchon Motel on Park Street. I think the charge was like $6 per night! We ate at a little Greek restaurant nearby. We walked trails on the mountains, even going to Goat Rock! On Wednesday we drove back home. I had taken $100 with me. When we got home, I had $45 left! But you must remember this was 1954.

We had rented a garage apartment from our school teacher, Mr. W. J. Austin, which was just up the street in front of Mercer's Goat Castle (motel) and that big sharp curve. It really **had** been a two car garage. It was small with only one closet with no door by our dinette table. One night we were eating supper when Marcia looked up and saw a little mouse walking across the coat hangers. She screamed, of course. I leaped up and stabbed him with my fork! (Where's the eraser on this computer anyhow?)

I went back to work at the bank and about six months later, Marcia was offered a secretarial job at the Louisiana Welfare Department, now called Human Resources, I believe. She worked there about four years, and up to two weeks before our son Bill was born. She was the youngest one on staff there. She typed reports from Dictaphones, which was modern technology in those days! She said some of those cases would tear your heart out, like when the authorities would remove children from poor or abusive family conditions. She recalls a true story about a black lady who really liked Mrs. "Woody" Long, her contact person. She told her, "I'm gonna bring you a duck, Miss Woody." A few days later she came in with a brown paper sack tied at the top and set it down by Woody's desk. She thanked her and continued her work. Suddenly, out of the corner of her eye, Woody saw the sack move…again, and again! The woman had brought her a LIVE duck! Marcia enjoyed working there for almost five years.

TRIPS TOGETHER

The following Labor Day weekend (1955), Roy and Kathryn went with Marcia and me up to Branson, MO. Of course, back then it was just a small town in the Ozark Mountains, but still a big vacation spot. In fact, Earl and Betty had gone to Rockaway Beach in the Branson area on their honeymoon. Table Rock Dam was under construction at that time.

We left Winnfield Saturday afternoon after the bank closed at noon with the long holiday ahead. We must have spent the night out somewhere along the way. On Sunday after a day of sight-seeing, we could not find a motel room. We drove up to a farmhouse on a hill after dark and Roy and I went to the front door. It was open but there was a screen door.

Today this is hard to believe! Upon knocking, a woman came to the door and we told her we were from north Louisiana, up with our wives for the weekend and were unable to find a motel room. We asked if it would be alright for us to park out front in the large open space and spend the night in the car. She said that would be alright, that her husband had gone hunting and would be back around midnight. She showed no fear of us. It was a full moon that night and around twelve the man did return. His dog circled the car and checked our tires. I sat on the floor on the passenger side and leaned against the door so Marcia could have the bench seat. Kathryn and Roy were in the back. Next morning we went to a service station for necessary activities and headed south to Winnfield.

The four of us also made a trip to Hot Springs, AR, one short weekend. I parked on a side street and we turned the corner on Central Avenue (Bath House Row). Roy looked up at a two story building and said, "Golleee, Mo! Look at that tall building." A man walking by smiled and shook his head. Embarrassin'!

Yet another trip was made to Baton Rouge, LA. The capitol itself is unique, being a 34-story building. No other state capitol is built like it. I think it was constructed in the late 20s or early 30s at a cost of four and a half million dollars! The old capitol looks like something out of King Arthur and the Middle Ages. They are both located a few blocks apart near the east bank of the Mississippi River.

When Hollywood made the movie about the massacre at the University of Texas at Austin (some guy got up on the tower and began shooting people), the tall Louisiana state capitol was used. But a time or two the cameraman, who was shooting film from behind the "shooter" raised up a little too high and you got a quick glimpse of the river. There is certainly no river like the Mississippi near the UT campus.

I took my two weeks' vacation at the bank and Roy apparently did from Tremont Lumber Company, and the four of us headed to California! Our destination was "The Old Fashioned Revival Hour" held in the Long Beach (suburb of Los Angeles) Municipal Auditorium. Mr. John T. had arranged with Dr. Leland Green who directed that great choir to have them sing my new song "Each Step I Take." Before

Dr. Charles E. Fuller brought the message, I was introduced to the crowd as the composer of that song. That was a thrill I will not forget. But my keyboard idol, Rudy Atwood, was not there that Sunday, as he and the OFRH quartet were on tour. I later met him in Cincinnati at a CBA convention, however.

To prepare for the long drive across the desert southwest, I borrowed an apparatus from Mr. Fletcher's friend, Russell Tullos (Dry Goods store on Court Street) that was supposed to help keep the interior of our '53 Buick cooler than the outside temperature! Ice cubes were put into it and it was mounted on the top of the passenger door with that window lowered an inch or so. Plus a canvas bag of water was hung over the hood ornament to hang in front of the grill to help keep the motor cool. PTL! Times have changed!

The four of us left Winnfield when we got off work, heading west on US-80 across Texas. We saw dozens, maybe hundreds of jack rabbits in our headlights along the roadway. I had my picture made standing by the town sign of "Elmo, Texas." We took turns driving while the others slept. The next morning when the sun came up we were still in Texas. But in southeast New Mexico we stopped and walked through Carlsbad Caverns. Needless to say we were all tired.

We spent the weekend in Los Angeles, even took the ship out to Catalina Island. We stood on the deck and watched flying fish dip their tails in the water and swish them back and forth, then go sailing above the surface of the water for a hundred feet or so. As the ship came into beautiful Avalon Bay, kids were treading water, yelling for people to toss coins down to them. Leaving LA we drove up Highway 101 along the coast. Just south of San Francisco we were stopped by the highway patrol. A sports car had gone off the high cliff down to the beach. The recovery team brought up two bodies using ropes and pulleys. We could see an ice chest caught on a scraggly tree a few yards down the precipice.

In San Francisco we went straight to the Golden Gate Bridge and crossed to the north side. There were steel and concrete bunkers built along hillsides above the beach, The US had feared the Japanese might invade our country. We went to Fisherman's Wharf for a seafood "dinner". We could see Alcatraz Island out in the bay where that notorious prison stood. We rode the trolley cars to Chinatown, then headed east across the Oakland Bridge and on to Yosemite National Park. The valley is so beautiful with El Capitan, Half Dome and the high falls on the Merced River plunging some 2,700 feet. Leaving there we climbed several thousand feet to the plateau on top, which was equally scenic with mirrored lakes and still higher mountains. The Tioga Pass Road to US-395 was a one-way dirt road then, with two-way traffic. The rule was that cars going downhill had to stop to let the uphill vehicle keep moving. There were no guardrails with 2,000 foot drops by the road's edge. Marcia and Kathryn (perhaps Roy, too) were nervous wrecks. We played in some leftover snow and then two hours later had the air conditioning unit on in our motel room!

In Las Vegas we drove down "the Strip." We found a motel room and I asked the clerk if the pool was still open. She smiled benevolently and said, "Mister, nothing ever closes in this town!" We went to the Thunderbird Hotel and Casino and saw Dorothy Collins, a singer on the radio show "The Hit Parade." We paid $2 for a coke (very high back then) in order to hear Pee Wee Hunt and his band play a while. We walked into Binions, famous for their display of one million dollars in thick glass, hung from the roof. Two tough-looking armed guards stood by. A suited man came up and asked Marcia how old she was. She told him and he said she was underage and would have to leave. I imagine Kathryn was too young as well. [A few years ago Johnnie and Bart were traveling with us and we went by Las Vegas. It's a huge city NOW!!!]

We came by the North Rim of the Grand Canyon and had to laugh at a man trying to slip up on a COW to make a snapshot! His car license was New Jersey. We were making pictures of all kinds of wild animals. Marcia and I have been to the North Rim 3 times and to the South Rim 3 times. It is breath-taking indeed. Later a patrolman stopped us but when he looked in the backseat and saw Kathryn and Roy he looked surprise. He explained that a couple had stopped at a gas station then drove off not realizing their little boy had gotten out. He could only say the car was blue and white, like ours.

Finally we got back home to Winnfield. Roy and I had put $200 each in the "kitty" to make the trip on. We each got $10 back. We had made a 5,500 mile trip in eleven days and nights, including motels, entrance fees and GAS for $380. Each couple paid for their own food. Think what a trip like that would cost today!

Other friends of ours had married and were beginning their families. I've mentioned Evie Sue and A. L. Shirley, and Kathryn and Roy Jones. There were three Johns boys: Billy, "Junior" and J. J. He and A. L. played "twin" electric guitars along with the rhythm guitar played by Billy. We really needed an upright bass, and perhaps a fiddle or a mandolin. We would meet at one of our houses to rehearse. I borrowed an accordion from Preacher Davis' wife, but couldn't get the hang of pushing the bass buttons with my left fingers. So I stood sideways to the audience and sang "Tennessee Border" as I played. "Lady of Spain" was a good accordion piece. I tore up the piano with Dell Woods' "Down Yonder." We did two "gigs." One was at the Winnfield Elementary Auditorium and the other down at Atlanta High School Auditorium. We had lots of fun. Bob Baker, with whom I worked at the bank, and I wrote a country song titled "Never Look Back."

PENNIES FROM HEAVEN

A rather unusual evangelist came for a revival. Everything he wore was black (like Johnny Cash did.) The sanctuary lights were cut off and the lyrics to the hymns were put on a screen set in the baptistery. I was playing the organ for the meeting and was instructed to play the hymn through one complete time. Then the congregation was to sing the words shown – there was no song leader. This guy read his sermons using a pen light! The house was full every night, probably with a lot of curiosity-seekers.

A boy, who lived at the LA Baptist Children's Home in Monroe, came home for the weekend. A local friend came in with him, and since they could find nowhere to sit they went up to the balcony. The local boy knew there was a "step-down" but the LBCH boy behind him did not. You know how it is when you go to take a step and the distance is further down than you expected. The little boy flailed out his arms and his outstretched hand hit the big wooden collection plate that had been set on the "railing," perhaps a 1x10 board. The heavy plate went *loopty-loop* on that board then fell over the side into the lap of Bro. Lee Jutzi. Had it hit him vertically on his head it would surely have killed him.

The *coins* in the plate spilled onto the floor loudly and began gaily rolling around the plank floor toward feet unknown. Marcia and I were sitting to where we saw the entire episode and we were almost rolling on the floor. The speaker stopped for long moments, and we feared he was going to unload on us poor sinners. Then he continued to read. I don't recall how the "invitation" was handled or if there was any response.

He was also a chalk artist. Every night the lights would come up long enough for him to draw a pretty picture with some object lesson. But one night two little boys about seven or eight sat about as close as they could get. As he drew one boy gave a "play by play" account. Finally the preacher looked at them and scolded, "Please don't talk while I am drawing!" They hushed – we suppressed another laugh.

OUR FIRST FLIGHT

Starting in May 1955, Marcia and I made annual spring trips to Nashville. Mr. John T. knew that neither of us had ever flown in an airplane before, so he told us to drive to Memphis and then fly to Nashville! We were so excited I forgot all about the gas gauge. We coasted into a gas station in Walls, MS, actually a southern suburb of Memphis. We got there in time for the flight, but severe weather cancelled it. The airlines put us in a Holiday Inn (that chain began in Memphis, I am told). We had to get up at 4 a.m. to make the flight on to Nashville, on a prop-driven plane. It took an hour!

One of their daughters, Carolyn (Callie) picked us up at the (old) Nashville airport. We were welcomed into the Benson home, rustic on the outside and comfortable inside. We found that Roy Acuff lived in the log house next door to them. That was about the time he ran for governor. Mrs. Benson (Miss Jimmie) squeezed fresh orange juice for breakfast. Afterward we all went to get ready for church, when suddenly a jet plane roared overhead.

When we got to the First Church of the Nazarene on Woodland Street in east Nashville, we heard that the plane had crashed on the campus of Trevecca Nazarene College on Lafayette Street, only about a mile from us. The pilot was killed but he had courageously guided the plane away from populated areas and he was a hero. In the next few trips up there, we got to know so many wonderful people in that church. Even the famous Speer Family attended. Mrs. Elizabeth Pate and Mrs. Amanda Jarrett played piano and organ, but on Sunday nights they would switch places. The Men's Quartet was good, and stayed together with no personnel change for 42 years. Mr. "Pek" Gunn, Tennessee Poet Laureate, was a member of the quartet. I arranged a song he wrote about Tennessee that is included in a book he had printed. It was sold in Cracker Barrel Old Country Stores across the country. {By the way, Fred Vick, a member of Park Avenue Baptist Church, drew the floor plan for Cracker Barrel}.

Mr. John T. led the singing at First Naz as it was called for 30 years. His father had led 25 years before that. He had a talent to get a congregation to sing out, and the choir as well. He was a gracious gentleman, but one day after a rousing song he thanked the congregation and stepped backward to where he thought his chair was, but missed enough to set down on his rear! Bob Benson told me that himself.

People were always sending their poems to Benson in hopes of getting them set to music. Often he would accept one and commission me to write a melody to go with their words. Sometimes I liked what I wrote so much I wished I could have kept it for myself!

One such case was the six poems submitted by Dr. Oswald J. Smith, pastor of the great People's Church in Toronto, Canada. This was while I was a staff writer and working at the Winnfield Bank. I composed music to all six of them and two were published. One is "I Would Still be Poor without Jesus" and Marcia sings it as a solo in our concerts and church services.

Marcia and I made annual trips to Nashville through spring of 1960. For a couple of days Mr. John T. and I would go over the songs I had written during that contract year. Some he turned down flat. He would suggest changes on others, but some he liked immediately, like "Each Step I Take," written when I was 19 years old. Another was "Lonely Road, Up Calvary's Way," written in 1957. We would leave with his check in my pocket, rejoicing all the way back to Winnfield.

In 1957 we built a new salt-and-pepper brick ranch-style house on Mr. Fletcher's garden plot. We bought it from him. The fence was torn down, but the little dog Trixie would still run up to where the gate *had* been to exit the area! The house has a wide chimney with a real wood-burning fireplace in the living room. Hardwood floors were everywhere except where tile was put in the two bathrooms and kitchen. It had three bedrooms and a separate dining room. There was a screen porch connecting the house with the carport. We had a well drilled in the backyard, and central heating. Back then, it was built for $12.500 by a Mr. Webby Sanders. I got some St. Augustine grass runners and when Hurricane Audrey hit the SW Louisiana coast, I was on my hands and knees planting them in rows in our front yard. Trees were bending and the rain was pouring.

Little did we know that about 200 miles south of us some 600 persons would die in that storm! We drove down to visit Earl and Betty a month afterward. He was pastor of Twelfth Street Baptist Church in Lake Charles. They drove us down toward Cameron, which was wiped out. Stoves, refrigerators, bathtubs, even boats were carried at least ten miles inland by the storm surge and stranded there. He showed us a rope on a tree that somehow was left standing where it was said a man tied the bodies of three of his family members to await transportation to a funeral home.

OUR SON IS BORN

We lived in the Austin garage apartment for two years as we had promised, then moved over a couple of blocks to a house on East Maple Street. It was owned by Miss Mary Riser. You will recall she was owner and publisher of the weekly paper, the Winn Parish Enterprise and both Earl and I had worked for her. While living there Bill was conceived. The house was later moved a short distance to North King Street and in June 2012 it was still standing.

We bought a black and white TV. Guys from the bank, Marvin (who lived across the street), G. W. and Bob would come over and watch the Friday night prize fights! In the mornings while Marcia and I ate breakfast and got ready for work we would watch the Jimmy Dean Show from, of all places, Washington, D. C. Two guitar players were in his band: Billy Grammar, whom I met years later at Park Avenue Baptist Church when I accompanied him on the piano during a time of special music. He had been saved in a Bob Harrington crusade sponsored by our church. The other was Roy Clark, who had not started singing as yet. Also many years later we met Jimmy Dean at a Benson picnic in Warner Park in west Nashville.

I bought a Wurlitzer studio piano while we lived there. My cousin, last name Ward, which was Granny Mercer's maiden name, owned a music store in Alexandria. I got a whopping cousin's discount of ten per cent! A man delivered it in a day or two, backed up to the front porch, and used a 4-wheel "dolly" to move it right in our living room. It was suggested that I stay out of his way and hold the door open.

Back in the fall of 1957 Marcia had a pre-natal visit with Dr. George Rogers. While I was sitting in the waiting room I wrote "The Way That He Loves." As it turned out, Bill was born seventeen minutes till eleven p.m., December 31, 1957 – a 77-minute income tax deduction. Dr. Rogers wanted Marcia to wait and win all the gifts the local merchants gave to the first baby born each year, but she said "no way!" Her due date had been January 15th and she worked till December 15th. Bill came two weeks early!

I was standing in the hallway outside the delivery room at the Winnfield General Hospital when I heard a baby cry. We didn't know if the baby would be a boy or a girl. It hit me like a ton of bricks! I was a FATHER…after over three years of marriage. He was named William Elmo Mercer, Jr. My advice is, don't ever do that! The "Senior" and "Junior" will get mixed up: bills, bank accounts, speeding tickets, you name it!

My parents had other grandchildren and were very proud, but Bill was the Fletchers' first grandchild! S. Q. was beaming and a few months later was telling folks that his grandson had quoted the 23rd Psalm…you just couldn't understand what he was saying!

Back then we used Birdseye diapers. Made of cloth, they had to be washed and hung out on the clothes line. I would come home from the bank for "dinner", and "Mammaw" would have cornbread, blackeyed peas, boiled okra, mashed potatoes or rice, squash, some kind of meat...whatever. I'm telling you now, there was nothing better than "mama-in-law" fried chicken, cooked in a skillet on a natural gas stove top. Then I would go out and hang diapers on the clothes line. Sometimes there would be a very cold wind that would flap them in my face. We saved our money and bought an electric clothes dryer!

Then in the winter of 1959 Winnfield received a twelve-inch snowfall - highly unusual! Bill was a little over a year old and couldn't decide if he liked it or not. Marcia's brother Bernard and I built a big fort, as did the Reeves brothers across the road, and we had snowball fights. We gathered some snow and made ice cream. Today with all the pollutants in the air I would be afraid to eat snow cream.

Marcia and I decided it was time to buy a new car. We sold our faithful blue and white '53 straight-eight Buick to C. W. Wardlaw, who did some repossession work for the bank. One time I went with him up to southern Arkansas to repossess a pickup truck. I knew he carried a pistol and sometimes repossessions can provoke tempers! The truck was there but the man with the keys was not so we went and ate lunch. When we got back, old tires had been put on the truck and Wardlaw was mad. I guess I drove it back to Winnfield.

Like I said, I sold our '53 Buick to Wardlaw for $300 that day. In about an hour he came whistling (his trademark) back up to my window and said, "I just sold your car for $400 and made me a quick hundred!" I guess he thought I would explode, but

I just said, "Great. I got what I wanted, and you got what you wanted." I later learned that the man who bought it made a dozen trips to California. I reckon if it had had a tongue it would have been hanging out over the grill like the water bag we used on our trip!

Not long after that we took Mammaw and Pappaw Fletcher with us to Hot Springs, AR one weekend. I told him I bet he wouldn't see anyone he knew. Well, we were walking along Bathhouse Row on Central Avenue when we heard a familiar whistling sound. It was Wardlaw, walking across the street. Pappaw guffawed at me!

We bought a black 1959 Chevy Impala, with the flared out back fenders, from Max Thieme Chevrolet in Winnfield. That's what we had when we moved to Nashville on New Year's Day 1961. God was at work in our lives! Woohoo! What a way to live!

PART TWO
The Move to Nashville

WE MOVE TO NASHVILLE

On New Year's Day 1961 we drove to Nashville, and this was before interstate highways were built. There was two inches of snow on the ground when we went through Memphis. We lived at Mercury Motel on Lafayette Street for several days. Then Mr. John T. moved his Air Stream trailer to a park on Dickerson Road where we lived about a week. Bob Benson drove us around looking for a house to rent. We finally found a suitable one on Groves Park Road. It ran off Eastland Avenue just before going over the railroad to Riverside Drive, near Shelby Park. The little house was the third one on the left. It had an attached single garage and fenced backyard, perfect for Bill to play in. There were two bedrooms, a bath, living room and kitchen. Not exactly what we'd had in Louisiana, but a new future lay before us.

We had some absolutely wonderful neighbors and grew to love the neighborhood. Next door to us (the second house) lived Mr. and Mrs. Holliman. She loved Bill and Marcia would take him over there often. Years later I sang "Each Step I Take" at Mr. Holliman's funeral at Fatherland Street Baptist Church in

East Nashville. I just looked at a knot hole in the back of the sanctuary, trying to keep my composure as I sang.

Across the street was the home of Dean and Juanita Baker. They had no children and loved Bill, too. We had several backyard outings with them. Directly across the street from our house lived the Pughs. Porter drove a cab – one of those long, green and white checkered foreign makes. He really took a liking to Bill. Mrs. Pugh was a large lady and smoked cigarettes. One Sunday night we came home from church. I had pulled into the single car garage and was about to pull the door down when I saw a big person standing on the front stoop, silhouetted against the inside lights, and smoking. I thought it was her and I said, "You've had a lot of company today, haven't you?" After a slight pause, a man's voice drawled, "Yeah, and I'm it!" I pulled that door down without saying a word. Marcia said that was the first time she'd ever known me to be speechless!

RIVERSIDE BAPTIST CHURCH

The first Sunday we decided to attend Inglewood Baptist Church on Gallatin Road, only about four miles from our house. No one said a word to us! On Wednesday night we drove to Riverside Baptist Church on the corner of Porter Road. We entered to find the service was in progress and sat on the back row. The pastor and those who looked around had surprised looks on their faces. He said, "We're glad to have you folks tonight. We're having our January Bible Study and were about to dismiss! Please introduce yourselves." I did.

After the closing prayer we were mobbed by the members and I eventually made my way to the organ. The organist said, "Do you play?" "Yes ma'am." "Please sit down and play some." I started on "Each Step I Take," and about the time I got to the chorus, she said, "What did you say your name was again?" I said, "Elmo Mercer…I wrote this song." She almost fainted. Her name was Mrs. Lamons and she worked at the Baptist Bookstore on Broadway and was quite familiar with my name and music.

Needless to say, the next Sunday we moved our membership there. That Sunday night the young man who *was* pianist, resigned in a huff. I was asked to "fill in", and about three months later we were out of town and the church voted for me to become the pianist! Jay Mick (wife Burdene) was the minister of music. They had come from the Nazarene denomination. The next New Year's night we had several couples over to our house on Leswood Lane in Parkwood Estates. At midnight we went outside to do fireworks. At that time it was legal! I threw a plain firecracker at Jay's feet but it bounced into the cuff of his pants. He did an Irish jig to no avail and it blew a hole in his pants. [A few years later he became minister of music at Grace Nazarene near where Opryland was built]. We had a great choir, full of talent. Mrs. Lamons and I played offertories that I arranged. I sang some of my songs…at that time Marcia and I had not started singing together. We fondly remember Mrs. Coleman who "kept the nursery."

We stayed at Riverside almost five years. One Sunday night (about 1963) the choir was singing my first Christmas cantata, "The Story Unchanged (through the Ages)" that Benson had just published. As far as I know that was the first cantata Benson had ever printed. I looked across behind Mrs. Lamons through the tall stained glass window and saw that it was snowing big flakes. It doesn't get any better than that!

Several friends, young couples we had come to love, were concerned about our getting home to Parkwood Estates. I told them the route I would take which was out of the way but had less inclines on it. Ann and Larry Link asked us to call them when we got home. I did and thought Ann answered. I went into detail about the trip home then a woman said, "Well, sir, I don't know who you thought you were calling, but I am glad you made it home safely!"

Two young men, Bob Portman (wife Barbara) and Lowell Smith (wife Bobbie) put up $200 each...I put in my $200 also...to help me make my first LP album. I recorded it at Globe Studios, upstairs on Broadway, in the same block as the famous Tootsie's Lounge and Gibson Guitars. I sang several of my best-known songs while I played piano. I also played instrumentals on the piano, then dubbed in the organ. We actually made about $200 each in profit, the retail price being only $2.98 back then!

We had church socials and parties both in Shelby Park and in Riverside's fellowship hall downstairs. One time some of us young couples put on a TV studio program. For instance, the weather man said the barometer was falling, and behind a partition someone broke some glass in a waste basket. A commercial sang, "You'll find out where the yellow goes when you brush your teeth with Polinos!" (?) Another was for a brand of cigarettes and it featured the emcee calling a man up to endorse the product. It was Mrs. Lamons' husband. He said a few words then broke into a coughing fit and had to go "off camera." I wrote the script!

One of those couples was Shirley and Buddy Smith. Around the mid-90s he had a heart transplant and is still living; now the doctors are studying him! Another couple after eighteen years of marriage finally had a baby! We enjoyed our Sunday school classes and Mrs. Carter, the pastor's wife was leader in our Young Married Training Union class.

Bill was saved when he was six years old, kneeling by his own bed at our house. Bro. Carter was having health problems so our associate pastor, Dr. Bob Byrd, a Belmont college professor baptized him. Sometime later Marcia was sitting out in the audience with Bill during a Sunday night service when he said, "Look, Mama, what I got." He had been outside in front of the church before the service and had gathered a pocketful of snails! Marcia was horrified and whispered, "Put those things down this minute." Mistake! They crawled all over the sanctuary.

Bill and Ola Mae Lamb (he worked for the phone company) became close friends although they were a few years older. They had a son and a daughter, and he loved our Bill. Every Sunday he would give him pennies to put in his pocket. He taught a young boys' Sunday school class and Jim Summers was a member.

Jim was minister of music at Park Avenue Baptist when we moved our membership there in September 1965!

JTB PUBLISHING COMPANY

Now I'll say a few words about the John T. Benson Publishing Company. Mr. John T.'s father had started it back in the early 1900s. He was born in 1904 and named JTB Junior. He had older brothers, but the first one given the name Junior had died. When he grew up and married he worked as a traveling salesman for the Benson Printing Company that his older brothers had founded. Their father's songbook company folded. Mr. John T. sold college yearbooks across the country. The printing company also produced Navy ship yearbooks and periodicals, like one that was called "Lighting." Miss Jimmie was left home to raise two boys and a girl mostly by herself.

Mr. John T. finally told his brothers that he was going to leave them and re-start the John T. Benson Publishing Company. They told him he would starve! That was in 1949. He signed Lois Irwin to a writer's contract. She and her husband Kenny lived in California and traveled nationwide preaching and singing. Her song "The Healer" is owned and published by a west coast company, Fiesta Music, now a subsidiary of the Zondervan Corporation. In March of 1951 he signed me as his second staff writer, while I was still on crutches getting over a broken left thigh.

In Nashville I rode a city bus to work most of the time, getting off on Union at Fourth Avenue North. Then I walked two blocks down Fourth Avenue, rain or shine, to the Benson office, located in the Benson Printing Company building. The "Batman" building stands there now. But sometimes Mr. John T. would phone and say he and Bob would be coming my direction so I was to walk down Groves Park Road to Eastland. You recall Mr. John T.'s house was on Brush Hill Road near the Cumberland River, and Bob and his family lived in the Dalewood area at the time. One such morning there was snow and ice everywhere. Mr. John T. drove his little Nash Rambler. After we crossed the old Woodland Street Bridge over the river and turned south on Fourth Avenue, there was a slight incline for about a block. Bob and I had to get out and push!

One morning I got off the bus and headed toward the office. A man who also rode the bus walked along by me. Out of nowhere, a pigeon "strafed" us! I yelled after him, "Go ahead, everybody else does!" My friend busted out laughing at me, hit from my left shoulder to my right knee, till I told him to look at his reflection in a store's glass front. He had collateral damage! When I got to the office I had to go to the men's room and try to get cleaned up. Embarrassin', plus it smelled bad, too.

A bunch of us men would sit in the back of the bus talking and having a good time. One day I looked across the aisle at an article in the Tennessean newspaper that read: "USS Providence Hit by Shore Battery." [This was in the late 60s during the Vietnam War]. I said, "Hey, my wife's brother is on that ship!" Bernard was an air traffic controller on the Providence and also on the Enterprise. My brother Ronnie and our sister's son Frank Rankin are Vietnam veterans. I had a distant cousin Hugh

Mercer, Jr. who was a jet pilot. He was shot down and rescued but died two weeks later in a Japan hospital.

I told Marcia I didn't want her to work, even though my salary was not great. We would tighten up and make it alright. I wanted her to stay home with Bill. Two weeks after we moved there, Mammaw and Pappaw Fletcher, along with Bernard, came up for a short visit. After all, we had taken their only grandson 550 miles away from them! A couple of months later, Marcia and I, along with 3-yr-old Bill went to Fall Creek Falls State Park, about a hundred miles east of us on the Cumberland Plateau. We enjoyed our time there and I believe there was some leftover snow in places. The high falls is 256 feet high, a ribbon fall, one hundred feet higher than Niagara! Some months later we went on to Gatlinburg, and in the early 60s it was still a quaint and lovely vacation spot, especially the Cades Cove area. We drove on up to Newfound Gap, then another seven miles to Clingman's Dome. We went down the North Carolina side to Cherokee, a very unique town.

In 1962 the people of Nashville voted in "Metropolitan" government, combining county and city. Highway signs now read: "Welcome to Metropolitan Nashville Davidson County." One afternoon I bounded out of the alcove to both Benson offices, heading up two blocks north to catch my bus, and collided with Roy Acuff as he left the Tennessee Café. I said, "Oh, 'scuse me, Roy." He said, "That's alright, young man!" We both kept going. Sometimes I would go to that café and get a hamburger for lunch. Lots of times ol' Bashful Brother Oswald would be sitting at a booth with three women...different ones every time!

The first mayor of Metro Nashville was a judge named Beverly Briley. Another morning on the bus ride to work, a lady was sitting near us (men) on the side bench that goes over the rear wheels. She was really running her mouth against the mayor. When it was my turn to exit the bus, I softly spoke to the men, "Watch this." I stepped down in the stairwell and said to the lady, our faces a foot apart, "Well, lady, I will admit UNCLE Beverly has his faults!" I pushed the doors and stepped out and walked up the street. That afternoon the guys told me they wished I could have seen her face. They said she never said another word!

One red haired guy that sat with us said a friend had taken him deer hunting early Saturday morning. He was so sleepy when he got to his assigned place he sat down and leaned back on a tree. He went to sleep but a noise roused him. A big buck was within feet of him just staring at him! He reached for his gun and of course the deer took off.

We lived on Groves Park Road perhaps ten months, while having our house constructed in Section II of Parkwood Estates. It was on Leswood Lane, which connected two other streets. Friends would tell us they could see our house but had trouble getting to it!

When we moved into our new house, I was back in Bill's bedroom trying to put together his bed frame. I had leaned the mattress up against the wall, but a little of it stuck out into the doorway. I was down on my hands and knees, getting frustrated I imagine, when little Bill came streaking down the hallway into the room. His arm hit the mattress hard enough (a pure accident) that it fell over on me, knocking me flat.

Somehow he, too, was under it! He looked at me and said, "Must be nice to be wanted!" That saved him a good spanking. The source of that statement was a TV commercial back then advertising some brand of milk I believe. A cat slapped at the tail of a mouse, but he got away. Then the face of a cow looked at you and said, "Must be nice to be wanted." We've talked about that many times over the years. About that time there was a "knot" came on my ring finger where it joins the hand and I was getting concerned about it. We were sitting in the den watching TV one night and I got exasperated with Bill's antics, telling him to settle down. He was wearing a scabbard with a toy steel pistol in it and as he ran by me (after Indians, no doubt) I swung my hand back to whack his rear. Instead my hand hit the butt of that gun and I thought I would die with pain. Then I discovered the knot was gone!

Our house was set upon a sprawling hillside, the street curving somewhat. Our driveway was steep getting up to the carport. There were three bedrooms, but we took the third (off the hallway by the kitchen) for a dining room. Several weeks later we were having a couple out for supper and when I walked in to set the table, my shoes squashed on a soaked carpet! We found that a nail had pierced a copper pipe in the master bedroom bathroom and we didn't know it! One Sunday morning as we ate breakfast, I saw steam pouring out under the utility room door outside. I dashed outside and pulled the electric plug. I don't know if I did anything else, but I could just see that thing going through the roof like a NASA rocket!

I brought a toe-sack filled with St. Augustine grass sprigs from Louisiana and set them out in the yard. They did alright till winter snow and ice took their toll. Earl was returning to Louisiana after a meeting in Washington, D. C., and he planned to stop over and spend a night with us. Well, we got about a six inch snow with very cold temps. He said the stewardess announced, "We'll be landing soon at Nashville, where the temperature is minus fifteen degrees!" He already had his pajamas on under his suit. We managed to make it to the (old) airport and get him to our house, then back the next day.

BENSON ADDS RECORDINGS

Six months after I started work Mr. John T. and Bob decided to enter the record business. At first they were just going to feature soloist, college choirs, etc. They came up with the name "HeartWarming" for the label and that's the way it was spelled. The first album was a male soloist from Ashland, KY with only organ accompaniment. Then Bob and I were sent to try to sign two others. The first was the Shorty Bradford Trio. We drove down to Rising Fawn, GA, just west of Chattanooga. Shorty and Jean took us down the mountain to a café for supper. Shorty strutted in and told the folks we were "music execs from Nashville."

When we got back home, Shorty told us there was an art show held annually near where they lived. People from all over the world, he said, would come to it. It was called the "Plum Nellie Art Show" because it was "plum nellie off the other side of the mountain." I think that was something he made up! Shorty took Bob and me to a cliff overlooking a beautiful vista, and started talking…not business. It was a full moon. Shorty said one night he and some friends were sitting at that very spot, listening to the Beagles chasing whatever. One shot by them with his nose to the ground and plunged right over the cliff. Apparently the wily creature had made a 90-degree turn right at the edge of the precipice but the hound was just in too big of a rush!

He said that late one night a quartet he was in was returning home and he was driving. He told the young man in the passenger seat that he had a headache and was going to take an Alka-Seltzer. He got one but with slight-of-hand gave the impression he had swallowed the big white tablet. After a few miles he heard the boy gagging and carrying on. He looked over and he was foaming at the mouth. Turns out he had (really) tried to swallow on. Shorty stopped the car and shook the boy upside down till he coughed it back up! Funny.

After a great country breakfast prepared by Jean, Shorty's wife, Bob and Shorty talked business, and I reckon agreed to a contract. Jean became a staff writer and wrote songs like "Lord, I Need You Again Today." Bob and I left before noon for Tennessee Temple College in Chattanooga, to try to sign the a cappella choir to a recording contract, which did not happen. On the way back to Nashville that night Bob said, "Well at least we've managed to spend Dad's expense money!"

It wasn't long until we started signing folks like the Speer Family; Ira Stanphill (he recorded "Each Step I Take" in a western style with steel guitar); Jimmie Snow (Hank's son) and Carol, (his wife, Wilma Lee and Stony Cooper's daughter); the Frost Brothers Quartet; the Tennesseans Quartet, etc. Actually, the printing product sales supported this recording venture. We did our recording at RCA studios on Music Row, now called Studio B on the Country Music Hall of Fame tour. We also had RCA in Indianapolis to press the albums and announced all this on the back liner…in other words, we clung to RCA's "coat-tails!" But when folks bought a HeartWarming album, they knew they were getting quality. Later Benson added other labels, including "Impact" when we recorded groups like the Imperials, Hale and Wilder, Truth, etc.

Captain Billy Burke (Air Force Dentist) came to Nashville in the early 60s. He and I wrote a Christmas song together called "Christmas time is here." The Johnny Mann Singers recorded it. He came by my office one day on Fourth Avenue North and I invited him to supper at our house. I called Marcia and she got some steaks out of the freezer. Then Billy mentioned he was a vegetarian (Seventh Day Adventist, in fact), so I called Marcia back to tell her that. *Cream of broccoli soup, anyone?*

My friend Ken Barlow was minister of music at Parkview Baptist on the Jefferson Highway in Baton Rouge, LA. It was a huge church. Like Park Avenue Baptist in Nashville it had a *new* sanctuary, an *old* sanctuary and an *old, old* sanctuary! They had a school, K through 12 and even had a football stadium! Louisiana school buses served the school also! Ken and I wrote a song together (I think it was titled "Praise Him") that Lifeway published in the periodical "Glory Songs." Phillip Willis who had attended the *Whachamacallits* had previously been minister of music there; later he went into evangelism and traveled a lot. On one of our trips there, the choir gave us a ceramic Siamese cat in which you could grow a plant. We had told about our Siamese cat (Sheba) that *used the commode!*

I must tell you about our new wireless telephone, along about 1977. I carried one to the piano in my music room at our house in Thousand Oaks Estates. I know I'm getting ahead of myself here, but when I thought of Ken Barlow I remembered this happening. I was working on music with my left elbow a few inches from the phone. It rang and I jumped a foot off the bench. I figured it was Marcia (upstairs) trying out the new phone to tell me she loved me, you know.

I picked up the phone, punched it on and said, "You just scared the crap outta me!" SILENCE, then a man's voice said, "Elmo?" I hit the "off" button, then dashed upstairs to tell Marcia. I said the man would likely call back and I was not home! She said this was no time for her to start lying and the phone rang again! When she answered she said, "Yes, he's around here somewhere. Mo-Ooo." In a few seconds I answered breathlessly. It was Ken Barlow. He didn't mention the previous call and I surely didn't.

His sister's son was Billy Ready, minister of music at First Baptist in Bogalusa, LA, but I didn't know that. He had us to come there for a weekend. When we finished choir practice on Saturday night I told the choir about that incident. I noticed a lady in the choir was laughing uncontrollably, and so was Billy. I asked what was so funny. Billy said, "That's my mother and Ken is her brother!" My face turned beet-red!

Well, Billy had us down to do music in a revival and the choir practiced and had a meal together on Saturday night before. We had our back to the door. Ken came in and went around the table speaking to a few folks. He was standing right behind us when he said to Billy, "I thought you said Elmo was going to be here." I had started wearing a hair piece and he did not recognize me. That was funny.

Dr. Carlton C. Buck resided in Eugene, OR. We co-wrote about 50 songs including an Easter cantata titled "Gift of Love." As a complete work it was not published, but two songs taken from it were, by Lifeway.

On one of our three visits to my childhood friend Jerre McBride's church in San Angelo, TX I got an idea for a new song from his morning sermon. He was pastor at First Baptist for 31 years. When we got back to his house I went to their grand piano and begin jotting down the melody. He asked what I was doing and I told him. He said, "Oh, let me write the words, ok?" The song "Rekindle the Fires of Faith" was published in a book by the Benson Company soon after that.

The song "Shine, Jesus, Shine" was written by Graham Kendrick, who lived in England. He made an album with Benson in the 70s.

"ON THE JOB" TRAINING

I had been a banker, for cryin' out loud! What did a music editor do anyhow? At first I sat on a "high" chair using an artist's board to arrange music on – without a piano. Soon Mr. John T. bought a Story & Clark studio piano for me, then quickly saw the immediate need to build a wall around me! One day he came in, handed me an album and said, "Take off Side II, Number 1," and started back out the door. I said, "Uh, do what now?" He said, "I want to publish that song. Transcribe it and arrange it in four parts."

What did "transcribe" mean anyhow? I finally figured it out, but it took about four days for me to do it. {Now I can do four a day!} I wish I could remember the title of that song. The phonograph was setting in the bottom of a wood cabinet and I had to squat down and place the needle on the LP. I'd listen to a line, stand back up and step to the piano and try to write down what I thought I'd heard! Repeat and repeat!

I began to study printed music by Ralph Carmichael, Stuart Hamblen, Johnny Lange, WORD Music, anybody that might help me learn more. I figured out chord symbols, and sometimes the guitar chord would be atop what the bass was to play. I slowly began to catch on how to write piano accompaniment. When I was a staff writer my compositions had been done in four-part harmony like in a hymnal. This was interesting!

About ten years later when the company had moved out on Broadway, Bob Benson brought me an album and the *conductor's score* of a Dave Boyer recording. He was a "Frank Sinatra-type," but God had saved him out of that life and he had become quite famous in the Christian music world. I was to reduce all that down to a solo line with piano accompaniment so the songs could be printed in an artist's 9 x 12 folio. Now THAT was a job! But I was determined to do it.

I would listen to a song and study the conductor's score, listening to what various instruments did, then try to capture the same "feel" in the reduction. I actually got credit in the song folio for doing the transcriptions. I was beginning to gain confidence and God was increasing my ability.

A songbook series really took off for John T. Benson Publishing Company. The title was "Songs of Inspiration" and the first book was compiled and published by John Daniel. He had a famous quartet in the late 40s and the book was released in 1949. Boyce Hawkins, who later became well-known as the WSMV Channel 4 weatherman, was their pianist for a while. Also Gordon Stoker, who later founded the Jordanaires, was also their pianist. [Gordon passed away in April 2013]. Mr. John T. bought the rights to the book and compiled a second volume, calling it "New Songs of Inspiration, Volume II."

When I began working in January 1961 Bob was compiling volume IV. I helped and even arranged some of the songs. They were printed in shape notes and that is another reason they were so popular. Many singers learned to read music by the shape of a note. The Stamps-Baxter Music Company especially taught them in singing schools across the south. Marcia went to one and later taught me! I got to where I could write them as fluently as regular "round" notes. Also for many years Bill Gaither printed his songs in shape notes, 4-part harmony

9 x 12 sheet music. I arranged his music from 1962 to 1971, more about that later.

One day, Virgil Brock and his wife, Blanche Kerr Brock, visited the Benson Company on Fourth Avenue North. Mr. John T. and Bob came into my office and we all enjoyed fellowship. In 1936 they composed the beautiful song, "Beyond the Sunset." Virgil told us his brother-in-law was blind and as they looked out over the Grand Canyon, he tried to describe the beautiful sunset. He said, "I just wish you could see it!" His brother-in-law smiled and said, "Oh, Virgil. I can see beyond the sunset!"

When they got back home, Virgil sat down and wrote those beautiful words and Blanche set them to music. What a testimony that is, and what a blessing, comfort and inspiration it has been down through these many decades. In fact, in 2012 I sang it at the funeral of our dear friend, Ray Newbill, in Hendersonville, TN. Our long-time friend Ethel Lunn accompanied me on the piano and later told me that was the first time she had ever played for me to sing. She was pianist at Park Avenue Baptist Church before we went there.

WHERE'S THE...*FIRE?*

Metro police chief (at the time) Joe Casey invited Bro. Bob to ride with him one night and Bro. Bob got a first-hand education. He was shocked at what went on in Nashville after darkness fell. On a Sunday morning sometime after that he had the chief come speak to our church. He gave some startling crime statistics. He also presented Bro. Bob with an honorary badge!

There is a permanent burning ban in Metro Nashville on anything like leaves, etc. Apparently Bro. Bob was not aware of this. One day he had raked up a pile of leaves in their yard and he proceeded to set them on fire, creating quite a smoke. They live perhaps four miles east of us as the crow flies, over some high hills. The fire truck arrived and put them out. Shortly after hearing about that I penned a little four verse poem in about ten minutes while waiting for Marcia to get ready for supper and prayer meeting. Remember the TV commercial when the little old lady buys a hamburger then asks, "Where's the beef?" Here it is:

"Well, I was drivin' around the other day when I spied a fire truck comin' my way, and he wadn't lettin' no grass grow under his tires! I took in after him, you see, but I wondered where he's a-takin' me, and most of all I wondered, 'Where's the fire?'

"With me close behind we rounded a curve, right then I nearly lost my nerve, the whole neighborhood was filled with awful smoke! And I remembered with a shock my pastor's house is in that block, and a lump in my throat just about made me choke!

"Sure 'nough we stopped in front o' his house, there stood Bro. Bob as meek as a mouse, you could tell he was hot 'cause he'd done rolled up his sleeves. To his surprise and embarrassment the firemen grabbed their hose and went to sprayin' water on his burnin' leaves!

"An irate neighbor turned him in and you bet there was some mad firemen, but Bro. Bob's honorary badge saved the hour!

Then he made me promise not to say what really happened there that day if anybody asked me, 'Where's the Fire?'" [This poem was printed in Park Avenue's Sunday bulletin].

One Sunday morning Bro. Bob said he was getting ready for church when he pulled the top drawer in a chest of drawers out too far. It fell and broke a big toe. He wore a slipper on that foot until it healed. He was preaching away one Sunday and when he made a point he stomped *that* foot then flinched it hurt so bad. So, I composed an appropriate poem, "Ode to a Broken Toe." He kept it under the glass on his desk for years.

BILL GAITHER AND ME

I was going through the morning's mail at the office in 1962 and found a letter from a guy named Bill Gaither. I thought that was a strange name I'd not come across before. I found out he was a school teacher in Indiana who also promoted gospel singings. A year or two before, he had written the popular song "He Touched Me." Bob and Mr. John T. apparently knew who he was. The Bill Gaither Trio agreed to record on a Benson label. And before long I was transcribing his songs either from a reel-to-reel tape or one of Bill's "lead sheets." I would make a 4-part shape note arrangement so he could get them printed in 9 x 12 sheet music. I did this on my own time at home with Mr. Benson's approval. He knew it would supplement my income. I did this for nine years. In 1971 John III and Bob Benson told me I had to stop arranging music for Bill, that it was a conflict of interest...?

During that time, Bill and Gloria penned some outstanding songs like: "A Hill Called Mt. Calvary," "There's Something About that Name," "The King is Coming," "Because He Lives," "Something Beautiful," "The Longer I Serve Him," "I Will Serve Thee," "Let's Just Praise the Lord," "Thanks to Calvary," etc. I arranged all that he wrote and published during those nine years!

Artist's folios became popular, accompanying the release of a new album, and that put a damper on single sheet music sales. Prices had gone much higher as well. Later, Benson discontinued sheet music altogether.

I did arrange several folios for the Gaithers that Benson published, usually titled after a song contained in them, like "Get All Excited!" "The King is Coming," etc. I arranged some instrumental collections of his songs for C-treble, C-bass, Bb and Eb instruments. Volume IV of the Crusade Choir series contained medleys of 18 of their songs, and I arranged it as well.

Mr. John T. paid my tuition ($150) at Peabody College in the summer of 1970 for me to take an orchestration course. The textbook was "Kennon's Book on Orchestration". I learned a lot. The teacher was Rick Powell who was arranging a lot of Benson's albums along about that time. So I became a 38-year-old teacher's pet! One assignment was to make an arrangement of any song of our choice for a string quartet (2 violins, a viola and a cello). I chose "My Faith Looks up to Thee." Four students came to the next class and played what we had arranged.

The kids looked back at me with thumbs up, and it was pretty and well performed. One boy had done his arrangement on something like "Mary Had a Little Lamb" but he called it "Bullfrog in Heat on a Flat Rock."

Here is a true story you might find interesting. Journalists call this a "human interest story:"

The Benson Company eventually had a large booth at the Christian Booksellers Association (CBA) convention, held in July in some large USA city. One year, I believe it was 1970, it was held in Minneapolis. I went by myself (Marcia and the kids did not go), and roomed with Danny Lee, a California songwriter who wrote "Jesus, He is the Son of God". He sat by me (at the Broadway office) on the piano bench and sang it phrase by phrase as I made a lead sheet from which I made the arrangement. In fact, I arranged ten of his songs for his artist's folio that accompanied an album he recorded on a Benson label.

At the Tuesday noon luncheon (some 1,500 attended) Doug Oldham sang for the very first time, Bill's song, "The King Is Coming." I was standing outside the doors when people were coming out. Bill started grinning when he saw me. He came over and said, "Elmo, were you in there?" I said no, that my ticket was for the next day…why? He said, "Doug just sang one of my new songs, and judging by the crowd's reaction, I believe it's goin' t' be a good one for me!" That was perhaps the understatement of the century?

He reached in his coat pocket and handed me a lead sheet he had used to accompany Doug. He said, "Arrange this for me while you're here and send it to the music typesetter. I've got to get this in print at once!" That night the booths stayed open until 11 pm, can you believe that? Then a group of us went out to eat a late supper. I got back to my hotel room about 1 a.m.

I sat at the desk and, without a piano, made the four-part shape note arrangement of "The King Is Coming." Next morning in the lobby I "ran into" Mosie Lister, a famous songwriter from Florida. I told him what I had just done and asked if he had a first-class stamp on him. I believe they were eight cents then. He did. So, I mailed the future Bill Gaither hit, arranged by W. Elmo Mercer, with postage stamp supplied by Mosie Lister, to the music typesetter. That song HAD TO BECOME A HIT!

Another incident occurred at Bill Gaither's "Praise Gathering". The first was held in Indianapolis, but he failed to book for next year soon enough, and the second was held in Cincinnati. Several of us were "hanging out" around the piano on stage one morning after breakfast and I said, "Hey, Bill, listen to this new song I just wrote and let me know what you think."

I played and sang my song, "There's Just Something about the Name of Jesus." I couldn't help but notice that sly grin come across Bill's face and he began slowly shaking his head as I finished. I said, "WHAT?" He just motioned for me to get up from the bench and said, "Let me show you how the Lord works. I've just written this one." And he started to sing,

"Jesus, Jesus, Jesus, There's just something about that name." That was amazing. Benson did print mine in 9 x 12 sheet music, but I think a year later there was 990 dusty copies still on the shelf. Bill's song became a hit and appears in many hymnals. All glory to the name of Jesus!

I can't help but believe I contributed even a small part to Bill's early success, and I'm thankful God allowed me to do that, and gave me the talent to do it as well. Marcia and I have many fond memories of our times with Bill and Gloria.

ALL-NIGHT SINGINGS

Marcia and I, along with 3-year-old Bill, started going to the "All-Night" Singings, put on monthly at the Ryman Auditorium by a man named Wally Fowler. [Years before he had started a quartet named the Oak Ridge Quartet]. Actually, the man who did the work involved in producing those programs was named George Thomas, who later worked for Benson. They were also done monthly in Birmingham, Atlanta and Knoxville. They would sometimes go on until 2 a.m.! We sat up in the balcony and munched on snacks we took with us. At 11 p.m. it was broadcast for one hour on WSM radio. It began with prayer (!) and one night Wally asked me to do that! I hoped the Winnfield folks were listening!

I went backstage just about each month and introduced myself as Elmo Mercer, the music editor of the John T. Benson Publishing Company. The name "Benson" registered on them. I guess

I eventually met everyone who came and sang there. In no time I was arranging their music, with Mr. John T.'s approval!

Wally Fowler's office was in the back of a building on Gallatin Road in east Nashville. I would have to go over there every now and then, probably to pick up sheet music or deliver songbooks. Ed Crowe ran the place for him. He told me he wrote the song, "Honey, Let Me Be Your Salty Dog" that Flatt and Scruggs made famous.

Some of those singers at the All-Night Singings were Hovey Lister and the Statesmen, James and the Blackwood Brothers, the Speer Family, the Happy Goodman Family, the Oak Ridge Quartet (with Smitty Gatlin and Herman Harper), the Oak Ridge Boys, Naomi and the Sego Brothers, the Jennings Trio, Wendy Bagwell and the Sunlighters, the Klaudt Indian Family (Marcia and I took them out to dinner one time), the Florida Boys, the Couriers, the Goss Brothers, the Hoppers, David Butler and the Sons of Song, the Blue Ridge Quartet, the Inspirations, the Orrells, the Rambos, the Hemphills, the Dixie Melody Boys, etc. I may have misnamed some of these and I apologize; also I fear I'm leaving some out as well.

Eventually those All-Night Singings faded away, but the memories remain. The annual National Quartet Convention was held in Memphis, then Nashville and now it is in Louisville. I believe in 2013 it will be held in Pigeon Forge, TN near Gatlinburg. Benson always had a booth there and I enjoyed meeting the people who attended and came by to speak to us.

Ted Davenport is a member of our church – Scottsboro First Baptist on Old Hickory Boulevard between Nashville and Ashland City. At age 14 he was singing with his family and at 16 started his own quartet! In later years he sang with other groups including the Blackwood Brothers. He traveled with James Blackwood for a time, too. He has a beautiful tenor voice and sings solos and with our men's quartet. We love to sit around and talk about "the good ol' days."

Three months after I started work on January 2, 1961 Mr. John T. put me in charge of sheet music sales. We were distributing for Ira Stanphill. We had about 200 titles altogether, selling around 200,000 copies per year mostly to bookstores. I began ordering the songs being made popular by these various singing groups, many of which I had arranged! For instance I ordered 10,000 copies per month of "The King Is Coming" from Gaither Music. He said he always rejoiced when a letter from Benson came in the mail! Eventually we had to move our steel shelving out of the office and the stock was kept out in a storage area of Benson Printing. [In a few years I had over 1,200 titles in stock selling over a million copies annually!]

One day I went back in that Benson Printing storage area to take inventory of the sheet music. There were several aisles between the steel shelving. Thick plywood was put on top of them for extra space; in fact, the zinc plates (16 songs up) for printing our songbooks were kept up there. I would abbreviate the book titles with a grease pencil on the big pasteboard boxes...all except one titled "Blessed Assurance." (!)

So, it was quite dark under there. There was a single light bulb on a long electric cord, in a wire "cage" with a hook on it, and I just hung it up on a pipe. I was working away when suddenly water began shooting from everywhere! Well, what would an old country boy from north Louisiana know about sprinkler systems anyway? I ran out to get help and eventually the water was cut off, but most of the music stock had to be thrown away. Thank the Lord for insurance. I don't think it damaged any of the printing company's stock. They printed a lot of WORD's books back then.

Lily was a black woman who worked for the Benson Printing Company. She would make coffee every morning and as employees would come in they would get a cup. John III made the comment that Lily's morning coffee would put hair on your chest, and take it back off around 3 p.m.! She was a stout woman and comical in her conversation. You didn't want to cross her! One day the big deep sink got stopped up and George Thomas ran a "snake" through it. He told Lily not to let anyone get around it for a few minutes while he went to the floor underneath to "blow it out." A man (name withheld) from the Printing Company side came to lay his coffee cup in the sink before Lily noticed him and about that time George "blew it out." Smelly slime shot all over this guy. He and George almost came to blows when he insisted George buy him a new shirt and tie. Lily got a kick out of it.

Back down one of those aisles Mr. John T. had an old recliner. Some days he would go there and take a nap. That was also the "wood shed" to which Bob and I were summoned at times.

Some days he would come in my office and say, "Now, young man, you go right ahead with your work, I'm just going to lie down for a while." A long built-in couch set on the street-side wall. He would take about three breaths and go to sleep. In about 15 minutes he would get up refreshed, work another hour or so and head for home.

He said he would get up some mornings at 4 or 5 o'clock and since he taught an adult Sunday school class he would prepare his lesson. He had a home library that would make any preacher salivate! He would dress and go to work. One morning he discovered he had on a brown shoe and a black shoe, and one had a blunt toe. Sometimes he'd leave for home around 2 o'clock in the afternoon.

Anyhow, we had to have more office space. Bob MacKenzie, who had been the PR man for the Nashville Symphony, was hired to be our A&R man and to produce recordings. Bob Benson naturally wanted his own office. Three rooms were built up on top of that steel shelving. A spiral staircase provided access. Bob hired a secretary, who created some excitement for those in the vicinity when she wiggled up those stairs!

Whatever needed doing, I was the man! I couldn't decide which title sounded better – Music Editor or General Flunky. I would be arranging music and the call would come to help unload boxes of new albums off a delivery truck. They were stacked in a cave-like area right underneath the Tennessee Café. I could tell when they were cooking turnip greens! But, I will say, that Bob was right in there helping me.

THE FAMOUS MAXWELL HOUSE

Mr. John T. told me (I'm sure he was joking), "Son, you may forget to ship the merchandise, but be sure to send the invoice!" He told me that I was considered an executive (!) and to always dress like one – coat, tie, shirttail tucked in, shoes tied and hair combed (I had some back then), etc. He never did any of those things, but then, he was the boss! He was of small stature with bushy eyebrows and a gracious smile.

Some days he would tell me to join him for lunch. We ate at various places and I remember one between the office and my Metro bus stop that featured an open-face roast beef sandwich. I'd never encountered that before! At the corner of Fourth and Church Street was the Noel Hotel and on the ground floor was a café called The Stirrup. {I passed the hotel one day just as Gene Autry and some others stepped out the doors}. When we went to leave The Stirrup, Mr. John T. discovered someone had taken HIS hat. He just took another one! Perhaps a month later we ate there again, went to leave, and *there was HIS hat!* He grabbed it!

The famous old Maxwell House Hotel was across Fourth Avenue from the Noel Hotel. They became famous because of the delicious coffee they served. I was told they hired a Benson Printing Company artist to design a newspaper advertisement. He thought for a while then drew a tilted cup with a drop falling from it. Under it he wrote, "Good to the last drop!"

That was a million dollar slogan for a $50 ad. At least, that's the way it was told around the Benson offices. Later I saw on a TV quiz show that President Teddy Roosevelt came up with that slogan? Who knows...and does it really matter, huh?!! I remember walking up the hill on Church Street and looking in the window of the Maxwell House Café and seeing Byrl Ives sitting there having lunch.

On the Fourth Avenue side of the hotel was, to me at least, a fancy restaurant. A black man in coattails would open the door for you. There was a black waiter, with a bright red vest, that waited on us one day. He made no notes when we gave our orders, and made no mistakes. That was amazing. Around the corner on Union Street was a café called Satsuma, and we ate there some also. I usually carried my peanut butter sandwich to work in my briefcase. OK, I looked like an executive... folks just didn't know what was inside! And some days I would go next door to the Tennessee Café and pick up a hamburger or a weenie sandwich.

Marcia's sister Johnnie's fiancé Bartlett Kennedy worked for the US Forrest Service (he later retired after 38 years) and right before they married he was transferred from Winnfield to Newberry, South Carolina. I played the organ for their wedding – the same date as ours but four years later – at the Catholic Church in Winnfield. All three of their children were born in Newberry. On Christmas 1961, we went over there. A friend of ours had made a little cushioned seat for Bill to sit on in the front seat between Marcia and me...no seatbelts back then, either! We had taught him choruses and as we passed through Cleveland, TN, we were all singing "Christ for me." We passed a hardware store with a neon hammer coming down in about four positions and Bill wanted to make sure we saw it. Our song went, "Christ...for...HAMMER... me!" as he pointed at it.

We stayed in Newberry until after New Year's Eve. That night we saw on TV the news that the Maxwell House in Nashville had burned to the ground! It was then discovered there was a tunnel that ran from its basement downhill four blocks, coming out on the rocky bank of the Cumberland River. It might have been a part of the "Underground Railroad" during slave days. Years later another was found at Harvey's store.

A new Maxwell House Hotel was built in what is called MetroCenter, an 840-acre tract of land along the south side of the River about 3 miles north of downtown. It is perhaps twelve stories tall and is called the "Millennium Maxwell House." The cast of "Hee-Haw" TV program used to stay there twice a year for three weeks while they taped sections of the show at WLAC Channel 5 in Nashville.

Third National Bank became our bank when we moved to Nashville. They moved where the Maxwell House Hotel had stood and built a big tall building. One day I walked in the new building's lobby and was greeted by a big, tall man who shook my hand. He was Bill Wade, former Chicago Bears quarterback! I had loved watching him play when we lived in Louisiana and chose the Bears as my favorite team many years before. He told me that he was hosting a devotional time at noon on Wednesdays on the third floor and invited me to attend. I did as often as I could. There would always be someone to sing special music and bring a short message. I sang "Each Step I Take" at one meeting. We became good friends, and a few years ago I talked with him in front of our Walmart store.

FIRST MUSIC CLINIC

I think it was in January 1962, Mr. John T. decided to hold a music clinic in Dunedin, FL, just north of Clearwater on the Gulf Coast. I don't recall how it was promoted. Dr. W. T. Watson, president of Trinity College was the host. Mr. John T., Bob and his wife Peg, Marcia and I and Bill went down there. We stayed at the Fenway, a huge wood structure on the bay that had been a fine hotel in the twenties!

Dr. Watson told us that young Billy Graham had attended Trinity for a while some years before. He also said that the famous composer J. W. van de Venter ("I Surrender All") passed away with his head in Dr. Watson's lap! There we met Dr. Albert Nash from Toronto, Canada and enjoyed times of fellowship. He was a dedicated Christian businessman who knew how to make money in real estate. He told us at lunch one day that he went up in an airplane two times one day looking at property and made a $65,000 profit! For years we exchanged Christmas cards. One year on their way to south Florida for the winter they came by the Benson Company. We were at the CN Tower in Toronto one time and I phoned and talked with him. Not long after that he passed away.

When we arrived at the Fenway, I attempted to remove a footlocker containing songbooks and materials for the clinic from the trunk of my '59 Chevy. I hurt my back, needless to say! Next morning I could barely get out of bed. The Nashville doctor said I had a herniated disc and for about five years I endured terrible pain. I would crawl on my hands and knees into bed at night. I'll finish this story later on.

Almost every day we would go to the Bay Drive-in for seafood. It was all you could eat of the "day's catch" for one dollar. O, my! I dearly loved red snapper. In Louisiana about all we ever ate was catfish or a fish called "buffalo." (I'm serious…it had lots of bones, though).

We are so glad we got to be a part of that week in Dunedin, Florida.

LAKE LOUISE, GA

R. G. LeTourneau made his fortune building giant earth-moving machines. Their wheels would dwarf a man standing by them. [He also tithed a tremendous percentage of his personal income]. In Longview, TX is LeTourneau College. He built a retreat in northeast Georgia, including a big lake, and named it Lake Louise. The building was shaped like spokes in a wagon wheel. Motel rooms went down a couple of them, meeting rooms down others and also a dining room and kitchen. The "hub" was the auditorium. People came and we had music classes…for directing, studying the rudiments of music, graded choirs, etc.

A trio of young men attended and sang beautifully. We kept in touch with two of them through the years. One is Gerald Turner who moved to south Florida, formed quartets and continues to sing. The other is Bill Cline who had us in his huge church and I'll elaborate on that later. I can't remember the third one's name.

One evening before the service, we were finishing supper, and someone stopped to talk with me. As I lifted a spoonful of ice cream and looked up at him, the brads (welds) in the metal folding chair I was sat on broke and in a split second I was flat on my back, still making eye contact and holding the spoon of ice cream! Everyone was so concerned about me (I was mortified), but I told them not to worry…I had fallen on my wallet and that protected me from injury – like it was packed with paper money! Not.

I remember a Mr. and Mrs. Thomas attended. Also we met another couple, named Happy and Harley. I asked which one was Harley. (See, I was building my reputation, right?). One day while there, Marcia, Bill and I drove over to Toccoa Falls and I made a snapshot of Marcia, pregnant with Kellye, standing on a rock at the foot of those beautiful falls. You may remember that years later, the dam broke one night due to heavy rains and many campers below it perished.

COURTED BY ZONDERVAN

In the spring of 1962, Mr. P. J. (Pat) Zondervan flew into the Nashville airport to talk with me about moving to Grand

Rapids and going to work for his company. He and his brother Bill had founded it many years before and had established a great reputation for great music and attractive Bibles. While we were talking in a café Marcia and Bill were sitting on an outside bench watching the planes. A single engine on take-off suddenly veered right toward them and the terminal. It turned again and crashed. The two persons in the plane walked away, but that was some excitement for Bill and Marcia.

I thanked Mr. Pat but told him Mr. John T. had been so good to me, I couldn't leave him now. Really, I didn't want to live in Michigan! He asked if I would do some arranging for him. With Mr. John T.'s approval I made about thirty choral arrangements in two and a half years. They were printed in several Zondervan publications. That was really the beginning of my choral arranging. Another arranger for Zondervan that I admired was Harold deCou, recently deceased. He arranged John W. Peterson's great Easter and Christmas cantatas. Peterson was my idol when it came to composing songs.

Then Mr. John T. had me arrange some choral books, a first for the company. Some early titles were "Singing 3 Parts,"/1966; and "Choir Impact,"/1968. They sold quite well. We had a series called "Special Songs for Special Singers" that had five volumes. I also composed my first Christmas cantata titled "The Story Unchanged (Through the Ages)". Benson printed and recorded it. In later years I composed another Christmas cantata with Jeff Jeffrey titled "Wise Men Seek Him Still," not to be confused with Lanny Wolfe's song "Wise Men Still Seek Him."

I also wrote two Easter cantatas – "Resurrection Celebration" was co-written with Jeff Jeffrey, printed by Benson, and "Eyewitness to Easter," written after I retired from Benson and published by Lifeway. I also compiled and arranged several shorter choral works. "His Last Days" by Dallas Holm was arranged by me and was a big seller for years. William (Bill) Cox and I compiled two folios for Senior Adults and I arranged them. The third one was titled, "Celebrate Jesus 2000," and had narration throughout the songs. Premiers were held in Atlanta, GA; Cherry Hill, NJ and East Texas Baptist College.

BENSON'S TALENT SEARCH

The Benson Company entered the recording business in June 1961, six months after I became music editor. At first, Mr. John T. just intended to record some soloists, college or church choirs, and some gospel singers. The first album on the HeartWarming label (that's how it was spelled) was a Mr. Whitmore from Ashland, KY. He had a beautiful tenor voice, accompanied by organ as I recall.

Very soon, Benson signed other artists like Jimmy Snow (Hank's son) and his wife Carol (Wilma Lee and Stony Cooper's daughter who lived on Riverside Drive close to our Groves Park Road rented house). Also Ira Stanphill, famous preacher and composer of songs like "Mansion over the Hilltop," "Room at the Cross," "I Know Who Holds Tomorrow," etc. He included my song "Each Step I Take," doing it in a relaxed country feel, using steel guitar. The Oak Ridge Boys, who were singing gospel music back then signed with Benson. [By the way, along about 1970 I played organ for their lead singer, Duane Allen and Nora Lee Stuart's wedding in Bowling Green, KY. Nora came from a family of singers. She and her two sisters were known as the Stuart Sisters Trio. Sometime later Nora and Carol (Snow) along with two young men, were backup singers on the Grand Ole Opry, known as the Carol Lee Singers.]

The famous contralto, Bette Stalnecker, made several albums with Benson. Rosie Rozelle, the high tenor with the Statesmen Quartet recorded an album that contained several of my original songs up to that time. He got a sore throat and I was sent "up town" to a pharmacy for a prescription. The druggist said, "Tell her to take this according to the directions." I replied, "It's not a HER, it's a HE." The man looked at me with a funny expression on his face!

We recorded Bob Newkirk and Cathy Taylor, singers on the long-running radio show from Chicago, "Bob McNeil's Breakfast Club." I was sent there to present their albums to them "on the air." Marcia, Bill and Kellye went with me. The show was broadcast from the top floor of Hotel Allerton and you could see clouds from Lake Michigan floating by the windows.

Bob McNeil said to me, "By the way, Mr. Mercer, how's your wife?" I said, "Compared to whom?" That, of course was preplanned.

We made another trip to the Chicago area to deliver one thousand choral books to the compiler, Lindsay Terry. At the time he was Minister of Music at Jack Hyle's famous church, First

Baptist in Hammond, IN. Marcia's parents were visiting us at the time in Nashville and they went with Marcia and me. A big pastor's convention was going on at Jack Hyle's church, some 3500 were present. The next morning I thought it would be neat to drive along Lakeshore Drive in Chicago, maybe even run up across the Wisconsin state line, so Mammaw and Pappaw could say they'd been in that state! I approached some orange pylons, then ducked between them and kept going. That was a bad idea because that lane went downtown! I noticed this black car on my rear bumper. I figured I had made a cab driver angry, but when I stopped at a traffic light, a big guy got out in a hurry and I saw the gun on his hip. A policeman, but he hadn't turned on his flashing lights.

He came to my window and said, "I ought to give you a ticket for every violation in the book!" When I asked what I had done wrong, in my most innocent, Tennessee hillbilly voice, he said, "But I'm just going to tell you the quickest way out of this city!" So help me, I'm telling the truth. He said, "Go up yonder to the fifth light and... No, that won't do it. I tell you, turn here and go two miles and... No, uh," so I quipped, "In other words I can't git there from here!" He just laughed and said, "Get outta here!" We enjoyed our tour of the city and we did make it to Wisconsin in time for "dinner."

One of our biggest artists was the Bill Gaither Trio. They recorded perhaps two dozen albums over the years. At first it was Bill, his brother Danny and their sister Mary. Then Mary needed to stay home with her family and Gloria took her place. I remember playing piano for Danny in Benson's recording studio out in the new MetroCenter building as he practiced "It is Well with My Soul." Later, Danny decided to go out "on his own." Sometime later he was diagnosed with cancer and passed away. Gary McSpadden, who had been with Jake Hess and the Imperials, took his place. They could thrill an audience. Then Gloria gave Bill a VCR camera for Christmas and the rest is history! (I'm just joking.)

I am on two of those Homecoming Friends videos sitting in the choir next to Wally Varner, pianist for the Blackwood Brothers Quartet for a long time. That was the first three day recording session Bill attempted and we (Marcia was with me, of course) got to see many of our "old" friends. David Ring, who had preached at Park Avenue when he first started his ministry, yelled at me across the yard. He walked up and said, "How is everything at Park Avenue?"

Henry and Hazel Slaughter were there. Remember they had lived a couple of blocks from us in Parkwood Estates for many years. They rode from the motel with us one day to Gaither's place, and the next day we rode with them. Bill provided a great lunch for everyone and one day in walked big Alvin Slaughter. Hazel (Slaughter) shouted, "Aaall-vinnn, come over here to see yo' Mama!" Everyone laughed. Dallas Holm and Praise were there for the first time.

Outside the recording studio one morning, Marcia and I were privileged to visit with Mosie Lister, his wife and one of their twin daughters, before Mosie was called in. I asked him what his favorite composition was and he quickly replied, "'Til the

Storm Passes By." {By the way, my favorite of the songs I've written is "Nailing My Sins to His Cross."}

The Imperials was another group that made a bunch of albums with Benson on the Impact label. Back in 1964 Jake Hess left the Statesmen and started the "Imps" as every one called them. Their bass, Armond Morales, who had been with the Weatherford Quartet, made a solo album also. For a time they backed up Elvis Presley in his travels and on albums. They also were backup singers for Jimmy Dean. One afternoon Benson held a picnic in Warner Park in West Nashville for all employees and in-town artists. Jimmy Dean came with the Imperials. Remember the pop song, "If I knew you were coming, I'd a-baked a cake?" When I shook Jimmy's hand (he wasn't nearly as tall as I imagined him to be) I commented, "If I knew you were coming, I'd a-bought some sausage!" Apparently he was too young to make the connection and it fell flat!

Jake gave me a reel-to-reel tape in the early 60s (while we lived on Leswood Lane) from which to transcribe a song. Some guy in New York had written what he considered a gospel song... something like "this morning I saw a bluebird and thought of God." He wanted the Imperials to record it! Well, in a seven month period, I had strep throat three times, and I wasn't feeling too good when I tried to work on it. After three days I gave up and took it back to Jake. He gave me his deadpan, disappointed look and said, "Why, Elmo, I thought if anyone could do it, you could." I took it back and said, "Let me try again." And I did it! You know, that was a milepost in my life. Afterward, when I encountered something difficult to arrange, my thoughts went back to that incident, and I kept on working till I finished the task!

Now TRUTH was something else! They used real instruments and real singers that could put on a program! I knew Roger Breland and got them to come to Park Avenue in our new sanctuary. For a couple of Sundays I admonished the congregation to "be there." Well, on the first number, the brass blew a couple of little old ladies out in the lobby. They got up, dusted themselves off and headed out the door. I almost got lynched!

A couple of years later I was the pianist for a series of services held in Hendersonville's high school football stadium. Called a "Starlight Crusade," it was sponsored by College Heights Baptist Church. The format was to have a different speaker and a different singing group each night. The only speaker I remember was Elvis' half-brother (step-brother?) One night the Imperials were there, and Truth performed another night. A black sax player, Dr. Vernard Johnson played "It Is Well with My Soul" and the crowd leaped to their feet; he had a black man accompanying him on the piano. The last night, I began the service singing, "Each Step I Take," then Ferlon Husky, Billy Walker and Jeannie Shepherd sang. The night Truth was there, after the close of the service Roger auditioned a young woman to sing with Truth. He had her sing "Amazing Grace" in about all twelve keys on the piano – and I was able to play them all! Then Roger rode with us to Shoney's. He said, "Mo, would you please tell Bro. Mowrey that I'm still saved!" We laughed about that, recalling their concert at Park Avenue that I mentioned above.

Re'Generation recruited some great singers down through the years also. Derric Johnson created that group. He had been director of music at a huge church in the San Diego area. They had eighteen singing groups and Ron Coker helped with them. Bob Clark was the sound engineer. Re'Gen sang with excellent soundtracks and had great costumes. They did a LOT of patriotic songs in the mid-70s as our nation approached its 200th anniversary. One time they were on a trip out west and got caught in a blizzard. They were taken in by a couple living on a farm and that was a memorable time for them.

I recall in 1975 our family went to the D. C. area to see historic sights – a year before our nation's 200th birthday. Bad choice. The city was PREPARING for the celebration. We stayed in a Holiday Inn only six blocks north of the White House and left our Cadillac in their garage. I flagged down a cab and told the foreign driver to take us to the Bureau of Printing and Engraving. He nodded his head and took off, then asked me again. I said "Where they print the money." He smiled real big and said, "Ohhhh!," changed directions and took us there. Besides printing currency they printed food stamps and US postage stamps! We would go to the Smithsonian around 3 p.m. every day.

One night just before 10 p.m. we walked in a cafeteria to eat supper. The serving ladies were tired I'm sure and kept saying, "Hurry, please!" I could see steam beginning to come out Marcia's ears. In a minute she looked at me and said, "I don't have to put up with this!" and shoved her tray toward a server. Bill, Kellye and I followed her to the already-locked front door and couldn't get out. The manager came over and sensed something was wrong. Marcia said, "I don't want to get anyone in trouble, just unlock the door so we can get out of here!" Late the next day I told Bill and Kellye, "Maybe we'll get to eat a good supper tonight if Mama will behave herself!"

Dave Wortman sang bass with Re'Gen for a while. He was from Iowa, brought up on a farm. When he left Re'Gen he went to work for Benson. He told me his family woke up one morning to several feet of snow, and huge drifts. He looked out and the old mule was standing on the slanting barn roof! His early morning job was to milk the cows and his brother helped him. As his brother walked behind one, she raised her tail and blew it out, all over him. Dave fell out laughing and his brother beat him up…he said! He lives in Nashville and we keep in touch.

Derric told me one time (true story) that he was standing in a crowd at a concert where several groups were on program. A quartet was singing one of my songs when a man sidled up to him and said, "You know Elmo Mercer?" He answered that he did. After a minute or two the man spoke to Derric again and said, "I know him personal." [Not personally]. After that when we saw each other he would point and say, "Hey, I know you personal!" Derric later was director of music at Disney's Epcot Center, and I believe a lot of Re'Gen singers sang there also. In June 2012 some Re'Gen alumni surprised Derric with an 80th birthday party. Dave phoned me about it but at the time we were in north Louisiana and could not attend. I later saw photos on Facebook. What precious memories!

Early on, I had told Mr. John T. that I didn't want to sit in on any contract talks, really didn't care to travel. I just wanted to work on music. I said one day at the bank in Winnfield, "I wish all I had to do was work on music." And I did. When I got to work at Benson they'd chain my ankle to the piano. {I'm joking}. I told Marcia I slaved over a hot piano all day long! I told them I didn't want a secretary – after all I typed 90 words per minute myself. When I got a phone call wanting something done, I did it right then, if possible. I had the cleanest desktop in the building. One day (in our new building in Metro Center) they bought me a new Olympia typewriter. I thought that thing was something. Then personal computers came along!

I did research on books and records that Benson released each year and entered titles in a publication I called "Song Finder." It was printed in 8-1/2 by 11 size. That was a big job to keep up with and still do all the other arranging required of me, but I enjoyed the challenge and was proud of my work. And still today I will go to a filing cabinet in my music room here at home and refer to the last one I printed to locate a song.

Also I started doing custom arranging and printing, with Mr. John T.'s approval. One time I arranged a song for a lady and the title was "This Do in Remembrance of Me"...but I spelled "remembrance" wrong. I had to reprint 1,000 copies of sheet music. I think I "went in the hole" on that job.

The most notable mistake was for Dottie Rambo. They had decided to form their own "Rambo Music Company," and left Benson. She wrote lyrics to Londonderry Aire and had me make a four-part harmony SHAPE note arrangement. She titled it "He Looked Beyond my Fault." I printed the first 1,000 copies of sheet music. When I proudly showed her a copy she exclaimed, "Oh, no, Mo! It didn't have an 's' on it." So, it is MY fault that people call it, "He Looked beyond My Faults" and Saw My Need."

Bob Benson made some comment about "He looked beyond my ankles and saw my knees." Our long-time friend Mark Sheldon (who was interim music director at Park Avenue for a couple of years) worked in the post office (he retired in early 2013 I believe). One day I got a package in the mail that had apparently passed by him. He wrote on it: "If you don't get this package on time, it's not my FAULTS!" The last song I arranged for Dottie was "We Shall Behold Him," one of her greatest, and she wrote many "hits."

I still remember the day, Buck and Dottie and nine-year-old Reba stepped through the front door of the Benson offices on Fourth Avenue North. Dottie said, "Mr. Benson, we're the Gospel Echoes from Dawson Springs, KY, and we want to make an album." I lost count on how many they did make. Shirley Cohron sang with them at first. Then Kenny Parker and Elmer Cole sang with them. Reba grew up and joined Buck and Dottie making it a family trio. They had the gift of electrifying an audience. Dottie penned so many great songs, such as "If That Isn't Love," "I Will Glory in the Cross," etc. Dottie went through several years of bad health but got "back on the road" again. She was tragically killed when her bus crashed a few years ago.

Benson recorded Doug Oldham, the first of many artists that Bill Gaither promoted. Doug told every audience how he had wandered away from God (his father was Dr. Dale Oldham, a radio preacher) but had come back "home." He blessed folks everywhere he sang. One of Gaither's songs "Thanks to Calvary" seemed to be his testimony. Some other artists that Bill helped start their careers were Mark Lowry, Michael English, Sandy Patti, Steve Green, Larnelle Harris, and many more.

New York City opera singers Robert Hale and Dean Wilder, with Ovid Young their accompanist, made many albums with Benson. Bob Hale was from Grant Parish, LA, where Marcia and I were born! {And Les Beasley of the Florida Boys Quartet was from Grant Parish also}. The first album was titled "Wilder and Hale" and we immediately saw our mistake! They sang at Belmont Heights Baptist Church one Sunday night here in Nashville and the church receptionist bought the album. When Dr. Bob Norman came in the office Monday morning, it was playing and he said, "Hey, that's Wilder 'n' Hale." She replied, "Why, yes it is, Dr. Bob, but you really shouldn't talk that way." Hale and Wilder would travel in concert nationwide about two months out of the year.

MY MARK LOWRY CONNECTION

I first met Mark Lowry when he was twelve years old. His mother (you've heard about her from his stories) brought him from their home in Houston to Nashville to make an album.

His voice had NOT changed and he sang beautifully...still does. [You know he wrote the words to "Mary, Did You Know?" and Buddy Greene wrote the music].

You will remember that Mr. John T. had paid for me to take an orchestration course from Peabody College, and he instructed me to orchestrate Mark's album, for which I am very proud. The soundtrack was recorded in London by symphony musicians and is really pretty. But it almost didn't happen!

Apparently I had to finish those arrangements while attending my first CBA convention, held in the city of Minneapolis, MN. On the Ozark Airlines flight back to Nashville, my luggage was lost...and those arrangements were in those bags! Dear Lord, HELP! About 15 minutes before I was to leave on vacation with my family, a cab pulled up at our Fourth Avenue offices with my luggage and the arrangements. Bob MacKenzie was leaving for London to record soundtracks. I was a happy camper. I went home and picked up Marcia, Bill and Kellye and we took off!

By the way, Mark's Mother, Bev Lowry, was a professor at Liberty University at Lynchburg, VA for a while. She also has written several songs, like "I Thirst," and "The Ground is Level at the Cross." I am so proud to see Mark has become so successful and such a crowd favorite, whether singing, telling his stories, or just "looking stupid." He is one of the very best and I'm grateful God allowed me to have a part in his early beginnings.

RECORDING AT RCA

What fun it was for me to attend recording sessions at RCA studios on Music Row. It is now called "Studio B" and is on the Country Music Hall of Fame tour here in Nashville. Sometimes I "ran" the sessions, especially when they went from 11 p.m. to 2 a.m.! I got to know the engineers and a lot of top Nashville musicians. For an old country boy from North Louisiana, it was hard to believe this wasn't a dream!

Here I was in the studio where so many famous people had recorded so many hit songs. Of course, Elvis would top the list, which would also include Chet Atkins, who managed the studio; Floyd Cramer, Boots Randolph, Eddie Arnold, Willie Nelson, Jerry Reed, George Jones, Patsy Cline, Kay Starr, Perry Como and the list continues. We never did get Chet to play on any of our Benson albums, but Boots and Floyd did.

I asked Floyd during a break if he'd let me watch his hands and he said, "Sure." I won't go into detail, but I observed three things he did to get that famous "slip-note" sound. He taught his grandson, Jason Coleman, his technique and he has CDs on the market. He must have used the same arrangements, maybe even some of the same musicians, because he sounds just like Floyd. You should "Google" him.

We met Donna and Rayford Hilley when we moved our membership to Park Avenue Baptist Church in September 1965. Rayford played football for Vanderbilt so they moved here from Birmingham. We raised our children together – took trips together. Donna worked her way up from Jack Stapp's secretary at Tree Music to eventually becoming President and CEO of SONY-ATV here on Music Row. A few years ago she invited us to accompany them to Maui, Hawaii, to a National Music Publishers Association (NMPA) meeting in about 2003 or so. We flew over to Honolulu for a day and at the airport ran into Boots Randolph. He told us he had been to Singapore for a "one-night-stand!" While all of us were talking I asked if he remembered playing on Benson sessions. He said he did and really enjoyed doing it.

We spent three nights in Four Seasons Hotel in Beverly Hills. The elevator doors opened one afternoon and there stood Richard Chamberlain in a bath robe headed for the pool on the roof of the 4th floor. We took a tour of Hollywood and saw where many of the stars lived. Well, I got off track a bit, didn't I?

Benson hired the best Nashville Union musicians. We usually got Harold Bradley (brother to Owen who ran Columbia Studios and was famous for his organ recording hits back in the 40s and 50s) on electric guitar, or Billy Byrd, who was Ernest Tubb's famous picker. Over a year or so, Billy taught me chord structure and chord progressions that really helped change not only my ability to play piano, but just listening to music! The drummer we usually hired was Buddy Harmon. He was in such demand for sessions that he had a drum set in several main Nashville studios. "Lightnin'" Chance or "Junior" Husky played the upright bass. Vic Willis of the Willis Brothers played accordion sometimes and "Pig" Robbins, Marvin Hughes or

Bill Purcell played piano. Marvin was great on the organ and also taught me some "rudiments of music." When the airplane crashed in Tennessee killing Patsy Cline, Hawkshaw Hawkins, Cowboy Copas and the pilot Randy Hughes, Marvin later married Randy's widow – she didn't have to change her last name!

Benson hired the best string players, brass, woodwinds and percussionists available, many of them members of the Nashville Symphony. I remember when my song, "Lonely Road up Calvary's Way," was being recorded one night, I saw a black man playing the violin while tears ran down his cheeks. We used varied arrangers - Bill Purcell, Ronn Huff, Rick Powell, Larry Mayfield, Don Marsh, Jim Hall, to name a few. Mr. John T. had me arrange some sessions for instruments and vocal backup. It all sounded great to me. But the Union President dropped by on a session one night and asked me if I'd made the arrangements. Thinking I would be complimented I said, "Yes sir." Instead Mr. Cooper said, "Well, if you're going to make any more you need to come see me!" I knew what he meant and told Mr. John T. the next day. I never got to join that union, but I wished I could have.

Benson also hired the top backup singers. The Jordanaires was one such group. Of course, they sang backup on many of the recordings made in those years. I was proud to get to know them all. Neal Matthews made all their arrangements and sometimes played guitar. In a session they did mostly "head" arrangements. After listening to the song to be recorded, they would make up their own backup singing parts. And since they used the shape notes they didn't need manuscript paper.

They would "stack the notes" on the back of an envelope or piece of paper. If the song happened to go up a fourth, the baritone and high tenor simply switched parts. Neal and his wife Charlsie were members of Park Avenue Baptist. In later years after Neal passed away, Charlsie would host monthly card games at her house. Marcia and I were among the eight who participated. When their daughter Lisa had heart surgery Marcia and I sat with them in the waiting room. Elvis named his daughter Lisa after Lisa Matthews!

Another backup group in much demand was the Anita Kerr Singers. Anita drew from about fifteen singers, but she also had a quartet (2 women, 2 men). Anita also made head arrangements. They were known for their fabulous blend, especially on the "Oohs" and "Ahhs." Millie Kirkham did all those HIGH soprano parts that you heard on a lot of hit songs by various artists, like "The Good, the Bad and the Ugly."

I digress here to say that Anita asked me to write some country or "pop" songs for her company, Poker Music. She and Bill Porter, an RCA engineer, formed the company: "Po" from Porter and "ker" from Kerr. I wrote 19 songs in three months! She was going to do a demo of four songs. She sent fifteen songs, (with the composer's names blacked out) to a guy in Pensacola she said sang like Al Martino. He was to choose four… three of them were mine!

This was in 1967. I took the afternoon off and went to the session at RCA. It was a big one, with of course the Anita Kerr quartet doing backup, lots of strings and other orchestral instruments. The studio lights were turned down to create the right atmosphere, I guess. Oh, I was on Cloud Nine! It was so beautiful. I just knew I was on the road to fame and fortune!

But God...don't you just love those words? They're in the Bible many times. But God had different plans and I am so glad He did. He slammed that door. I never even got a tape of the session! And I don't know what ever became of the songs. Later Anita married and moved to live in Switzerland! RCA built a big 3-story building with a new studio next door. Some of us from Benson went to the Grand Opening. Al Hirt was the featured guest. A few years later it was closed down! God must have influenced Mr. John T. to have me do more choral arranging. And in 1970, after he had retired, Jack Price and I came out with "Crusade Choir, Volume I" and I've already mentioned its popularity.

On a few sessions we used Tom Paul and the Glazer Brothers as backup singers. While doing a session one day at RCA, Connie Smith dropped in. She was standing at the coke machine and Lightnin' Chance asked her what she wanted. She said a Diet Coke because she was watching her figure. Lightnin' said, "You git yourself a regular coke, and I'll watch your figure!"

In 1979 Darryl Hicks interviewed me at my office in the new Benson building in MetroCenter, for a book he was writing. I forgot about it until twenty years later (Egads!) when I discovered the book had been printed and released. Others written about in the book were Larry Gatlin, Connie Smith, Wes Yoder, Jessi Colter, Mike Warnke, Jimmy Snow, Donna Stoneman,

John & Debra Brown, and others. One night after a concert at First Baptist in Okeechobee, FL I was at our product table when Lois Cammon looked at my picture in that book. She made the comment that it didn't look like me. A little *eight*-year-old boy looked at it and said, "Mrs. Cammon, I've known Mr. Mercer since I was a *kid* and that's not him!" But it was...I was wearing a hairpiece, a big checkered sport coat and had no beard. I would have disowned myself!

Our pastor, Bob Mowrey, asked me to accompany him and a grandson from Dallas to the new downtown Country Music Hall of Fame. If you are a country music fan, you must go there! As a part of the tour, you board a bus that takes you to Studio B which is the original RCA recording studio. When we entered it I saw that same old Steinway grand piano with the cigarette burns on it. I asked the guide if I could play it. She gave permission and I walked over, sat down, and started playing "Last Date" in Floyd Cramer's style! Folks rushed to me. I told them he had played on some of the Benson company sessions and I learned that from him.

Mary Lynch was RCA's receptionist. She would answer the phone in a soft, slow and VERY sexy voice. One morning Lightnin' Chance said he phoned the studio and by the time Mary finished her greeting, he said, "Aw, (bleep) Mary, I done forgot what I called about now!"

George Beverly Shea (soloist with Billy Graham Crusades for decades) was in town one week to record a new album at RCA. Marcia and I were invited to the session when he was to record

"Each Step I Take." Bev asked his A&R man Darryl Rice where it was on the schedule. He stumbled around, looked in a file and finally said, "Uh, Bev, I made a substitution on that song." Bev told them all to wait a minute. He took us out in the hallway and apologized, and talked with us for ten minutes or so. However, later he did record it, not once but twice. It was included in a Billy Graham promotional CD.

I MEET JOHN W. PETERSON

The National Quartet Convention was held in the early 60s in Memphis, Tennessee, at the famous Ellis Auditorium where Elvis performed. Mr. John T. took me with him, probably in the fall of 1962. We stayed at the Peabody Hotel, famous for its "duck walk." Daily at 5 p.m. several ducks parade through the lobby, then swim in the fountain pool.

I guess it was the first morning of the convention. Mr. John T. and I approached the auditorium and I saw two men who appeared to be waiting for us. I recognized one to be Mr. Pat Zondervan. The other guy was very tall. Mr. Pat greeted us and said, "I'd like you to meet John W. Peterson." I looked up at him and said in awe "John W. Peterson?" We shook hands. Mr. John T. said, "I'd like you to meet Elmo Mercer." John looked down at me and said, "Elmo Mercer?" We had us a mutual admiration society forming right there. I'll always remember meeting my songwriting idol.

Later that day we attended an ASCAP luncheon at The Four Flames restaurant. I got to talk with him for a little while.

Later I read his life story "The Miracle Goes On!" and I recommend it to everyone. I found he was eleven years older than me. What a talent he had. He wrote such songs as "I Believe in Miracles" (lyrics by our friend Dr. Carlton C. Buck), "It Took a Miracle," (written as he flew planes over the Alps), "Heaven Came Down," "Surely Goodness and Mercy," etc. His beautiful Christmas and Easter cantatas were arranged by Harold deCou. That is the only time I got to spend with him.

Benson always had a booth at the Quartet Convention. Sometimes I would stand out front and talk with people passing by. One time at the Nashville Municipal Auditorium (after the QC moved here) we met a couple who lived in Vermont, a mile south of the Quebec border. In later years they came out to our house for a visit and we just happened to have a big snow on the ground! We went by to see them in Vermont, too.

The Happy Goodmans had just bought a new purple bus from Sweden. They even had matching suits, as well as Vestal's dress. Bob Benson looked up and saw them heading our way and he quipped, "They ought not to be backing that bus down through here!" Rusty was writing some great songs then, like "Who Am I?" "Had It Not Been," etc. One of his best was "I Wouldn't Take Nothin' for my Journey Now." He gave me a reel-to-reel tape and I made a four-part shape note arrangement for 9 x 12 sheet music. He named his music company Journey Music, later purchased by WORD.

Paul Downing married Ann Sanders when she was singing with the Speer Family. They started their own singing group called, appropriately "The Downings." One night at Ellis Auditorium in Memphis, Paul and I happened to be in the Men's Room when two policemen came in and said, "Alright, everybody clear out, now!" I asked, "What's going on? Is the building on fire?" He said, "No, Elvis has to come in!" Well, Paul didn't like that one bit but it was kinda funny to me. I didn't see Elvis myself that night. We had seen him on the Louisiana Hayride in Shreveport a few years before. I never met him personally.

In the early 60s, Mr. John T. took me with him to Atlanta, where he was to meet with the LeFevre family to discuss his purchase of their company. We all went out to a fancy restaurant for supper, after which Mr. John T. and I went back to our hotel room. I don't remember the name, but it was a broad, red brick building about ten stories high in the east part of downtown.

It was COLD that night...outside and inside our room! Mr. John T. slept in his clothes with his raincoat laid over the spread! I didn't sleep too good myself. The next day, discussions were held. Mr. John T. decided not to pay their asking price, and we caught a bus back to Nashville!

Again, in the early 60s, Mr. John T. took me with him to Knoxville...on a Trailways bus. Its route took us on US-70 South through that part of the Cumberland Mountains. The scenery was beautiful but the bus felt top-heavy to me! We enjoyed the long night of great gospel singing by various artists after which Hovie Lister preached an hour or so. It was late when we got back to the hotel where we all stayed.

The real purpose of Mr. John T.'s visit was to talk business, I'm certain. He might have hoped to sign them to recording contracts, I don't know. J. D. Sumner had gone to his room, and Jake went down to get him. He told me to go with him. Jake knocked on the door and said, "Gawky? Gawky!" I assume that was his nickname for J. D.! Anyway, neither quartet ever recorded on a Benson label, although Rosie Rozelle and Jake Hess did make solo albums with us, recording several of my songs. The next day Mr. John T. and I caught a ride on the Speer Family's bus back to Nashville.

STUART HAMBLEN

Phil Drake lived in Nashville a while and, among other talents, he was a piano technician. He tuned the pianos at the new Benson building in MetroCenter, plus my Wurlitzer at home. We discovered mice had chewed up straps, etc., but did at least put them in a neat pile. Phil did extensive work and the charge was only $60, but that was decades ago! He was a great pianist also, and told me that Readers' Digest had contacted him about doing an album of pop songs they were producing. I don't know if that occurred.

Anyhow, Phil and his wife invited Marcia and me to go with them to the lounge at Shoney's Inn near Music Row to hear a guy named "Fingers" Carlyle. He played electric guitar, but laid it on his lap like a steel guitar, then "walked" his fingers over the strings! It was amazing. He even played "Orange Blossom Special" which is a fiddle tune!

A man walked between us and the stage and stumbled over an empty chair. I told Marcia that he reminded me of Stuart Hamblen. In a few minutes the emcee for the show said, "We have a famous composer here tonight." I began adjusting my tie and coat, believing Phil had slipped around and told him I was present. My pride bubble burst when the emcee said with a swing of his hand TOWARD US... "Mr. Stuart Hamblen!" Wow. I had talked with both Stuart and his wife Suzy on the phone many times before, ordering sheet music for Benson, and when we would be in Los Angeles. They lived on Mulholland Drive up in the mountains overlooking the city.

OUR DAUGHTER IS BORN

Our wedding was October 2, 1954. Kellye was born October 6, 1962, in Baptist Hospital. We show no baby pictures of her! She had a pointed head, for one thing, and we discussed trading her back in! She arrived over eight years after we married, and is almost five years younger than Bill. Marcia was in the room with the wife of a TV personality and he said he would hate to come up "cold" on the name "Marcia Mercer" as he would surely get his tongue twisted. We do have some cute pictures and home movies of Bill and Kellye.

Later in our concert travels I would tell the pastor or music minister to give her top billing... to say Marcia and Elmo Mercer. Because if they said Elmo and Marcia Mercer the people would fall out in the aisles! I told them she was 72% of "the act." But then I added that since she'd had tarsal tunnel surgery on both feet so she couldn't tap-dance on the piano any more. I got some funny looks, believe me!

In 1961 we decided to build our new house up on Leswood Lane in Parkwood Estates. I asked the salesman what the vacant space was that went through the area. He said that was where Briley (first mayor of Metro Nashville-Davidson County) Parkway would be built, but added "that's at least 8 to 10 years away." Would you believe it was more like thirty years?! We lived there about three and a half years then decided to build a second house north of that proposed Parkway on Masonwood Drive. The houses on the north side of the street backed up to a huge cow pasture owned by a Mr. Jackson who lived on out Brick Church Pike. This house had a full basement and double garage. I built a wall between the garage and the rest of the basement creating a rec room, (or was it "wreck" room?).

We put a ping pong table down there, a pool table, a couch and TV along with the washer and dryer. I enclosed the stair steps, ran a carpet down them and then built a closet under them. I think our pastor, Bro. Bob must have majored in ping pong at UT-Chattanooga. I thought I was good and invited him to play a game while Marcia and Peggy were putting finishing touches on our meal. He let me score two points!

As for the pool table, Kellye was pre-school and could beat me! She shot with her *left* hand for some reason and could barely see over the rim. I've seen her sink four straight balls. She'd say things like, "Why don't you sit down, Daddy, till I miss?" and "I don't have to practice to beat you, Daddy!"

The main floor was over 1300 cubic feet, as I recall. It had three bedrooms and two baths, a den and kitchen combo. My piano, moved up from Louisiana, was in the living room, positioned so I could watch TV that was in the den. I arranged many a famous song while watching TV shows like "Gunsmoke," "Bonanza," etc. The brick was mostly orange/tan. In 1974 we added a 20x21 foot room upstairs, connecting with the den and kitchen. It had a real fireplace in it with a heat-o-later (?) installed. There was an outside stairway down to the ground. There was another open fireplace in that area, but I don't recall ever using it. A car could be parked under there as well. I remember one Sunday we were running late to leave for church. I told the family I could not stop the clock and since I was pianist I HAD to be on time. In a tizzy, I backed the Cadillac out of that space and put a dent in my GMC pickup truck driver's door! Of course when we arrived at church we had our halos on straight with smiles and soft greetings! You've all "been there, done that", admit it!

One Saturday Bill and I decided to climb to the top of Taylor's Knob, a mile or so east of our house. It was said to be the highest point in the county. [A big hospital is built in that area now]. We discovered there was stalks of poke sallet everywhere. We had no bag but I used my shirt to gather a bunch of it. I left the shirt by the washer in the rec room. Next morning we found a dead mouse on it – he had apparently eaten some of the greens somehow left on that shirt! You have to parboil the greens before cooking them to eat. Another cold and snowy day, Bill and I went over there again to sled down a portion of the hill. Two men were there using the hood off a car for a sled. They had no control and once it spun around and slung them off. One guy got a portion of his body caught on the hood ornament or latch and quit sledding - ?

I remember one time while we lived there, Marcia, Bill and Kellye went to Winnfield for a visit. In my haste to get to Riverside Baptist Church in East Nashville where I was pianist, I locked myself out of the house and of course, the car keys were on the same key ring. I had to climb in the small front bathroom window which was quite high off the ground. I was wearing my favorite green iridescent suit and almost plunged headfirst into the commode! I did make it to church on time even though I had to change what I wore.

GOVERNOR JIMMIE DAVIS

Jimmie Davis, twice governor of Louisiana, and Mama went to school together in Jackson Parish (north LA). He was one year older...born in 1899, he lived through the 1900s and died in 2000...he lived in 3 centuries! He was also known as a songwriter and singer.

On his campaigns he always had a live, country band and would sing his songs, like "You Are My Sunshine," "Worried Mind," etc. A great western-swing, rock and roll piano player, Moon Mullican would tear up the keyboard. During the first two campaigns, the Plainsmen Quartet also traveled and sang with him. They also recorded on Benson's HeartWarming label. On TV, Jimmie would lean back on his desk, look into the camera and just talk to you. He had no trouble getting elected for two 4-year terms. Louisiana law required him to skip four years, and then he tried for a third term. This time, the famous Speer Family traveled with him. He lost the election, but not on their account. I'm telling you, Louisiana politics was "something else," and still is. Chicago had nothing on Louisiana! {I'll not get into Tennessee politics!}

Jimmie and his first wife were married almost 50 years when she passed away. They are buried behind the Jimmie Davis Tabernacle in Jackson Parish (more on that below). Later he married Anna Carter of the "Chuck Wagon Gang," and they were married perhaps 25 years or so. When he had gotten quite old, he said he and Anna would attempt to walk some out in the yard, and if he went down, she went right with him!

The two of them came into the Benson office on Fourth Avenue North one day in the late 60s. Marcia happened to be there also and when she and Jimmie walked across the shag carpeting and shook hands, the static electricity snapped and Marcia screamed! Jimmie quipped, "Well, I didn't know I still had such an effect on young ladies."

He had a "lifetime" contract with Decca Records, and Anna had a "lifetime" contract with Columbia Records. More than once, I would be working away at Benson and my phone would ring. "Elmo…Jimmie Davis. Can you come up to my suite at the Andrew Jackson Hotel after you get off work today and rehearse with me? I'm recording a new album tomorrow." He would have a spinet piano brought up to the 12th floor and we would go over the songs he was to record. We had a great time together. Then I'd call Marcia to come pick me up. I rode Metro buses for ten years, even after Benson moved out on Broadway, but switching buses downtown (in front of the state capitol) became such a hassle, we bought a little '68 Dodge from a TV personality's wife. Back then gas was like 34 cents a gallon. I'd put $4 in the tank and run all week!

In the early 60s, Jimmie's close friend by the name of Buddy Billips got a campaign going to build a "Jimmie Davis Tabernacle" near his old home place in Jackson Parish. Buddy owned the Rose Oil Company, "the sign of the friendly hand." For only $500,000 a beautiful building was built – a cathedral in the pines. Jimmie asked me to play the organ for its dedication. Marcia, Bill, Kellye (she was hardly two years old) and I drove down in our 1961 white Cadillac I'd bought from my Sunday school teacher at Riverside Baptist Church.

That day was a blast! Jimmie had the Statesmen, the Blackwood Brothers, the Chuck Wagon Gang and I believe the Happy Goodman Family there to sing for about 2,000 people. The night before, 65 pigs had been strung up by their feet and slowly cooked over a fire so there was plenty of pulled pork. There were barrels of "dirty rice," all kinds of veggies, soft drinks and desserts. About 4 p.m. I went and told Jimmie we needed to head back up to Nashville, some 500 miles (no interstates then). Bill had a perfect attendance record…in fact he did for ten years of school. Kellye later had five years of perfect attendance. As I shook Jimmie's hand, I felt him pass something to me and I thanked him very much for having me play for the dedication. I stuck it in my pocket and when we got around the curve from the church I looked and it was a hundred dollar bill, a lot of money back then!

Jimmie's big Palomino horse was named "Sunshine." A friend borrowed her one day, but had a wreck and the horse was killed! Oh, my! Think of the courage it took for him to go back and tell Jimmie. The first time he was elected governor, as a publicity stunt he rode Sunshine up the steps of the capitol building. There are 48, one for each state (then). Later Hawaii and Alaska were just added to the top steps. He rode Sunshine into the lobby and down the hall into the governor's office while cameras rolled. Next day the newspaper article said that as far as they knew, that was the first time the entire horse had been in the governor's office! A bale of hay was sent to his office with a note: "This is for Sunshine and all your other jackass advisers!" If you get the chance, read Jimmie's autobiography. It will crack you up. In my opinion, he was a great man.

LIFE ON MASONWOOD DRIVE

We moved in the house on Masonwood Drive in March 1965. It was lightly snowing that day. We lived there about ten years. We got to know the families living around us. There were a lot of music people who lived in Parkwood Estates. Henry and Hazel Slaughter lived two houses from Jack Green of the Grand Ole Opry only about three blocks from us. Jim Hill who wrote "What a Day That Will Be" lived a couple of blocks from Henry. Herman Harper of the "old" Oak Ridge Quartet lived down the hill from us. The "Ragin' Cajun," Jimmy C. Newman lived around the corner from us, next to our friends Bob and Linda Coombs. Bob was organist at First Baptist in Madison for many years, later doing the same at Two Rivers Baptist across from Opryland Hotel.

Jan Crutchfield (Jerry's brother) lived 3 doors to our west. He wrote "Dream on, Little Dreamer" that Perry Como recorded. Also Ronnie Dove and Ray Pillow lived in Parkwood Estates but I'm not sure where. All the kids went to Brick Church Pike Elementary, Ewing Park Middle School on Knight Road and Maplewood High School just east of Dickerson Road. Bill was a Cub Scout and I carried him over to a Presbyterian Church in Parkwood Estates for those meetings.

One morning Kellye phoned Marcia from Brick Church School to say there was a little puppy running around the parking lot. She asked Marcia to come take it home till they could find out who it belonged to – well, you know how that goes, we never found out. We named him Major and he grew to be a big German police kind of a dog. We had a chain link fence around the backyard and when another dog trotted along Masonwood Drive Major would bark something fierce. I opened the gate and booted him out and said, "Sic 'em!" But he dashed back inside, reared up on the fence and began barking again! He was a better "doorbell" than a protector of life, limb and property.

Schools in Nashville were integrated, of course. In the fourth grade there was a big black girl who would come up to Kellye on the playground and say, "Let's fight!" Kellye said she didn't want to, and ignored her as best she could. But it became a problem. She told Marcia about it. Full of motherly advice, Marcia said, "Next time she does that just say, 'Ok, let's fight!'" Well, the girl backed off, and from then on was Kellye's friend and protector!

We got a kitten from Marcia's Uncle Leslie (Aunt Bea) who lived in Smyrna, GA (northwest Atlanta). He was an executive with the Atlanta Hardwood Lumber Company at South Cobb Drive and I-285. You've heard of "Nashville Cats?" Well, we had an "Atlanta Cat." He grew up to be a big yellow cat and we named him Luke, why I don't know. Once after our family left the CBA convention in Minneapolis, I had a trip planned for us to go the route over Lake Superior in Ontario, Canada. We spent the night at a small motel just south of the border. The next morning I found out the lady who owned it was organist at her church and was familiar with my arrangements. There was a big, almost-purple looking, Persian cat lying around. Kellye loves cats (and dogs) and she was stroking it when the lady said, "Yes, that's Sir Cedric of Wedgewood," the name of the motel. Well, I was not about to be outdone and I blurted out, "Now, isn't that something! Our cat is St. Lucas of Masonwood!" (We later had a Siamese cat, Sheba that used the commode! Honest).

We crossed at International Falls and really enjoyed the long drive through the Canadian woods. We would cross rivers where logs would be floating down. There were beautiful provincial parks along Superior. We spent the night in Wawa, Ontario. Outside our motel was a HUGE statue of a Canadian goose. Next morning we heard a parade coming down the street. It was the Polish Alliance of Canada. It was very colorful. At Sault Ste. Marie we crossed back into the USA and stopped to watch ships go through the Soo locks, connecting Lake Superior and Lake Huron. We enjoyed going over the 5 mile long Mackinaw Bridge, dividing Lake Michigan and Lake Huron. Marcia and I, many years later, made two trips out to Mackinac Island. It is a Michigan state park.

A couple of days before we got back home to Nashville we discovered Bill had an ailment. He became lethargic and slept a lot. Our doctor at home said he had a kidney infection and later refused to give permission for Bill to play high school football. But when he entered Middle Tennessee State University at Murfreesboro, he was a "walk-on" football player and made the team! He got hurt and never played in a game.

Kellye might have been four years old when Gail Knight (of PABC) told Marcia she wanted her as a flower girl in her wedding. The night of rehearsal Kellye was shown how to walk slowly and drop the petals around on the carpet. The next morning Marcia looked out the front window and there was Kellye slowly walking on our sidewalk and dropping flowers. Where did she get flowers? Well, she had gone next door to the Cooper's yard and plucked all her tulips! You know, it seems like they moved right after that!

Into that house moved Mr. and Mrs. Hugo V. Trosky. We think they were Polish! He fell in love with Luke. Early one morning Marcia heard him say, "Mornin', Luke. You comin' over?" The Troskys would go to Sarasota, FL during the winter. One day she called and when Marcia said hello, she said, "How's Luke?" No "Hi, Marcia, how y'all doing?" Marcia and I went over for a visit and I started to sit down in a yellow chair in their living room. She quickly informed me that was Luke's chair! She said one day she kept hearing a noise and when she opened their kitchen door to the stairs going down to the basement, Mr. Trosky was sitting in their electric power chair holding Luke in his lap, going up…and down, up…and down! When they returned from Florida, we'd have a big "Welcome Home" sign taped to their basement garage door. Years later when Luke died, Mr. Trosky came inside our basement for the first and only time, bringing a bouquet of flowers! We buried him between our house and asphalt driveway. And would you believe? When we moved away, Bill and Kellye wanted us to exhume that cat and move him to the new place in the Bellevue area.

Across Masonwood Drive and up the hill a little piece lived the Naby family. One son, David, was Bill's age and they played together a lot. His little brother was mentally challenged and he kept calling me "Wally." One day he came to our front door, Marcia said, and asked if Wally could come out and play. In later years David became a naturalist and was killed in a car crash. His name is on a historical marker at an overlook in Fall Creek Falls State Park in the Cumberland Mountains of Middle Tennessee. On the other side of the Trosky house lived a family who had three sons. Bill and the older boy got in a fight one day and the father came out to pull Bill off. He didn't fuss at Bill but simply said to his boy, "Can't you do any better than that, son?" as they walked away from Bill.

Down the street in the opposite direction lived a family who had a son and a daughter. The daughter and Kellye were very close friends and later she was in Kellye's wedding. [I played for HER wedding at Jackson Park Church of Christ in October 1982. After shaving for that occasion I grew my full beard which I still have today!] Anyhow, her brother was a bit older than Bill and liked to pick on him. One afternoon they got off the school bus at the top of the hill. Apparently the boy had been harassing Bill on the bus. As the door closed and the bus moved off, Bill suddenly turned and buried his fist in the boy's stomach. He cried out and ran for home. Soon the father knocked on our door and complained about what had happened. Marcia said she told him, "You take care of your son, and I assure you I'll take care of mine!" After that incident our families became good friends. When Kellye would come home from Florida we would visit them in their house off the Ashland City highway. Sadly the boy passed away some 25 years later.

Doug and Betty Hale (son Trent) lived next to us on the east side. They had a big brown Boxer dog in their backyard and we shared a common chain link fence. Bill thought he was retarded. One day his football went over in that yard. Bill checked out the dog and figured he could retrieve the ball and get back over the fence unharmed. He threw the ball back in our yard and ran for the fence, noting that the Boxer was gaining on him. He went to vault over the fence but got tangled up somehow and fell awkwardly on our side, breaking his left arm!

We took him to our family doctor, Bill Pettit, at Miller Clinic on Gallatin Road. While he was checking Bill out he asked,

"How in the world did this happen, Bill?" So help me, if Bill didn't pause, sniff and look up at him and say, "Child abuse!" How do you refute that? Fortunately the doctor knew he was joking! I reckon Bill is a "chip off the old block," huh?

One Halloween night I walked with Bill and Kellye as they went to the houses on Masonwood Drive. A cold front was coming through and it turned very cold before we got back to our house. The next morning we woke up to a six inch snowfall! We usually have one such surprise almost every winter.

Behind our house was a large pasture on which there was an authentic Indian mound. It was perhaps 300 yards from our house. One day the land owner discovered that the mound had been "raided". Perhaps historic artifacts had been stolen. A big hackberry tree was just outside our chain link backyard fence. Bill built a tree house about fifteen feet off the ground. He spent a lot of time there. One Sunday afternoon Marcia and I woke up from our afternoon nap to find a storm was upon us. I looked out the back bathroom window and Bill was up there "ridin' it out." I went through the upstairs den we had recently added to the back of the house, opened the door and stepped out on the steel stair landing. I yelled, "Bill, get down and get in here now!" A gust of wind ripped my hairpiece off my head and so help me, folks, I jerked my left arm up and caught it in my hand! Had I not, it likely would have gone all the way to Butcher Holler, Kentucky!

When we did get a good snow, the kids on the street loved to ride their wood and steel sleds down the long hills. One day they were racing down our street when a friend stiff-armed Bill off to the right. He actually went UNDER a school bus parked against the curb! A tornado touched down two blocks south of Masonwood Drive doing extensive damage, especially to Love's Chapel Methodist Church on Brick Church Pike.

Our phone number was ONE digit off from the Nashville Crisis Center. Marcia said that every now and then she would get calls from desperate people. Before she could tell them the correct number to call they would threaten suicide! She would give them the number and encourage them to call the NCC for the help they needed. Back then we had one black wall phone in the kitchen by the door going down to the full basement. Now we must have ten throughout the house! And how did we ever live without cellphones?

We had our Cadillacs serviced at a place on Dickerson Road, not far away. At that time Joel Hemphill and family (originally from around Bastrop, LA) lived in a beautiful home on Dickerson Road up on a hill not far from our house. Bill dated Candy Hemphill. She married a man whose last name was Christmas.

One evening the service attendant was changing oil and we got to talking. I told him I was in the gospel music business and we usually used RCA studios. He said, "My wife is makin' demos of new songs here in town. She's sittin' out there in the car waitin' for me to get off work."

It was Jeannie C. Riley before she became famous with "Harper Valley P.T.A." Later she was converted and made an album with Benson and was a guest at a WHACHAMACALLIT at Opryland Hotel. Even though I had no connection with her career I thought this was an interesting memory anyway.

PARK AVENUE CHURCH

While we were serving at Riverside Baptist Church, a big church in west Nashville known as Park Avenue, asked me to be pianist for a revival they were going to have. Afterward they asked me if I would consider becoming their church pianist. They needed one. Marcia and I talked and prayed about it but decided we were needed, as well as contented at Riverside. Then Park Avenue sponsored Cliff Barrows, Billy Graham's crusade music minister, at the War Memorial Auditorium across from the state capitol for a one-night service.

Mrs. Sue Neeley was organist, Jim Summers was music minister and I was on the grand piano. The place was packed, about 2500 I believe. The choir sang beautifully. When Pastor Bob Mowrey introduced Cliff, he strode out on stage smiling and with outstretched arms said, "Oh, friends, before I preach, let's all stand and sing that old favorite 'Amazing Grace, how sweet the sound!'" I had begun the introduction as soon as he called out the title and the place rang with that great song. So, not only had I been privileged to play for B. B. McKinney, I now had accompanied Cliff Barrows!

Again, Park Avenue asked me to become their pianist and I declined. But Marcia and I decided to "put out the fleece", like Gideon did in the Bible. If PABC came back the third time and asked me, I would agree to it and we would leave Riverside for Park Avenue. Marcia enjoyed the Women's Missionary Union at Riverside plus it was twice as far to go to PABC. Well, they did come back and ask me to play for another revival. On the second Sunday in September 1965 we moved our church membership and I became their pianist. We look back now and marvel at the way God directed our lives.

At that time there was a string quartet that sat on the platform on the piano side. Robbie Mowrey, Bro. Bob and Peggy's older son, played the viola. He was in high school, a graduate of Blair School of Music and a member of the Nashville Musicians Union. He played on a lot of albums including Floyd Cramer. While at Princeton University his roommate was Bill Frist from Nashville who later became a US Senator. Robbie is a successful corporate attorney in Dallas. His younger brother David has worked for CSX Railroad for over 35 years and they have always lived in Nashville.

I discovered other musicians in the church so we expanded into an orchestra and I made the arrangements. We played songs like "I Asked the Lord," plus favorite old hymns. Our son Bill played the drums. When he was younger he would overturn our wastebaskets in the house and play them like drums, so we went to Miller Music on Charlotte Avenue and bought him a used set of Slingerland drums. One Sunday night Marcia and Bill raced home from church to get his drums. On the way back he was tuning them. I didn't know a drum needed tuning, did you? Marcia said our next kid was going to take up the harmonica! In our orchestra we had a trumpet, trombone, sax, clarinet, rhythm and lead guitar and drums, plus piano and organ. Eventually the string players stopped playing. They played my arrangements and the people seemed to enjoy them.

There were about fifty in the adult choir. We made the listening album for "Crusade Choir, Volume I", the first one Jack Price and I did together. Ronn Huff's wife, Diane, played piano and it was recorded in the new RCA studios on Music Row. We were nominated for a grammy, but didn't win. That book, in almost 22 years on the market, sold over 500,000 copies. PTL! Jack and I did a Volume II and III; the fourth in the series I arranged as medleys of eighteen Bill and Gloria Gaither songs. Sing and Share Volumes I and II rounded out that Price and Mercer series of six books. In August 1980 the Zondervan Corporation of Grand Rapids, MI bought Benson to make it their so-called "Christian contemporary music" division. Bob MacKenzie was made the president. On February 17, 1981 Jack waltzed into my office to tell me he had just gotten permission from MacKenzie for us to do a Volume VII. I leaned back in my chair and shook my head. He said, "What's wrong?" I said, "Jack, I just laid my letter of resignation on Bob's desk!" He was flabbergasted. As you may know, Jack started his own company, Prism Music and did quite well. Billy Jack Green, a prominent Baptist minister of music was on his staff.

Bro. Bob Mowrey did have some great evangelists to preach revivals. Some of them were: Dr. J. Harold Smith, Clyde Chiles, Eddy Martin, Bob Harrington, Richard Hoag, Mel Dibble, Hyman Appleman, Angel Martinez, E. J. Daniels, etc. Our daughter Kellye was saved at home and made her public profession at an Angel Martinez tent revival on PABC grounds. Some of them came more than once, and I played for all of those meetings. As a teenager I had listened to J. Harold on a powerful Mexican radio station. He preached a revival in our home church, FBC Winnfield, LA. He had been in our home in Winnfield. During a PABC revival in one service over one hundred came forward at invitation time. His famous sermon was "God's Three Deadlines." Once I boarded a plane in Nashville and saw him sitting back there. He was on his way to speak at the first graduation ceremony at Jerry Fallwell's Liberty University.

Dr. R. G. Lee came to Park Avenue around 1975 and preached his famous sermon "Payday Someday." And Evangelist E. J. Daniels launched his TV ministry at Park Avenue during a revival. The Director's loud truck was positioned right in front of the steps up to the second floor auditorium. Large cables ran all through the church to cameras and lights. They didn't finish on Tuesday night so the large choir was told to remember where they were sitting and to wear the same clothes on Thursday night. E. J. had a leer jet and on Saturday took several children up at a time for a short flight from the Smyrna Air Field (active in WWII). I said something to him about his quarter million dollar jet (the price back then) and he said, "How'd you know it cost that much?" I am told he had a big ministry with several preachers and singers in the organization. He also printed many newspapers. He was headquartered in Tampa, FL, I believe.

Evangelist Clyde Chiles' music man was Jim McNeil. He made albums on a Benson label. Rick Powell was the arranger and Jim led him (Rick) to Christ. Eddy Martin's mother came with him and faithfully visited and witnessed. Bob Harrington's music man was Jack Price. He told me if I ever saw him on a plane to never yell, "Hi, Jack!" Richard Hoag had a band with him and identified especially with the young people. Mel Dibble had been in show business and was "groomed" to replace Jack Parr. Dr. Hyman Appleman was a saved Jewish preacher. During an invitation one night he asked all who were Christians to sit down. That left standing many Jewish people who had come to hear him preach!

In 1976 PABC moved into our new church building with the address 4301 Charlotte Avenue, but it fronted on 43rd Avenue. Now remember the church name was Park Avenue! Go figure, huh? When we joined there in 1965 the church was located at Park Avenue and 44th Avenue. The auditorium in the new building seated about 1,300 with 90 seats in the choir loft. Church offices and the library were on the 43rd Avenue side, and a full-size gymnasium was on the 44th Avenue side. The choir room faced Charlotte on the second floor. Beneath it were restrooms and storage space off the gym. So the choir had to go up steps, then down steps to get to the choir loft. By that time we had almost forgotten what the special music was!

A covered walkway connected the new building with the old educational building. Before it was constructed the alley between the buildings was open. One night a lady was walking there heading up to the new building when a stranger ran by, snatched her purse and took off. She screamed and our son Bill took off, gaining on him with each step. Jim Corbitt had begun dating our organist Lyndal Lavendar, but still had not met a lot of our members. He immediately thought Bill was the culprit and tackled HIM! It was kinda funny... Lyndal and Jim married and she took over as church organist...we worked together for MANY years. I arranged a bunch of offertories (like "You'll Never Walk Alone") that everyone seemed to enjoy.

MY PROGRESSIVE DREAM

I started having this dream when Marcia and I moved to the Mary Riser house on East Maple Street in our home town of Winnfield, two years after we'd married. It seemed to progress as it came to me over a number of YEARS. In the dream a girl in a slinky dress was standing at a gate in a picket fence and seemed to be determined to come in and attack me!

After dreaming that for a while it progressed to where she was walking in the yard toward the front steps. And then she walked across the front porch to the front door. As the dream progressed, she was coming in the hallway and turning toward our bedroom door.

I had been telling Marcia about this each time I would have the dream. We now lived in Nashville and were members of Park Avenue Baptist Church! I had it again and she was on her hands and knees crawling up the foot of our bed about to "get" me! Marcia said, "Don't worry about her. Next time I'll kick her out!" I thought, "Well, Darlin' Baby, it's time to ACT!!!"

One night we were with Donna and Rayford Hilley and I told them about the dream. Rayford said, "That is a demon. Next time you have it, say 'Demon, you have no power over me; get out of my life now!'" Well, when I'm having the dream I can't do that!

Several months after that, the four of us were together again. I guess Donna or Rayford asked me about the dream. I looked at Marcia and said, "You know, I haven't had that dream in a long time." Marcia smiled and nodded at me and quietly said, "I know." Like Gary Coleman on the "Different Strokes" TV sitcom I said, "Whatchu talkin' 'bout?" She said, "Well, I knew you couldn't do what Rayford said, so I did it for you!"

Great. Now I'll never know what that ol' gal had on her mind. Maybe I should say, "Thank you, God!" and thanks to Rayford, too! I've never had that dream again.

MY 1967 BACK OPERATION

Remember that in 1962 I had hurt my back down at the Florida music clinic when I got a loaded footlocker out of the trunk of our '59 Chevy. When we got back to Nashville I went to a chiropractor in East Nashville that George Thomas knew. He was German. I could just imagine him looking and smiling at me, cracking his knuckles as he said, "Ya, Herr Mercer, ve vill get your back in order quite painfully!" I did get temporary relief. After a while it hurt me so bad I would have to crawl into bed on my hands and knees. But I did NOT want to have an operation.

Finally, I was in agony 24/7 so I went to an orthopedic doctor near Baptist Hospital. This had been going on for five years! The sciatic nerve was pinched and the pain had slowly gone from my left hip down my thigh and calf to my toes. I was more-or-less dragging my left leg. The doctor told me that if the nerve was severed I could become *paralyzed!* That word got my attention immediately.

He sent me to Parkview Hospital on 25th Avenue, just east of Centennial Park where the replica of the Greek Parthenon is located. A milogram (sp?) was scheduled. You do know that those steel tables you lay on are kept in a freezer, right? There I was lying flat on my stomach, exposed to the world and especially the nurses as they flitted about.

The doctor came in with a needle about the size of rabbit ears on an old TV set. He explained to me the procedure and I blurted, "You're gonna do WHAT?" He inserted that gadget into my spine about my beltline and wiggled it! It felt like I got hit with 110 volts, to be honest. He asked, "Tell me where you felt that?" and I said my right forefinger. He wiggled it again and asked the same question. I said in my left knee. He wiggled it again and asked again…but I wasn't about to tell him and those nurses where I felt THAT jolt but I almost rose up off that cold slab and did a Mexican hat dance. Ooo-wee!

After that episode I was told to lie flat on my back for **three** days – this was in the hospital! I was told not to lift my head up but I still got the most awful headaches. I am told this entire procedure has been updated and fine-tuned. I pray that is true, but I want you all to know I was one of the pioneers for that procedure.

The operation was done in February 1967 at Parkview. They had found exactly where the problem was and made a small incision there, knocked out half the fourth disc and "uncorked" the sciatic nerve that had been pinched for five years. They said the recovery period could be about as long! In the spring of 1975 I was back in again for two weeks of therapy due to back pain again. I was doing four exercises amounting to 240 an hour. Figure that on a fifteen hour day. Why, I didn't even have time to watch "As the World Turns!"

Then they put me in a room with a Mr. Lee from Cookeville. Bless his heart, he passed away! So they thought: we'd better put this guy in a room by himself quick, what with the adverse effect he has on our patients. Now I'm up on the fourth floor with a great view of the downtown skyline. Only one thing – my commode exploded! Alright, settle down now. Keep reading, it gets better.

It was pouring down rain and still dark when I got up one morning and went to the bathroom. I flushed the commode and started to plug in the cord to my electric shaver. {BTW, I started shaving when I was 13, shaved 3 times that *year*...cut my leg all 3 times!}. I had taken an early morning shower and put on the clean pajamas Marcia had brought me the day before. Suddenly the vertical pipe (I don't understand hospital plumbing) just separated and water gushed to the ceiling like Old Faithful Geyser. I was immediately soaked in my fresh pajamas.

Forgetting my bum back, in about three leaps I was to the phone beside my bed. Forget the nurse's call button. Actually I was the first room from the nurses' station and should have just yelled! I picked up the phone and a sweet voice said, "Good morning, Mr. Mercer, what can we do for you?" So, in as calm a voice as I could muster, I simply replied, ***"Come quick! My commode exploded!"*** She said, "Your WHAT?"

By the time she raced around the corner, my house slippers were riding the waves coming from the bathroom and about to collide with the foot of my bed. She rescued me, stood me out in the hall as she yelled for someone to call Moses (the black resident repairman). I said, "The way that water's risin', you'd better call Noah, too!" She wasn't amused. I kinda thought it was funny myself...<u>and</u> appropriate!

They all began packing towels, quilts, whatever they could find, under the doors of the other rooms on that floor, not knowing if those patients could tread water. Eventually the water was shut off. I later learned the "flood" had gone all the way to the first floor operating rooms! Like I said, I'm standing in the hallway leaning against the wall wiggling my toes in the current while watching all the lifesaving activity. A nurse comes up to me with a wheelchair and said, "Come with me, I've got to get you into dry clothes." I had hoped for a life jacket myself. Down the hallway we went and I'm reading the signs on the doors as we fly by. Then it hit me – she's gonna put me in one of those dadgum skimpy hospital gowns...I called them "See-more" gowns. And sure enough she wheeled into the supply room. I raised two fingers like Churchill's "Victory" sign and said,

"I'll take two, please: one for the front and one for the back." She didn't even smile.

I don't remember if I got one or two but then they parked me where I could see the nurses coming in with their umbrellas for the 7 to 3 shift. Their dresses were wet and they lifted hemlines to the steam heater. I told them it was wetter inside than it was outside. I mean, nobody appreciated my comments, so I just hushed!

I was demoted to the third floor again, at least temporarily. There was a young man already in that room awaiting appendicitis surgery. I told him to have no fear I would not be a permanent resident; I had been put there because the commode in my room exploded. He said, "Your WHAT?" as he grabbed his side. I warned him to get control of himself or he might not need the operation.

About that time in walked MY surgeon. He resembled the actor Raymond Massey who played Dr. Gillespie on that TV show... baggy cheeks and bushy eyebrows. He frowned and asked me, "Well, what are you doing down HERE?" I said, "My commode exploded upstairs." He snapped, "Your WHAT?" Why did people keep saying that? I was speaking plainly.

I continued, "And furthermore, I'm not doing these exercises you've got me on till I get back in a room...I'd moon the whole wing of this building!" I was eventually put back in another room on the fourth floor. Marcia came later to visit me then went down on the third floor where Dottie Rambo was in a room. As she passed the nurses' station she heard the nurses talking about someone's commode exploding upstairs. She smiled.

A couple in Park Avenue church brought me a quart of buttermilk and a half pone of cornbread. Another lady brought me a pint of white beans. Egads! Surely that's not what caused my commode to blow up!!!

This was during the "Praise Sing" at the Baptist building downtown. Folks came from all over the convention to sing through the entire new 1975 Baptist Hymnal. On page 193 was the chorus to my song "The Time is Now." A former Park Avenue church music minister, John Nading, was there to participate, and he came to the hospital to see me. I really appreciated that..

TRANSCRIBING AND ARRANGING

A big part of my duties as music editor for Benson was to prepare songs for publication. I would be given a reel-to-reel tape, then later a cassette, of an album that had just been recorded. I was to transcribe those songs, at least all of the new ones, and arrange them for publication. Transcribe means I would listen to a phrase or two, then write that down on the music staff, and repeat the process. I would make a lead sheet first. A lead sheet has three things: the melody line, the chord names and the lyrics. From that I would make an arrangement, depending on the instructions. Some would be 4-part harmony like in a songbook (maybe in shape notes), it might be melody (lead) line with piano accompaniment, it might be a choral arrangement, it might be as an instrumental piece, etc. It might be printed as a single 9 x 12 sheet of music, in a songbook or it might go in an artist's folio along with pictures to be released simultaneously with the album.

I am reminded of one case in particular. DALLAS HOLM AND PRAISE spent three days in the Benson studio recording a new album. The cassette was brought to me with instructions they wanted the arrangements done "yesterday." [I loved my work but not the pressure]. I think it was the fourth song that was entitled "Rise Again." That meant nothing to me at the time, but I noticed immediately he sang it in the key of C. In the chorus, when the lyric says, "Yes, I'll rise" ... "rise" is on a G natural, far out of the reach of the average singer. So I moved down a third to the key of Ab. In about three months that song was ranked the number one gospel song in the country. No one could sing it like Dallas Holm and Praise.

Benson had the three top songs...GMA (Gospel Music Ass'n) Dove Award winners, for six years running, each of them for two years each. I transcribed and arranged all three. They were:

"Learning to Lean" was written by JOHN STALLINGS. He also wrote "Love Grew Where the Blood Fell," and many others.

"Rise Again" was written by DALLAS HOLM. He also wrote "Here We Are," and many others. His Easter work "His Last Days" was a big seller for several years – I arranged it also.

"Sweet Beulah Land" was written by SQUIRE PARSONS. He also wrote "He Came to Me," "Redeeming Love," and many others.

Some other Benson writers and recording artists for whom I arranged were:

STEVE ADAMS – "Peace in the Midst of the Storm," "All Because Of God's Amazing Grace," "Where the Spirit of the Lord Is," and many more.

LANNY WOLFE – "My House is Full," "Surely the Presence of the Lord is in This Place," "Whatever it Takes," and many more.

DOTTIE RAMBO – "If That Isn't Love," "He Looked Beyond my Fault," "We Shall Behold Him", etc.

GORDON JENSEN – "I Should Have Been Crucified," "Jesus Will Outshine Them All," and many others. [Note: "Redemption Draweth Nigh" copyright is owned by Silverline Music, an Oak Ridge Boys' company].

JOEL HEMPHILL – "Consider the Lilies," "He's Still Workin' on Me," etc. They are Louisiana natives.

DANNY LEE – "Jesus, He is the Son of God," "Little Flowers," and many more. Danny sat by me on the piano bench and sang phrases of these songs as I made lead sheets. We were roommates at a CBA convention in Minneapolis.

PHIL JOHNSON – "When I Say Jesus," "Lift Up the Name of Jesus," "More (Than You'll Ever Know)," and many more. His office was next to mine on the third floor of the new Benson building in MetroCenter.

As music editor, I arranged the songs of many others, who may not have recorded on Benson labels.

Mr. John T. acquired songs and copyrights for years. He owned and published such titles as "Love Lifted Me," "Blessed Redeemer," "The Last Mile of the Way," "No One Ever Cared for Me like Jesus" etc.

In the 60s I was told to make a choir arrangement of "Love Lifted Me," and it sold quite well. Later when Kenny Rogers and the First Edition recorded it, I transcribed that very arrangement and it sold well. Then when Ray Stevens [*] recorded it, I did the same thing, and it sold well! My three arrangements were published by Benson in a ten year time period and all sold well!

[*] "Ray Stevens" is a "stage" name. He is also an accomplished organist. He played the organ, and was leader of the session, on a Jake Hess album Benson recorded at RCA. Jake recorded "Lonely Road up Calvary's Way," which I wrote back in 1957 soon after composing "The Way That He Loves." Jake was guest soloist at my 10th anniversary at Park Avenue church and sang, "Lonely Road," as only he could.

Also, as Benson music editor, I decided to contact copyright owners of highly popular songs and got their permission to make arrangements in FOUR-PART HARMONY, SHAPE NOTES. They were printed in 9x12 sheet music and sold well. Some of those titles were:

"Bridge Over Troubled Water," "O Happy Day," "People Got to be Free," "I Asked the Lord," "Somebody Bigger than You and I," etc. The last two I listed were written by Johnny Lange, who also wrote "He's Only a Prayer Away." He lived in California and founded Fiesta Music that owned Lois Irwin's song, "The Healer." Would you believe he also wrote "Mule Train" that Frankie Layne made famous. Johnny and I got to be good friends...on the phone!

We met John Stallings in 1964 at the Benson company offices on Fourth Avenue North. He was an Assembly of God pastor/ evangelist. He told me his mother had been a star in silent movies! He wrote several songs that Benson acquired and published. One song "Learning to Lean" became an instant "hit." Before it was published he met with Jimmy Swaggart and showed it to him. Jimmy said "If you'll write two verses that are more positive, I'll record it." John did, and Jimmy did. When we printed the song (I made the first arrangement) we included all four verses!

Not long after that he wrote "Love Grew Where the Blood Fell." What a beautiful thought! I made a choral arrangement of it that was sung in churches all over the country. John lives in Orlando and one time on our way to or from Okeechobee we stopped by to visit. He plays piano "on the black keys." He sang a song for me: actually it turned out to be the chorus, and said, "It needs a verse, don't you think?" I agreed and sat down on the piano bench. I said, "Let me make sure I remember what you did so I can work on a verse." I played – on the white keys – what he had played in F#. He exclaimed, "Hey, I gotta be more careful! You could steal my song(s)!"

I did write a verse to his chorus and it is titled "It's His Life." It was recorded by the Revivaltime Choir from Springfield, Missouri. Some years later John was interim pastor at an AG church in Orlando and had us come by for a concert.

Benson distributed Jimmy Swaggart's recordings for a while. We also printed two books by Jerry Lucas, the famous NBA star. I met him when Bob Benson was showing him around our offices. In the Art Department a young woman who worked there looked up at him – he was very tall and said, "Gosh, you ought to play basketball!" One day Terry Bradshaw was being shown around as well. When we shook hands I told him I, too, was from Louisiana. He looked at me, paused a little bit then said, "You're fired!" Terry recorded an album on a Benson label!

THE "CHAPLAIN"

In 1970 Bob Harrington walked into the Benson office on Fourth Avenue North. He had a red tie, red handkerchief in his coat breast pocket, and red socks. He called himself "The Chaplain of Bourbon Street." He said his office was next door to Pete Fountain's. He was preaching revivals across the nation with his music man, Jack Price. They needed a crusade choir book and the Benson sons agreed to take on the project. Mr. John T. had retired on his 65th birthday. (See the following article).

Jack compiled it and I arranged it. This came as Billy Souther's great choir books were beginning to fade. We must have done something right. "Crusade Choir, Volume I" sold over 500,000 copies in 22 years.

Park Avenue had the team for a revival under a huge tent on Charlotte Avenue, where our new building was later built. I remember one night before a service, the choir was practicing. Platforms were built for the choir and the stage. The organ and piano were moved out of the old auditorium. Suddenly, the bottom of the piano bench fell out, and so did lots of books and loose music, sliding all over the place. Sue Neeley, organist, looked over her glasses and said, "Well, Mercer, you dropped your bottom!" I guess it came out a little different from what she intended to say.

The two back "legs" of the metal chair Bobby Strickland was sitting on, slipped off the top row in the choir. We heard a shout and looked up in time to see the soles of his shoes going over backwards! Bobby displayed such wit and talent and was a great church party emcee. He attached a commode seat to the neck of a guitar and called it his "gittoilet." At the retirement party for financial secretary Mary Donihi (32 years), Bobby was the emcee and said the church was sending her abroad (a joke, of course) then commented, "I wish somebody would send me a broad." Bobby served as deacon chairman several times and taught a Sunday school class. He retired as a public school teacher and worked for many years at SONY-ATV when Donna Hilley was President/CEO.

Our church later sponsored Bob Harrington at the Nashville Municipal Auditorium…twice. It seats 10,000. He was rather controversial and Metro Police were everywhere, watching the crowd. Four men came up in the sitting area behind him and sat down. Tensions rose. About that time a burst of hard rain fell on the monstrous roof and Harrington jumped like he HAD been shot! He quipped that at the Rapture he hoped to get higher than that!

Along about 2007 he preached a revival at First Baptist Church in Okeechobee and I led singing from the grand piano. We were spending the winter at our condo there. Kellye and her family lived eight miles from us. Many souls were saved in those services.

BENSON MOVES TO BROADWAY

In April of 1969, Mr. John T. was leaning back in his chair at the office, with his feet on an open drawer. He sat up, kicked the drawer closed and said to his sons John III and Bob, "This is my 65th birthday. I'm out of here. This business is yours now… sink or swim!"

They decided to acquire computers, and back then they just about filled a room, and were noisy and hot and sometimes contrary. Two young women were hired to run them. We began getting monthly printouts on how we were doing! Rev. Jerry Fallwell, pastor of Thomas Road Baptist Church in Lynchburg, Virginia, even came down for a couple of days to observe the use of computers!

Sometime during 1971 (I believe) the Benson brothers decided we were too crowded at our present location. We had about 25 employees and rented some space upstairs from R. L. Polk Company. The Roy Orbison building at 1625 Broadway was purchased, located just west of where Broadway splits off at 16th Avenue. West End Avenue begins to the right. It had seven floors and only a freight elevator. The warehouse was on the top floor! Before we made the actual move, I was sent out there for some reason. I parked in the alley and climbed up the stairs to the loading dock. No one was around so I walked inside further. My eyes tried to adjust from the bright sunlight. Suddenly I looked down and my toes were at the precipice of the elevator shaft! It was perhaps ten feet down to the bottom. I thanked the Lord I hadn't taken one more step.

Benson rented a double-decker bus like in London and we rode around downtown Nashville proclaiming we were moving the business westward! A big red and white striped tent was put up on the ROOF of the building and we had a party up there. Frank Brooks, a young black man who handled our shipping of product at Fourth Avenue North, called me over to look down to the street. He said, "I think I'll jump! I always wanted to make a 'splash on Broadway!'" That was funny.

The building was refurbished to the Benson brothers' specifications. Orange/red/yellow/brown shag carpets were put everywhere on the ground floor. My office was at the end of the hallway, perhaps ten feet underground! East of my office was the freight elevator. In front of my door the stairs went up to what we called "the Mezzanine" because of its low ceiling. Some offices were there along with the computer room. There were no windows on that floor. A copy machine used a thin tan onion-skin kind of paper. I guess I had copied too much at one time and the last piece came out with *flames* on it! I grabbed it and headed for the sink in a kitchen-lunch room area but didn't make it. I invented a new St. Elmo's fire dance and stamped it out on that blasted shag carpet!

By then I was wearing perhaps my first hairpiece. It was pouring down rain one evening when I came out to that loading dock to run to my little '68 Dodge. Frank Brooks was standing there, too. We talked a minute then I said, "I sure don't want to get my hair wet." I ripped it off and stuck it under my arm and dashed to the car. The next day Frank said, "Mr. Mercer, you like to a- scared me t' death yesterday. I didn't know you wore a wig!" Another time Marcia and I were at a Nashville Sounds (AAA) baseball game when it started to raining. Henry Slaughter was sitting by us. I took my hairpiece off and protected it. Henry just sat there, rain dripping off his. He wasn't about to take his off!

We would have dinners sometime and one time a newly-wed brought a macaroni and cheese dish that was rather watery. One of the guys quipped, "Daisy, did you bring any straws with you?" It was at this location that I got sheet music titles to reach over 1,200 titles selling over one million copies per year! Our son Bill started working in the warehouse at age fourteen, along with Rocky Jones, one of our salesmen's sons who lived across from us on Masonwood Drive in Parkwood. On a box cutter Bill carved the words, "Little Mo from Tupelo." I still use that knife at times. I had to sign a paper releasing Benson from any liability. He continued to work at Benson after we moved to MetroCenter, even while he was going to Middle Tennessee University.

Bill moved up from the warehouse to the third floor as a telephone salesman, working Mon-Wed-Fri. He went one semester at MT on Tuesday and Thursday and took nineteen hours. He seems to do his best work when he is under pressure. In three months he was the top salesman. His conversations went something like this: "Hello, Mrs. Jenkins? Yes, this is Bill Mercer with the..." "Mercer, did you say? Are you related to..." "Yes ma'am, he's my Dad. Listen, the Imperials have a new album releasing next week and..." "I'll take ten." "Well, that's great, but I'm telling you, this one is their best ..." "OK, send me twenty!"

Bill really enjoyed his work for the Benson Company. We rode to and from work together.

ANDRAE CROUCH VISIT

One afternoon at the Broadway office, Andrae Crouch came for a visit. The piano from my office was rolled down the shag-carpeted hallway to the reception area and he sang about thirty minutes for us.

Naturally he did his own songs, and most of them were already hits in the gospel music field. Then he said, "I would like to sing for you now a brand new song I've just written, that came from some turmoil in my life." And he started singing, "I've had many tears and sorrow, etc." His great song "Through it All" became such a blessing to millions of people.

John III and Bob decided to take all the employees on two leased buses down to Cleveland TN, Lee College gymnasium, where Andrae Crouch and his singers along with the Imperials, were in concert. It was awesome, and loud! We were on our feet most of the time. On one song both groups were on stage rocking it on down and I shouted in Marcia's ear, "How are they ever going to stop?" About ten minutes later they brought it to a close! We all spent the night at the Admiral Benbow Inn in Chattanooga.

But on the trip down there on I-24, we pulled into a Rest Area. Bob had announced earlier that one bus would compete against the other. We were to unload and on signal run around the bus three times counter clockwise. (I'm serious). I don't remember who won, but I do remember that John III's personal secretary Mary Davis' husband Eugene, ran head first into the big rear-view mirror as he rounded the front of the bus on the first lap and had to drop out of action!

I recall our flight to and from Minneapolis on Ozark Airlines for a CBA convention. I was on the aisle seat and Mary and Gene were in the middle and window seats. Mary had never flown before and she was a nervous wreck. The jet vibrated as we took off and she grabbed Eugene's wrist and said, "Do something!" When we came in for a landing (we were served nothing on the flight) I yelled, "Hey, Cap'n, can you pull into that McDonald's down there? We're hungry!" Oh, well…

BILL AT H.S. AND MTSU

Our son Bill could not play high school football as I've said previously. He was diagnosed with nephritis and the doctor would not give permission for him to start practice. Maplewood High was only a couple of miles from our house on Masonwood Drive. He drove our '73 silver and white GMC pickup. He later told us that he would take lunch orders from his friends and run up Dickerson Road a half mile to a Burger King. He would charge a wee bit more to make it worth his while. Students were not supposed to leave the campus, but back in those days it was wide open.

Bill turned in one day coming back from Burger King and there stood the assistant principal. He figured he was caught when the man flagged Bill down. Instead he jumped in the passenger seat and told Bill to "follow that car!" He was after someone else who was leaving campus!

There were about 425 in his graduating class in the spring of 1975. The ceremony was held at the Municipal Auditorium downtown. The guest speaker was **Oprah Winfrey**! At the time, Chris Clark at WTVF Channel 5/CBS had hired her as an "on-the-spot-reporter." She went on from there...

In the fall of 1975 Bill enrolled at Middle Tennessee State University because of their top-rated aerospace program. He wanted to become a commercial pilot. He was a "walk-on" trying to make the football team, and he did! But he got hurt in practice and had to leave the team. He got his pilot license before his 18th birthday! He told us he "buzzed" our house one day! {One day at MTSU a boy "streaked" through a dining hall and Bill drove the "getaway" car – the only red Firebird Formula on campus! That was not too bright.}

He even flew two-engine planes. Then it was discovered that he had an irregular heartbeat and high blood pressure and was told he might as well forget about becoming a commercial pilot. His world caved in. He broke up with Renee Fuqua, a Cohn High School cheerleader that went to Park Avenue Baptist church. He changed his major to Biology, but went on to complete the aerospace course with a 4.0 average. He was a research patient at Vanderbilt Hospital for a week. Bill completed the 1976 fall semester and had a shoulder operation over the Christmas holidays, but was unable to make the spring semester. He started back in the fall of 1977 but got sick with mono. When he got over that the doctor and professors said he was too far behind to "catch up" and stay current, so he missed that semester, too.

Back when he was in Vanderbilt Hospital, he told me he would really like to get a 4-barrel Holly carburetor, a new manifold and high jackers for the back axle on his Firebird. I had no idea what he was talking about, but this was "my little boy" in the hospital! So for about $1100 we fixed that car up. We later found out no Metro police cars could catch it. [He also wired it so all lights, including the brake lights, could be shut off with the flip of a switch under the dash]! I'll finish that story later.

I remember one time we made a trip to Louisiana and stopped to gather plants along the way for Bill's Biology class project. It called for fifty wild plants and he had to list their scientific name *and* common name. He also took a bunch of Criminal Justice courses. He loved to go to Night Court down at the Metro courthouse. In fact, he was there so many times, the night judge (done by rotating lawyers) asked him over coffee *early* one morning what law firm he was with. He said he was an MTSU student just interested in criminal justice. If the morning paper was on our table we got up we would know what time he came home!

He was **selected** as one of seven General Sessions Court Judges on the university campus and served for three years. The university gave them power to act. For instance, a boy was convicted of a drug charge about three weeks before the semester ended. They agreed to let him finish, but told him not to return. Kellye [*] had her textbooks stolen and a boy caught with them was to come up before Bill (her brother!) and the other judges. Those books miraculously re-appeared!

[*] Kellye got to MTSU as a freshman before Bill got his degree. He crammed four years into six! They were lab partners and for a long time were thought to be husband and wife. Kellye said,

"Heavens, no! He's my brother." We had told Bill to try to keep a watch over Kellye. Bill lived on the third floor of a dorm with three other boys. They would answer the phone, "Disco 320." Every Thursday night they would crank up the music and students would gather for a jam session. Kellye was standing on the outside corridor talking with a boy and the music was so loud, the boy closed the door. Bill opened it immediately and told him the door was to stay open!

Kellye would sometimes drive home during the week…it was about 50 miles one-way. For her senior year in high school we had bought her a 1979 Ford. One night when she got back to her dorm and carried some things in from her double-parked car, she got distracted and forgot about it. Next morning she happened to look out the window and a campus cop was about to have it towed. She jerked on shorts and a t-shirt and ran down just in time. Kellye went three semester then got her "MRS" degree and moved to south Florida.

One year Bill ran for Student Council president, as the "unknown candidate" with a paper sack over his head. But a "Watergate" occurred the night before the election was held and his identity was made known.

He was told if he didn't hurry and graduate, the school would have to put him on the faculty. Well, he did teach canoeing for three semesters! When he finally walked across the stage to receive his diploma, some of the professors stood and applauded. PTL! We feared he was becoming a professional student. I mean, we had two kids in college and I quit my job!!!

Go figure. Marcia and I stepped out on faith! When August rolled around, Bill told us one morning, "I think I'll run back down to school today." "Why, you graduated!" "Yeah," he said, "but the freshman girls are coming in today and I might help with orientation!" His second semester as a freshman he was recruited to be a Student Orientation Advisor, or SOA. I reckon it could have been worse...

Bill sent resumes to Wildlife and Fisheries Departments in 34 states. Florida was the only one that responded! He went to work as a Wildlife Specialist on the Corbett Reserve located on the east side of Okeechobee Lake, instead of the Fisheating Creek Reserve on the west side. He and two other men were in charge of 56,200 acres! They surrounded the 10,000 acre plot where the Pratt & Whitney airplane engine plant is located. Bill and his dog, Magnum, lived in a 3-bedroom/2-bath double-wide house trailer in the middle of nowhere. He walked only a hundred yards to work!

Marcia and I loaded his stuff in Nashville on a four-wheel steel trailer we owned and pulled it behind our Oldsmobile the 850 mile trip. We got in NO rain until we backed up to his front door – and the bottom fell out! Especially the mattress got wet along with a chest of drawers, etc. After getting all that moved into his trailer, Marcia and I slept on twin bunk beds. As I climbed up to the top one I commented, "I hope I don't fall outta this thing!"

There was an eclipse of the moon about 4 a.m. and we all got up to see it. Then we went back to bed. I fell back asleep quickly and the next thing I knew I was sailing downward rapidly! My chin hit the top corner of the chest of drawers and I bit my tongue. My right elbow and left knee were bruised badly. Marcia said she heard a noise and looked up to see me holding the thin mattress like a parachute. Well, it didn't help! In fact, it fell on top of her. I went to the bathroom mirror and tried to stop my tongue from bleeding. There was blood all over my t-shirt. I said, "Well, I guess that was kinda funny, huh?" Marcia was about to bust a gut controlling herself. She erupted then! I lay down on the floor but don't think I went back to sleep!

I remember we were spending a night with him one time and Pratt & Whitney fired up an engine to test it in an underground cylinder I guess you'd call it. The ground literally vibrated and shook. That was a bit scary.

Bill told us that one night the three men were taking a deer survey. One drove the swamp buggy (it had HUGE tires), one sat in the passenger seat keeping count on a clipboard, and the other manned the powerful spotlight. Suddenly, automatic weapons fire started clipping leaves and twigs all around them. They turned around and took off. Bill said they had likely come upon a drug-drop area. About a year later at the Fisheating Creek Reserve a 25-year-old female Wildlife Specialist was found shot through the head.

I rode with Bill in the swamp buggy. You talk about a swamp! And this was northwest of West Palm Beach, not in the Everglades! Snakes, wild hogs, alligators, plus drug-drops??? No way could I work there.

Bill would get off work some days and decide he wanted fresh fish for his supper. There was a pond that was created when dirt was needed to set the trailer on and to cover septic tank field lines. Sometime he would pull one in, but sometimes an alligator would leap from the water and get it! That happened to Kellye when we visited Bill once. She dropped that pole and screamed all the way to the trailer!

His left knee really got to bothering him and eventually he had to have an operation, at Good Samaritan Hospital in West Palm Beach. Marcia and I went down there. There was a single car shed behind his trailer and I don't know why we insisted parking our car there! When we left the trailer about 9 a. m. we would forget to turn on a light. We got permission to stay in his hospital room all day and we'd leave about 9 o'clock at night. We had been told to be careful walking there at night. We would stumble over a big eucalyptus tree root and I just knew I'd lose a hand to a gator!

A TRIP TO NEW YORK CITY

In the mid-70s Park Avenue voted to stay at our present location in Sylvan Park rather than move out somewhere and build. Mr. and Mrs. C. E. Francis, who were faithful members and also in the real estate business, gave much of the funds to buy the northern half of the block that fronted on Charlotte Avenue. A gas station and several houses were removed and our new building became a reality. In 1976 we moved in it.

Mrs. Francis came to me earlier and said she was going to buy a new grand piano for the new sanctuary and what brand did I want? Oh my! I said, a Steinway!

Street Piano Company in Nashville paid the fares for Bob Ward (minister of music at the time) and me to fly to New York City. The Steinway factory is in Queens borough. We did all this in one day's time! I mean, we were two old country boys flying into LaGuardia airport. You could look out the window and see secretaries working in the buildings. If you landed too soon you'd go in the water; if you landed too late you wouldn't have enough runway and would crash into a concrete and steel barrier! We made it, PTL! Then we caught a cab to the Steinway factory.

I noticed wood stacked out in the open like the lumber companies back home did. Maybe they were seasoning it, or whatever, but I don't know why those boards would cost so much later on! I had five pianos to choose from. One must have been built for a funeral parlor...it was so soft and muffled. I would have pounded my fingers to the bone. I tried them all, and picked the fourth one. It had a bright, even brilliant sound, perfect for evangelistic, old-time singing at our church.

When Bob and I left the factory, we were directed to a subway and we went up to 57th Street in Manhattan to the offices of ASCAP (American Society of Composers, Authors and Publishers). I had been a member since July 1957. [Back then you had to have a song published or recorded, and be recommend by two members, in order to be accepted. They had 75,000 members. Today there are well over 300,000 I am told].

We thoroughly enjoyed seeing what we did of New York City. We caught a Yellow Cab back to LaGuardia. Oh friends, I will never forget that ride as long as I live. We flew back home, right proud of ourselves, but a bit on the tired side as well. About a month later it was delivered and the serial number checked to make certain we got the correct one. I played it the next Sunday. It sounded so great. God had blessed us again!

The spacious lobby in the new building was later named in honor of "Skeeter" Daniel. In his younger days he played baseball in the famous "Sulfur Dell" ballpark near the Cumberland River. He and his wife would invite friends over to their house for some "baloney and crackers," but we knew it would be much more than that! He was a great cook. They always decorated the inside of their house at Christmas time...a village scene with an electric train, etc. In the church lobby he gave out wrapped candy to the children and after many years was giving out candy to the children of those children! He was a great saint of God and is greatly missed.

We would have supper at church on Wednesday nights, with sometimes 200 in attendance. Some wonderful, hardworking ladies faithfully made that possible. One cook was Connie Fuqua who later became Bill's mother-in-law. He would sidle up to her and get some more meat or dessert.

We had so many wonderful and close friends in Park Avenue church. Often we would go to the home of Mr. and Mrs. M. D. Lavender. To many he was, "Junior"; and Elizabeth was "Nan." Oh, what a feast! Their daughter Lyndal and family would be there. Sometimes other couples would be there with their children. The Lavenders visited us at our Okeechobee, FL condo one time and we all went to the beach. One winter we had been down there only a few days when we got a phone call that Junior had suddenly passed away. We went back home (800 miles) and I played for his funeral. At the grave site, Bro. Bob called on Marcia to say the closing prayer. Bill and I prayed that she'd get through it. She told Bro. Bob to hold her up! She made it. Bill and Junior were close, too.

PABC PERSONNEL

I cannot attempt to name all the persons who served on the staff at Park Avenue Baptist Church while we were members there (42 years). But I will mention some:

Ralph Harris was associate pastor when we moved our membership to Park Avenue. Our families became close. They later moved to Columbus, Ohio when he became pastor of South Parsons Baptist Church. We visited them three times. The first time we stayed in a high rise hotel across the street from the state capitol. Mammaw and Pappaw Fletcher went with us. He didn't like staying on the eighth floor. I asked him why and he said a fire truck's ladders would only reach to the 7th floor! (I wished I hadn't asked him). Sunday morning as we walked out on the sidewalk, a hippie strolled by and Kellye, maybe five or six years old then, wolf-whistled him. He turned and smiled and kept going.

That afternoon Kellye was trying to learn how to ride Diana's bicycle. She fell into the kiddie's pool. Our family of four would always sing in the services. One Sunday afternoon I had to chip the ice away from the car's headlights when we left to drive back to Nashville, so Bill and Kellye could be back in school Monday morning and maintain their perfect attendance records.

Jim Summers was minister of music and instrumental in getting me there as pianist. He and his wife, Sandra had a big thoroughbred German Police dog. He was born and trained in Germany. They had us over for supper one night. Jim had me come out in the yard to show me his dog, who only understood the German language. He told me not to be afraid then gave him a command. The dog would have attacked me had Jim not held him firmly. Then he spoke something else and said, "You can pat him now." I exclaimed, "Are you kidding? I make my living with these hands!" He convinced me he had commanded the dog not to bother me. I reached out my fist and then patted his head. Wouldn't it be great if Christians obeyed God like that!

Jim made the decision to enter the preaching ministry so he and Sandra moved to a large church in northern Illinois where it really grew under their leadership. A move to Miami followed in a few years and now for over 30 years he has been pastor of the great Northwest Miami Baptist Church. He told me there are over forty nationalities in the church. We have remained friends through the decades. He has been guest speaker at Scottsboro First Baptist Church many times.

During the mid to late 60s there was racial turmoil in Nashville. Police put a curfew in effect and our church held its Sunday evening service at a time when people could reach their homes before it started. We were tipped off that a group from Tennessee State University was coming to a Sunday morning service. Bro. Bob instructed the deacons and ushers to welcome them and tell them to sit wherever they pleased. Sure enough, it happened. Next Sunday they did not come back. Had our men blocked the doors, not only would they have returned in mass but the news media would have come as well. Thus a situation was averted.

A few Sunday mornings after that, however, Bro. Bob was preaching away (our services were on radio) when a huge white Boxer dog came trotting down an aisle! How many white boxers have you ever seen? Jim leaped off the rostrum, grabbed the dog's collar and ushered him through the stained glass swinging doors behind the organ and out the other door onto Park Avenue. He later said he had seen the dog in the community. Anyhow, Bro. Bob paused as that was happening, then he said, "Well, I declare…and he's white, too!" He never made any further explanation and I imagine the radio audience wondered what he meant by that!

John Nading, who was still a student at Tennessee Temple University in Chattanooga was minister of music for a while. Dr. Lee Roberson was the beloved president and also the pastor of Highland Park Baptist Church. Their code of conduct was quite strict. The first time he drove up to our church for Wednesday night supper, prayer meeting and choir practice, he was mortified to discover some women were wearing slacks! We would have at least 400 in prayer meeting. We had about 35 in the choir and always did a choir special. One Wednesday night we had seven additions!

I well recall one Wednesday night when John turned to the choir and said, "Don't ask any questions. Stand and go sit in the audience." After the service some people came to him to ask why he'd done that. He said someone told him there was a big wharf rat in the choir loft. A young man who later became a paramedic, asked, "Where's 'e at?" They found him and the man whipped out a big pocket knife, flipped it and pinned him to the floor! We had gotten home from church one night when our doorbell rang. It was John asking if he could borrow $3 for gas to get back to Chattanooga! Gas was about 30 cents a gallon then, and he drove an Olds 442. We bought Bill a new 1977 red and black Olds 442.

David Busby was associate pastor for a while and he cultivated a close relationship with our youth not known before. They loved him because he loved them. He spoke straight with them. He took them down to Titusville, FL one time and several were saved on that trip, including James Edwards. James had been brought up in PABC but, like so many of us, had wandered away from God. He and his wife Sherry are active members at our Scottsboro church now. Bill spent many hours talking with David and he greatly influenced Bill's life. David passed away much too early, but he left his legacy.

David Werner was also a minister of music. His wife's name is Jean and she plays piano or organ well. She started a group of women singers called "The King's Daughters." During Dave's time with us he organized a great youth choir and I talk about that in more detail later in this book.

When Bro. Bob was pastor of First Baptist in Ft. Payne, AL (prior to coming to Park Avenue) a teenage girl brought her 16-year-old boyfriend to talk with him about being saved. His name was/is Bobby Welch. The girl was Maude Ellen, whom he later married. Bobby was genuinely saved and later became Park Avenue's associate pastor for two or three years. They lived in the house that Mrs. Francis gave to us! [That gift will be explained later]. One Sunday morning Bobby stepped to the pulpit and just stood there eating an apple. He made that an object lesson, but I can't remember what it was now! One Sunday night Bobby was running late for a baptismal service. He pulled on his waders and began baptizing, only to feel water seeping in them due to a split in the feet. Several years ago Bobby and our friend Ronnie King rafted down the Colorado River through the Grand Canyon. I think it took about a week. They both agreed it was *quite an experience!*

As a promotion and witnessing tool, Bobby had wooden coins made about the size of a half dollar with the words on it, "Round-to-it." When a person would ask someone to come to church and they'd say, "I will when I get around to it," you'd hand them one! Then you'd say, "We'll look for you Sunday, ok?" Bobby did a great job with our bus ministry. He left Park Avenue to pastor First Baptist in Daytona, FL, and was there

32 years. For two years he served as President of the Southern Baptist Convention. In 2011 he accepted a position with the Tennessee Baptist Convention and they now live in Brentwood. In early October 2012 we attended a revival service at Parkers Creek BC at Burns, TN, where there were two speakers EACH night! That particular night Bro. Bob Mowrey preached first, followed by Dr. Bobby Welch! What a service it was!

In early November 2012 Bobby and Maude Ellen unexpectedly showed up at our Scottsboro church. Bro. Bob naturally called on him to come to the pulpit and speak briefly and then pray. As he stepped to the mike he pointed to me at the keyboard and said, "I've come this morning to get rid of this guy!" The crowd roared. Bobby travels around the world twice yearly, exhorting churches and Christians to carry out Christ's great commission in these last days.

Kellye was really too young (she's almost five years younger than Bill) but she wanted in on some of the excitement she knew was going on, especially after Sunday night services. So one night we let Bill take her with him and some of his friends. They "rolled" someone's house. Up here, believe it or not, that is a "sign" that you like a person, when you decorate their trees with toilet tissue! As they were throwing rolls up over the limbs in the front yard of the chosen house the outside lights suddenly came on. Everyone ran except Kellye! She was wrapping the shrubs around the front door and hid behind one.

A couple of blocks down the road, someone yelled, "Where is Kellye?" Bill circled around and picked her up. She said she was about ready to surrender and tell the home owner, "I'm gonna need a ride home, ok?"

Bob Ward was minister of music for three or four years, and our new associate pastor was Todd Zieger. They would always sit on the front row right in front of the pulpit. One night at a youth party, we (?) decided to slam a cream pie in Bob's face. I engaged him in conversation while another slipped around behind and with both hands flipped a towel over him like a barber would do. Just then someone pushed the cream pie onto his face. He took it good naturedly…actually, soon after that he entered the ministry and left! He had Marcia and I come and do a concert at Washington Avenue Baptist in Cookeville, TN. We later did a revival together at Parkway Baptist in Knoxville, TN when Walter Davis was pastor. He was a former PABC staff member and his wife's name was Dody. She played guitar and sang.

One Sunday night Bob was preaching at their church in Cookeville when his wife, Yvonne had to take their younger son out for discipline. The auditorium was built in a half circle and they walked around the curved back. Yvonne knew there was an apple tree outside. The little boy led by his mother's firm hand, said out loud, "Uh, I don't need a whippin', Mama, I'm gonna be good now." But that was not the end of it by any means. When they came back in the door, he announced to all, "Oh, God, I wisht I'd a-wore my long britches tonight!" Yvonne was taking their younger daughter in her arms out the door to Bob's right as he was preaching one night. She grabbed onto the door with both hands and yelled, "Help me, Daddy!"

I think he dismissed the crowd early. For many years Bob has been doing mission work in Romania. I am serious!

Steve Smith was our minister of music for about eight years and everyone loved him. He played piano and accompanied himself on solos. He was a songwriter also, and I put one of his songs in a Benson songbook.

Mark Sheldon served a couple of years as interim music director. He also played piano, and we all loved to hear him sing "He Looked Beyond my Fault." He had a singing family, too – all grown up now.

From Lifeway, for a year or so, we had Randy Smith as our interim minister of music. He and I became close friends because Lifeway was printing a lot of my music during that time. I was on the sixth floor of the "tower" downtown one day and stepped into a vacant office and hit the first part of "Last Date" as Floyd Cramer played it. I paused awhile and sure enough, I heard Randy in his office pick up the tune for a few bars!

William (Bill) Cox was our interim music director four or five times. He is such a great guy, has a booming voice and a big heart. Everyone loves him, even his wife Catherine! He's just a "big teddy bear," someone said. We loved to hear him sing Gaither's "The King is Coming!" Also Roger Matthews (Neal's brother) was interim music director for a while. He and Jane and the family moved around the United States since he worked for IBM.

During an Eddy Martin revival in our new building one night a couple and their daughter came – she was in her 30s. All three were mentally challenged. The daughter came out of the sanctuary and went to the ladies' room. She came out in a few minutes and her hair was wet – she must have washed it. The man got bored, I guess, took OFF his baseball cap and began twirling it on his cane, above his head! It's a wonder Eddy didn't call him down. In a few minutes he got up and went out in the lobby. For some reason Marcia and Peggy (our pastor's wife) happened to be out there also. They noticed in a few minutes the old man was sitting in a chair. He would put something in his mouth, and then throw paper on the floor.

A deacon, John Evans, was out there also and Marcia asked him what the man was doing. He said, "Aw, he's picked up cigarette butts on the street and is gettin' the tobacco out of 'em." That little job completed, the man stood and headed back to go inside again. Peggy said, "Oh, Mr. (name withheld) please don't go back in there now, the service will be over in just another few minutes." He looked up at John Evans and said, "Who in the (bleep) does she thank she is?" Now I learned this first-hand because Marcia was an eye-witness. I later asked John, "What did you do?" He said, "I done my best to keep from laughing OUT LOUD!"

I want to mention here that Bro. John Evans also served as our bus ministry director in its early stages. I don't remember who started this practice but the bus pastor who had the least number of riders for the month got to take a live chicken (or rooster) home with them for a week! Believe me, that was an incentive! John went with our family and the Blankenship sisters every

Christmas for several years, as we went to the homes of shut-ins and delivered poinsettias and sang carols. John's wife was Miss Ruby, a sweet Christian lady. These are sweet times to remember. For a while John would lock up the church after the night services. Many of us would be standing around talking and he would blink the lights – in other words "would you please leave!" I yelled one night, "John, you're going to ruin the fellowship of this church! Stop that!"

Bro. Charles Cooey and his wife Charlene were faithful and active members of Park Avenue. He is blind and does a lot of work with Lifeway for blind curricular. I remember when Benson was on Fourth Avenue North he would make his way from where he worked to my office during his noon hour and we would sit and talk music, play some on the piano. He is a remarkable person.

Dr. Leonard Ravenhill conducted a great week of Bible study at Park Avenue in the 80s. He made a comment one night that gave me an idea for a song. He said although Jesus repeatedly told his disciples he would rise up from the grave…when it happened NO ONE WAS THERE to welcome Him! The song was published and recorded and Marcia sings it as a solo, especially around Easter. I was told that back then he lived at Lindale, Texas. Other residents of that town were Dallas Holm and Jimmy Owens!

THE BUS MINISTRY

It was decided that Park Avenue should start a bus ministry. John Evans took on the director's job. Several from the church went up to Jack Hyles big First Baptist Church in Hammond, Indiana. I think they operated well over 200 buses! We eventually had over twenty buses running at one time. We started with old school buses, then we bought some Metro transit buses that had been replaced with new models. Our son, Bill drove one of those buses. One morning as he got off an interstate exit he realized the accelerator was stuck. Fortunately no vehicles were coming on the cross street and he shot across and up the entrance ramp! He reached down and somehow got it un-stuck! Ray Saddler was recruited by Bro. Bob to take over as Bus Director. We began running over 1,500 in Sunday school. One young black boy, Jeff Knight rode the bus, was saved and became a preacher. He has been a pastor in Detroit for many years.

Each bus had a driver, a bus "pastor" and an assistant. On Saturday they would faithfully visit on their routes. Over the years we had men like Bobby Welch, Ray Sadler, Bobby Sadler, John Evans and Ron Chilton to head up the bus ministry. Men like Grady Bowman, Gene Scott and Tommy Dodson kept those old buses running. We were still driving Cadillacs and Grady was a Lincoln man. He tried his best to get us into a Lincoln. I told him one day, "Grady, if I'm gonna spend that much money I'm gettin' a Cadillac!"

Ray Sadler felt led to leave Park Avenue and form a team to travel the country, encouraging churches to start a bus ministry. Not long after that the private plane crashed that carried the team. Two were killed and Ray died four days later. I played for his funeral in the "old" auditorium and many were saved at the end of the service. Andrae Crouch's song "Through it All" was sung in the service. That auditorium was named the Ray Sadler auditorium and his portrait was hung on a wall.

Bobby Sadler became Park Avenue's bus pastor. He and his wife Joyce had a burden to bring children to Christ. He later pastored Peytonsville (TN) Baptist Church for about thirty years. He frequently preaches at Scottsboro church when Bro. Bob is out of town.

Bob Ward was our minister of music for about four years during which time we moved into our new sanctuary at Charlotte and 43rd Avenue. He did a great job with the choir. Todd Zeiger was associate pastor then.

Ron Chilton was another associate pastor who also headed up the bus ministry. His wife Lana would venture into some dangerous communities on Saturday visiting and witnessing. She became known as Lana Banana. After she died, Ron moved to become pastor at Southside Baptist in Shelbyville, TN. Bro. Bob and I did a revival there for him soon after he got there. He later re-married and I believe he has retired now.

Ron frequently did baptisms, especially those who came through the bus ministry. In a service one Sunday night he *attempted* to baptize a stout black woman, taller than he was. He said the appropriate words and went to lean her back with no success whatsoever – Grady Nutt said it was like trying to baptize a stump. After quietly saying something to her he tried again and this time she threw both arms around his neck! I reckon she didn't know how long he might hold her under. She said something and Ron told the audience she said she had arthritis in her back. By this time the congregation was about to lose Christian control of themselves. Well, on the third attempt he managed to get her under, except for her elbow sticking up like a periscope.

Another associate pastor was Benny Bond. He was engaged when he first came. Soon he and Beth were married. They were fun to be around. At a big church social in our gymnasium (in the new half-block building) one night he presented a dramatic recitation. He was to end it down on his left knee with his right foot out front and arms outstretched to the people. It was to be a big ending, and it was, but not like he intended. His extended foot slid off the platform and he just crashed off the stage. Folks exploded in laughter thinking that was part of the performance.

An elderly lady was in the hospital. Her daughter worked for Impact Books at the Benson building in MetroCenter and told me what happened one day when Benny came to visit. After talking awhile he asked if he could have prayer – oh yes, please do. He prayed some appropriate sentences then said, "Lord, we thank you for the 84 years you've given Mrs. (name withheld) to serve you." His mind slipped into neutral but his mouth kept going. (Pause) "And…and Lord, we just pray you'll give her another 84 more years to serve you!" The lady said, "O God, don't do that!" When Benny would make announcements in the morning service it appeared the congregation would all lean forward in their seats, knowing that somewhere along the way he was puttin' his foot in his mouth!

Marcia and I passed through the Shreveport, LA area years ago and went by the church where he was pastor. We sat in his office and talked a short while. I said, "Uh, you and Beth have two children, right?" He cocked his head to the ceiling, thought a second and said, "Yes, two." Like I said, we loved them both!

There were some faithful women working at PABC as well. Mary Donihi was receptionist and financial secretary. She had a placard that read "This office is protected by an attack cat." Lois Hinckley was Bro. Bob's personal secretary. After Bro. Bob retired she moved back to Lewiston, Maine. On one of our trips to New England, Marcia and I had lunch with her. She had re-acquired her Maine accent! Joan Means was the visitation secretary and always had cards laid out on tables for us to pick up. It seems Marcia and I always chose cards of people who had problems.

One night I knocked on a door and stepped back down the steps. When the door opened I was nose-to-nose with a Great Dane. He had a quilt in his mouth that he shook like it was a handkerchief! I wrote on the card, "Beware of BIG dog!" We would have 150+ coming for supper and visitation on Tuesday nights. Danny and Bonnie Wagonfield, a young couple who joined our church, were always there on visitation nights. We have lived within a mile of each other for many years. They are attending another church and are now proud grandparents.

One Wednesday night, right in the middle of prayer meeting, a man burst through the stained glass swinging doors behind the organ and a shocked look came over his face. He was carrying a typewriter, and walked quickly up an aisle. About the time he got to the back of the church, two deacons came through those doors and yelled, "There he goes!" Come to find out the man was stealing a typewriter out of the church office! And one night a lady came out to her car in the parking lot and it was sitting on blocks with all four wheels missing! After that men volunteered to patrol our church property during services.

I won't attempt to name all the ministers of music and associate pastors that were there during my 38 years as pianist. Bro. Bob was pastor at PABC for 35 years and tried to retire. He was interim pastor at First Baptist in Cookeville, TN for two years then did the same at FBC Sparta, TN. He later went to Scottsboro First Baptist Church, a small church on Old Hickory Boulevard located between Nashville and Ashland City. This became his second longest pastorate. In April 2013 he celebrated 12 years there. I have been leading the singing from the keyboard there for several years. This church consistently ranks 9, 10 or 11 (out of about 185 Baptist churches in the Nashville Baptist Association) in number of persons saved and baptized, the criteria being five in a year! We usually have around 35 to 40 each year and we still have spring and fall revivals. It is quite shameful that a lot of prominent churches are NOT even on the list!

I was instrumental in getting many of the music people who recorded on Benson labels to come to Park Avenue for concerts.

I'll attempt to name as many as I can remember: the Speer Family, J. D. Sumner and the Stamps Quartet, Jake Hess, Henry and Hazel Slaughter, the Downings, ReGeneration, Truth, etc. I can't remember if we had Bill Gaither's Trio or not.

I just remembered this, although it happened in the early 70s. I went up to the Portland, TN Methodist Church. Before the service they had watermelon down in the dining room (can you believe it?) and without thinking, I ate "my fill." On the way up the stairs to the auditorium, a teenage girl told me, "I sure hope all that watermelon don't git to you 'fore church is over!"

MY "HEE-HAW" CONNECTION

I'm sure you remember the TV show called "Hee-Haw." It was taped at WLAC studios in Nashville. When it first started it showed two young men running in and out of a barn, the speed much faster than real time. Bill Grine was a Music Row photographer and he also did shots for Benson album covers. Jimmy Moore was also a photographer and Benson published a book of his still shots called "A Value of Time." Those two were the guys at the beginning of Hee-Haw. The show was video-taped twice a year for 3 weeks at a time.

The cast stayed at the new Millennium Maxwell House Hotel in MetroCenter. This was during the time Benson was located at 1625 Broadway, a block north of the Music Row area. When you entered the lobby, Bob and John III's private offices were located to the right. On the left was McKenzie's office as A & R man and Director of Publications' was on the left. A long hallway went straight to the door to my office, some 10 feet underground at the back of the building! So if I was sitting at my desk you saw me immediately when you turned down that hallway.

I would look up twice a year and see my friend Bickley (Bix) Reichner coming down toward me with that sly grin on his face. He'd say, "Hi, Mercer, how ya doin'?" He was of German descent and lived in Malvern, PA. He had a music company called Malvern Music. He wrote the beautiful song, "If You Know the Lord," that many have sung and recorded. Then he'd say, "Hey, I got some good ones; you got time to listen?" He was the guy who came up with all that funny stuff and one-liners, cornfield popups, the Culhanes, the barbershop, etc. on "Hee-Haw." Of course I would stop and listen.

He had a yellow legal pad in his hand and would read off a joke. If I was obviously not amused he would mark through that one. But if I busted out laughing, he'd smile and put a checkmark by that one! So, you know? I'm wondering if maybe I had some effect on the jokes that made it on "Hee-Haw?"

HENRY CHEERS ME UP

At the Benson office on Broadway one day I was, for some reason, depressed and discouraged. I might have been having a pity party! Henry Slaughter dropped by, and sensing my mood he just sat there talking to me. He said, "You know, Elmo, Hazel and I have been working the same two rows in God's garden for many years now. I could see folks on the other side doing much better than we were. But God said 'I'll bless you where you are!' So Elmo, you hang in there and keep trusting!" I never will forget that.

John III or Bob told me to take four of Henry and Hazel's albums and choose ten songs to make a choral book. My arrangements were to match the soundtracks on the album. There would be an accompaniment track available. I was doing fine till I got to the eighth song where Henry "picked and grinned" a verse. That meant I had to try to copy his style. It took a while, but I think I did it alright.

Sometime after that, Henry and Hazel did a concert at Park Avenue in the "old" auditorium. Henry and I "made this up" to do. When they got through singing that song ("Before I Found the Lord" by Lanny Wolfe) I jumped up from my front row seat and said, "Shoot, Henry, I can play like that!" Our congregation gasped to think I would do such a thing. Henry got up from the bench and with a flourish of his hand he said, "Well, Mo, be my guest." I sat down and just about duplicated his style, and the crowd applauded, realizing then what we'd done.

Later, when Marcia and I were traveling, I imitated three of my favorite piano players: Rudy Atwood (the Old Fashioned Revival Hour pianist), Floyd Cramer and Henry Slaughter. I would say a few words about each before I played their style.

We had Henry and Hazel to sing at Scottsboro church several years ago. I love to hear them sing "I've Never Loved Him Better than Today," (he wrote that) as well as their signature song "We've Come This Far by Faith" by Albert Goodson. They are such a sweet couple who have faithfully used their God-given musical talents. At one time he was choir director from the organ (!) at Rex Humbard's Cathedral of Tomorrow in Akron, Ohio. He succeeded Audrey Mieir, who has written beautiful songs like "His Name is Wonderful." When the Weatherford Quartet left the Cathedral Henry went with them as pianist. Then George Younce and three men in the church started a new quartet and became known as "The Cathedral Quartet!"

Henry became the first pianist for the Imperials. In 1964 Jake Hess left the Statesmen and started them. Later Henry and Hazel did the "warm-up" for the Bill Gaither Trio concerts that preceded Homecoming Friends videos. And believe me, they still have faithful fans across this country. For many years now they have lived between Ashland City and Pleasant View. We keep in touch by e-mail, Facebook and phone; sometimes we see each other at restaurants or stores. Our friend Jeff Jeffrey had us on his (www.cpradioonline.com) hour-long program in the summer of 2013. We were guests on his live show "Jeff Jeffrey's Country and Gospel Jubilee" on Friday nights at the KOA Camp on Briley Parkway near the Cumberland River and Opryland.

THE SPLIT CROTCH CAPER

In the early 70s Bob and John III decided to do a music clinic in California! Jeff Jeffrey flew on out to help get things set up.

Marcia and I flew to Los Angeles, and Cathy White (the company's PR person) went with us. At LAX airport we noticed and heard a big crowd up ahead in the concourse. Out came an electric vehicle carrying a man and woman. We recognized him to be actor Jack Lord, the star of TV's "Hawaii 5-0." I guess fans wanted his autograph and to have pictures made with him.

I looked at Cathy and commented, "I'll bet half the people here don't even know who ***I*** am." She laughed at me, saying I was so silly! We went on to our connecting plane to Santa Barbara. It was packed because a flight to Las Vegas had difficulty and those passengers were then put on "our" plane, of all things!

When we got to Santa Barbara, we were driven east to the Ojai (pronounced O-hi) Country Club. Marcia and I knew we were in "high cotton." Beautiful trees and vineyards sprawled over the rolling hills. There were lovely grounds around the fabulous place. I felt like the Apostle Peter at the Mount of Transfiguration…can't we build us a place and stay here awhile? The actress Loretta Young had a house in the area we were told.

That evening, a "get acquainted" time was held as we met the California leaders of the music clinic, along with their wives. Food was laid around and you can imagine I checked it out. I graciously met the ladies seated around the low coffee table on which the snacks were set. I would bend over and get a bit of this and a little of that. I want you to know: when Marcia and I got to our room around midnight and I removed my pants, the whole seat (crotch) was ripped out of 'em! I HAD MOONED

THE ENTIRE BUNCH! And even today I still check the crotch of my pants before pulling them on…

While we were there, we were awakened very early one morning by shouts and running feet outside on the lawn. We found out later that Immigration Authorities had raided the place! The manager assured us we would still get top service, it might "just take a little longer."

OK…on the return flight Cathy was again with us. We had to change planes in Dallas. A man was in the window seat, Marcia sat by him and I was on the aisle. Across from me sat Cathy. So help me, I am telling the truth! This man leaned out, looked at me and said, "You're Elmo Mercer, aren't you?" I just turned and looked at Cathy. She liked to have died. I wouldn't have taken a "skint monkey" for that incident! It turns out the man lived in Nashville and did, in fact, know me.

Another incident just came to my mind. I don't remember the year but the CBA convention was in Denver that July. Benson always had a big booth and usually many of our recording artists would be there. One night John III and Bob hosted a big dinner on the top floor of "The Top of the Rock" building. Afterwards we stood by the GLASS elevators to go down. I did not know that Bob Benson feared heights. He got on first but bowed his head and covered his eyes.

Doug Oldham, Hale and Wilder with their accompanist Ovid Young then stepped on. Seems like there was another heavy-set one or two got on. John III had been talking with someone then turned to get on and suddenly stopped. He gasped and said, "Uh, I think I'll wait for the next one!"

Benson had an excellent relationship with all their recording artists.

THE 'WOMANLESS' WEDDING

Well, I don't know if you're old enough to remember the "Minstrells" the Lion's Club (or whoever) used to put on sometimes. They would black their faces and put on a show. "Mr. Interlockater"... Ok, that went out of style decades ago. I guess the "womanless" wedding has also, but we had one at PABC one night, and it was probably in the early to mid-70s.

Men are the "stars," there are no women in it at all. Naturally, I played appropriate music as I sat in my beautiful evening dress, borrowed from Carolyn Campbell, Chet Atkins' secretary. I couldn't zip it all the way up in the back and had to wear a light something-or-other (shawl?) to keep the folks from knowing that.

It was a military wedding – well, there was a shotgun there. The bride's daddy carried it over his shoulder as he followed "her" and the groom down the aisle. Their baby (Bobby Walton) was properly diapered and sat in a "customized" baby carriage that was pushed by a brother of the bride. Our pastor,

Bro. Bob Mowrey was a bride's maid and had trouble keeping his wig on because he'd bend over when he laughed so hard.

The groom (Tommy Atwood) was a short fellow and when the preacher (Bobby Strickland) pronounced them husband and wife, the bride (Jack Owenby) picked up the groom, slung him over "her" shoulder like a hundred pound sack of potatoes and ran up the aisle, whooping it up. You know, I don't believe there is any way we would do that nowadays.

Also I remember one week a conference was held in our "old" auditorium and prominent men attended. Two I recall were Dr. D. James Kennedy and Dr. Peter Lord. It would seat, including the balcony only about 750 people. During revivals folding chairs would be put in the aisles and folks stood in the lobby. When we started going there, PABC was having an 8:15 a.m. worship service, then Sunday school at 9:30 followed by a 10:45 a.m. service. The church had an agreement with Yellow Cab to pick me up at our house on Masonwood Drive in Parkwood Estates, so Marcia and the kids could come later for Sunday school and church. My dear friend from RCA recording sessions, who helped me understand chord structure and chord progression, BILLY BYRD (he played guitar with Ernest Tubb's band for years) was the driver! He and I had great fellowship on those 13 mile rides, sometimes in snowfall. {Years after Billy passed away we saw his wife in a local rehab center}. Park Avenue church would send a bus to Belmont College for students and they usually sat in the middle right down at the front taking up several rows of pews. One of those students, now Peggy Reams went on that South Korean Mission trip with us!

Marcia has always had the misfortune of snagging something when she walks by it. Well, one night she was sitting in the PABC choir, crossed her legs and the buckles on her shoes got tangled together! The lady next to her had to reach down and get them apart.

The Park Avenue Men's Quartet sang often. We had various personnel over the years. For a while, our high tenor was Roger Matthews, brother of Neal Matthews who sang with the Jordanaires – he made all their arrangements and sometimes even accompanied them on the guitar. Bubba Campbell, William Coleman and Bob Dodson were the other guys. We would go to one of our houses for practice and great fellowship. Every now and then we'd have a cookout before our practice, with wives attending. One night we were invited to sing out at the facility in southeast Nashville where the criminal-minded offenders were housed. Bill Coleman forgot he had a knife in his pocket – he picked it up on the way back out. Guards had no guns or weapons of any kind, but were standing all around. I spoke quietly from the piano bench to the quartet and told them to smile and sing purty! As we left someone shouted, "Y'all come back now. You just like one of us!"

RONNIE RETURNS HOME

Keep in mind that Ronnie and I were together at home on South King Street in Winnfield from August 1946 (when Mama and Daddy adopted him) until Marcia and I married on Oct 2, 1954...eight years. I have written about our times growing up. He went to Winnfield schools and was popular.

Daddy left the T&G railroad and worked twelve years at the LA Highway Department erecting highway signs. When he retired from that job they moved some 35 miles south to Dry Prong, near our "family roots" in the Big Creek community. Ronnie graduated from Dry Prong High School and entered the Navy since he had joined the ROTC there. The older sailors told him he needed to go to the Aleutian Islands in Alaska...there was a woman behind every tree! Ronnie was actually sent there! The truth was...there are NO trees up there!

In the meantime, Mama and Daddy decided to move up to Jackson Parish where Mama was born and raised. They built a nice little house just east of US-167 between Hodge and Ruston. It was on the loop road to the Jimmie Davis Tabernacle. When Ronnie got out of the Navy he headed home to Dry Prong. You've heard the joke, right? Well, this actually happened. He found his parents had moved! He walked up the highway to Mr. Johnson's store to find out what was going on. Mr. Johnson told him where they had moved, some eighty miles north. He even loaned him his station wagon to drive up there!

While in the Navy, Ronnie learned job skills that were very helpful in civilian life. He married Janice Holland from Jonesboro. They have two daughters and are proud grandparents. For many years he has worked for a gas and oil well drilling company, working mostly in east Texas, north Louisiana and southern Arkansas, commonly called the ArkLaTex. He is what is called a "mud logger." Sections from the drilled hole are brought to him, he analyzes it and enters the information on computers (he has five of them in the on-site trailer). He and

Janice have lived in Crossett, Arkansas for many years. He's about ready to retire and travel some in their motor home.

STRANDED ON I-75

In the winter of 1973, Marcia and I, along with Bill and Kellye were on our way to visit her brother Bernard and his Japanese wife Keiko. He was in the Navy, and was stationed at Glencoe base at Brunswick, GA. It is now a training facility for the US Secret Service. When Marcia and I were traveling in church music evangelism, we had dinner one night with a man who had worked there as an "actor". They would have him to act as the president (or some big executive) while the SS were being trained. He said it was quite an experience because sometimes they got quite rough with him!

We were driving our pale green '72 Cadillac when south of Atlanta on I-75 we began seeing trucks with snow plows on the front. We wondered what in the world was going on. In a few miles we encountered heavy snow! We were stopped in the southbound traffic for almost three hours; back then it was a four-lane interstate. A man in front of us got out of the driver's door and got a liquor bottle out of the trunk. He poured some in a glass, and then scooped up a handful of snow to cut it and chill it!

I stopped at a gas station and convenience store at Forsythe, just north of Macon and filled the gas tank. We always carry a sack full of food and snacks when we go on a trip. It's a good thing we did. We got maybe a mile or so down I-75 and stopped again. It was midnight and it began snowing heavily. Marcia had put blankets in the trunk so I hit the release button...nothing happened. Kellye and I got out and the trunk was covered with an inch of ice. Forget the blankets! Kellye was in the back seat with Marcia. Bill and I were in the front (bench) seat. We used our jackets as "cover." Every 30 minutes or so, I would crank up the motor to run the heat. I would **push** my door open, step out and try to remove the snow from the windshield. We'd wait till the car got really hot then cut off the engine. It was quite a night!

When dawn came we turned on the radio to find that **19 inches** of snow had fallen. It must have been a small town radio station and the guy was at the station all by himself who was likely snowed in also! He said, "Well, let's call the sheriff's office and see what's going on." They talked awhile and then he said he would check with the funeral home, so on and so forth! A man came from the northbound side in a Ford Bronco (new in those days) and drove across the median (slight ditch) to a pickup truck we found was loaded with pigs! We had not heard a squeal out of them all night. He hooked the truck to his Bronco and made his way between vehicles and pulled them back over to the northbound side, which amazingly was open... to two-way traffic!

A highway patrolman drove by over there and we yelled, "Get the snow plows!" and I think he yelled back, "What's a snow plow?" We heard on the radio that a pregnant woman was flown out by helicopter. We used a large drink cup as our "bathroom," and noticed yellow snow by many vehicles! We sat there 12 hours. We found out later there was a fifty mile traffic jam in the south-bound lanes!

Bill trudged down the highway a mile or so and came back to tell us that some truckers were helping cars go across the median to the two-way traffic northbound lane. He said a state trooper came up and told them it was against the law to cross the median and they were to stop immediately. The truckers told him, in colorful language to get back in his car and leave. We thought it was worth a try, but then stalled cars became a problem. We made it to the place and a trucker told me not to give it any gas until they yelled for me to. The guy in front of me didn't do that and tore one side of his rear bumper off...he just kept going. We made it over with no problem. Sometimes we would be driving on the left side of the road like the British do!

We were finally directed to go over a bridge and get back in the southbound lane. Snow was almost window-level deep on that bridge, with barely room for the car to go through (one-way). We made it to Bernard's on Saturday evening. Keiko was pregnant with their older son Lee. Sunday morning we had to start the long trip back to Nashville. We debated going west to Birmingham to hopefully get out of that snow band, but ended up going the way we had come. All along the way in the area where we had been stopped, we saw big snowmen that people had built while stranded. We even saw some on the roofs of cars as they drove the highway. We stopped at an exit and got out and enjoyed a snowball fight! This was an experience we have remembered, and talked about for many years.

THE STALNECKERS

In the early 70s, Park Avenue had Ed and Betty Stalnecker, along with David Tyson (piano) and his wife (organ) for the music team in a revival. Ed preached and Betty sang...she has a beautiful contralto voice. She made albums with Benson also, and recorded many of my songs.

The team would park their motor coaches on a church parking lot and hook up to facilities. One night after the service was over, Ed headed for their coach and paraded two huge dogs down the sidewalk as people left the service, holding a leash in each hand like he was Ben Hur driving a chariot!

Their two sons later married and formed a revival team. They came to Park Avenue's new sanctuary. Their services were quite "contemporary," even setting off smoke bombs for some reason! Many people vacated the premises! In later years, Bette sang at Bellevue Baptist Church east of Memphis where her friend, Dr. Adrian Rogers was pastor for many years, having followed Dr. R. G. Lee.

THE FUNNY PHOTO

Two teens, David Williams and Tony Stewart came to Park Avenue church one Sunday looking for girls but they found the Lord! Pretty neat, huh. We had a very active youth program in the late 1970s. They became faithful members of the church.

I believe it was David's senior prom where he and his date had their pictures made in front of a big sign on the wall behind them that read "**CLASS of 1978.**" (Forgive me if I'm wrong). You know when you look at a picture you look at yourself first, right? David did and thought it was an excellent shot. But Tony laughed uncontrollably, pointing at the picture. Finally David discovered what was so funny – his head was blocking out the letters "CL." (Just picture it, ok?)

THE 'WHACHAMACALLIT'

Bob Benson came up with the idea to start a minister of music conference. A title could not be agreed upon so he just called it the "Whachamacallit." The title was not copyrighted, however. The first one was held in the winter of 1972 at Montgomery Bell State Park, west of Nashville on US-70. We rented the entire park's facilities, yet many could not come because it wasn't big enough. At that event we met Bro. Dick Whipple and his twin brothers, David and Danny from Florida. Bro. Dick was pastor for 30 years at First Baptist in Okeechobee, FL.

For the next five years it was held at Lake Barkley State Park in southwestern Kentucky, a very lovely place. It is located on the "Land between the Lakes," created by dams on the Cumberland and Tennessee Rivers. A two-story motel was shaped in a wide "V" and attached to the back of the huge lobby was the dining room with beautiful views. One year the lake froze over and then a snowfall followed. It looked like a giant cow pasture!

We made so many new friends there. A man served the meat and I got to know him really well! He had four names just like Mama's brother, John Daniel Morgan Johnson. One day Marcia was in the Gift Shop and got to talking with a music minister's wife, Brenda Eades from South Carolina. Ever since then she and her husband Dean have been our close friends. He said I am the brother he never had. We've stayed in each other's homes many times, sang and played in each other's churches, been on staff for senior adult week at Ridgecrest, NC and Glorieta, NM (Baptist conference centers), took a big western vacation together, etc. Now they are known as the "Dulcimer Couple." Dean builds them in his basement shop on Lake Keowee near Seneca, SC. He conducts dulcimer workshops, and by the way, is available. [864.882.7791]. He uses different kinds of wood to build them, and everyone can afford one, though he does make some pricy ones. Some people hang them on their walls in a room or hallway.

Another couple we always looked forward to seeing was Mildred and Jack Coker from Okeechobee, FL. We would traditionally squint at their name tags and say, "Where in the (bleep) is Okeechobee?" Jack was in the beef cattle business (one time he had 10,000 head on a feeder lot in west Texas) plus he was a building contractor. Little did we know that a few years later they would have us sing at First Baptist Church and Jack would introduce Kellye to her future husband, Bruce Jeffers. Jack and Bob Bell, a friend of his, built the condos in Oak Lake Villas where we owned one for 28 years or so.

And everyone who was present remembers the night at Lake Barkley when we witnessed Ronn Huff and Bill Gaither working on "Alleluia! A Praise Gathering for Believers." Several men brought their wives with them, so we had a well-balanced choir to read through it. Ronn was perched on a stool down front, and sometimes he would call us to a halt, grab his pencil and say, "Hold it! That's just not gonna work." He would make a few notations and we would continue. This went till midnight or after. The success of that work added to our special memory of that particular night.

Marcia and I would either pick up late comers at the Nashville airport, or maybe get them back to an early departure. The park would only accommodate about 275, including several cabins that would hold eight each. But some guys would come and sleep on the floor, so as not to miss it. One man, Tillman Singleton, liked to talk like an Englishman and told funny stories. We were to carry him back early to catch a plane. He was staying in a cabin. We drove there, I opened the door and shouted in my best Mae West, "Hey, big boy! Why don't cha come up 'n see me sometime?" A very large man stuck his head around a door facing and said, "Oh hey, Brother Elmo." I could have died on the spot! Tillman got a big kick out of it till I asked him if he wanted to walk to the Nashville airport.

The last four years the WHACHAMACALLIT was held in Nashville at the Gaylord Opryland Hotel – no space problem there! And all four years it snowed. Benson always gave a generous 40% discount off the retail price for music purchases made while there. A lot of men said they spent almost all their music budget at these conferences.

One year we had Ralph Carmichael and his entire orchestra to come for a performance. In late October 2012, Marcia and I, along with our daughter Kellye sang at Allenspark, Colorado Community Church's Sunday morning service. Afterwards while talking with many of the folks a man approached me. He was Col. Denny Dakane, USAF retired. He told me that for many years he played piano in Ralph Carmichael's orchestra! He told me he traveled to 43 countries and had played various pipe organs in 19 countries. I wish we could have talked longer.

These conferences were cancelled after those ten years... February 1981 was the last. A few days after that, I put my resignation on Bob MacKenzie's desk. I had been a staff writer for ten years, then music editor over twenty years. Marcia and I had decided to "go out on our own" in church music evangelism. Bob Mac said they didn't want to lose track of me and I agreed to arrange ten choir books for them over the next few years. I ended up working for Benson another seventeen years while Marcia and I traveled the USA. This made a total of 47 years!

I just thought of this. One year Bob and John III had a brunch at Blue Grass Country Club located north of Hendersonville and invited a slew of recording artists. Marcia helped Bob's wife Peggy with the centerpieces on the tables. I think it was a bouquet of artificial flowers sitting in an aluminum "plate." Lanny Wolfe was the winner at his table and as he was walking out Marcia noticed the plate was missing. Without thinking she yelled, "Oh Lanny! You've dropped your bottom!" He grinned and said, "Well Marcia, I certainly hope not!"

THE FRANCIS FARM YEARS

Marcia and I had become concerned that Bill and Kellye were growing up in the city (more or less) and missing out on the kind of upbringing we'd had. One Sunday I asked Mr. and Mrs. C. E. Francis to ride up toward Gallatin with us and look at a 40-acre plot of land that I'd found was for sale. We got in our new 1970 red Cadillac and made the scenic drive up there.

It was in the spring and it looked great to us. But Mr. and Mrs. Francis had made their money in real estate, both commercial and house rentals, and I valued their opinion. I got it. He pointed out that it looked great now, but wait until the hot and dry weather came. There was no stream of water on it and the ground was rocky. It was on a hill, and finally was really too far away from our house in Nashville.

Then he said, "I have a little farm down at Spring Hill I'd like to show you. We'll go down there next Sunday." This was years before the Saturn assembly plant was built there. The next Sunday we turned off US-31 at the Church of Christ Children's Home in Spring Hill, and went south about two miles on Kidron Road. We turned right on Denning Road which was gravel and dirt. I found out that it passed his farm, went by the University of Tennessee Experimental Farm then rejoined US-31 about six miles north of Columbia.

His farm was 165 acres. There were 100 acres south of Denning Road and 65 north of it, with a tunnel under the road for cattle to go through. There were three springs on it, with beautiful pastures and wooded areas. He was currently leasing it to a Mr. Luther Quirk who was running a few head of cattle on it. We absolutely fell in love with the place and I believe the next Friday night we drove down there and spent the night out under a big tree in a little tent we had. A beagle appeared to join in the fun. We found out later it belonged to the Smiths who lived on 34 acres across the road and around the curve. At the slightest noise he would bark and bay for half an hour.

Then Mr. and Mrs. Francis invited us one Saturday to go with them down near the Alabama state line to a horse auction. She bought a big sorrel for Kellye, (named Annie) and we bought a shiny black for Bill (named Princess)...both of them mares. Bill's had a five week old colt that we named Thunder. Pappaw Fletcher called him "Little Man." As he grew older, while Kellye would hold a feed bucket, he would paw with a front hoof. We became afraid that he might injure Kellye and we sold him for $50. He surely made somebody a great horse.

Marcia and I bowled on a Park Avenue church league Friday nights, and would get down to the farm about midnight. At the bowling place the children from other families would play together, mostly outside. Bill and Kellye have told us since then that Bill would load our Cadillac up with girls and drive around the parking lot area, while Kellye stood in that parking place to keep others from parking there!

We had not gone down many times when one Friday night it was storming. The four of us went on down and I had the bright idea of driving into the hallway of the HUGE barn.

Bill opened the lot gate and the double barn doors and I drove in. We listened to the hard rain on the tin roof. Bill and I were in the front (bench seat in those days) and Kellye and Marcia were in the back. We talked a while then I nudged Bill and said, "Look, Bill! There's three little ghosts dancing up on that rafter!" Kellye shot up, "Where? Where?"

The next morning we realized a mistake had been made. When I attempted to back out of the barn and the lot, my rear (drive) tires started spinning and sliding toward the woven wire fence. We finally found a rope and tied it to the back bumper. Bill and Marcia pulled hard on it as I tried to ease back out again and we made it that time!

At an old home place on the property there was a small log cabin that was written up in the Columbia paper as being the oldest structure in Maury County (pronounced Murray). It had been where the slaves lived. In the large barn mentioned above there were stalls on each side. There was a tack room with wooden flooring. A smaller barn was between the slave house and the big barn. Mr. and Mrs. Francis didn't seem to care what we did, so we started spending Friday nights IN that slave house. We cleaned it up and took an old iron bedstead down for Marcia and me to sleep on. Bill and Kellye had sleeping bags. We'd build a fire in the old fireplace on cold nights. Marcia would wrap hamburger meat, some carrots and a potato in aluminum foil and we'd either set them on the hearth or put them among coals. It was delicious. The cold winds would blow in through open crevasses between the logs. We got some big sheets of plastic and nailed them up on the north and west walls one

Saturday. I forgot Misty had been tied by the reins to a post at the corner of the cabin and when I hit a nail with the hammer, she tore down a section of fence and the gate!

Bill's friend, Dale McWright would go down with us most of the time. One night about midnight the three of us decided to go hunting – rabbits, 'coons, 'possums, whatever jumped in front of our flashlights. We had lots of fun. While we were gone one night, Marcia and Kellye retired. Marcia heard a noise that was scary. There it was again! She found out it was Kellye snoring in her sleeping bag. We were talking one Friday night about how many slaves had likely been born and even died right there in that room. There were narrow steps against a wall that accessed an attic area. The flooring up there was unbelievable. Boards were like one inch thick and 20 inches wide, and I bet you could NOT drive a nail in them!

Mr. Francis talked with Luther Quirk about putting our two horses on the farm and he said it was fine with him. We became close friends with him and his wife. He drove a big red six-wheel cattle truck and Kellye would see him entering the front gate on Saturday mornings. She would run across the pasture to meet him and he would let her sit in his lap and steer the truck down the road to the big barn. Kellye was around nine and Bill was about 14.

Marcia and I were sitting in folding lawn chairs under a big shade tree while Bill and Kellye rode their horses one day. We looked toward the front gate and Bill was galloping toward us.

Misty was so pretty when she stretched out, with her mane and tail flowing behind her. Bill reigned in and said, "Kellye got bucked off, come quick!" We imagined the worst, jumped in the car and sped across the pasture to a grove of oak trees. She was up, crying, and appeared to just be shaken up. We spied a stream of blood on Annie's right flank and assumed a horsefly had stung her. Kellye had been sitting with both legs on the left side and when Annie bucked she hit the ground with her arms crossed. After a while she climbed back up and rode more.

The next morning we went to Park Avenue but during Sunday school Marcia was called to get Kellye. She was undoubtedly in pain. At the hospital it was determined BOTH forearms were broken and she was put in two casts! Marcia would take her to school, get her books out of her locker and take her to class. During the day teachers or friends would help her get a drink of water, carry her books, go to the restroom, etc. Marcia would pick her up and write her homework. Her six weeks' grade on penmanship was a "C". Thanks, Mom!

I really can't explain it, but Marcia and I decided to "go into the cattle business." Mr. Quirk said we could put some cows on the farm. We bought a registered Black Angus bull, a registered Black Angus cow with a calf. Mr. Francis, upon learning what we bought, said not to fool around with the "registered" bunch, just buy some good grade cattle. We bought six more cows. Bill and Kellye got an education quickly on animal husbandry. We named our bull "Buster." I kept adding to our herd. I even bought a pair of cowboy boots!

There was also a 3-room house on the farm, between the big barn and Denning Road, but several hundred yards from it. A black family had been living in it and they moved out. We all took one weekend to clean it up GOOD! We shoveled and scrubbed, painted, etc. It was made of concrete blocks with hardly any eaves on the roof at all, likely built during WWII. It was shaped like a "T" with the crossbar being on the front. Each room had an outside door and three windows that cranked open. It had a real fireplace that we thoroughly enjoyed on cold Friday nights. We would get down there about midnight and get the fire going. We'd rotate so that one or two could become toasty, while others behind them were freezing.

We had three single beds in the living room that was 25 feet long and about 12 or 14 feet wide. At the north end of the "T" was the kitchen which we'd painted a bright yellow. Marcia cooked off a 2-eye wood heater until Mrs. Francis found out about it. She gave us the electric stove out of her kitchen! A short hallway led to the back bedroom. A small bathroom was on the right off the hallway. Harvell Campbell from Park Avenue came down and installed a lavatory for us and a commode. We ran a 4 inch plastic pipe down the hill behind the house, dug a pit and put pieces of tin over it. We got a small secondhand bathtub but never hooked it up.

Benson went on a 4-day workweek (it lasted 5 years) and Marcia and I got down there Friday morning. As I walked down the hallway I caught movement to my left. There was a mama cat with a bunch of kittens. She had apparently climbed in a window where a part of the pane was broken out and had her kittens. By that time Marcia had gone in the kitchen to discover a mess. The cat had gotten into whatever she could find, tearing up a 5-lb bag of sugar even! We named her Glutton. She stayed there a few weeks then disappeared.

One day while Mammaw and Pappaw Fletcher were up visiting us, I bought six Black Angus yearlings, and borrowed some cattle racks for my GMC pickup. Pappaw went with me to transport them to the farm. I forgot to air up the rear truck tires and they were down quite a bit for the half-mile ride to a gas station. We had been putting numbered tags in our cows' ears in order to keep information on them. Push-pull and the tag was installed that quickly. I wanted that job done before I unloaded them. As I leaned forward to insert the tag in the last yearling's ear, tragedy struck! The rear end of one was up against me and the one on which I inserted the tag jumped. It scared the other one and she shot out crap all over the front of my pants, draining down into the cuffs! I thought Pappaw was going to bust a gut he was laughing so hard! I did what any old Indian would have done. I walked gingerly down to the big spring and washed them out really good, scrubbing them on a flat rock. I hung them on a wire fence to dry and then worked in my boxers till they dried. We were several hundred yards from the road anyhow.

Mr. Luther's brother was named Jesse. He took a liking to Bill like Luther had to Kellye. We let the pastures grow and hired Jesse to cut and bale hay. I think he made 1800 bales and at 50 per truck load, it took a while to get it all picked up and put in the huge barn. Kellye would grab those strings and lift it to where she could bump it with her knee and then up over her head it would go. Someone would be on the truck to stack it. Bill and Dale figured out a way to keep hay available to the cows during the week while we were gone. They got some of those wide boards and secured them to where we could stack bales of hay (the loft had a high ceiling) and, as needed, they would slide slowly down those boards into the feeders on the wall below.

One Friday night Kellye's friend at Park Avenue, Sherry Pewitt, came down. About 1 p.m. they were coming back to the barn from a moonlight ride. I had gotten a sheet and climbed up on the sloping roof of the smaller barn. Then the thought occurred to me I might spook the horses, so instead of moaning or yelling "Boo" I just stood there. They both saw me about the same time and Kellye said, "Go to bed, Daddy!" Quite often Sherry would come down with Kellye. One night the two of them galloped down Denning Road near the two UT farm houses yelling, "The British are coming! The British are coming!"

We asked Dale's parents if they wanted to help us make a garden down there. Mr. Jesse was using half of a 4-acre plot to grow a tobacco allotment on, and he said we could use the rest for a garden. The rows were about 150 YARDS long! I bought an 8-horse power garden tiller from Sears. I pulled that cord and that thing tore out across the two acres with me barely hanging on! My hat flew off and finally when I lost my footing and collapsed, the thing stopped. I discovered my right hand controlled the throttle! I should have read on to learn how to stop the dadgum thing. Maybe I wasn't cut out to be a gardener!

Then Mr. Francis told me of a 92-year-old woman who lived a couple of miles north of Spring Hill, who wanted to sell her tractor, a double turning plow and a disc. We went up there about 10 o'clock one Saturday morning and she was in the hot sun hoeing in her garden. She wanted $1,800 for the three items. Mr. Francis told me that was a good deal. The tractor was a Ford Jubilee, said to be 29 horsepower and built in the mid-50s. At the time our president was Gerald Ford, so we named our tractor Gerald.

Those turning plows did the job, too. Then Bill ran the disc over it and broke the ground up good. He got to where when he would get to the end of a row he'd hit the hydraulic lever. The disc would come up in the back causing the front two wheels to come up off the ground. He would hit the left brake and the whole thing would do a 180 degree turn. Then he'd get off the brake, hit the hydraulic lever to drop the disc on the ground and away he'd go again. It was fun to watch. We also made about a four foot wide "walk-way" mid-garden that made the rows be like 75 yards long on each side of that division.

We had some "English peas" (Snow peas, whatever) on part of the first row in the garden. We noticed something was definitely eating on them. One Saturday morning I got up to the garden just after daylight and found a big rabbit having peas for his breakfast. I shot at him with my .22 rifle. He jumped in the air but kept on eating. I shot him three times and he finally collapsed. When I picked him up I had hit him every time!

The ground hogs gave us fits in the garden, too. One time the four of us were on a western trip and stopped to eat in a café in Iowa. On the menu was a "groundhog sandwich." Well, it was pork, I guess. But I wanted Mr. Francis to see that, so I took it home with us. He got a good laugh out of it, then I mailed it back to the café and told them what I had done!

One year we had 228 hills of squash, 351 tomato plants and 300 feet of okra! We planted four 150 foot rows of potatoes and about the same in pumpkins. The kids were going to "truck farm." Then when school was out, Bill, Dale and his younger brother David got summer jobs. We parents were left literally holding the hoe! At a day-old bakery we bought 500 bread sacks and would fill them with one vegetable – like okra, squash, beans, tomatoes, whatever. And we sold them for fifty cents a bag! (Remember that was the mid-70s). We gave the kids about $200 a piece, including Kellye who had helped us. Can you believe we did that? I asked a man who came in the Broadway Benson offices one day if he wanted some pumpkins and he said, "Yeah, I'll take about nine yards worth!" Mrs. Francis' nephew later took pumpkin seed we gave him and grew some pumpkins on that same plot that won a blue ribbon at the middle Tennessee state fair! We also grew sweet potatoes that would run under the ground for a foot or so and I'd just chop them off with the shovel. In about ten yards you could fill a bushel basket with butter beans! The first time I picked okra I did not wear gloves and the next morning at church I played piano with ten band aids on! I learned the hard (ouch) way!

Kellye loved to plant seeds and hoe but when it came harvest time she was hard to locate! On Friday nights we would sit in the living room and watch "The Rockford Files" while we shelled peas or whatever! We never spent a Saturday night there because we had to be at Park Avenue early Sunday morning. I have mentioned that we had an 8:15 service, followed by Sunday school, and then a 10:45 service. Soon it became necessary to have Sunday school and the church service at the same time. A person could either go to early Sunday school or early worship service. As church pianist, it was necessary for me to play in both services.

Prior to that, for many years Marcia and I helped Gene and Anna Bea Turner in the 4-year-old department in Sunday school. I would tell the Bible story once a month and would enlarge on it... "Paul jumped in his jeep and drove over to Macedonia," etc. The kids would almost fight over who could sit by me on the piano bench. We had fun singing. One day Marcia overheard a little girl tell another one, "Oh, I saw one of your friends the other day." The other little girl asked, "You did? What color was she?"

The lady from whom I bought the tractor put her 160-acre farm up for sale. She told Mr. Francis she wanted to move to Nashville and for him to be on the lookout for a place – but he had to keep two things in mind. The rooms had to have ceilings at least eight feet tall to accommodate her antiques like her bed headboard. And she wanted an acre or two so she could set out some fruit trees! She was 92! Well, two burglars broke in on her one night and demanded money. She said she didn't have any. They slapped her a time or two, and left! When she was a hundred years old her maid of 60 years, shot her twice and killed her. She was convicted.

In the early spring the cows began having calves. We were in business! Mr. Harold Slaten, a deacon at Park Avenue church had a 40-acre farm west of town on Hwy 100. He also ran a community grocery store in Sylvan Park not far from Park Avenue. When we would see each other on Sunday morning across the sanctuary we'd hold up fingers as to how many new calves had been born that week! Late one afternoon we discovered one cow was in distress. Bill rode to get Sam and Francis Smith across the road. His brother was a veterinarian. Sam discovered the calf was breach (feet coming out first). He was able to turn the calf and literally pull it out. Marcia tore some strips of cloth and Francis cleaned out its mouth, cupped her hands and blew into its mouth. The calf would be okay but the cow left the scene! Sam told us to round her up and get her in a stall in the big barn. He picked up the calf and carried it, perhaps 30 yards or more, to the stall. We all headed after the cow and somehow managed to get her through the briar patches to the barn as well. But she refused to have anything to do with that newborn calf! Sam said the calf needed that first milk. He tried to hold it up to suck with very little success.

We thanked them for all they had done for us rookies and they went home. It was already dark. We watched TV for a while then about 10 p.m. Marcia and I lit a lantern and walked through Spring Valley back to the barn stall. I put my left knee against the calf's rump and with my right hand tried to raise its mouth to suck. I became exhausted. Marcia said, "Here, let me see if I can do it." The minute she entered that stall, the cow cut her off and began licking the calf and letting it suck! Marcia said she guessed the cow sensed Marcia was a mother, or something like that and she took to her calf and protected it. After that everything was okay. One year we had a cow to birth twins; another cow had two calves in one calendar year which is rather unusual.

It came time to give the yearlings their "black leg" shots. We all rounded them up out of the pasture into the big barn. Then Bill and Dale would alternate bringing one out at a time and throw them to the ground where I would pop him/her with the shot. They told me there was one more in the hallway of the barn. Dale drawled, "I'm gonna let you have that one, Bill." Soon the double barn doors flung open and out came Bill, both feet in the air in front of him, holding to the neck of that overgrown calf. Dust was a-flyin'! It took both of them to get him on the ground and when I went to administer the shot he flinched and I almost gave it to Dale in **his** leg. I told him at least he wouldn't have had to worry about getting black leg!

Mr. Quirk picked out about ten of our animals to send to the sale barn in Columbia. He even used his truck. One steer had caused us a lot of trouble. He was the last one to be loaded and he obviously did not want to make the trip! In the stall he leaped over a half-wall and had he turned left he would have gone free, but he turned right and was still in the stall, stomping his front feet and eyeing me. Mr. Quirk said, "If I was you, I'd git outta that stall!" I did. Then we called a friend in Nashville and he was down there in a couple of hours and put a 30.06 bullet between his eyes. In an hour he had him strung up and quartered. Every bite Bill and Kellye would say, "Good ol' Butch!"

One night the strangest thing happened. We had entered the gate to the hundred acres and started driving down the curving road through the pasture toward the house. Suddenly everything lit up like it was high noon, for at least several seconds. We never heard anything about it, maybe it was a meteor, falling star or something like that. It was weird and scary. I drew a map of the hundred acres and named sections so when we talked we would know where we were talking about!

Plus there were screech owls down there that could chill your blood. A lady, "Doodles" Miller would come down a lot. She drove a big Cadillac. Kellye and Sherry would sometimes ride down with her. One Saturday afternoon we had to get back early and left Doodles, Kellye and Sherry down there. Doodles insisted on cooking supper and as it was getting dark, a screech owl hollered very close by. It sounded like a woman was getting murdered out in the back yard! The girls insisted Doodles stop cooking so they could "git outta Dodge" immediately, if not sooner!

Once we were using our Ford tractor and it got stuck. The next weekend when we got down there we found Sam had rescued it with his big John Deere and had it parked under the machinery shed, cleaned up and ready to use again. Dale, Bill and I went over and helped Sam get his hay bales in his barn. They were stacked high on his wagon and for some reason I was riding on TOP. He went down a slight incline and the load shifted. I rode "the tide" down to the ground. Then we had to reload because it still wasn't to his barn yet! The Smiths became great friends and often helped us out a lot.

Bill and Kellye invited their friends from Park Avenue to come down on Friday nights and Saturdays and of course they wanted to ride horses. We bought two from Kathy Batson's parents (she was Bill's girlfriend at the time). It was a mare (Sugar) and her filly (Chica), both white Arabians. Then we went over to Haines Haven to look at one. That is the property where the Saturn plant was later built. However, they did not raze the old southern-style home, barns, etc. Her name was Molly and she was a brown and white paint. They were asking $350. About that time a girl in a riding outfit rode by on a big horse with its bobbed tail. I said, "I'm just wondering how much that one is?" The man answered, "Thirty thousand!" I pointed at Molly and said, "I believe I'll take this one." Soon after that we bought a black and white paint (Lady). She was stout and short in length and had a colt we named Sundance.

Bill loved Chica and rode her a lot instead of Misty. Late one afternoon we discovered our registered Black Angus bull (Buster) had broken through the old wire fence in the back pasture. He was fraternizing with a herd of Holstein cows next door to us, on a 350-acre farm owned by George Jones and

Tammy Wynette. Her Dad ran the dairy, but sometimes we would look over there (another colonial home) and see a big Fleetwood Cadillac and figured one or both were over there. That house is where General Hood was when the Battle of Franklin was raging. It is said he was drunk!

It was November and a storm was moving in. It began to rain lightly. Bill and I were riding horses trying to head our bull back through the gap in the fence – should have known it couldn't be done! We were "using the fence" to help herd him along when suddenly he veered off and around the pond. Bill and Chica cut **through** the pond to head him off. Bill said he suddenly realized that Chica was swimming! We eventually had to take down a section of fence so that (bleep) bull would go back on "our" property.

We wasted money buying four saddles. The kids would put a halter on the horse, grab some mane and swing up on them like a wild Indian. They liked to let the horses stand in a creek at the south end of the farm and the kids would dive off their rumps. Also the youth from church came down a few times. The girls wanted to sleep on our hay wagon (bought new from a Mr. Robertson in Dickson County). Bill and Dale gave them time to drop off to sleep then lifted the tongue to give them a wild ride. So a chaperone took the girls to the big barn to sleep on the hay. Our big dog Major was down with us. After a while the lady said, "Alright, Bill, I know you're around here somewhere, I can see Major's ears!"

Just off the Francis farm was an OLD cemetery. Some hogs had rooted all over it and tombstones were tilted and turned over.

One said, "Pvt. Holland, Tennessee Volunteers 1824." Another was made of concrete about an inch wide with a rounding top on it that simply had the word "Mother" on it. There was an area enclosed by an iron fence. It could have been the graves of the ones that lived on the Francis farm. There was a big tombstone for the man, and on either side were graves. One was his wife and the other was his consort (or companion). We took the youth over there around midnight. Bill and Dale had been small trees over and tied cans on them. When they walked by they'd cut the string and they'd make a loud noise, scaring the youth. We also took them on a hayride. We told them to stay ON the wagon. But one girl bailed out just as we went to cross a little stream and she slid all the way down the bank! Later on we also had the young married (our age) to come down and they behaved worse than the youth, especially on the hayride!

I liked to ride a horse, stand up in the stirrups of the saddle and try to count my herd! We had a total of 86 head of Black Angus cattle and it was a pretty sight. I was on Annie (the big sorrel that Mrs. Francis bought for Kellye) when she decided to head for the barn. I saw she was heading for the burdock trees. We called them "bodock", and they had big thorns on them. So I pulled back on the reigns and yelled "Whoa!" Annie planted her front feet and I promptly sailed over her left ear. I bounced three times while in a fetal position and my hairpiece never came loose!

Mr. Francis had all those bodock trees bulldozed and piled up. With his permission I was going to burn them. I sprinkled some gasoline around and threw the match in. It flared up and we were enjoying the sight (it had gotten dark) when I saw the 5-gallon gas can still sitting there. I guess it was foolish, but I swooped in and got it out safely, PTL. But another time I was going to burn some woodpiles in the pasture in back of the house. I sprinkled gasoline around, then wadded up newspaper and poked it in…I should not have done that. When I struck the match the explosion tumbled me back head over heels. My eyebrows and forearms were scorched.

Marcia was called to Lufkin, TX, because her mother was in the hospital. Johnnie, Marcia's sister, kept her at their home as long as she could but eventually the doctor told us she had to enter a nursing home. Marcia flew down there and I was left to work and care for Bill and Kellye. We went on down to the farm and worked that Saturday but Bill got to feeling bad with a sore throat. We headed back home where I stopped by a drugstore in our neighborhood and got some medicine that the pharmacist recommended. When we got home and got out of the truck I dropped it and it broke, so we had to go back for more.

At some time, I discovered I had left my hairpiece down at the farm! Why did I wear it in the first place? I wasn't about to go to church the next morning without it! I got Bill and Kellye in bed then took off down there to get it…an 84-mile round trip. Solomon was right…all is vanity!

This reminds me of the time our church treasurer, L. C. Green, bought his first hairpiece. He was completely bald. He sidled around the door facing to pay for supper on Wednesday night and everyone saw him! But one night he was driving on Lafayette

Street and was rear-ended by a dump truck. It knocked his hairpiece off and it apparently flew over on the passenger side. The truck driver ran up to the window and said, "Hey, man, you okay?" L. C. was bending over feeling around on the floor. He straightened and said, "Yeah, I'm just looking for my hair." The man exclaimed, "(bleep) man, you ain't got no hair!"

One Friday Marcia and I went to the farm and worked in the garden. We needed to get back earlier than usual and I needed a shower. Earlier we had hooked up a piece of garden hose to the lavatory and hung it out the bathroom window that was high up off the ground. That location was quite private. But I guarantee, before you stepped under that hose with running water from that big (cold) spring, you'd better EXHALE because when it hit you, you would have a gigantic intake of breath!

We were several hundred yards from Denning Road, plus there were hills and trees. That was about the time the college kids were "streaking", so...yes, I DID! I went tearing around the front of the house. Marcia was sitting there reading. She looked up and said, "Go get dressed, we need to go!" The honeymoon was over.

We watched the Alfred Hitchcock movie "The Birds" one Friday night at the farm house which made it hard to go to sleep! This is the truth - Saturday morning we woke up to find a black bird flying around inside the house! I guess it somehow got through that same broken window. We opened the front door but while trying to shoo it out, he demolished the flimsy curtains we had put up in the living room.

And that brings to mind...as part of our sprucing up the inside of the house we bought some rolls of wallpaper and glued them to the ceiling, leaving an equal distance between each one showing the white ceiling. To us it looked great and we were proud. Next morning we got up to find most of them hanging by one end from the ceiling, so then we had to clean it all up and ditch that brilliant idea.

Mrs. Mary Taylor (Mimi) came down quite often on Friday afternoons. Sometimes she would bring a big oblong pan of pork chops in gravy. Her husband Don, a Metro fireman died from a heart attack, in his late 40s I believe. They had two daughters. They were always having a bunch of youth over to their house on Murphy Road, including Kellye and Sherry. On Saturday we would work in the garden, but Marcia and Mary Lee McWright would quit early and go to the house to fix "dinner." One of us would volunteer to ask the blessing but if they prayed too long we would say, "Scratch Dale," (or whoever). We wanted FOOD! Along with the meat we had fresh vegetables. Mimi passed away in the summer of 2012 and Mary Lee McWright passed away in the spring of 2013.

The fox squirrels (reddish with bushy tails) were smart, no, they were deceptive! We would go to pick corn and find most of the kernels had been eaten, but the shuck had been pulled back up around it. Kellye and I were taking the chain off the wide garden gate early one morning when we heard a loud "plop" behind us. As we whirled around we saw a mouse racing away from a big black snake. They had undoubtedly fallen out of a tree by the gate.

For Bill's sixteenth birthday we gave him a "Sweet Sixteen" shotgun. He promptly shot a big fox squirrel like Pappaw Fletcher taught him. When we were growing up we ate a lot of squirrels. He proudly told Mr. Francis at church the next day and he exploded, "Don't you be shootin' MY squirrels!" One cold day on the farm we looked out in the field behind the house and there was a man and (I guess) his two sons, hunting. I yelled that Mr. Francis didn't allow anyone hunting on his farm. The man said that didn't matter to him. They had a bunch of rabbits. I told Mr. Francis at church Sunday and he was quite furious. He knew who they were.

Mr. Francis had a big McCullough chainsaw, and it was heavy. I sawed down a big tree for him one day that was obviously dead. We tried to "keep up" the farm for him, but the fences were in bad need of repair or replacement. One morning we woke up and looked out our back bedroom window. There were about fifteen strange looking cows, not Black Angus. I lifted my eyes upward and said, "Thank you, Lord!" Marcia said, "You know we can't keep those cows." Later that morning a neighbor, a Mr. Reed came over to reclaim his cows! Then we had to find the breach and repair it as best we could. It's strange how we got to "know" our cows. Mr. Quirk certainly knew his. One day we noticed another strange one in the herd and she looked like the devil. She had short horns, too! We named her Devilena. I honestly don't know what happened to her.

We sold some cows at the Columbia Livestock Auction barn, and when they were tested, one "banged" out on us, meaning she had brucellosis. It affects milk, not meat. We were alerted that the "government man" would be out on a certain date to test our entire herd. Marcia and I went down on a weekday and walked all over that hundred acres rounding them up. It was cold and overcast. I hung the toe of my boot on a tree root and sprawled down in the branch coming from the big spring. We must have had maybe sixty head then.

The test showed six were positive and their jaw was branded with an "S", meaning "suspect." They were sent to market. The man came back in six weeks (we had to round them up again) and I believe four showed they were positive. We just called the Columbia Livestock barn and they sent out three trucks. We sold them all but one which we put in the freezer. We were OUT of the cattle business, *we thought.* We'd bought when prices were high and had to sell when they were low.

BENSON MOVES TO METRO-CENTER

I believe it was in June of 1976 that the Benson Company made the move to the new building they built in MetroCenter, an 800-acre plot along the south bank of the Cumberland River three miles north of downtown. Ten acres had been purchased and it set on half of them. It was two big warehouses with very high ceilings, offset perhaps 20 yards or so and perpendicular to the river. In between on the second and third floors was office space. On the first floor was where stock was kept, the shipping department and three loading docks. At the front of the western-most building was the recording studio, said to be the best in town for the string sound. I was involved with several recording projects there over several years even after I left Benson.

My office was on the third floor on the west side overlooking the Cumberland. Often I would see river boats with several barges going up or down. Sometimes in staff meetings I would become so frustrated I could hardly keep my emotions in check until I got back to my office. Upon telling Marcia about hitting my desk with my closed fist, she bought me a little 6-inch rubber man for me to hit instead, and he ricocheted off the walls many times! In 1979 I was diagnosed with occupational stress and high blood pressure, and early in 1981 I retired after being affiliated with Benson over 30 years. I continued to do work for them another 17 years, however.

A SUDDEN DEATH

We had been using the Francis farm for five-plus years when suddenly one morning in 1976, Mr. Francis fell dead in his bathroom. Their house was directly across from the entrance to Hillwood Country Club in West Nashville. They had no children. I played the organ at Park Avenue for the big funeral.

They had given so much money to Park Avenue toward the purchase of lots on Charlotte Avenue where our new sanctuary was to be built that it was named "Francis Auditorium." Our family purchased brass letters about ten inches high that read "Francis Auditorium". They were placed on the wall in the spacious lobby between the two entrances. Mimi Taylor gave money that specifically paid for the baptistery in memory of her husband, Don.

Mr. Francis' death changed our situation. We felt we should get off the farm and started looking for another one. We found one down in Humphreys County. It was 70 acres – half pasture, half woods, with a small barn and a pond. It was in the Bold Springs community and about eight miles from Loretta Lynn's place. Our exit off I-40 was called Bucksnort, perhaps 65 miles west of our Parkwood Estates home. One Saturday Marcia and I, along with Mammaw Fletcher made two round trips between the Francis farm and our "Bucksnort farm," moving the four horses we had. We traveled a total of 280 miles on curvy, almost-mountainous roads. The three of us were quite tired that night!

I honestly don't know why...but we bought another Black Angus bull, four cows and three calves and put them on that farm. We bought a house trailer for $3,500 from its location at Nashville Shores (on Percy Priest Lake east of town), had it moved down and set up. It was nice, with a raised living room, shag carpeting and a free-standing wood stove. It had a nice kitchen, washer-dryer combo, nice bathroom, and a king-size bed in the bedroom. We got a man to drill a well close by for $2,500. He said he must have hit an underground river. Water shot in the air with enough "for the city of Nashville." He had to get a dozer to pull his rig out!

It looked like we were set up on our own farm...but we got down there one Saturday and discovered our herd was missing. We found where they'd broken through the fence. Our neighbor owned 4,500 acres and told us there was a wild herd on it that he couldn't even round up to take to market. Bill, Kellye, Tommy (her boyfriend who was the center for Cohn high school football team) and I got bridles for the four horses and mounted up – no saddles - to try to find them. Bill thought he spied them and we took off. But we got to a steep hill and just gave up. Bill was pulling back yelling at Misty but she couldn't hear him because he had slid down/up on her neck covering her ears! We took them all off our income tax that year as a loss.

Then the gas crunch descended on the nation. Kellye got to where she didn't want to go down and Bill was in Middle Tennessee University so Marcia and I were left "holding the bag" again. Mr. Harold Slayton took his truck and I took ours and we hauled twenty crossties down and made a bridge over a "wash" just inside the front gate. One snowy day I got a phone call while working at Benson from our neighbor, Mr. Reynolds, who said our horses were out of the pasture and standing in the dirt road. It so happened that Bill and Tommy could go with me and we were successful in getting them back through the gate. Then we had to find out how they got out. We had to shout at each other as we trudged through the six inch crusted snow and ice. Oh, the joys of farm life!

We had paid $250 an acre in 1976 for the Bucksnort farm… unbelievable, huh? In 1985 we decided to sell it and a couple in Arizona bought it at $450 an acre, sight unseen. Of course the trailer and the well went with it. We'd owned it for nine years. Out of the farm business? Nope! I forgot to mention that we had already concluded it was too far from our house, so we had bought a twenty acre farm just south of Dickson, about 35 miles from us. We called it the "Dickson farm." It had about a three acre pond on it in the shape of a comma and a high earthen dam. It also had beautiful oak trees. We had hoped to have a contractor build maybe five nice houses around the lake, but that didn't happen.

Marcia and I fished down there a few times. Twice, about a year apart, Marcia caught a two pound catfish. She jerked that pole up and that poor fish went sailing over her head as she backed up and stumbled flat on her back! Both times! I don't remember how long we'd owned the "Dickson" farm, but we sold both of them in 1985. They were just tax shelters anyhow...we made one annual payment.

We believe our years "of farm/country living" helped keep our family close together. We surely had a lot of happy days and nights together and learned a lot, too.

THE GIFT

While Bill was in Vanderbilt Hospital in 1976, after our morning worship service at Park Avenue, Mrs. Francis came to me and said, "Mr. Mercer, I want to give you all a house." I smiled and said, "Well, that's mighty – you WHAT?" She smiled and repeated it and said "When do you and Marcia want to go look at it?" I said, "How 'bout tomorrow!" And so we did.

It is located twelve miles west of downtown Nashville in Thousand Oaks Estates at 301 Forrest Valley Drive. It is the last house on the right and sits up on a hill with a steeper hill immediately behind it. It was a split-level on an acre and a half lot. Adjoining it was 48.22 acres and she gave us that, too! The deed states, "Due to my affection for Marcia and Elmo Mercer..." They had owned a hundred acre plot of land that fronted on Sawyer Brown Road (the popular band was named after that road!). Interstate 40 went right through it. They had no access to the acres on the north side. When the 301 FVD house went on the market they bought it.

When Bobby Welch was our associate pastor at Park Avenue, he and his family lived in that house. Later, friends of ours from Jacksonville, FL lived there for two years. Lee and Dianne Turner had songs published by Benson, including a children's work called "They All Sang Jesus." In more recent years, his song "Glory, Hallelujah, Jubilee!" was sung by the Billy Graham choirs in various crusades. George Beverly Shea recorded his song, "Who Moved?" Lee can play any style of piano from classical to rag-time. He had hoped to become a Nashville union musician in demand for recording sessions. Ten percent of the local musicians do ninety percent of the studio work, and he never could break into that business. They moved back to Jacksonville.

Thousand Oaks Estates is accessed off Charlotte Pike (US-70 North), one mile west of Old Hickory Boulevard, off I-40 Exit 199. Well, needless to say we were just flabbergasted that Mrs. Francis wanted to do this for us. As I said, they had no children and she gave the farm we had been on to her nephew, who built a nice home on it and installed new fences. She told us, "I want you to move in as soon as you can, and don't sell it while I'm living. Maybe it will make you some money someday!"

About a year earlier we had added a 20x21 upstairs den to the back of our house on Masonwood Drive in Parkwood Estates where it was a 26-mile round trip to Park Avenue church. Marcia kind of hated to leave it, but a house and fifty acres had just been GIVEN to us! The property taxes on the house and land was much more than our annual house payment, but we felt God had a plan! So we packed up, rented a truck and with the help of some of Bill and Kellye's friends made the move. We believe one main reason she did this was so Kellye could attend Bellevue High School. It was the second highest academic school in town. In the spring of 1980 she graduated. The high school closed so the following fall she could not return to football games or whatever! It became the Bellevue Middle School and later our Nashville grandchildren attended it.

Mrs. Francis had always been very fond of Kellye, buying her expensive clothes and things like that. When PABC was selling bonds to finance the new building, she bought a thousand dollar bond and gave it to her.

Now as we look back, we can also see that the rent income from the two cell phone towers up on the ridge helped us to take our music ministry to small town and rural churches, where we asked only that a "love offering" be taken for us. Isn't God amazing!

THE 3 A.M. PHONE CALL

In addition to the WHACHAMACALLITS (choir clinics) that were held at Lake Barkley Resort in SW Kentucky, Benson hosted other retreats. We held a bookstore dealer retreat, introducing them to new product plus having seminars to help them learn how to improve their business, create ads for radio, TV and newspapers, etc. We also had artists' retreats where folks got to be together, exchanging ideas, plans and stories. This was done for several years, and it was like a vacation for Marcia and me.

I guess this happened in 1976 when Kellye was up there with us for one night. About 3 a.m. the phone in our room rang. We knew something was wrong and when Marcia said, "Hello," she heard Bill say, "Mom?" and then the line went dead. That scared the pepper sauce out of us! Did the house burn down, was Bill in jail, or back in the hospital? WHAT?

After a few agonizing minutes the phone rang again. A few weeks earlier, Bill had a fender bender on MTSU campus and we had taken the Firebird to a repair shop near downtown. They parked it in their lot but left the keys in the ignition! Duh! It had been stolen. The Metro police saw a rear taillight was out due to the wreck and attempted to pull the driver over. He floored it. Bill and the cops knew each other by first names! These two probably thought they were chasing Bill. They told him later they were topping out at 120 mph on East Nashville streets and he was pulling away from them! So that's what that $1100 did to Bill's Firebird!!!

Not knowing where he was, but getting there fast, the boy headed down into Shelby Park along the Cumberland River. There were icy spots everywhere and he slid into a tree. The passenger side was crunched in to the console! The car spun out on the frozen lake. The boy leaped out and attempted to run, as did the police. It must have looked like the Keystone Cops. The car broke through the ice and it blew the engine.

The boy (from Kentucky) was apprehended and the police phoned Bill to come to the precinct. He was calling so I could talk to the police and tell them that it was indeed our son's car and that the boy had no right to be driving it. We didn't even have to press charges...Metro did.

And what did we do? We special-ordered him a new 1977 Olds 442, black and red, his favorite colors. Is that kinda dumb, or what? We didn't have to do anything to that car...it came HOT from the factory. A lot of NASCAR drivers drove them back then. He and I repainted his bedroom walls black and red, leaving three 2-inch white strips horizontally, then did a 45 degree upward slant to connect with the back window and reversed the colors on the other two walls. We got him black and red (shag) carpeting.

FUNERALS

Bro. Bob Mowrey, our pastor at Park Avenue, asked me to sing at the graveside service for a 100-year-old woman one day. I had to do it a cappella and it was at the huge Woodlawn cemetery in south Nashville. I made it alright and Bro. Bob was nearing the end of his short comments when seemingly from out of nowhere came a terrific wind gust. Perhaps a cold front was coming through and that was down-drafts. It blew the flowers over, and the tent collapsed. Frankly, we all took off, leaving that dear lady there.

While we were living in Winnfield, LA, I played for two military funerals a few years apart at the same church! Coulee Methodist Church was about 15 miles west of town on US-84. I will never forget the bugle playing taps. Another man was perhaps a hundred yards away in the woods and he echoed what the graveside bugle played. It chilled your blood but also made you feel so proud and patriotic.

Just around the curve from there was Lakeside Baptist Church. One day Pappaw Fletcher was driving by and needed to use the bathroom. Churches were not locked back in those days, so he walked in. When he tried to come back out the door was locked – it absolutely would not open. He had to climb out a window! I couldn't believe he even told us about it!

A 'CAROL BURNETT' WEDDING

I've played for hundreds of weddings and hundreds of funerals in my lifetime. I'm reminded of many stories, some of them humorous. This one tops them all, and it is TRUE.

In September 1975 a couple in their mid-30s came to Bro. Bob and talked with him about conducting their wedding. Both had been married previously but after talking with them he agreed to do it. It was to be a small wedding with family and close friends, and was to be held in the Smith Wall chapel of our church.

At the short rehearsal the night before the man asked Bro. Bob, "How about the kiss?" Bro. Bob chuckled and said he'd performed weddings for many years but had never been asked about the kissing part! He said, "I'll tell you when it's time to kiss your bride." Well...we *should* have rehearsed it!

At the end of the ceremony Bro. Bob smiled, nodded his head and said, "I believe it's time for that kiss!" Friends, that ol' boy grabbed ahold of her and bent her over backwards and commenced kissing on her for maybe 15 seconds? I thought I was watching the Carol Burnett Show on TV. Bro. Bob looked at me and nodded for me to play the recessional or Yankee Doodle - anything to break 'em apart! I realized my mouth was hanging open while my eyes bulged out.

Finally I started playing and they broke and went out, for air, probably! As it turns out, about 4 p.m. that afternoon my brother Earl had phoned me that our Daddy had passed away. But I stayed to play for that wedding. I told Bro. Bob, then picked up Marcia, Bill and Kellye and we drove all night to get home.

But wait! There is a second verse to this true story. The girl had told me earlier, "I want you to play a song at my wedding. I think Bill Gaither wrote it and it goes something like, 'I just feel like something good is about to happen,' do you know that?" I am serious. I thought to myself, "Reckon so, I made the first arrangement!" My quick mind jumped from the gutter and through barely controlled lips I said, "Yeah, but wait! You told me you wanted background music downstairs during the reception? Why don't I play it then?" She said that would be perfect. I kept my word but "embellished" it as much as I could. Lyndal came over and hit me on the shoulder and said, "You dog! What ARE you playing?" I told her the bride had asked me to play it. She didn't believe me, but I believe Gaither would have been proud.

A PRAYER MEETING TO REMEMBER

Friends, this is a true story! In prayer meeting one night at Park Avenue, from my place at the piano I looked at Marcia sitting in the choir. She ran her forefinger under her nose and with her eyes and jerk of her head, plainly indicated to me that I should sit with Bob Ward and Todd Zeiger. They always sat on the center front bench, "at the feet of Bro. Bob," as it were. I realized then that a couple and their daughter (I spoke of them earlier) were in the service. All three of them were mentally challenged. The daughter, perhaps in her 30s, sat on the front pew over on the wall side where I usually went after the song service. Well, I had never gone and sat on the middle front pew before. I didn't want it to be so obvious, so I decided to simply sit on the aisle side of the same bench. God, I wish I had done what Marcia told me to do (and I am talking TO God when I say that)!

Remember we would usually have 400 in prayer meeting with 35 or so in the choir. That night when the special music was done, I went and sat down on the aisle side of the pew, thinking I would surely be safe there. Wrong! We had no cushions, just polished, slick wood to sit on. I settled back and looked up at Bro. Bob, ready to receive the message. The next thing I knew something slammed against the left side of my body! I was told later she stood up, took a couple of quick steps and hit the pew sliding in for a landing!

Well, I looked around, startled to say the least, and our noses were four inches apart. She looked at me like, "I gotchu now, baby!" An object crashed inside my stomach and I knew immediately it was my heart. Silently I prayed…no, silently I yelled, "HELP ME, GOD!"

Bobby Sadler (Bus Ministry Director) and his wife Joyce were sitting right behind me. When I turned back to look up at Bro. Bob, in my peripheral vision I could see his red head shaking, hardly two inches above the aisle carpet. I knew all 400 people in that congregation had seen what just happened, and were watching to see how I would manage the situation. I crossed my right leg over my left knee…my cowboy boot prominently protruding out between us. I also put my left hand on my beltline, swinging my elbow out for upper protection. I was thinking, hoping, *praying* that the neutral zone would hold. I became very interested in Bro. Bob's sermon, saying a nervous "Amen" here and there, I hoped at the right places. Or perhaps I would laugh, again hoping it was at the right place, because actually I wasn't hearing a word he said! I was *crying out to the*

*God of all Ages! The same God that delivered Daniel from the lion's den, and the three Hebrew children from the fiery furnace, and....*well, you get the picture. *Don't you see me down here, God? I'm dead if you don't send help, like NOW!*

I felt movement on my cowboy boot and just had to look. She was running her finger along the design on the upper side of my boot. I mean, how sexy can you get? I jerked my leg down and looked back up at the pastor. He later told me he did not realize what was going on. I told him he might as well preach that sermon again because there wasn't a person present who heard a word he said, including Bobby Sadler.

Sensing movement again (Hey, my "senses" were on HIGH alert...and going higher every second!), I cut my eyes over in her direction and found she was leaning forward and just looking at me! After a while she grew quiet and I chanced another look. Folks, I am telling you the truth. She apparently had the "makings" and had rolled her a cigarette, just licking it as I looked. She dropped the tobacco sack down her bosom! I almost died! IF she had a-lit up, I know I would have.

The choir was watching the show, too. Marcia just had a smile on her face. Even Bob and Todd were having trouble controlling themselves. I knew the feeling for I was having the same problem. This had to be the way Wendy Bagwell felt as he looked for a back door in that snake-handling church service!

Bobby Sadler told me later that she put her arm on the back of the pew behind me. Had I known that, Lord help me, I honestly have no idea what my reaction would have been! Where was my guardian angel?

Mercifully, invitation time came and I shot up to the piano bench, hoping surely she would not follow me up there. Bro. Bob selected, "Since Jesus Came into my Heart" and when we started singing, the girl began to clap her hands and sway with the beat. Her skirt was three or four inches above her knees and SHE was also wearing cowboy boots! She was in her element. Bob Ward noticed her and unconsciously started swaying along with her.

After the service one of the church bus drivers got a "delegation" together and approached me. He had acquired a little golden trophy of some kind, likely used in VBS, set it on a hymnal and said, "Bro. Elmo, we would like to present this trophy to you for your cool performance tonight." I said, "Cool nothing. I was froze stiff!"

Now, in order for me to get from choir rehearsal in the basement to the grand piano on the opposite side of the auditorium, I had to pass through a church office and go behind the baptistery. I saw a rolled-up umbrella on a desk and grabbed it, holding it up like a club. I slowly opened the stained glass swinging doors, poked my head in and looked over the crowd. As I walked to the rostrum carrying my "weapon" and sat down on the piano bench, a murmuring swept over the congregation.

Just sitting here typing this, I have re-lived the entire episode! On to brighter memories!

DEBUT OF "MO'S BAND"

On New Year's Eve, Park Avenue always had a big party – a musical extravaganza of church talent plus a big chili supper in the dining room downstairs. On one of those nights, we were still in the old auditorium, and the debut of "Mo's Band" occurred. Others were singing songs like "How Great Thou Art", etc. We decided to do something different, <u>very different.</u>

We opened with "The Wabash Cannonball", featuring Dave Dunham on sax. At the time he was playing and singing backup with Sonny James. Then we slowed it down and I was featured on the piano doing "Moon River" (lyrics by *cousin* Johnny Mercer) in Floyd Cramer style. The little old ladies were falling out in the aisles! Our closing number was "Alley Cat," featuring the whole band.

As we finished eating downstairs some ladies came to me and asked, "Can y'all play some more when we get back upstairs?" I said, not too reluctantly, "Well, we did rehearse one more… Let's go!" We tried to get back upstairs before too many came in. We played "The Stripper", but those ladies didn't know what it was, and neither did Bro. Bob! We rocked it on down. Instead of praying in the New Year like we did in Louisiana, we blasted it in. A Mr. Johnson always did fantastic fireworks at midnight – that was before Metro banned them.

Many years later we got another band together with some different personnel, for a big show in the gym. We imitated different singers and bands. We had a spotlight on the featured acts, and even showed lyrics on the back wall, while the crowd thought we had memorized it all. On the platform, each member of the band had their own music stand with a big piece of white pasteboard bearing the cursive initials "MB" We had matching costumes. I made the arrangements for both instrumentals and vocals. Hey, somebody had to take Lawrence Welk's place, right?

We had "The Andrews Sisters." "Frank Sinatra," with fedora, came strolling in under the spotlight, doing "New York, New York." It was Ron, Rayford Hilley's brother, who was a New York Opera backup singer for many years. And I, of course, was Floyd Cramer on the piano as well as the emcee for the evening. I can't remember what all we did do, which is probably just as well.

Leroy Armstrong was a genial blind man at Park Avenue who sang bass in the choir. He could bust the bottom out of a double low C, and he learned songs, even cantatas, quicker than sighted people! One Sunday morning Marcia was coming from Sunday school over to the new sanctuary when she saw Leroy with his cane trying to find his way. She took him by the arm and they talked as she brought him down the aisle. He commented, "Just wait till tomorrow when I tell folks at work that the *purtiest* girl in town was seen walking me down the church aisle!" Marcia said, "Now, Leroy, you don't know but what I'm the *ugliest* woman in this church!" I played many times for him to sing. One of my favorites was the old song, "The Ninety and Nine."

Another blind man was Billy Manning. He had a mellow voice very much like Jim Reeves. I accompanied him when he sang and the congregation always gave him a loud standing ovation. Bubba Campbell and I were helping him down the steps to his seat and I'd say, "Billy, they're all standing up for you, man!" He'd say, "For me?" Both Leroy and Billy have passed to their heavenly home.

GMA IN CA

For a while in the early 70s I was a member of the GMA (Gospel Music Association) Board of Directors. We flew out to Los Angeles for a particular meeting. Hal Spencer (son of Tim, Sons of the Pioneers and movie star) was the host and was late for the first meeting. It was pouring rain...and you know it "never rains in southern California."

I don't know how it came about...maybe the night before it was raining and we all bought sunglasses, but when Hal walked in the room we were all sitting around the long table with our shades on! He said, "Aw, come on, fellas!"

Hal owned Manna Music, Inc., and they were instrumental in getting "How Great Thou Art" translated from Swedish to English. The arrangement was copyrighted, printed and distributed by Manna Music. By the way, other beautiful Swedish songs are, "Day by Day," and "Filandia (Be Still, my Soul)."

Around that period of time, I was on the Nashville Songwriters Association International Board of Directors. Others on that board were "Whispering" Bill Anderson, Mrs. Danny Davis (Danny's band was called the Nashville Brass, I believe), she was the widow of Jim Reeves, Wesley Rose of Acuff-Rose Publishers who owned Hank Williams' songs, Maggie Cavendar, a remarkable woman, and I believe Tom T. Hall ("Harper Valley PTA" and other hit songs). As an employee at Benson, I was a member of NARAS and voted on who got "grammys." I had been inducted into ASCAP, the American Society of Composers, Authors and Publishers, in July 1957. God has been good!

SNOWS ON FVD

In 1976 we had four address changes – house, farm, church and work! We moved into the house Mrs. Francis gave us at 301 Forrest Valley Drive in August 1976. We were told our street name had two "r's" in it because it was named after Confederate General Nathan Bedford Forrest.

A half mile off Charlotte Pike our street starts curving left as it comes over a hill and is still curving at our driveway where it stops. It amounts to a 90 degree turn! The old woven wire fence that came down the hill on the east SIDE of our house actually becomes the BACK fence for the houses going toward the entrance to Thousand Oaks Estates. We cleared out that fence and cut trees and bushes and expanded the width of the front yard. It is probably a 20 to 25% grade and great for sledding. A few years ago we had to have installed a new copper water pipe. The plumber said it was 60 yards from the meter up to the house. The leak was discovered to be under our concrete driveway. The snow melted where the leak was!

Bill and Kellye had sleds, of course. Their friends from Park Avenue would come out to our house. We would build a bonfire at the bottom of our yard and roast wieners and marshmallows. And it would be freezing cold! I was right out there with them till midnight or later knowing I had to be at work the next morning at Benson. There were six persimmon trees, two at a time that made a perfect route to go down in the front yard. One boy bailed off his sled and wrapped himself around a tree trunk at the bottom.

We all sledded a lot. We would take off at the top of the hill on our street where it was a half mile to the entrance off Charlotte Pike. The track was better if it had melted some during the day, then frozen back. And then you would go fast! I would drive down in my '79 Ford F-250 4-wheel drive pickup and bring them back up to do it all again.

One night I just had to try sledding for myself. I shoved off from the top of the hill lying flat on my stomach. As the road curved I realized I was going much too fast, and this is at night. Too late to do anything now and I wasn't about to bail out! Ice was thick and I hit a contrary rut that shot me off toward a neighbor's driveway header. Arms and legs were flying everywhere and I knew they were mine! I crashed, was shook up, but okay!

The next day (Sunday afternoon) after lunch, Bill and I went out. I had him go down the hill on his sled and I drove the truck perhaps 20 yards behind him, keeping equal distance. I got up to 35 mph! I guess that's how fast I was going when I crashed the night before. Some of the kids would go up Forrest

Valley Court about a hundred yards and start from up there. The problem was negotiating the turn onto the main road. Some of them left only one set of blades, meaning they were tilted when rounding that curve!

Late one afternoon after a good snow had fallen a close friend of Bill and Kellye's called to say he was going to come out. He worked at Harold Slaten's community store. He asked if there was anything we needed that he would bring it when he came. Marcia quickly said, "Yeah, we need a fifty pound bag of dog feed." (She was joking, of course). She said there were moments of dead silence on the line and then he said, "Aw, you're joking, right?"

Later that night, Kellye (younger than the others) and Mike Russell decided to race down the curving hill toward the entrance. Suddenly he yelled, "Bail out, Kellye! Some idiot left his car parked in the middle of the road!" After they got up from the ditch he discovered it was his own car that had slid down from where he had parked!

We made huge snowmen during those times, too. We saw some on TV but they couldn't compare to ours, but no cameras came out our way. We had our share of snowball fights, too. Marcia and I bought four bookcases to put two on each side of the piano in my music room that had been the single garage. We found that those pasteboard boxes were excellent to get into and slide down our front yard. They were one foot by two feet by six feet...about like a casket! The others would hold it while a person lay on their back and inched their way down in it.

Then the top was closed and it was shoved off. Bill went off the right side of our driveway culvert into about a six foot ditch (filled in since then) and couldn't get out the top. He had to kick open the bottom so he could slide down out of it. It was funny to the rest of us.

One of our friends, a man younger than me named Fisher, was out here that night. The boys called themselves "Fisher's Boys." He and I had been helping the boys get down in the boxes. I eased over to Fisher and said, "You know what's coming next!"

Sure enough they demanded that we go down, so I got in first. They shoved me off but I couldn't take it not knowing where I was headed. I busted open the top and peered over the box, but thank the good Lord, I made the trip safely, and Fisher did also. Fisher drove a church bus, and so did Bill. We had well over twenty buses bringing hundreds of children to Park Avenue every Sunday.

One Sunday night the boys wore dark suits and ties and Bill drove our Cadillac up to a Shoney's Restaurant, then on Murphy Road. They had intended to have Fisher play the part of a "mob boss" and they were his body guards. He didn't make it that night so they got a man named Bill Spain to take his place. We were inside Shoney's watching through the window. Two "men" got out and entered, obviously "casing the joint."

They returned to the car and one opened the back door and out stepped Spain in his suit and tie. The boys flanked him as they came in and escorted him to a table, standing by like the Secret Service or the like. All in there were aware of their actions...the boys got a kick out of doing it!

We watched the TV weather reports to try to know if snow and ice was expected so we could park our car down at the bottom of our driveway, or even up at the top of the hill. If our car WAS up behind our house, it was rather dangerous to try to get it down the driveway. It was best to put either side of the tires off it and in the yard and ease down a foot at the time. If you ever started to slide, that was it...but praying helped. Marcia said one day Kellye was going to drive down and Marcia was in the passenger seat. When she put her foot on the brake the car began to slide helplessly. Marcia kept yelling for her to "get your foot off the brake!" Well, that's not easy to do, especially when your mind is telling you to hit the brake! But the moment she did, the car turned the way the wheels were heading and they made it down to the street alright.

A realtor in West Nashville and a member of Park Avenue was Ed Groves. We got him to list our house on Masonwood Drive in Parkwood Estates after we had kept it through the winter. It sold within a week and he came out with papers for us to sign. There was snow and ice on the ground and he parked on the driveway when he could not get up any further. Upon leaving we found that his car had slid backward about ten yards and was parked right over the culvert! One time we were standing near our driveway when suddenly our neighbor's son's car came sliding fast down their steep driveway, shot across the road and into our yard! It scared all of us!

Years later Kellye and her family flew up and there was a big snowfall. We picked them up at the airport, but I couldn't get any further up the driveway than the sidewalk to the front door which was seldom used. I held the brake on while their luggage was unloaded from the trunk. Then Bruce (her husband who owns an auto repair and tire store) told me to turn the wheels sharply to the left. He suddenly shoved the left front fender and the car did a 180 and I drove back down the driveway!

In 1977 we got 17 inches of snow in February alone! The driveway was gravel then and we got up it three times that winter when snow was on the ground! Bill got our Ford tractor (Gerald) from the "Francis farm days" and plowed our street to the top of the hill. We had a grader blade that hooked on the back. Right after we moved out to this house the front yard was eroding badly and Bill and I shoveled a lot of dirt from the woods onto our rubber tired wagon to dump in there. When the weight on that wagon started shoving the tractor down the hill, even with Bill jamming the brakes, going at a 45 degree angle I yelled for him to jump. He did and rolled out of the way just as the wooden "tongue" on the wagon splintered and the tractor turned a complete flip downward, landing on its wheels again. We thanked the Lord over and over for protecting us that day. I should have known better.

We thought the tractor was alright but a few weeks later we discovered the steering wheel had quit working. We did get that fixed, however. We sold the tractor, with the bush hog connected behind it and mounted on our 4-wheel steel trailer, with the disc on the truck bed, to R. O. Stone's father who lived at Chattanooga but across into the state of Georgia. [R. O. and Angie Stone were song evangelists and their three sons played trumpets. He later had us in his church in Ocala, FL]. We delivered all this, probably getting maybe eight miles to the gallon in our Ford F-250 4WD truck.

THE NATIONAL BAPTIST HYMNAL

In January 1979 a group of men from the National Baptist Convention came to talk with Bob and John III about publishing a new hymnal for their denomination. It had been forty years since they had printed a new one! The denomination has over five million members. As they were leaving, one of them said, "Oh, by the way. Our national convention is in June. Could we have it by then?" John III said, "No problem!" When the men were out the front door downstairs, he yelled, "Ellll-mo!"

With God's help, even though I worked several Sundays, I met the deadline...doing about an 18-month job in four months! Their only instruction was to put the old hymn, "Holy, Holy, Holy" on page one, and to include certain "spirituals." They also wanted my song "Each Step I Take" in the book and another one of mine entitled "Do You Need a Friend?" They wanted responsive readings, their creed, and both a topical and general index.

On a page in the front of the book was a list of all who had worked on the project. Topping that list was a young man named T. Boyd III. Listed was John T. Benson III. Well, the head of our Art Department was listed as Bob McConnell, but he had me change it to Robert B. McConnell III. My name, W. Elmo Mercer, was listed between two prominent National Baptist women's names!

Many of the songs I had to arrange. I laid out the sequence of the book, checked all writers' names and the copyright notices placed at the bottom of the page, securing permissions where needed. I ended up with 545 songs. The actual printing could not be done at Kingsport (TN) Press as planned, so at the last minute we had to go to Fairfield, Pennsylvania. It is located about eight miles west of Gettysburg. Glenn Smotherman and his wife had driven to Kingsport to oversee the job and then drove on up to Fairfield. John III told me to fly to D. C., rent a car and drive up there to check each form in the book before printing.

The man in charge of printing at Fairfield Press was of Polish descent. He offered me a pencil from his desk that had an eraser on both ends! There were two huge rolls of paper at one end of the press. In about thirty yards the completed book came out. It was amazing and they said they would print the 50,000 copies in about two hours! Before the process started they would bring me a signature, or form of 32 pages, for me to closely check to see if everything was in order. Dear Lord, what a responsibility...what pressure I felt. Everything turned out alright, thank God!

I checked page numbers, position on the pages, etc. On a page in the front of the book where the copyright was listed there was a symbol looking something like a snowflake. I marked that it was too far to the left...well, it looked that way to my "naked eye." It was found to be 1/32 of an inch too far left! Naturally, I am very proud of my work on that project, and thank God for allowing me the privilege. Editions printed were for the pew, the pulpit (leather binding) and the accompanists (3-ring binder). Numerous printings have been done over the years, needless to say.

The Benson Company was first bought by the Zondervan Corporation in Grand Rapids, Michigan. I left Benson in early 1981 and Marcia and I started our travels nationwide in church music evangelism. One day John III called me to his Triad Music office in a Music Row office building. He asked if I would do a similar hymnal job for the Church of God in Christ that he had contracted. I declined – for several personal reasons.

BETTY, THE BARMAID

When Glen Smotherman, his wife and I were in Fairfield, PA for the printing of the National Baptist Hymnal we ate dinner one night at a quaint restaurant. It was an OLD historic structure and there were tables throughout the rooms. On a table in the hallway were big books. They asked us to sign in and look through the books. Some dated back in the late 1700s – politicians, businessmen, drovers, etc. When we started to leave, the cash register was at the end of the bar. [All kinds of liquor was stacked behind it].

The lady asked where we were from and Glen said Nashville, TN. She said, "Oh, Music City! Country music is okay but I really like gospel music." Glen pointed at me and said, "This man composes gospel songs." She kept talking, "My favorite song is called 'Each Step I Take,' you ever heard of that?" Glen sputtered, pointed again and said, "He…he wrote that song!" [I can't help but believe Glen set that up]. The lady said she had a little Magnus chord organ and was going to bring it the next morning. She told us to come back for breakfast and she wanted me to play and sing!

The next morning when we finished breakfast and went to pay the bill, sure enough that little organ was setting on the end of the bar. She insisted that I play and sing. So I sang a verse and chorus of "Each Step I Take." Men were sitting at the bar and were flabbergasted! Then I played "How Great Thou Art", "Just a Closer Walk," and another one or two.

Christmas came and I got a Christmas card from "Betty, the Barmaid." I tried to explain it to Marcia. I said she was a LARGE blond, probably a grandmother!

The next time we took one of our famous trips, the four of us went to that place! We stayed in the same motel (Liberty, next to an alpine slide down a mountain). For supper we went to that café and thank God, Betty, the Barmaid, was there! Whew! We enjoyed talking a while. Later Marcia noticed there were flowers on every table except ours! The next morning at breakfast we were taken to a different room to a table that was the only one with no flowers on it! Marcia noticed that also, and I can't explain it myself!

PITTSBURG AIRPORT

In the mid-70s Jeff Jeffrey and I conducted music clinics in eight towns in Pennsylvania on eight Saturdays. The Benson representative for one area was Clyde White, who met us at the airport. I commented, "These are beautiful mountains, what are they called?" Clyde said they were the Poconos. I said that sounded like an Indian name. But Jeff spoke up and said, "No, Mo, that's Italian, don't poke-a-no girls today!"

These music clinics were done in American Baptist churches. One late Saturday afternoon we went in a restaurant in the Pittsburg airport. We were on an expense account so we ordered a steak, feeling like we had earned it! So help me, we were half-way through when we looked at each other and both spoke at the same time, "This ain't gonna get it! Let's order it again!" (The meal cost only about $5.95 back then).

We got the attention of the waitress and told her we wanted to order the same thing again. She said, "Aw, come on, guys. This is my first day on the job!" We convinced her we were serious. She even brought clean silverware wrapped in a napkin.

RIDING WITH THE ARTISTS

John III and Bob had the bright idea one time that we "executives" should ride on the buses of our recording artists and get a taste of that life! Our offices were on Broadway at that time. I was assigned, quite naturally, to Bob Harrington's big bus. "The

Chaplain of Bourbon Street" was in big letters on the sides. Bob did not even ride on it, but flew to the destinations. We did a one-night-stand in the big Greensboro, NC coliseum. I believe I played organ and Steve Adams played piano. Jack Price was the music man. The bus driver's name was Max Carter. A big time was had by all that night.

The next morning Harrington caught a plane to D. C. for a meeting with Secretary of Defense McNamara – apparently they were friends. The four of us rode Harrington's bus over one Appalachian range of mountains after another headed for Akron, Ohio and the Rex Humbard Cathedral of Tomorrow. When we pulled in for lunch somewhere a guy ran up and asked, "Is Ray Price on this bus?" WHAT? Why would he think that? I said, "No, but we got a Jack Price!" He turned and left.

Before the service that night, a man played the organ beautifully - old favorite hymns, standard hits and new gospel songs. Afterward I asked about him. I was told he was a miracle, a phenomenon! They said he had the mind of a four-year-old!

The second bus I was assigned to was the Kenny Parker Trio. At the time Elmer Cole was singing with them. He wrote "Ten Thousand Years," that Benson owned and published. He also drove the bus. We passed the National Football Hall of Fame in Canton, Ohio, on our way to an event held outdoors near Lancaster, PA. They were just one group of many. I remember Jerry Goff and his singers were there. Jerry married the LeFevre's daughter. We were in Amish country and the food was great, especially Shoo-fly-pie. On the way back to Nashville Elmer was barreling down a divided four-lane highway when he discovered he had no brakes. He was approaching an intersection with a traffic signal. He started blowing the horn and we made it through alright. The brakes were repaired and we continued our journey home. We saw him later, in 1996, at a Gaither Homecoming Friends taping in Alexandria, IN.

Somehow, somewhere I got a wooden sign and put it on my desktop. It simply read, "It's hard to be humble when you're as great as I am!"

BROADMOOR PARTY

Bill and Ola Mae Lamb, with their son and daughter, moved to Memphis. (Remember we met them at Riverside Baptist Church in Nashville. I believe it was the late 60s or early 70s. He was transferred there by the telephone company. They joined Broadmoor Baptist out on Austin Peay highway. It was a big church with musically-talented people. The first Friday night in December each year they held an adult Christmas party. The men gathered and grilled steaks. Green beans and baked potatoes along with the drink and dessert was the meal. We went 12 consecutive years. I remember one time we were rehearsing a Lanny Wolfe song "The Year When Jesus Comes" as we drove down I-40 west of the Tennessee River. We didn't even notice the car I was passing till we got beside it. The man was wearing a TN Highway Patrol uniform. Thankfully he exited into the Rest Area...I guess he was also speeding to get to it! I said,

"Thank you, Lord!" not that he made it but that I didn't get a ticket!

Usually about 450 adults attended this Christmas party! The first part of the program was country or pop music acts. The pastor, Jack May wore chaps and a 10-gallon hat, picked a guitar and sang a Hank Williams song. A man and woman, sitting on opposite ends of the stage talking on telephones, acted out Conway Twitty's "Hello, Darlin'" as the record played. A girl played drums and sang Karen Carpenter's "Top of the World"...these are just examples. I played piano with some of the acts. About 10:30 (honest!) we would take a 15 minute potty break and then the second part of the show was seasonal. Ensembles and soloists sang Christmas songs. A lady with an accent always read a Christmas story; another lady sang "O Holy Night." Marcia and I along with Bill and Kellye would do two or three numbers also.

We always spent that night with Bill and Ola Mae. On Saturday morning Bill would crank up the reel to reel tape and we'd listen to most of it again. Then after lunch we'd drive back to Nashville for church on Sunday. Those are priceless memories.

Bill and Kellye used to sing "duets" in the Park Avenue Sunday night services. One of the songs was "We have a wonderful guest at our house." They were so cute. I remember when Bill was ten years old, he was invited to sing one night at Evangelist Eddie Martin's crusade in Fraser (Memphis) TN. I played for him but can't remember what he sang. Eddie told him if he would learn 8 or 10 songs, he would take him with him throughout the summer to sing in his crusades. What an honor! But that didn't happen.

PABC YOUTH CHOIR

Park Avenue had an excellent graded choir program, headed up by Carolyn Campbell, who was Chet Atkins' secretary. They regularly sang in the services. Dave Werner was minister of music then and he had a great youth choir. They loved to do musicals, which was a popular thing to do in the 70s. In one of them, Bill was to sing a line. He "milked it" for all it was worth...with outstretched arms and eyes to the ceiling he bellowed, "Give my regards to Broadway!" That kid was a "ham" - like father like son, I guess.

The youth choir would go "on tour", singing in three or four churches, sometimes going into other states. Dave would drive the church bus. One time they went down near Columbia, MS, just above the Louisiana state line. The 200 acre site was owned by a friend of ours, Jim Cagle, who was an Eastern Airlines pilot working out of New Orleans. On this property was a high and long red clay hill that had become severely eroded. The kids loved to slide down it. They took old clothes for that purpose. But that era did not last long. The attention given the youth waned and they in turn began to lose interest in coming to church!

On July 4th and New Year's Bill insisted on "doing" fireworks... everyone else was although there was a ban in Metro Nashville.

We especially liked the bottle rockets because they shot so high into the air. It made mowing the lawn a bit more interesting, too. There was another that when laid on the ground and lit, it would chase after you. After one New Year's party, I cleaned up outside on the "turnaround," then wondered what I should do with it. Without thinking I just threw them into the fireplace in the den. When the next fire was built, we were sitting there watching TV and unexploded fireworks started popping all over the place and we scattered! DUH!

BREAK A LEG

For a while we kept three horses here on the 50 acres that Mrs. Francis gave to us. Bill, Tommy (Kellye's former boyfriend) and I strung barbed wire around about ten acres of our land. We used my chainsaw occasionally and one day I was carrying it back through the woods in my right hand. It was not turned on, thank the Lord when I tripped over a root or vine. I stumbled forward and the bar hit the lower front of my left shin and the teeth made a cut which bled profusely even down into my sock.

One of the horses was named Lady, a black and white paint like Little Joe rode on the Bonanza TV program. One Saturday Kellye decided to ride her in the neighborhood. It had rained some and Lady slipped and fell going from our yard up to the asphalt street. Well, you know a horse tries to get up immediately. Kellye was attempting to get off and had one foot on the ground when Lady sprang up and flipped her in the air and out onto the street. She landed awkwardly and her left leg was broken near the ankle!

She yelled for help. Tommy was with Bill up behind the house doing something. He ran down the hill and when he picked her up in his arms, her left leg flopped over at a terrible angle. He saw it and said, "(bleep), it's broke!" He carried her all the way up our long, curving driveway. She was on crutches for quite some time, needing help at school once again! For her 16th birthday we gave her a party out back of the house, inviting many of her friends. The phonograph's external speakers were pointed toward the woods so as not to disturb our closest neighbors.

GRADY NUTT

I first met Grady Nutt at a Belmont College (now University) luncheon. He was one funny guy! Benson printed a book he wrote titled "So Good, So Far." He also recorded an album with Benson in our new studios. He sang a quartet by himself – overdubbing all four parts! On a couple of songs he wanted choral backup so Bill and I were called along with other employees to be in that choir. We stood on either side of Brock Speer! That was fun.

Marcia and I sang at a church in Huntsville, AL. The pastor said he and his wife lived in an apartment next to Grady and his wife when they attended seminary. Grady's wife was expecting any time. The pastor said they heard noises during the night from Grady's apartment so they put on housecoats and opened their door. Just then Grady's wife stepped out their door followed by Grady with his golf clubs. His wife yelled, "Grady!" and pointed at them. He threw them back inside and said, "Oh Lord, I thought I had your hospital suitcase!" We also had Grady to speak at a Benson WHACHAMACALLIT at Opryland Hotel. You will remember him being on "Hee-Haw" also.

When the baby was born, a nurse (who knew Grady well) brought to him a black baby wrapped in a blanket. Grady took a look and said, "Oh well, she burns ever'thing else!" That Huntsville pastor said he'd had Grady down for a banquet. They left to fly back home. Grady had two pilots. It was freezing that night and the plane crashed soon after takeoff because the flaps or something were frozen together. That's the way he told the story...if I am wrong, please forgive me.

JERRY WAYNE BERNARD

At my office in the new Benson building in MetroCenter Jerry Wayne Bernard and his two older daughters came by to see me. He was an evangelistic singer and did some revivals with James Robison. Robin was on General Hospital soap for a while. Crystal was on Happy Days, then Wings, and later starred in "made for TV" movies. In one of them Jerry played the part of a funeral home staffer! Both girls did a little song and dance for me. That had to be after 1976.

Jerry was adopted and later found his birth mother and led her to Christ!

Along about then the team of Bernard & Robison did a five night revival in Vanderbilt's 16,000 seat gymnasium. Cowboys head coach Tom Landry came one night and gave his testimony. Afterwards I was invited to go to the Fifth Quarter with them. There were five of us – Landry, Bernard, Robison and me. The fifth was a PR man and I assumed it was for Tom Landry. He sat at the end of the table to my right.

I finally got up the courage to ask him what the Cowboys thought about Don Meredith's sports announcing on Monday Night Football. I can't recall his answer but he said ol' Don was quite a character. He said in one game a big defensive lineman sacked him and said, "Get used to it, Meredith. I'm gonna rub your nose in the mud all afternoon!" Flat on his back, Don reached and grabbed the guy and said, "Kiss me, you sweet thang!"

Another time, Landry said, Don came up to the line, crouched behind the center, paused a minute and said, "I ...forgot...the play. Hike, hike!"

BRO. BOB'S 20th ANNIVERSARY

For Bro. Bob's 20th anniversary in 1980 as pastor at Park Avenue, we had a big party in the gym. We had 500 or so around tables. "Skeeter" Daniel was in charge of the food and service. It went like clock-work. Doug Oldham was the guest singer and Steve Adams was his accompanist. Several dozen colorful balloons, filled with helium were floating above the crowd...well, they were supposed to. They all migrated up to the return air vent in a corner of the gym.

As Doug was ending a rather spirited number, one of the balloons began to lose helium and float down to the platform. He saw it and timed it just right...on the last note he skipped and kicked it back into the air.

On stage that night was our dear friend Donna Hilley (President and CEO of SONY-ATV on Music Row) who had planned the program. Only ***five days before*** she had given birth to Whitney, she and Rayford's third daughter. Well, the show must go on, and she was a real trouper!

VBS AT PABC

Soon after moving to the split-level house on fifty acres of land Mrs. Francis gave us in August 1976, we bought a small puzzle of the world for Kellye. [She loves puzzles to this day, especially horse pictures with 500 pieces]. When the last piece was inserted, the song "It's a Small World" began to play. It got packed into a box and stored in the 24x29 garage we added on to the house, which is now a part of our apartment.

This is unbelievable and I can't explain how it could happen. Years later we were cleaning out the garage and a box tumbled down from its storage spot. That dadgum song started to play! "Bunny" batteries, you think?

Each summer Marcia and a lot of her friends always helped with Vacation Bible School at Park Avenue. Hundreds of children came. One little boy was quite rowdy and Marcia told him if he didn't settle down and behave himself she was going to make him sit on her lap. He cut up again and she made him do it. But he was so proud, looking at the others like, "Hey, Mrs. Mercer is holding ME on her lap!" He just needed love.

The same boy did something in prayer meeting that was actually ingenious. A spinster took it on herself to sit by him. Remember, we would have 400 or so in attendance. During an extended prayer time, people who could were urged to kneel at their places in the pews. The lady did and so did the boy. She looked over at him after a while and he clasped his hands as in a prayer stance. When she looked away he poked a big glob of bubble gum on the floor under her shoe. When prayer time was finished and she stood to turn and sit back down, she could not. She was stuck to the floor and I guess had to get out of her shoes. I don't know the end of that story...

Another boy in VBS had body odor problems and came from a poor family in west Nashville. It was said they didn't even have running water in the house. Marcia said to the children, "Now let's all go home and take a good bath tonight, ok?" She told the other workers what she had done and one of them said he'd probably come down with a cold. He did not show up the next day, but was there the next. Marcia noticed his face looked like it had been scrubbed clean. She asked him why he missed the day before and he said, "I got a cold!"

MY WAYNE WATSON CONNECTION

In 1979 Marcia, Bill and Kellye and I were in Winnfield, LA visiting Mammaw and Pappaw Fletcher. Mrs. J. R. Byrnes, wife of the local Ford dealer, called out to their house to talk to me. She said, "My son-in-law writes and sings gospel songs, and..." [How many times had I heard that?] She continued, "Would you mind if I brought him and my daughter out so you could listen to some of them?" I said, sure, come on out.

I was introduced to Wayne Watson. He strummed his guitar and sang some for me. I was very impressed, and told him to record a cassette (at the time) and send it to me at the Benson Company in Nashville. His songs were in the Christian contemporary genre. Even though I had attempted to write and arrange in that field, I was not particularly fond of the style. Our daughter Kellye has told me since then that this is the way THIS generation sings praises to God. In fact she was a regular in two church Praise Teams in south Florida.

When I got back to the Nashville Benson office I got Bob and John III together, perhaps some others as well and we listened to the cassette. They also were impressed and signed him as a writer and recording artist. I recall in the summer of 1980 seeing Wayne at the company one day at noon when he and some others were having lunch on the patio area overlooking the Cumberland River.

We talked for a while. He was already getting his career off to a great start. Among his many songs is one called, "People of God" that I later included in the Best of Country Western Hymnal. I have seen it in other publications including hymnals. Some years later, Marcia and I did a concert at a northeast Louisiana church and we met Wayne's mother and brother. I am pleased to have had a small part in Wayne Watson's early beginnings in the gospel music field.

After the Zondervan Corporation purchased the Benson Company in August 1980, it was made their Christian Contemporary music division. Marcia and I talked and prayed about it. I thought about retiring but we had two kids in college! One day at noon I was sitting on the grass on the east side of the huge building in MetroCenter thinking and asking God for direction. I looked to my left and there was a bush with dozens of bees going into it then coming out. It was like God told me to just trust Him to guide and bless us – that He was going to *send us out* and people would be *coming to us!* We began traveling the nation in church music evangelism and people did come to hear and meet us! What a thrill it is to live in God's will for your life!

I retired from full-time work as Benson music editor in early 1981. Zondervan made Bob MacKenzie president after their purchase of the company. Previously they had bought Paragon Music that was founded by MacKenzie, Bill Gaither and Gary Paxton (who wrote "He was there all the time.") MacKenzie and I had worked together for many years. He said he didn't want to lose track of me and contracted me to arrange ten choral books in the next five years. I arranged books for the Hemphills, Squire Parsons, Dottie Rambo, Steve Adams, Dallas Holm and others. I also arranged a choral book for the Hoppers one winter when we were in Okeechobee.

Our decision had been made. Marcia and I moved out into an exciting yet unknown future. We trusted God to lead and bless as he had so many times in the past.

PART THREE
We Start Our New Ministry

A NEW DIRECTION

I was now free to send original songs and arrangements to other publishers as well as do work for them. LIFEWAY published many of my arrangements and some original songs in quarterly publications "Glory Songs" and "The Senior Musician." FRED BOCK Music in California published my song, "One More Hill, One More Valley" in octavo form and had me arrange two SAB choir books. BRENTWOOD Music published some of my original songs in octavo form for choirs to sing. DERRIC JOHNSON's company did likewise.

The LORENZ Company of Dayton, OH published about ten of my original songs and PD arrangements in octavo form. I wrote a wedding song for our daughter Kellye called "Because of Love" and Lorenz included it in a 9x12 folio of wedding songs. Marcia and I wrote a song for Bill's wedding called "In God's Time" but it was not published.

In 1987 I became associated with Bible Truth Music of Newport News, VA. The founder and president is Evangelist Byron Foxx (he says the second "x" is silent). BTM has printed many of my original songs and arrangements. Through the years I arranged songs he acquired from other writers. They put out excellent product, both print and CDs.

The word spread that I was available for concerts, revivals, banquets, etc. We went into every state numerous times and sang in 37 of them! I told Marcia she was going to have to "sing for her supper." We traveled by car – a '79 Olds 98; an '83 Olds 98; an '86 Olds 98 (that was a "lemon"); an '87 Buick LeSabre; an '89 Olds 98; a '93 GMC Safari mini-van; a '99 Olds Silhouette mini-van and a 2006 Toyota Siena XLE.mini-van. I would love to trade again but I'm about to the age I don't buy green bananas anymore! I dearly love to drive. I love to research and plan trips, typing out the itinerary on computer and putting it in a binder to refer to as we travel. We have seen the USA and a lot of southern Canada.

We felt that our ministry should be directed to the small town or rural church. We went on a "love offering" basis. Most did not pay anything on expenses, but God always provided our needs. We made friends all over the country and keep in touch with a lot of them by phone, letter or e-mail.

Our first "date" was a week's revival at a Baptist Church at Owens Crossroads, AL. I count a revival as ONE date. It was the last week in March. [*By the end of October we had done 33 dates! God began blessing our new ministry*]. We stayed in the home of a Mrs. Moore, a widow who owned a bakery. Her son's name was Dwayne and he led the music at the church. You may recognize the name Dwayne Moore from a great book he has written on church music and choirs. Each night before he preached the dear old preacher would kneel by the pulpit and pray. God gave us a memorable time during those days.

One night the invitation stretched out to perhaps six invitation songs and the young pastor kept pleading, apparently for someone he knew was there. Soon a man in his mid-30s stepped out and started down the aisle. A lady in the choir shouted and so did the man's mother, I assumed. Scared me speechless! Listen y'all, the pastor started running laps around the little sanctuary! A lost sheep had been found! What a meeting that turned out to be after that, and **we believed God had led our lives to this new ministry.** But we had no idea what lay ahead for us.

NEW DOORS OPEN

I was pianist for Senior Adult Week at both Ridgecrest, NC and Glorieta NM in the same year. It was indeed my privilege to be pianist for "Gospel Music Reunion" held at the Lifeway building one spring. That was fun.

William (Bill) Cox, who worked at Lifeway for many years, and I, compiled three Senior Adult songbooks that Benson printed and distributed. The first was recorded by studio singers; the second by the First Baptist Church choir in Huntsville, AL. Bill and I went down and sang with the choir. The third was titled "Celebrate Jesus," released in 2000. Its premier was held at a big hotel near the Atlanta, GA airport. A second premier was at a Cherry Hill, NJ large hotel, actually a Philadelphia suburb. We attended both.

Around 1987 I began to arrange music for a new company called BIBLE TRUTH Music of Newport News, Virginia. The founder, Byron Foxx had phoned me in 1987 to say he was working at a church school but felt led to go "out on his own," and start a publishing company that would help preserve "Bible truth" music. I encouraged him to do so, and it is a big company now. I attend their annual staff meeting as a "consultant!" I have arranged perhaps hundreds of songs for him, and he has published a lot of my original compositions. He published two solo piano books for me, plus a piano and organ duet book. Benson had published about ten volumes of each when I worked for them. BTM has an excellent church hymnal also, plus children's music and activities, cantatas, etc. Byron is also a powerful evangelist and travels extensively.

PHIL WALDREP sponsored a senior adult conference at the Lawrence Welk Theatre in Branson, MO. Our friend Bill Cox was the music director and I was asked to be the pianist. I played that big white grand piano on stage before each morning's service. During the concluding service Marcia and I sang a couple of songs.

When we arrived, I asked if I could display our books and CDs in the lobby. We were told that was alright, but their staff would work it and receive ten percent. We agreed. We could not believe the sales amount. We sold out of most all of our product!

Reba McIntyre's sister was a guest speaker...we really enjoyed her. Lawrence Welk's golf cart was parked in the lobby and on the front were the words, "Wonerful, Wonerful!" A few years before we had visited his museum in Escondido, CA. Marcia made a picture of me standing by his life-size bronze statue by a fountain as though we were discussing a sheet of music.

During those early years of travel I still remained pianist at Park Avenue Baptist Church, and was for over 38 years. However, one year we were there only seven Sundays!

THE EARLY 80s

We had met Tim Langley at the Benson WHACHAMACALLIT. He invited Marcia and me to do the music in a revival at the First Baptist Church in Idabel, OK. We stayed in the home of an elderly widower, Mr. Earl Pryor, and will never forget that sweet experience. Six months later we passed within fifty miles of Idabel and went by to see him. [Tim also had us at churches in St. Joseph, MO and Moline, IL]

I believe it was in 1982 we got a call from Jack Griffin in Portland, OR, asking if we could come out for a weekend. He is the brother of my niece Jonnye's husband Danny, born and raised in Alaska. Marcia and I drove from Nashville and thoroughly enjoyed our time with them and Mill Park Baptist, located in the eastern part of Portland. The views along the Columbia River Gorge were breath-taking. Along I-84 and US-30 (The Lincoln Highway, America's first transcontinental highway) there are numerous waterfalls, including Horse Hair and Multnomah Falls. Mt. Hood is in the immediate vicinity south of the Columbia River.

We did a Saturday music clinic at Broken Arrow, OK, sponsored by a Christian Bookstore owner. We stayed in their home, and Kellye made that trip with us as it was right before her wedding in March 1982. The lady gave us a beautiful painting of "The Last Supper" showing the elaborate table stretching into infinity. It hangs on a wall in our house. David Ingalls came to that clinic just to see us. He is the composer of many gospel favorites such as "He is My Everything," and "There's a Whole Lot of People Going Home." He had a singing group called the Viscounts at one time. Also attending was Darrell Archer, a fine young writer himself from Oklahoma. For a few years I arranged his music and he printed a solo piano book of his songs that I arranged.

A professor at Oral Roberts University was there also. At the time he was on the ASCAP board and that gave us a "connection." He invited to show us over the Oral Roberts University campus Monday morning. We gladly accepted. When you drive onto that campus it's like entering a futuristic world (and this was back in '82). The buildings are very modern. The "River of Life" flowed from the building behind the pedestal of the praying hands statue. The two big hospitals were behind that. Inside the administration building we saw the offices of Oral and his son Robert up through the atrium on the second floor.

The Sunday morning we were at Broken Arrow we sang at the church the owners of the bookstore attended, I believe it was "Faith Baptist." Sunday night we did a concert at 16th Avenue Baptist Church in Tulsa nearby.

Early in 1982 we did music in a revival in a big country church near Jasper, AL. We were told that sixty-two millionaires lived there. We drove down there and saw the birthplace of movie actress Tallulah Bankhead and "Guber" of the Mayberry TV show. Believe me, the houses were quite different.

We stayed at a lake house owned by a doctor and really enjoyed it. There was a floating dock down the hill on the lake that had an enclosed room on it. In the center was a space cut out and enclosed by a low wall so you could sit there and fish...after some "fish food" was thrown in! I picked up some acorns and planted two in our yard and they are now tall oak trees.

One day they took us up to a famous restaurant along a state highway for lunch. They insisted we get the steak and when it was brought out, steamy vapors rose above it. When you poured the juices on it, it would really make noises! It was tasty, too. They took us by the power plant at Earl Smith dam. That was really interesting to tour. The lake had a huge earthen dam, and when it was completed and the gates closed it began to fill so quickly that some huge earth-moving machines could not be removed, and are now at the bottom of the lake, which is some 350 feet deep in places.

LINDSAY TERRY

I did two concerts WITHOUT Marcia! My good friend, Lindsay Terry, invited me to sing in North Carolina and Texas. Lindsay had been music minister at Dr. Jack Hyles big church in Hammond, IN for a number of years. We delivered a thousand of his newly printed choral books to him there. A pastor's conference was in progress and I believe over 3,500 were in attendance. Then Lindsay went to Dr. Jack Hudson's big church (Northside Baptist) in Charlotte, North Carolina. At a later date he was at Dr. Gary Coleman's big church (Lavon Drive Baptist) in Garland, TX.

Each time they had a mystery guest speaker and a mystery guest singer. I was kept in his office until after the morning service started, then escorted to the upstairs door through which the choir entered and waited to be introduced. When I walked to the piano and sat down, I said, "Sorry, folks. I know you were expecting John W. Peterson!"

Lindsay authored at least two books. In one he put the story behind "Each Step I Take" and in another he included the story behind "The Way that He Loves." Lindsay has been a great friend to me.

OKEECHOBEE, FL

FBC Okeechobee had a great Senior Adult program, which was strongest during the winter months. We took trips together on the new church bus – to restaurants, points of interest, even boat rides. Once a month we all met in the church dining hall to eat and have a special guest do some kind of program. Marcia and I usually sang some then. Mary Esther Kemper (husband Ned) from Windfall, IN could play two trumpets at the same time… one out of each side of her mouth! She played soprano and alto on "Power in the Blood" verse! It was amazing! She said "That's not talent, that's just showin' off!"

One month the ladies put on a Style Show. For instance, a sun dress would have several suns stuck all over it, etc. A sweet lady called "Aunt Dot" (see paragraph [*] below) got a "moo-moo" dress and asked Marcia to wear it. It was black and white Holstein complete with bag at the bottom front! Marcia cut a slit in the bottom of a black trash bag and pulled it over her head so when she first strutted into the room you didn't know what she was wearing! I was playing Eddie Arnold's "Cattle Call" when suddenly I switched to "The Stripper." Marcia jerked the bag up over her head and slung it about 3 times above her and let it go. It wrapped around the head of one of the men there and the place became unglued. The minister of music, Mike Zierden, grabbed a waste basket and set it under the bag on Marcia's outfit where she stopped. She left! All of them came back in for the judge's decision, and Marcia did not win! Bummers!

Mike had an embroidered sign on his office wall that read "Where two or three Baptists are gathered there will be food." He also served as Senior Adult minister and they went on some fabulous trips across the US. He wore a ball cap with two bills on it and a caption that read "Which way did they go? I'm their leader!" I must tell you about Mr. Cook, but I don't recall what state he was from. Folks said he "drove his age!" He asked if I would remember his name the next Sunday and I said "No problem." Next Sunday I thought a few seconds then said, "Hello, Bro. Ham!" I knew it had something to do with food.

[*]Aunt Dot" Williams was widowed many years but still spoke of her husband. Her return address on envelopes was a drawing of an ant followed by a big dot! She taught the 8-year-old girls' SS class and quite often you would see her come down the aisle with one of them to receive Jesus as Savior. She and I wrote a song together called "Hallelujah! He wrote it down" and Bible Truth Music published it as a choral octavo. Instead of saying, "Amen," she would say, "Hot Dog!" And if she did not and Bro. Whipple had expected it, he would look over her way and say, "That's a Hot Dog, isn't it, Aunt Dot?" She's in heaven now, we'll see her again! Surely there'll be hot dogs there, don't you think?

One winter, Marcia and I decided to put on a "Variety Show." Whew! That was a job, but loads of fun! We chose various recording artists and I made cassettes of the song I wanted someone to imitate. For instance, I had Liberace, Chet Atkins, Harry James and many others. We had one rehearsal on difficult "acts." I gathered up REAL instruments to use and the person would pretend to play it while the cassette played. Everyone got into the thrill of the event, and the people in the show dressed according to their parts. Marcia and I were emcees and wrote the script.

We had backdrops, too. We had our web site displayed and a sign that read, "A Mo-Mar Production." We had two cameras recording it, plus snapshots. It came off like clockwork and was a hit. The crowd numbered 105, double what we usually had. We made a still photo of the cast after the show, but sadly, many have passed away.

RUSTY GOODMAN

We met the Happy Goodman family in the early 60s...Howard, Vestal, Sam and Rusty. They could electrify a crowd. Rusty was the songwriter. "Who Am I?" was one of his first and best. I made the first arrangement in 4-part harmony, shape notes, for sheet music.

"I Wouldn't Take Nothin' for my Journey Now," was a big crowd favorite. Rusty gave me a reel to reel tape and had me to arrange it. He later named his music company "Journey Music." It was bought by WORD several years afterward.

Rusty told me one time, "Mo, I tell you what you need to do. Get Jimmy Swaggart to record one of your songs." I said, "Yeah, right!" The only connection Jimmy and I had, we were both from Louisiana and Benson distributed his albums. If I remember correctly, on one of Jimmy's albums there were four of Rusty's songs! The gospel music world lost a major part of its soul after all four members of the Happy Goodman family passed away. You can still see them on Bill Gaither's Homecoming Friends videos. I'm on two videos, not featured, just sitting up in the choir.

Once our son Bill had (yet another) knee operation. This was at Southern Hills hospital in south Nashville. I came out of his room to discover Vestal in the hallway. Howard was a patient two rooms away after having had both knee replacements. Come to think about it, I don't think Vestal had her handkerchief that day!

WHERE'S THE BATHROOM?

Eudora, Arkansas is in the extreme SE part of the state, a small farming town. Before interstates were built we crossed the Mississippi River at Greenville, MS and went through Eudora on the way down to Winnfield. In the early 80s we did a weekend there at First Baptist Church – a Saturday night choir practice, Sunday morning and our concert that night. We stayed in the small home of the young music minister. They had a little 2-year-old daughter and that first night Marcia rocked her to sleep. We had no grandchildren then. The mother had a hearing problem and left the child's bedroom door open. It was across from our room.

As we went to our room I made a quick note of the floor plan, in particular the way to the bathroom. When you take BP medicine, and I had been since 1979, you learn to check such things out beforehand! During the night Marcia and I "had to go." We carry a night light with us, but when we closed our door (why did we do that anyway?) it was pitch dark in that hallway! I hung back a couple of steps not wanting to run up Marcia's backside in the darkness.

When I got in the bathroom I said, "Just a minute, I gotta find the light switch." The light came on, I turned around and Marcia was nowhere in sight! She had taken a left turn but quickly discovered she was in the kitchen. She turned back and was about three inches from my face when I opened the door, cupped my hands and whispered, "Marcia?"

We both got so tickled neither could use the bathroom for a while. She thought I had gone into the parents' room, closed the door and turned on the light. Heavens, what would I have done? Cancelled Sunday services, maybe? Next morning we told them what had happened and they cracked up also. And you know, we went back to that church a couple of times in the following years, plus this young man had us at another church in southern Arkansas.

In that same area, I think it was Hamburg, we did a concert and I did my piano impersonations which include Floyd Cramer's style. Afterward a lady came up to me and said she had been Floyd's piano teacher when he was a child. (Well, he elaborated on those lessons, didn't he?). Floyd got a job at KWKH in Shreveport playing on the Louisiana Hayride where so many country stars got their start, including Elvis. A couple of girls screamed and ran down the aisle and it went on from there! I've seen Hank Williams (Sr) do seven encores on "The Love-sick Blues." Jim Reeves was an announcer on the program, but sang a song one night. A talent scout in the audience signed him up and he had a great career before his plane crashed in the Radnor Lake area south of Thousand Oaks Estates where we live.

CUTTING I-440 RIGHT OF WAY

The M. D. Lavender family was dear and close friends. Elizabeth and "Junior" were the parents and Drew was their son, Lyndal was their daughter and organist at Park Avenue.

We often were invited over for a big Sunday "dinner." They invited other friends over at other times, including Rayford and Donna Hilley. Junior talked with a man who was surveying for I-440 which was coming very near their house. He asked about cutting some trees for firewood. The man said that would be alright, to just be sure to stay within the red-flagged stakes.

One Saturday Bill and I went over to help Junior and his son-in-law, Jim Corbitt, cut some firewood. We had two chainsaws going, mostly operated by Junior and me. Jim and Bill loaded the pickup trucks and then unload them at their house or ours. Elizabeth fixed a big pot of home-made soup for dinner. We cut seven truckloads that day! Toward the end of the day, Junior didn't notice the tension on a limb he sawed off and it slapped in the forehead. He had to go to the ER and get stitches but was dismissed to go back home. Now the busy, divided six-lane I-440 runs where we were cutting all those trees, but about twenty feet deeper!

DR. DON WILTON

Dr. Don Wilton came to the USA from South Africa, and his parents fled the country some time later. He was the evangelist in a revival in Livingston, AL and Marcia and I were to do the music. We drove into town and found a dilapidated building with the sign, "First Baptist Church." Surely not, we thought! There was a big nice church where the sign read, "Livingston Baptist Church." Thank the Lord that was the right one! Livingston College is there, which dates back into the 1800s.

We enjoyed Don's preaching with his South African accent. When he said "pastor" it sounded like "pasta." One night after the service we sat in our motel room talking. He suddenly snapped his fingers and said, "That's it! I like you two because you remind me so much of my PARENTS!" I jumped to my feet, pointed my finger at the door and said, "Git outta here!"

A few years ago we attended the morning service at First Baptist in Spartanburg, SC, where he was pastor. They were recognizing all graduating seniors. He was wearing a robe like a professor would do during graduation exercises and started his sermon. An obvious cell phone rang, likely done through the sound system. He acted embarrassed for not having shut it off, then took it out of his pocket and said, "Hello." Then in an astonished voice he exclaimed, "GOD???"

Listening for a while, he said, "Well, yes God, I can tell them all that. Goodbye." Then he preached a sermon to those who were graduating that was a sort of "Ten Commands for Graduates." After the service we got to talk with him briefly and he remembered us from the Livingston revival. Dean and Brenda Eades (Dulcimer couple) were with us that day. We were visiting in their home near Seneca, SC.

SOUTH KOREA TRIP

In October 1981, I went on an 18-day mission trip to South Korea with about eighty Southern Baptists of all ages. Four from Park Avenue made the trip: Bro. Bob preached, Beulah Peoples worked with the women, Jeff Calk (a 17-year old whose mother passed away a month before we left on the trip) worked with children and youth, and I was the musician. Most of them were from Middle Tennessee, and I knew many of them.

Dr. Carl Duck was our "leader." He told me when he received my picture in the mail (to get a passport) he said out loud, "This can't be the Elmo Mercer I know!" I had decided NOT to wear my hairpiece. I mean, having only two hands I didn't want to have to keep one on top of my head every time the wind blew! We were told to carry only one suitcase, and later found out why (explained later). Around our clothes and personal items we stuffed some American "goodies" to give to the missionaries over there.

I believe the air traffic controllers were on strike and we had to leave the night before, flying to Atlanta and spending the night in a hotel! The next day we flew non-stop to Minneapolis, then on to Seattle. I kept my watch on Nashville time, and we chased the sun across the Pacific. It was 4 a.m. before the sun went down. I tried to forget there was a whole lot of water below us. We crossed the international dateline and flew non-stop to Seoul. I remember expecting to see a metropolitan city all lit up, but saw very few lights. Planes were told to stay out of the "blue zone" which was where the government buildings (etc.) were located. We discovered we had lost a whole day in transit!

We split into three groups. One group stayed in Seoul (for both weeks). Another group went to Pusan on the southern tip of the country. Our group of nineteen journeyed by FAST train two hours south to the city of Daejeon. We stayed in an 8-story hotel two blocks from the church. Bro. Bob and I roomed together in a 7th floor room. That night we discovered there was a bowling alley on the floor above us! I believe most of them lofted the balls halfway down the lanes and when it hit the pins our ceiling shook. The province is landlocked and there was a curfew from midnight to four a.m. We learned that over there the number 4 is superstitious, so there is no 4th floor in any building!

I can't remember the name of the church. It was a "store-front" in the middle of the block. But inside it was totally unbelievable. They had 3 morning services, 3 song leaders or choir directors, 3 different choirs, 3 different choir robes, an excellent sound system, yet in the restroom there was just a hole in the floor! The pastor, Bro. Ahn later visited Park Avenue but Marcia and I were "on the road" that Sunday. When a member entered they got their card from "cubbyholes" on the wall and filled it out. Also on the wall was posted for all to see the amount of money each person had given to the church the previous Sunday! Wow!

That Sunday morning I sang "Each Step I Take," and told how I had come to compose it. When the service ended people came to me and could not believe I was the person who had written it. They showed me their hymnal and it was in there! They carry their own hymnal along with their Bibles. When they arrive at church they begin to sing. That night the four of us walked from the hotel to the church, about 2 and ½ blocks. We began to hear them singing "Each Step I Take." I don't know how many times it had been sung, but they motioned for me to come to the piano. They sing all verses of a song and they sang it SIX more times. Folks, that means I played it 18 times.

By the way, I made a copy of it…hey! It's MY song and I'll copy it if I want to! I also have it in Spanish (Ray Robles recorded it on Christian Faith label in the 50s). I have it in Swedish (Carl Olivebring recorded it on either WORD or Christian Faith in the 50s also). Praise God, it has been recorded hundreds of times in many languages around the world. People of Indonesia were among the first to "adopt it." I think I've told you that Slim Whitman ("Indian Love Call") from England was the first to record it. George Beverly Shea recorded it TWICE!

I will NEVER forget the experience of their 5 a.m. worship service. They meet each day of the week, sing a song or two, the pastor preaches, and then they disperse over the sanctuary and begin to pray - out loud. We were sitting in the middle about halfway back. In order to remember it, I raised my head and looked around. One woman was sitting, but moving her upper body back and forth. Someone said that Buddhist did that, so she may have been converted from Buddhism. A man kept beating his fist on the back of a pew, as though he was praying for a lost family member or his nation since they live in daily peril. Suddenly I realized what was playing over the sound system – "The Hallelujah Chorus!" I was almost raptured through the roof right then!

The revivals were from Sunday morning through Wednesday night each of the two weeks we were there. Each morning the four of us would get with our visiting partners and go out, returning around 4 p.m. Two men went with me. Lt. Pee took his two weeks leave from the Army and Mr. Chung provided the car. In each home we were offered a dainty cup of coffee. I knew it would be impolite to refuse, so somehow I managed to sip it. (Remember when we were children Mama gave us castor oil with coffee). I would begin by saying, "I have come from America to tell you about Jesus." That would be translated. Thirteen people made professions of faith in our visits. I believe our team of four saw over one hundred saved during our work in two cities. One day we were invited into a big corporation conference room where Bro. Bob told the gospel story to all the executives sitting at an oblong table.

Lt. Pee and Mr. Chung took me to a restaurant for lunch. In broken English they asked if I liked "such and such" and I said yes. I did not know they would order all that! We had plenty to eat that day and I was somewhat embarrassed. When we left Daejeon I told them I would always remember them and they grinned and said they would remember my appetite!

Beulah Peoples, Bro. Bob and I walked through a Daejeon market place one afternoon between visitation and church time. Long dried fish was stacked like cord wood. A chicken, complete with beak, comb and feet had somehow been cooked and set in a store window for sale, standing tall and proud! We saw a bunch of puppies on a street corner and thought how cute they were. We were told they were for sale...to eat, that it is a delicacy there.

There must be no building codes there. Poverty would be right next door to riches. We went to an elegant house for a meal.

It was furnished with Mother-of-Pearl furniture, hardwood floors, a beautiful staircase, chandeliers, etc. In Korea the tables are hardly a foot off the floor and the first time we ate sitting "Indian style". You would just reach out – with chop sticks, and eat what you wanted. The next morning Bro. Bob and I could hardly walk. We had discovered thigh and hip muscles we didn't know existed! The next time we ate somewhere, he and I were permitted to slide our legs under the table and then our shoes stuck up on the other side. They laughed at that!

You would take a strip of meat and wrap it in a square of seaweed. They made a soup from seaweed, too. We really enjoyed the Mongolian barbecue and rice. But we couldn't eat the kimchee – and that may not be how it's spelled. We learned it was cabbage that had been put in containers and buried in the ground. Next spring you would take it out and eat it or drink the juice from it. Are you kidding me? Some businessmen lived in Daejeon (3 million) and worked in Seoul, a two-hour FAST train ride north. Seoul's population (1981) was 9 million and swelled to 12 million each work day!

We observed them building a five-story building. Even the scaffolding was made of wood, not metal. The streets were very crowded with cars and people. At traffic signals, when vehicles stopped at night they would turn off their headlights! City buses would be jammed with passengers. They said as many as one hundred twenty-five would be jammed on one bus! School children rode them and we heard that being low in stature, some had even suffocated!

On Thursday Pastor Ahn and some members took us on their church bus about fifty miles north to the tombs of an ancient dynasty. We passed the entrance to a Korean military base and I snapped a picture. I saw the guards jump and look after us. Lt. Pee told me I should not have done that! I looked out the back window for a while to see if we were being pursued. They told us prisons there were terrible. Even the family had to bring prisoners their food.

We forded rivers due to bombed bridges not being repaired (and this was 28+ years after the war) and saw women doing laundry on rocks near the banks. We drove through villages where people crowded the streets with no concern for traffic. We walked up dozens and dozens of rock steps to get up to where the tomb was located. In a glass case was one of the queen's teeth! On the grounds there we had a picnic. The ladies who went with us pealed pears that were big and shaped like our apples...they were SO delicious.

Gary McCoy was a music missionary down in Pusan, located at the south tip of the peninsula. He heard that I was in the group at Daejeon. He got word that he wanted me to ride the train (3 hours) there, meet the other missionaries and spend the night with him and his wife. Bro. Bob said that would be alright. When I got off the train, Gary was not there. I almost panicked! In a few minutes he came up and apologized for being late – that the traffic was terrible...and it was. That night he and his wife (about nine months pregnant) took me out to the US army base for Mongolian barbecue. We watched the men prepare it, using blocks of wood to flip it around over the flames. They set it on a bed of rice and it was really delicious.

That night all the missionaries in the "compound" came to their house. I played piano and sang some, then we all sang some old hymns and talked a lot then retired for the short night. At 8 a.m. I was put back on the train for the five hour ride north to Seoul. I quit counting tunnels and rivers. Lord, help us! That train went FAST. The windows were perhaps three feet high and maybe eight feet long.

A "hostess" came down the aisle pulling a 2-wheel cart with snacks and canned drinks for sale. The man sitting by the window asked me if I would like a drink. I said, (this is the way I spell it) "Cahm suh hahm nee dah," which meant "Thank you," but I SHOOK MY HEAD no! [By the way, "Tay don he cahm suh hahm nee dah" meant "Thank you very much"]. He bought me one anyway.

He ripped the plastic off the top and chugalugged! I ripped the top off mine and took a sip. Have mercy! I'll bet it was that kimchee! Oh, it was awful. I smiled at him, nodded my thanks again, and chugalugged, too. Ugh. You know, maybe he really didn't like it either...but then why would he even buy it?!

About that time a bunch of loud teenagers came noisily down the aisle. One of the girls said, "Oh, hi Bro. Mercer!" and on they went. I thought, Dear Lord, here I am on a fast train in South Korea and someone speaks to me by name! It was one of the missionary kids from the night before.

All the teams met back in Seoul for the weekend. Sunday we began our second week of revivals. We were sent to a much smaller church. I remember standing up on the top steps and looking down into the bright little faces of those Korean boys and girls as they huddled around Jeff. He taught them to say, "Good *marning!*" Every church in South Korea has a BLUE NEON cross up on the front. The houses are jammed together with an alley behind them. A man with a two-wheel cart comes along and empties the buckets of human waste into the cart. This is called "the Honey Wagon". Egads! Why was it called THAT?

We had a wonderful time at that little church also. Some other teams told us they were in churches that had no pews! In fact one of the men with us gave $750 to buy pews for that little church. On the following Thursday we were encouraged by Dr. Duck to go to Etawon (?). It was a huge shopping area. We found a big leather suitcase on wheels for only $12 American. Now we knew why we could take only one suitcase over with us. I bought several string necklaces of silk beads that had become very popular in the USA for about $25. I paid $8 each for them. I bought a framed silk picture – very pretty, for only $8.

Bro. Bob and I caught a cab back to the Lotte (pronounced *Low-tay*) Hotel where we stayed in Seoul. We could see it off to our left but the driver went all over the place to get to it. We told him we knew he was just running up the fare! The Lotte was about thirty floors tall with a glass elevator. Adjoining it was a ten floor store, open in the middle with escalators going all the way up! Thursday night we rode to the top floor restaurant. We didn't eat, but walked around gazing out the windows. Still it was not lit up like any large American city.

We stepped in the elevator first and were quickly jammed against the glass side. Bro. Bob raised his hand and said, "Uh, folks, I don't believe any more can get on here!" I told him they couldn't understand a word he said! We were told it would take a North Korean jet only 45 seconds to streak across the DMZ to Seoul! And you may recall there was no peace treaty signed – the North and the South are technically still at war! Underneath the city is another city! I guess it was built as bomb shelters for the population. They have intersections (pedestrians, no vehicles) and blocks, various shops and stores, etc. Bro. Bob bought beautiful dresses for their two granddaughters.

It came time to leave South Korea. All of us got on two buses to be taken from the Lotte Hotel out to the Seoul airport for the trip home. Looking out the window we saw the baggage men throwing the suitcases and stacking them high. Those people who had bought breakable items cringed as they recognized their baggage.

There was a man and his wife with us who lived at Huntsville, AL. His name was Col. Peltier. [They later had us do a concert at their church, University Baptist]. His toes had been frozen in the Korean War and he wore shortened shoes. He told us he had hunted pheasants, ducks or geese all around the area where the airport was now. By the time Bro. Bob and I got through customs we could not see any one of our bunch to follow to our plane. It was to depart at 6 p.m.

We panicked, fearing we would be left behind. We rushed along and a man herded us on a BUS! Well, I knew that bus would not drive over to Japan and I protested, saying "America, America!" He nodded and herded us onboard. Come to find out, our plane was out on the tarmac! Before we made it to our seats that plane was heading down the runway! It was a huge plane, with about five seats in the middle plus the outside seats by the windows. We landed at the Tokyo airport and I tried to look out the windows. They mostly reflected the room behind me. But I can say I have been to Japan! We slept during the long flight to Hawaii.

As we landed in Honolulu, I started singing, "God Bless America," and many joined in. The runway jutted out into the ocean and for a while we thought we were going to land in the ocean. We rode to our hotel that was right on Waikiki Beach next door to the pink Royal Hawaiian Hotel where top officers came for R&R during WWII to hear Glen Miller's orchestra. On the way we passed the setting for "McHale's Navy", a TV sitcom. We left Seoul at 6 p.m. and arrived in Honolulu at 10 a.m. OF THE SAME DAY. We had crossed the International Dateline heading east over the Pacific. That was weird.

Built into our schedule was two days of rest in Honolulu. We had to wait for our rooms to be prepared. When we finally got to ours Bro. Bob went to bed! Jeff and I caught a city bus out to Pearl Harbor and really enjoyed that trip. {Later Marcia and I accompanied Rayford and Donna Hilley to Hawaii for an NMPA meeting. I write about this elsewhere}.

Believe me, it was "culture shock" time on Waikiki Beach. In South Korea the ladies dresses went from below their chin to their ankles. On the beach the women wore very skimpy bikinis! We went to a luau the first night and watched the performers dance with fire, we ate roasted pig – did the "the whole 9 yards!" In our rooms we had fresh pineapple, macadamia nuts and orchids!

Our group of about eighty people left Honolulu in three groups and we had a choice. One went back through the Great Northwest but we chose the Dallas route. I think we flew over northern Mexico. We had a five hour layover at the Dallas airport! So we sat around and shared some of our experiences. When we finally got off the plane in Nashville, I was a walking zombie! We had experienced three "days" that were actually 27 hours long. I mean it was that long from the time we got up till we lay back down. And this flight home from Hawaii was the third one. I was exhausted. It was Sunday afternoon, but Bro. Bob told us to get some rest, that we could give our reports to the church at prayer meeting Wednesday.

Marcia picked me up and when we got home and into the house, Bill showed me a plate at the table with a cover over it. I just wanted to sleep but Bill said that this would help me to sleep even better. He lifted the cover off with a flourish and there lay a dead woodpecker! They had been driving us crazy pecking on the vertical stained wood on the front of our upstairs bedroom, starting about daylight. He had slipped out undetected by the critter and shot him...just for me!

I made well over 400 snapshots and one day in Seoul I had to go buy some film. It cost a small fortune, too. Then I walked around the area and stepped into the courtyard of a Buddist temple. He glared down at me! I wouldn't take a million dollars for that missionary experience, but I don't think I could do it again, especially in this day and time and at my age now!

UPSTAGING REX NELON

One winter while we were in our Okeechobee, FL condo, we were invited by our longtime friend, Bill Cline to come to his church in the Clearwater area. [Bill was a member of the trio we met at Lake Louise in north Georgia in the early 60s]. They had a senior adult meeting with lunch and a program every Friday. Eight hundred or so were there, seated at tables facing the stage.

Marcia and I drove over from Okeechobee and got there early. Bill said he had a demo cassette he wanted me to listen to and tell him what I thought about it. It started playing and I began to have doubts. It was a mixed quartet and they lacked a lot of things including talent. Then they hit the chorus with an alto lead "If your hair's too long (others repeat) – there's sin in your heart!" I knew I'd been "had." Bill was proud of himself!

We were actually the "warm-up" group for the main guests, the Rex Nelon Singers. Remember, years before Rex was a part of the LeFevre Family singers. We sang for perhaps twenty minutes.

At the close of our time I told the folks I wanted to sing the first song I ever wrote. I sang my "Lonesome in my Saddle (Since my Horse Died)" song written when I was thirteen. The crowd went wild…for a while. When Rex finally walked to the mike, he looked out over the audience and said to me, "Elmo, that's the first time I've had to follow a song about a dead horse!"

"DOODLES'" MOM

Remember Doodles, who came down to the Francis farm a lot? She also did some bookkeeping for Mr. and Mrs. Francis. Her mother was in Miller Hospital in East Nashville and passed away while Doodles was out of the room. Marcia, however, was there.

The doctors and nurses came running in and started the process to revive her. Marcia said, "Her daughter told me that her mother did not want to be resuscitated." They kept on working, but told Marcia their oath required them to try and save lives. About that time Doodles came in and cleared the room!

She wanted me to play for the funeral and also be a pall-bearer. I told her there was no way I could do both. She appointed me as lead pallbearer on the left side. [I don't remember who played for the funeral]. It so happened that day we had about a six inch snowfall on the ground and it was treacherously icy as well. I just knew I was going to slip and plunge butt-first into that open grave! But I made it, PTL! That was the second time I had ever been a pallbearer, the first being when the bank president in Winnfield passed away in 1955.

"I'M GONNA BE GONE!"

In the mid-80s we did the music in a revival at First Baptist in Baldwin, MS in the northeast part of the state. The choir was very talented. One night I had them to sing my arrangement of Lanny Wolfe's song, "I'm Gonna Be Gone." In the choral book at the bottom of the last page of music I suggest that at the end of the song, and without music the choir sings the words, "I'm gonna be..." We did.

The pastor, Bro. Leo Barker AND the evangelist who were sitting in platform chairs, jerked around and looked! That was the affect I wanted it to have...to make it appear the Rapture occurred right then! The organist at the church was a sweet lady about 90 years old, and she was talented. Her husband, still living at the time, had been a "circuit-riding-postman!" He figured he had ridden over 100,000 miles over the years.

One afternoon Bro. and Mrs. Barker took Marcia and me in their car out on a country road looking for a certain type of tree Marcia hoped to find and take back to Nashville. We spied one and went to get it. I dug the shovel into the ground around it and tried to pull it up but could not. Leo said for us both to pull on it. We bent over and pulled, but suddenly his elbow jerked back in direct contact with my forehead and I literally staggered backward. They all just died laughing! It took a while for me to decide which eye went where!

The Barkers moved to Philadelphia, MS where he became that Baptist association's Director of Missions. We had done music in a revival at First Baptist there prior to that. A faithful family in the church lived on a small ranch north of town. We stayed in their home. He was in the National Guard in transportation, and his unit was the first to arrive in Iraq in 1990 (Desert Storm) with the necessary equipment, then was the last to leave!

There was a donkey out in the pasture and I asked him about it. He said he used it to "train bulls." Around their necks he would tie about a 4-foot rope between the donkey and the young bull. I didn't see this but he told me about it. He would take feed and dump it in the trough. The bull and donkey, out in the pasture, would make their way to it. A few feet from the trough the donkey would plant his front feet and throw his head back, and that bull would fall flat on his back. When he got up the donkey would lead him back to where they had been standing, as much as to say, "I'll tell you when you can go eat, buddy!"

DEMONS & MILLER TIME

In a small town in north Louisiana we did the music in a revival. The pastor told us that the church's sound system had quit working the week before. They rushed to Monroe to obtain one for the meeting. The store manager told them that he had one but it had been previously used in a honky-tonk. They brought it back to use anyway. Actually, the church was small enough we could have done without...especially this one!

It caused trouble and embarrassment from the start. We were singing one night before the message when suddenly it blasted out a deep, sharp, loud, electrical sound that I cannot begin to describe. We were looking at the audience as we sang a poignant song (one of mine, of course), and the entire congregation, as one, rose a couple of inches from their pews while maintaining *their positions.* If an arm was draped over the end or back of the seat, it remained in that stance...up, and back down!

The Lord...I know it was the Lord...helped us to keep a straight face and finish the song. We picked out a knot in the back wall paneling and concentrated on the lyrics and made it through. But oh! I will never forget that service.

Bro. James Miller was pastor at First Baptist in Converse, LA and had us to come for a weekend. When we finished our medley of songs in the morning service, it was time for him to preach. I looked at the crowd and said, "And now comes Miller time!" All 75 people roared! James signs his e-mails "Miller Time."

It may have been that weekend that I practiced with the choir to sing my song "One More Hill, One More Valley." The lyric concludes, "...and... then...home!" Well, some bass would not pause after "then" and I said, "Now I want us all to get home at the same time. Remember to 'break' after the word "then," ok?" In my opinion that just emphasized that we'd be HOME. I further stated that if someone barged on through, we would flip them over into the baptistery! I want you to know as we approached that place, something happened...I don't remember...a baby squealed out, a car horn blew...something – and ***I plowed right through it!*** And would you believe it? That bunch of folks wanted to throw ME over in the baptistery!

James Miller has been a true friend through the decades. He has had us come to about four churches where he has been pastor. One was right across the road from a GREAT fried catfish place in Spearsville, LA. On January 13, 2013 as they celebrated their 50th anniversary at the church, Shirley suddenly passed away!

TEXAS

We have done concerts all over Texas, and especially "deep east" Texas. In Tyler a pastor friend invited us to his church. After lunch we spent the afternoon with an elderly couple. They had a beautiful ranch just out of town. He said that his son sold a large number of cattle each week and delivered them in tractor trailers that had his last name in lights on the front.

Another church just south of Tyler was a bit unusual. A member of the church was in the marble business. The church office had a marble counter top. The restrooms had marble walls, if I remember correctly. Even the toilet seats were marble…and HEAVY. That could have been somewhat dangerous!

We visited the Brookshire Brothers museum in Tyler. They were a large family and have many grocery stores all over east Texas…some are Brookshire Brothers and some are just Brookshire's. Another big grocery chain is called H. E. B. The founder was Howard E. Butt, who was a dedicated Christian and a Baptist. Also Tyler is known for its huge flower gardens.

We went to the First Baptist in Diboll, just south of Lufkin where Marcia's sister Johnnie and family lived, five times over the years. We always had a great time at that church. I can't begin to mention all the churches we went to in east Texas, but there are a bunch of great folks living there!

Another friend had us come to a Methodist church for a banquet in Big Spring, TX. And the spring IS big! We stayed in their home. He rode a motorcycle. Previously he had us at a church in the Wichita Falls area. We stayed at a Baptist conference grounds called the Ponderosa. Another friend got us to come to a church where he was interim pastor in Big Lake, TX. In a C-store we saw bottles of water labeled "Okeechobee water." We told them we had a condo in Okeechobee, FL and that the name meant "big water." We sang at churches in Ft. Worth, Weatherford, Mineral Wells, Paris, etc.

A HEATHEN HORSEFLY

At Pontotoc, MS First Baptist Church the unexpected happened. The choir had run through our special number from one of my choral books, and I headed for the sanctuary to play a prelude. After I began I discovered I had left all my music in the choir room! Fortunately, Marcia brought it all out but when she set it on the book holder some of it fell on my hands. Here I am trying to keep my fingers going and all the while keep smiling up at the closed circuit TV camera.

During the invocation, a HORSEFLY invading our area, buzzing around the piano and then it spied Marcia. Alarmed and taking NO chances, she grabbed a hymnal and took a swing at him. I looked toward her and whispered, "Marcia, stop that!

We're on TV." It didn't matter to her, but thank goodness the horsefly flew off in the direction of the choir. The organ must have been 15 yards across from us!

After church in the choir room we heard a lady say, "Did y'all see that horsefly in the choir this morning?" Marcia and I didn't open our mouths! Whoa, now that's hard to believe!

GLEANING THE FIELDS

Another "snowbird" couple was Ned and Mary Esther Kemper. Over the years we became very close, in Okeechobee and in their Windfall, IN home. It was a two-story frame house and our room was upstairs. One morning I got up and looked out and everything was white. Snow had fallen over night. They farmed hundreds of acres of corn and soy beans. An electric line lay across their driveway alerting them when a vehicle drove up. Their little dog was named Dixie. They always had a good garden next to their house. Mary could whip up a meal in no time. Then we would clear the table and start playing card games!

Some of the corn farmers in the area grew popcorn for Orville Reddenbacher Company. One afternoon Mary said, "Let's go over to a field and pick up some popcorn." That sounded good to us. It was very cold and bits of freezing rain or sleet were on the ground. We picked up the ears of corn that the combine had missed. You could step on a shuck to see if there was a cob inside it; if so you'd bend over and pick it up. I told Mary and Marcia, "Hey, this is like Naomi and Ruth gleaning the fields." Mary looked at me and said, "Yeah, and you must be Boaz!" I had a full beard. In fact I've had one since late October 1982.

The next day we shelled the corn we'd gathered. They had an OLD corncob shelling outfit that was patented in the late 1800s! You crammed cobs in the top and turned a big crank... not modern but it did the job. Mary would be turning the crank for a while and she kept reminding me, "Little end down, Mo!" Then we'd switch. When we got finished, and it took perhaps 2 or 3 hours, we weighed the sacks of shelled corn. It came to 130 pounds! They insisted that we take some home with us and we did. If our car had caught on fire going down I-65 we would have blocked it with a mountain of popcorn!

They also drove us around central Indiana. We'd drive in to Tipton, the county seat, and eat at Pizza Shack. We'd usually see friends there, too. But we never did go up to Shipshewana where a huge flea market is a favorite tourist destination. The Kempers lived a mile or so south of Windfall on SR-213. That town was mentioned in a national TV commercial several years ago.

The little church they attended was located in the edge of a cornfield north of Windfall. We sang there many times, even did music for a couple of revivals. They had such a wonderful fellowship there. They would have a "pitch-in" every now and then. Down south we called it "dinner-on-the-ground." One time a lady brought persimmon pie and it was delicious.

In Okeechobee during the winter months we spent a lot of time at each other's homes eating and playing card games, sometimes just the four of us. One year a tornado hit southeast Okeechobee and Marcia and I slept through it! It was said to have done $20 million in damage. A lot of citrus fruit was on the ground. Ned called us to bring our electric juicer and come help them. But the police had Taylor Creek Isles blocked off and would not let us in. We went back home and called Ned. He said he would meet us there and lead us to his house, and that was allowed along with the warning to watch out for fallen electric lines. We worked ALL day and put gallons of juice in our freezers!

By the way, they sold that place later. Would you believe another tornado came through there and ripped their glassed in back porch (the length of the house) completely off. We had all experienced many good meals and fun times in that room. At one meal, Mary served what she called lemon pie. We loved it. Then she told us she made it out of little grapefruit she pulled off a tree in their backyard that was dying!

BIRTH OF A SONG

I get song ideas from everywhere: prayers, sermons, conversations, bumper stickers, billboards, the Bible to name a few. Since we spent our winters in Okeechobee, FL for over 25 years, we were very involved in First Baptist church there. I played for the services (sometimes organ, mostly grand piano) during the winter months we would be there. Elsewhere I have written about our orchestra, etc. But the "contemporary Christian" music took over and the orchestra wasn't needed any longer.

One night pastor Dick Whipple and I were talking as we walked up the hallway toward the auditorium. He asked if I'd ever thought of writing a song on the "shoulders" of Jesus. I said I had heard songs about his eyes, his hands, etc. He gave me three ideas and soon I wrote the three verse song with chorus, simply titled "Shoulders."

1st – The Shepherd bringing the lost sheep home on his shoulders; 2nd – Jesus' shoulders bore the cross for you and me; 3rd – On His shoulders will rest all authority one day throughout all eternity. I also made a piano/organ duet arrangement of the song. It is one of the best loved songs in our concerts.

Our friend Jack Evans for many years has been pastor at Ebenezer Baptist in Greenbrier, TN. He married Diane, the younger daughter of Mimi and Don Taylor. Before that he was pastor at Siloam Baptist in Meadeville, MS located between Natchez and McComb on US-84 [it runs through our LA hometown also]. Marcia and I did the music in two revivals during the nine years they were there. Bro. Bob Mowrey was evangelist for one of them. He decided to ride a Greyhound bus down there and his luggage was lost! A member of the church went back to McComb the next day and retrieved it. Mary Taylor rode down with us. We had a great time together. Jack and Diane's son was a few years old then. He is now a member of the Tennessee State House of Representatives, already having been re-elected. Diane's sister, Marcie married Tom Wainman and he later retired from Ford Motor Company in Detroit. They live in Ashland City, TN.

FIRST TRIP TO ALASKA

In early August 1985 Marcia and I went to Fairbanks, Alaska where I played for the 40th anniversary of the Alaska Baptist Convention. My niece Jonnye's husband, Danny Griffin arranged for us to sing at four churches in Anchorage. He was the youngest son of Dr. Felton Griffin who went up there during WWII and planted scores of Southern Baptist churches there. In fact, Marcia and I stayed in his home while there. My sister Gertrude (Jonnye's mother) and husband Dan Rankin also flew up for that time together. They stayed at Jonnye and Danny's house. We flew out of Dallas about four hours apart.

The next morning at the breakfast table at the Griffin's house we saw the morning paper headline about a passenger jet crashing at DFW airport due to wind shear. God had indeed watched over us. Anyhow, I will never forget what woke us up that morning. It never really got **dark** there but we had closed the curtains and somehow went to sleep. Suddenly this gruff voice yelled, "Hey there, little feller! Wake up! It's time t'git goin' t'day!" I popped up in the bed looking around. It was a clock "Griff" had put in our room with the alarm set, and it was the Grouch off Sesame Street's voice! We found he was a collector of unique clocks.

One day Marcia and I borrowed Griff's T-bird and drove around Anchorage sight-seeing. We went to the I-Max and saw a great film about Alaska. We ate soup for lunch at a café…$9 (that was 1985). Everything is expensive up there. One night all of us went to a huge wooden mill-like structure to eat and

I ordered fish. It came to me whole and laying on the platter looking up at me! They had a player piano that portrayed digital red lyrics as it played songs. Big moose, elk and bear heads were hanging everywhere – there was no ceiling in the place and the rafters could be seen. Houses are built with foot-thick walls surrounded by varied beautiful flowers. Ornamental cabbages were at least two feet in diameter. An "average" house was $250,000...and that was in 1985.

During the 1964 earthquake in that area the houses across the street from Griff fell into the Cook Inlet. There is an "Earthquake Park" along there now where you can see pipes, concrete, etc. just below the surface. Danny said that when it happened that morning everyone ran out of their houses. A friend of his lived across from them and his mother yelled, "Oh! We left the baby in the highchair!" His friend said, "I'll get him," and ran back inside. Suddenly it all collapsed and disappeared into the inlet and their bodies were never recovered!

Danny borrowed a Volkswagen bus (like the hippies in the 60s drove!) for us all to ride in up to Fairbanks for the convention. We would almost creep UP the mountains, then joyously race down the other side! All at once Danny said, "Oh, no! The speedometer quit working." He suddenly hit his open palm on the dash and yelled, "HEAL!"....and would you believe? It started working again for the rest of the trip. I remember going over Hurricane Gulch, at least a thousand feet deep.

When it came "potty" time there were no Rest Areas, of course. We stopped at a huge white dome-shaped building but it stunk so bad we drove on a bit and then took to the woods – men to the right, women to the left. Along the way at a gift shop I bought a tie clasp that looked like a trap – a mosquito trap they told me. In fact, you could actually set it. I did that only once!

Arriving in Fairbanks Danny drove us to a LONG apartment complex with several alcove entrances to it. He had made arrangements with a friend, a worker there, for us to spend two nights in his apartment. Danny, Dan and I freshened up and went to the First Baptist Church, across from the campus of the University of Alaska. I was about ready to start my prelude on the organ when Danny handed me the keys and said "Can you run over and get the girls?" I said, "Are you kidding? I doubt I could find the place and I've never driven a VW bus!" He insisted and I started praying. God answered, too, but not like I expected…

God did help me turn at the right places and find the building. However, I ran into what I thought was the right alcove, flung open the door and said, "Hurry! We've got to get to the church quick!" A blond was sitting on the couch with her back to me watching TV and turned to look at me. I threw up both hands, palms out, and said, "Oops! Sorry, wrong apartment!" As I went to dash back out the door she said (so help me!), "Wait a minute, it may not be!" As I recall I yelled, "MARRRR-SUHHHHH!"

About 150 delegates were there and we had a memorable time. Dr. Lloyd Elder from "the Board" in Nashville was there and I had my picture made with him. We were given a heavy gold-colored pan like the ones used by miners to "pan" for gold in the creeks. It was engraved with the "40th anniversary" information. After the business session, Danny and his friend, Larry Russell sang "It is well with my Soul" and the windows in the building rattled! Then Griff preached his famous sermon, "Come Hell or High Water"... the condensed version that took only an hour and a half!

We drove to North Pole and saw the HUGE Santa statue, then on up to the Alaska pipeline so we could say we had seen and touched it! We saw an enormous machine that scooped up the earth, searching for coal or gold or something. It was unbelievable – the workers lived on it also! On the way back to Anchorage we found it had snowed. Danny said it was the first of the season (around August 10th or so) and was referred to as "Termination Snow" – summer workers gave their two weeks' notice to head back to the lower 48. We did not have time to drive the 90 miles or so out to Denali National Park. However, from Griff's house in Anchorage that huge mountain could be seen as a big white lump...about 160 miles to our north!

We went to a place where we could "pan for gold nuggets". That was a tourist trap if there ever was one! We did discover they have mosquitoes up there. They ran us crazy along the banks of the stream! In fact, Danny said there are 31 varieties of them there. One landed at Elmendorf Airbase in Anchorage and they had put 140 gallons of jet fuel in him when they discovered it was not a jet. (You believe that, don't you)? Later, on the banks of Shipp Creek near Anchorage we saw lots of salmon, up to 3 feet long lying dead on the rocky banks having been overcome by exhaustion trying to get upstream.

Danny took us down to Alyeska Ski area south of Anchorage. Parts of that area dropped from 20 to 90 feet during that 1964 earthquake. We rode the ski lift that was actually three lifts. From the summit we had an amazing 360 degree view of the Chugach mountain range. In a building at the base of the ski lift was a big piece of jade. An electric diamond-tipped saw was sawing it in half and was about half-way through. We were told it had started cutting over two weeks before! Wow! Nearby was a mountain outcrop of jade!

Dr. and Mrs. Griffin were remarkable Christians used of God in a mighty way. He had started the First Baptist Church of Anchorage, which grew to over 1,200 members. It is said one out of five families own a sea plane. At Anchorage there are two lakes – one to take off from, the other to land in. Signs on roads read "Aircraft have right of way." One day Griff had taken a preacher friend up in his single engine plane to go to a remote area. The engine suddenly quit and Griff said, "Well, Brother Sam, the motor's stopped. What would you do?" The man replied, "Uh, I think the more important question, Griff, is what are YOU gonna do?" He set the plane down in a lake that was later named Griffin Lake!

THE LATE 80s

Roger and Edna Stagner were from Granite City, IL, east of St. Louis. They had a wonderful family and one of their daughters played the organ at their church. We sang there twice over the years. Roger always had a great garden behind their house. He was of German descent and was in charge of the computers at the Granite City Steelworks.

They owned a place in Okeechobee with lake access. We visited in each other's homes during the winter. He was known to be an excellent fisherman. One time he was telling about catching the limit and someone asked him where it was. They went to the place the next day and didn't even get a bite. I told him his name was now Roger "Muddd" spelled with three "D's." He passed away a few years ago.

Dean and Brenda Eades, who live in NW South Carolina, got several dates for us. We met them at a Benson WHACHAMACALLIT at Lake Barkley KY and have been very close since then spending time in each other's homes. One of those dates was at a Baptist church called "Bounty Land," not far from their house near Lake Keowee. It is a large church surrounded by a huge cemetery as I recall. The pastor was called "Wild Bill!" I learned immediately I could not compete with him. He was a riot!

At Calvary Baptist Church in Erwin, TN (near the North Carolina state line) we did a concert on Sunday. We stayed in the pastor's home. They had two sweet little girls. Their mother was going to put them to bed and I said, "Wait. I bet I can do something you can't do." I ripped off my hairpiece and their eyes went wide. Then we all laughed...but I got to thinking I probably should not have done that. Those girls may be having bad dreams because of that to this day!

Over the years we did concerts in many churches in east Tennessee. For three straight Sundays we did three concerts on Sunday, doing one at 2:30 in the afternoon. One year we particularly remember being at Skyline Baptist in Johnson City. We stayed in the home of Paul and Ramona Seay. They would dress up like clowns and appear at events all over the area. They called themselves the "Art-cats." At a later time they invited us to spend three days in Gatlinburg with them at their time-share. We played cards, drove around some and had a big time together. Sadly, Ramona passed away in 2012.

JUDGE MO & THE GOVERNOR

We went to First Baptist Church in Dresden, TN several times to sing and to attend "singings" held there. Those folks love to sing good old gospel songs, AND they love to sing my songs. Judge Tommy Moore was church pianist and liked my solo piano books. He was "instrumental" (pun intended) in getting those dates for us. By the way, some folks there just call him "Judge Mo."

Their house is across the street from where Gov. Ned McWherter lived. A big plum tree was in the judge's front yard, but the fruit was being taken, he believed, by school kids or joggers. Tommy told his wife Carol he was going to get up early the next morning, sit on the front porch and tell people to stop taking his plums. They wanted to make jelly/jam out of them. After all, it was **their** tree on **their** land.

The next morning when he opened the front door there stood a shadowy figure of a big man with his back to Tommy. He was wearing a "gentleman's cowboy hat" and was picking and eating plums! Tommy thought, "Ah ha! Caught one red handed!" He yelled out, "**HEY**!!!" The figure jerked around to face him. It was Gov. McWherter! Tommy said, "Oh! Mornin', Governor. Let me get you a sack for those!"

On one of those times at FBC Dresden we were having a choir practice on Saturday night when in walked Larry Orrell. He formed a trio, aptly called "The Orrells," with Gordon Jensen (Benson songwriter) and another young man I can't recall. I said, "Larry, what are you doing here?" He had relatives in the area. His father was a gospel music promoter from Detroit. [I recall other concert promoters at the time were Sonny Simmons and J. G. Whitfield]. Dresden FBC bought a new grand piano and I was invited down to play for its dedication. We love those Dresden church folks.

SAN FRANCISCO BAY AREA

On a west coast tour one year Marcia and I did twelve concerts in fifteen days/nights in the San Francisco Bay area. A lot of them were secured by my niece Jonnye's husband Danny Griffin. At the time they and their four children lived in San Pablo at the NE corner of the bay. Danny was attending Golden Gate Seminary.

During that time we stayed at Bayview "Elegant Retirement Living," located further east off I-80. It was a beautiful setting with views of the bay and surrounding mountains. It had three guest rooms. A resident's husband had recently passed away and she paid for twelve nights, thinking that was correct. Later we went to pay for three more nights and the manager said to not worry about it! *(See further explanation following – {*})*

The building was three or four floors with beautiful landscaping and covered parking. Inside there were chandeliers, porcelain or carved wood animals and live plants everywhere. The dining room was spacious with big windows. There was a black baby grand piano that shined like patent leather shoes! At our first meal we waited until residents were seated so we wouldn't get someone's table. After they found out I played piano and what we were doing "in town" some of the guests would cut each other off "at the pass" in order to sit and talk with us. It was about a five course meal and took almost two hours, but what else did we have to do!

There was one couple that sat with us every chance they got! He had retired from AT&T and they were traveling extensively, many times on *merchant ships!* They said sometimes they were the only guests on board and would eat at the Captain's table. They said the rooms were larger than those on cruise ships. Interesting.

Our room was excellent and spacious. All rooms had microwaves, no other cooking was allowed. But our room had no television set. We went driving around searching for a rental store. While I was looking at signs I got too near a curb and blew out the left front tire! I phoned AAA and they came in

20 minutes and put on the extra tire. The poor guy said that was the 15th one he'd changed that day! We went to three stores trying to find the right size for our Olds 98 and could not.

So the next morning (Sunday) at Jonnye and Danny's church I told a man what had happened and asked him where I might find a tire. He said Montgomery-Ward should have it. I asked for directions. He told me to "get on I-80 West and get off at the Dam exit." I said, "What?" He said, "Oh, sorry! It's the San Pablo Dam Road and people around here just shorten it." We bought a new tire and rented a TV also.

[*] Two couples served as "managers" of the place, one there while the other was off. One couple was familiar with my music. He even had the sheet music of my song, "I Heard a Little Prayer" recorded by Elmer and June Childress (Wichita, KS) on Benson's HeartWarming label. I autographed it for him. He asked us to do a mini-concert at supper one night.

So we sang some and I played some. They began to eat their meal and I continued playing dinner music – some old pop tunes, WWII songs and some hymns. While I was playing a hymn Marcia became aware that a man not far from her was softly whistling. She walked over and said, "Go up there and whistle louder so everyone can hear you." He said, "Oh, I might not know what he would play." Marcia said, "Come with me."

I suggested we do "In the Garden." It was beautifully done and the folks obviously enjoyed our duet. We did "How Great Thou Art," and some others. After the meal was over and people were leaving the man said to us: "My name is Frank Fuller and my life will be fuller after tonight!" What a blessing we had been to each other. One of the ladies told Marcia later she was glad Marcia got him to do that. His wife was to go into a nursing home the next day and he would go with her although he did not need to. We saw him a day or two later and he was still at Bayview, and I'm not sure what the outcome was. We will always remember him. The manager told us to stay with them anytime we were back in the Bay area. That was a nice offer.

On one of our three "days off" we drove by the city of Richmond and then passed San Quentin Prison where Charles Manson was incarcerated. We had a good view of Alcatraz Island in the bay where a notorious prison was for many years. We crossed the Golden Gate Bridge into the city. After riding the trolley cars to Chinatown we went down to Fisherman's Wharf for seafood. After the Northridge earthquake (I believe it was) the Embarcadero was so badly damaged that it was propped up for a while. Embarcadero means "to embark". It actually runs under the western approach to the Oakland Bridge, going north along the port of San Francisco all the way down to Fisherman's Wharf.

After that earthquake, when the upper level of I-880 fell on the lower one, the people of Oakland just called it I-440. They still had a sense of humor. In 2012 at the American Baptist Women's annual convention held at the New Millennium Maxwell House hotel in Nashville, Marcia and I talked with a woman preacher from Oakland. She said she had just exited the Oakland Bay Bridge to make a cell phone call when suddenly her car was violently bounced around. She looked back and saw the interstate collapsing!

We then drove north through Berkeley and back to Bayview. One of our concerts was at a church in Livermore on I-580 east of Oakland. During the concert I mentioned something about my sister living in north Louisiana. After the service the pastor asked where and I said, "I'm sure you've never heard of it, it's a little town called Pelican south of Shreveport. He said, "I, too, have a sister living there!" We couldn't believe it. We recognized her name...she was Gertrude's best friend and lived in a half mile of them!

WE VISIT "SNOWBIRDS"

In Okeechobee, FL we met many "snowbirds" from several northern states that came down for the winter. Back home they were members of various denominations but would attend First Baptist while down there. We had a condo in Oak Lake Villas just off Eagle Bay Drive and would also spend most of our time there during cold weather at home. Two or three nights a week a bunch of us would meet at someone's house (meal optional) and play all kinds of card games. They surely taught us some new ones.

One night Barb Strahl stood up at the table and shook herself. I said, "What's the matter?" She said, "Nothing, I just had to stand up to let my underwear straighten out!" She and Dale were about the oldest couple and were the first to sell out, go back home to Columbus, IN and stop coming down. Marcia and I went by to see them several times after that when we would be traveling near them.

During a game one night at the Kemper's house, her cousin Madonna Renbarger looked at me from the opposite end of the table and said, "You know, Elmo – there ain't no justice in this here land. Why, I just got a divorce from my ol' man. But I had to laugh at the judge's decision – he gave him the kids…..and they ain't even his'n!" Funny. Her husband's name was Bob. They lived a few miles north of the Kempers in Indiana.

Dale and Betty Salsbery were the first couple to have Marcia and me in their home AND church. He farmed hundreds of acres of corn and soy beans and also had a big pig farm. I wanted to see the inside of it and he told me I should jog through because the smell would get in my beard! We did and I saw to my right the largest sow I've ever seen laying on her side. He said she was to "give birth" any time. We went to a nearby pig farm when a truck came to pick some up. They were big "piglets" but I was told they were only three weeks old! They were being taken to a feeder lot. We had another friend in the area that lost hundreds of pigs due to electrocution because of a short in a huge fan in the end of the long building.

In Dale's barn where he kept his implements was a new John Deere combine that had never been in the field. I climbed up and it was awesome. Years later on the day he had planned to retire, he finished work in an area and headed home. The land is flat and laid out in square miles with a connecting shell road every half mile. As he crossed a bridge that had solid concrete sides to it, he was almost jerked out of the cab! He had forgotten to turn the combine head from side-ways to length-ways to follow behind him. It about tore it up, but thank the Lord for insurance. He was somewhat embarrassed!

We visited them another time when we were in north central Indiana. They drove us up to Winona Lake. I knew of the place because that is where the Rodeheaver Company was located. Homer Rodeheaver led singing for the Billy Sunday revivals and played the trombone. We saw the old tabernacle, then went into the museum and among other items we saw his trombone! There is a lot of history and precious memories there. The beautiful lake is surrounded by houses. I'm so glad we got to go there.

The Rodeheaver Company owns copyrights to 31 of my original songs that Mr. John T. did not choose to take. I believe WORD Music acquired Rodeheaver many years ago. The Lillenas Company in Kansas City, MO (it is the official Nazarene Publishing House) owns three of my original songs. In the 50s while I was a Benson staff writer – the songs Mr. John T. rejected I was free to send elsewhere. So I sent them to Lillenas and Rodeheaver. The ones they refused, I would reverse and send them THOSE songs. The songs that were not taken by any of them I labeled "TTL" in my card file which meant "three time loser!"

Dale and Betty's church was Hemlock Friends Church located just east of Kokomo, IN and north of where they lived.

I thought women were to keep quiet in a Quaker church and had Marcia practicing to keep her mouth shut. (Yeah, right!). They had a supper Saturday night in fellowship hall and shoot, they were just like Baptists...sat there and goss-....I mean.... talked about everyone and everything. We went to their church twice and enjoyed it so much.

Dale and Betty had a son and two daughters. The son, for years now has been pastor of a big church in the general area. He had us at that church one Sunday for a concert. Another Sunday afternoon we dropped by and Wayne Hilliard's Trio were their guests. The older daughter and her husband live in a beautiful two-story home on a small (man-made) hill, with a nearby pond, of course. We were visiting one day and she got up and removed the strip of wood in front below the piano keys, gave me a felt pen and said, "Autograph my piano!" I had never been asked to do that before. Her husband farmed thousands of acres and was also a hot air balloon enthusiast. He went up one day in January (?), apparently got up in the jet stream and finally brought the thing down...in West Virginia!

The younger daughter married a Friends' preacher, who Dale said would ride his bike for miles to visit her. They had us in their church in north Indianapolis. When Dale and Betty were in Okeechobee during the winter they would take us out on the lake or maybe just the rim canal on their pontoon boat. They caught a lot of fish, too. We were playing cards at our condo one night and Dale asked Marcia when she was born? She said, "'36." Dale said, "Was that 18 or 19?" He never beat Marcia in a game called "Up and Down" (or "Oh heck") on her "own turf."

He played guitar and sang old funny songs, but sometimes he'd do a love song. He sang to Betty one night at Bob and Louise Vierling's house when they put on their annual "rabbit feast." Betty's health declined and they had to stop coming down to Okeechobee, and later on she passed away. One winter our doorbell rang and when I opened the door, there stood a grinning Dale. What memories we all have!

Bob and Doneta Williams live north of Elwood, IN and farm hundreds of acres. Their three sons have taken over now, however. They got us seven concert dates in a twelve day period and we stayed in their home. On Sunday morning we looked out in the field behind their house. A big sow had gotten out and one of their sons was on a 4-wheeler herding her back. They were going over the rows and sometimes he would bump her on the rump. It was funny.

Only one of the concerts was in a Baptist Church! We did a concert in their Christian Church in Elwood on Sunday morning. I offered to mow their large lawn and was told to dump the grass in their big garden plot behind their house. One time I went to do that and there was nothing in it…I had forgotten to engage the grass-catcher mechanism! Marcia and I got to ride in the tractor cab as Bob plowed a field. It was big, with four double tires on it. Some days he said he would place a can of food on the manifold (or motor) and when he was ready to eat lunch it would be warmed. Other days, Doneta would call him on the two-way radio and find out where he was working so we could carry his lunch to him.

Zondervan contracted me to compile "The Best of Country Western Hymnal." They had published the first volume in 1972 and had asked me to compile it. John III and Bob said it would be a conflict of interest, so I suggested our friend Fred Bock in California. He did the job. I believe Harold Lane (Speer family) did one volume for them. I don't recall who may have compiled the other three volumes. While Marcia and I were at the Williams' house those days I searched through those five editions and on yellow legal pads titled "MUST" and "MAYBE" wrote down titles and locations. Somehow I must have turned two pages at once, because I left out "Each Step I Take!" My brother Earl wrote me about that! I rushed to look through my file copy and oh, friends! It was not in there! I was devastated.

In the late 70s Benson went on a 10-hour four-day workweek. I was regarded as an "executive" (kinda funny, huh?) and was to work from 7 a.m. to 6 p.m., taking an hour for lunch. At that time I was driving Kellye to Bellevue High School where classes started at 7 a.m. In the winter he was still dark! (And it was dark when I got home from work, too). School dismissed at 2 p.m. (!) and she rode the bus home – to the top of the hill anyway. Her senior year we bought her a new '79 Ford. When we had snow and ice on the ground we had to carefully make our way down our front yard to where our car had been parked. I was wearing cowboy boots and she would crack up when many times I would slip and bust my rear. Anyhow, I told John III and Bob that I would take Kellye to school then arrive at work around 7:15 and would just take a shorter lunch break.

FRED BOCK

Fred knew how to live a full life. He loved music – from school bands to gospel/church music to classical. For 14 years he was minister of music at the prestigious Bell Air Presbyterian church in Los Angeles. After that he held the same position at Hollywood Presbyterian church for 18 years. He edited several hymnals including Bill Gaither's "Family of God" hymnal which sold three million copies.

I needed to talk with Fred about some publishing business and when I got to work around 7:15 a.m. I gave him a quick call. I heard a sleepy "Hello?" and it hit me…it was only 5:15 a.m. in California! I apologized. He had told me one time that when the big Northridge earthquake hit in California, it sloshed two feet of water out of his swimming pool!

At a Bill Gaither Praise Gathering one year a big choir was singing my arrangement of "It will be worth it all." Fred and I were standing back stage. He listened a while then asked, "Did you arrange that?" I said yes and he said, "That's very good!" I was pleased because he is also a noted arranger. We all lost a dear friend when he passed away several years ago.

OKEECHOBEE

Lois and Lee Cammon lived in Olney, IL. Lee did not like catfish. One day while fishing off his pier in Taylor Creek Isles in Okeechobee, he caught a 2-pounder. He called to see if

I wanted it. BJ, Joey and Kayla were at our villa so it must have been on a Saturday because they usually spent Friday nights with us. They climbed up on the tall barstools to watch. I had seen my Daddy do this, so I figured I could do it. I got a board, a nail and a hammer! I set the board to the left of the sink on the counter and laid the catfish on it. Marcia had the VCR camera rolling. I put the nail on his head and came down with the hammer. In a split second that big fish jumped right between my legs and I jumped and yelled, "Goshdogit!" Well, Marcia had jumped too and did not get it recorded. That would have gone viral on you.Tube had it been invented back then. I just thought I'd mention this to you before the movie comes out.

BJ, Joey and Kayla loved to play kickball in our small enclosure at the villa. Of course, Papa (me) had to play with them... it was my idea. With our back to the sliding glass door in the kitchen, we'd kick the ball and head for first base at the corner of the living room. The second base was straight across from that at a certain wide plank on the privacy fence. There was no third base, so with the next kick the runner headed "home." The boys would throw "wide" of Kayla sometime so she could safely reach first base. She wore glasses back then.

We did have one BIG problem. Just outside at the corner of the fence was a big bougainvillea bush that was several feet tall. It had absolutely beautiful wine-colored flowers all over it, but the branches had long thorns on it. Several branches hung over the top of the fence into our patio. They would deflate a brand-spankin' new kickball in a heartbeat!

BJ and Joey kept bicycles inside the fence at the condo. They liked to ride them on Saturdays out on the private street coming off Eagle Bay Drive into what is called "Oak Lake Villas." Jack Coker had 3 or 4 big dump truckloads of dirt brought along that road, but nothing was ever done with it. Eventually grass and weeds grew on it. The boys liked to race their bikes and ride over them, but sometimes they didn't make it! Also they liked to get up speed and go over the speed bumps on that road, jerking up on the handle bars.

Marcia and I bought a Ruby Red grapefruit tree when we first got down there and although it grew, it had no fruit on it for a few years. A friend of ours told Marcia to "spank it!" She said to take a rolled up newspaper, or a piece of old water hose and go around spanking the limbs and/or leaves. Marcia told our next door neighbor, Wesley Mobley (wife Faye) what she planned to do and he said, "Don't you touch my tree!" He had been fertilizing and watering it. He even mowed our yard for us year 'round! Well, one night Marcia slipped out there and gently spanked the limbs. Next year we almost had to prop the limbs up! Wesley passed away in April 2013. He and Faye were good neighbors.

Many of our friends and neighbors in Oak Lake Villas have passed away as the years fly by.

WHAT'S IN A NAME?

We were doing concerts in north central Mississippi right after that and Marcia told the story to several folks as we ate lunch.

Betty Shearrer and her husband Ed published a weekly newspaper in Water Valley. She put that little story in a column since lots of folks (Baptists, at least) in the area knew us. We stayed in Ed and Betty's home several nights over the years. Ed played a great sax and if we were doing a concert anywhere close they would show up. He and I would play music beforehand. Ed was killed in a highway crash a few years ago. We miss him a lot.

I told Marcia one day I was thinking about changing my first name (William) to "**The**" Elmo Mercer. It just has a ring to it, right? She replied, "You'd do better changing your last name to "**Who,**" everybody asks 'Elmo **Who?**'" Well, perhaps I should be called "Forgetful" Mercer. Several times, Marcia and I have packed, loaded and gone to various parts of the country only to find the first night out we had left something behind! One time we went to Columbus, OH to visit Ralph Harris, his wife Jeri and daughter Diane (Kellye's age). We discovered we had left the bag of shoes for Marcia, Bill and Kellye. During Sunday School Jeri took them out to a store to buy new shoes! At that time "blue laws" were still enforced in Nashville.

We went to do some dates in Louisiana and were going to stay at my sister Gertrude's house out in the country near Pelican about 50 miles south of Shreveport. We discovered we had left a bag of clothes and had to go buy some. In a church west of Atlanta we were to do a concert. Upon arriving at the motel I raised the trunk of our van to get the "hang up clothes" bag and it was not in there. Marcia said she could "make-do," but we had to go to a mall and buy me pants, shirt & tie, and sport coat! Marcia said, "By the way, Merry Christmas!"

A friend of ours had us come to his church in Bossier City, LA (across the Red River from Shreveport). All of us decided to take a Sunday afternoon nap. Marcia was already lying down and when I sat on my side to take my shoes off, it fell through to the floor. She got up, we adjusted the slats and springs/mattress and I want you to know, the same thing happened! I think we just napped at an angle that afternoon.

In Savannah, GA one Sunday afternoon (back for the second time at this church) we tried to nap upstairs and it was just too hot. It was a new house and the downstairs was cool. I don't know what the problem was. We finally got up, dressed again for the concert that night and drove to a cooler, shady spot and waited. I think we ate a couple of ice cream sandwiches apiece trying to cool down!

In the mid-2000s we did a weekend at a church in a community south of Tupelo, MS. We stayed Saturday and Sunday nights in the home of Joanne and Arthur Roy Reed. It is located on the west side of a state highway, and is an antebellum home with large columns that sits on a hill, with a lake between it and the road. White lathe fences frame the asphalt driveway curving up the hill. In their backyard is the biggest gazebo I've ever seen. The foyer goes to the second floor ceiling. On the second floor (overlooking the foyer) they have lots of memorabilia, such as an operating nickelodeon. Out in his garage Roy has a very old restored car.

We enjoyed a tour of Tupelo and the Elvis Presley grounds and museum. Like Huntsville, AL it is a progressive city with a symphony orchestra and interesting sights to visit. We thoroughly enjoyed our stay with them and keep in touch by e-mail. All over that area we have sung in various churches and provided music in many revivals. Several Town and Country Music Clinics were also held in that region.

OTHER LATE 80s DATES

In Farragut (west Knoxville) we sang at a big Cumberland Presbyterian church three times over a few years. We met Atlee Hammaker who was a pitcher for the San Francisco Giants then. He had BIG hands! Between our second and third visits they built a big new sanctuary. A friend sent us a video tape of the following:

A group of children were standing on the steps up to the rostrum singing, when two little brothers in the first row started jabbing each other. It led to fisticuffs! The congregation was cracking up but the pastor, who could not see them from where he was seated on the platform didn't know what was going on. When the song was finished he called on a man to pray who was sitting with him there. It was the boys' father. The congregation exploded with laughter.

A second incident happened. The big choir was singing one of my arrangements where I changed keys and added a measure, but they came in too quickly. The minister of music was playing the piano and kicked over an imitation potted plant. It rolled down the steps. He jumped up and said something cute and set it back in place, then said, "OK, choir, pick it up at Measure 32," and that situation was remedied quite intelligently!

At First Baptist Church in Gulf Breeze, FL (across from Pensacola) we did music in a revival. It is a beautiful location and we had a great revival there. We stayed in the home of a couple, both of them retired school teachers. One night they had the revival team over for "supper." Marcia and I, along with the minister of music and his wife, sat on the floor (I don't know why) around the coffee table and ate.

Marcia knew there was a jar of pickles on the table where the others were eating and asked me to get it. I got up and asked our hostess to "please pass the pickles." She grasped the top of the jar with her right hand and CRACK! The bottom fell off and pickle juice spread everywhere over her beautiful tablecloth. [She had told us it was like one that is in the White House!] I'm glad I didn't do it!

We have been to Crestview, FL so many times and just love that area of the panhandle located some 50 miles east of Pensacola. The Director of Missions is Bro. Eugene Strickland, his wife is named Marsha. One night we were staying in their home and I said, "Come on, Marcia, let's go to bed." Eugene said, "Mrs. Strickland, you keep your seat." When Gene was pastor at FBC in Chattahoochee, FL (on US-90, also in the panhandle), he had us for two revivals. I'll cover those stories elsewhere.

Gene got us several dates around Crestview and we stayed in the Econo Lodge by I-10 for ten days/nights. We sang in a church at Baker, a few miles to the northwest and later did music in a revival there. We met Marvis and Jewel Carr and have been keeping in close touch since then by phone as well as going by to visit in their home. They have traveled to other places when they knew we would be there, even to northeast Georgia! They came to Okeechobee for a few days and visited us.

At Milligan Baptist Church just west of Crestview, we did a couple of concerts there. A member of the church looked just like "Barney Fife." He had an old police car just like on the Mayberry show and appeared at events all over that part of the country. Mr. S. L. Garrett, who owned the Cleaners by First Baptist in Winnfield when we were growing up came from Milligan. His sister who still lived there had us over for a meal a couple of times. She said she remembered when US-90 was a dirt road and travelers had to take a ferry across the Yellow River just east of Milligan! We also did a revival at a church where Bro. Bill White was pastor, and stayed in their home. So we can truthfully say we have stayed in the White house!

We did music in two revivals at Port St. Joe, FL on the Gulf coast. The first was at Long Hollow Baptist and they put us in a cabin in a small state park on Cape San Blas Island. It's about a hundred yards wide but a few miles in length. Gulf beaches were to the west and the bay to the east. Across five miles of shallow water we could see the church steeple but we had to drive 22 miles ONE-WAY to get there. With both a morning and night service I estimate we drove almost 500 miles during that revival!

Arriving at the park after dark, we had to carry all our stuff from the car to the cabin on a raised plank walkway. Raccoons were everywhere and we thought they were cute. The next day someone said they might be rabid and to be careful! From then on they would chase us to our cabin's screened-in porch! Almost every day helicopters would fly very low down the length of the island. Guys would be sitting in the door with their legs hanging down! They were likely from Ft. Rucker in SE Alabama, (an interesting museum is there), or maybe Eglin AFB near Crestview. It covers most of three counties! We woke up one morning hearing men's voices and I spotted two a quarter mile out in the bay. They stood perhaps knee deep in water and had sacks on their shoulders. They were picking up crabs, shrimp, or whatever was edible!

The second revival was citywide and was held in the high school gymnasium. Each night a thick plastic covering had to be put down, and taken back up, to protect the hardwood floor. Barbara Fairchild was the guest singer for the entire meeting. I believe our friend Jimmy Kearse led the singing. I played piano and Marcia and I sang some as well. The large choir was great, as was the attendance each night. The football coach from Lowndes County High School in Valdosta, GA came one night and gave his testimony. At that time, I believe that school had the best record in the US.

For that revival we stayed at the Governor Hotel, right on the beach but several miles west and in the Central time zone! We crossed a big bridge over the Apalachicola River on US-90. We kept our watches on Eastern Time for those days. We enjoyed sitting on the balcony and watching the sea gulls and the waves.

In the southeast part of Louisiana is the town of Bogalusa. We sang in four churches in that area. The town is laid out in quarters of NW, NE, SE and SW and right in the middle is a huge paper mill. Most residents work there. But, oh! What a smell! I asked a local man one day, "How do you stand the smell?" He said, "What smell?" and grinned. I guess you get used to it when it provides your paycheck!

Marcia and I went to Rose Park Baptist Church in Holland, MI four different times! Our "snowbird" friend, Chuck Rich arranged these dates. He sat out in the lobby looking at 4 TV monitors as he directed the cameras for their closed circuit television audience. We've been in his home many times. He is a ham radio enthusiast. Several other dates across southern Michigan he secured for us.

One night, we went to a Cracker Barrel in Battle Creek (or was it Kalamazoo?) after our concert to meet with Millie and Ray Overholt. He composed "Ten Thousand Angels." In his early years he was on a TV show for children in California. As he was writing that song, he said he came under conviction and was saved! He played guitar in their concerts and wrote other songs including "God's choir in the sky."

One of the founders of AMWAY had a fabulous home in Holland along the Lake Michigan shoreline. We walked out to a lighthouse on the lake. [Did you know that it is the only "great lake" totally within the boundaries of the USA? And Lake Okeechobee is the second largest fresh water lake in the country. The Great Salt Lake in Utah is larger but it is salty, not fresh!] The western part of the state along Lake Michigan is a beautiful area. On one trip we drove along the northern part of the Upper Peninsula. It has many lighthouses along the rocky shore. We've gone out to Mackinaw Island twice.

At one of Holland's malls there is a BIG windmill operating. I saw a store named "WEM Ties." We walked in and I told the lady that was my initials so how 'bout a free tie? She wouldn't give me one! In fact, she didn't even smile! By the way, I do have a T-shirt that reads, "W.E.M.", but underneath in smaller letters it says, "West Edmonton Mall, Alberta, Canada." They wouldn't give me a free one either!

We did a revival at a church near Cookeville and stayed in the pastor's home. Sunday morning we noticed a pretty white dove hanging in front of a pastoral scene painted on the back wall of the baptistery. During the sermon Marcia nudged me and said, "That dove is moving!" It was suspended on a fishing line, I guess. We enjoyed eating at members' homes. We got to see a lot of those beautiful Cumberland Mountains. One day the pastor took us out in his pickup truck, and we forded a creek, and went by in the mountain country.

Guy Bates (raised in Nashville) was minister of music at FBC Athens, TN, on I-75 north of Chattanooga. During our morning concert, I had forgotten to bring up something from the front pew that I needed. I scrambled down and back up the five or six steps. Guy leaned over and said, "You know we're on TV, don't you?" (They had closed circuit TV in the area).

In the space of only ten years, we did music in five revivals at Immanuel Baptist Church in Lebanon, TN. Bro. Don Owens was pastor. One night, I was running late (Marcia did not go that night) and Kellye was driving while I made out an order of service. We had just bought a new '79 Olds 98 and she had not been driving too long. Noticing she was going fast I looked over at the speedometer and the indicator could not been seen! When she saw me looking, she eased off the gas and the indicator began rolling down to 85 mph.

Evangelist "Junior" Hill preached one of the revivals. Before services we were invited to eat in the home of the church pianist's house. It was immaculate. Junior looked over at Bro. Owens and said, "Hey, preacher, this house ain't nearly as filthy as you said it would be!" At a meal in another home he said, "Why, preacher, this food's not nearly as greasy as you said it was gonna be!" He was like that, so funny, but a dynamic preacher. Park Avenue had him two or three times also. At the close of one meeting he said, "I just want to thank all of you for being so nice to me. We've had a great meeting – great attendance and great music…No, wait a second, I take that back. Elmo did sing one night, right?"

At Ridgecrest, NC a few years ago, I was pianist for Senior Adult week, and Marcia and I sang some also. Junior was guest speaker one of the nights and it was so good to see him. He had lost a lot of weight and we almost didn't recognize him.

Deborah Burnet from Lifeway was in charge of that week and the couple in the audience who had been married the longest (62 years) was determined. She asked them "their secret." They looked at each other, and finally the man said, "Well, I guess we just learned to tolerate each another!"

We sang at Christ Church Pentecostal on Old Hickory Boulevard in south Nashville for about 15 minutes. Some of the members of their band also played in Amy Grant's band. Their huge choir became famous and sang at Carnegie Hall and in Israel. Landy Gardner was the choir director. I also played piano and sang at Shirley Bosch and Gerald Ward's wedding in the chapel at Christ Church many years ago.

We did a weekend at a church in Morgan City, LA, down near the Gulf, and Monday morning we were on our way back to Lufkin, TX where Marcia's sister Johnnie and family lived (for 41 years). The weather became boisterous. The tall sugarcane was lying almost horizontal and we became concerned. Finally we got to I-10 and headed west toward Lake Charles. An 18-wheeler right in front of us almost turned over when the left wheels of the trailer lifted off the pavement. Luckily there was an exit there and he drove down it, regaining control. A few miles on down the interstate an 18-wheeler WAS laying crossways on the highway and we had to go off on the shoulder to get past him.

Then we noticed everything was still, not a leaf was stirring. I told Marcia I was really scared now. We got off at the next exit and went inside a pizza place. It had a big screen TV. We sat and watched a Lake Charles TV station report that a bad tornado had hit just 15 miles north of where we were! God took care of us that day.

I honestly don't remember how many times we have been to Niagara Falls, both US and Canadian sides. The first time Bill and Kellye were with us. Bill was a student at Middle Tennessee at Murfreesboro TN and Kellye was a junior at Bellevue High School. Our motel was on the Canadian side. One evening we took a long walk along the river gorge up to the falls. We came back to walk through different part of the city back to our motel. Bill told us to wait there a minute and he walked down the street a little ways. He came back and said, "We don't want to go down that way." I said (tongue-in-cheek), "But all those young ladies are waving at us!"

Naturally we took the boat ride that chugs right up to the falls. You are given rain coats and hats. You've likely seen the TV commercial advertising a product that protects the observation deck. We also took the tunnel trip that ends with a cut-out window back UNDER the falls. Every now and then a deluge of water blows in. Both the Canadian and American falls are beyond description. We drove in our car downstream where a huge whirlpool is located. A tram went over it, but we did NOT ride it...not with my kind of luck!

On one trip, Marcia and I were standing at the top of the falls on the US side when a woman's voice behind us said, "Well, Mr. and Mrs. Mercer!" We turned to see some friends named Renbarger, who attended Ned and Mary Esther's church in

Windfall, IN. In fact, this man was a son of Mary Esther's cousin, Madonna and Bob Renbarger. They had three sons and one did missionary work overseas. We were surprised to run into each other there of all places!

We did three concerts in the Salt Lake City area on a trip out west. One was at a Nazarene church, I believe. Another was at the SLC Rescue Mission. When we arrived at Ed and Shirley Carnell's house (he was the director) he said we had a message to call a doctor in Nashville. Our son Bill was in the hospital with five tubes connected to him! And we were about 2,000 miles away. The doctor said his digestive system had shut down but there was no need for us to interrupt our western trip. That night after our concert at the mission I told the people there about it and most of them came to us to say they would be praying for him. That really touched us. Here these folks were in destitute circumstances, yet they would pray for Bill. The crowd was mostly youth to middle age, not like it was 30 or 40 years ago. They reached capacity and gave quilts to the rest, telling them to lay by the building that night.

The third concert was in a Conservative Baptist Church in Sandy, actually a southern suburb of metro SLC. We stayed in the pastor's home Saturday night. Sunday morning after breakfast he said I could ride with him to church as he had an early meeting with the "deacons" to discuss an urgent matter. The congregation had just moved into a new church building and the Mormons had volunteered to help them lay sod on the lawn. It was discussed and they decided to decline their offer. I believe most of Utah citizens are Mormons.

On another western trip we drove I-10 toward Tucson, AZ. At Benson we drove south to Tombstone and walked the streets. We went to the OK Corral where that famous gunfight took place. We did a concert at Sabino Canyon Road Baptist Church in Tucson, AZ. We got there early so we drove to the end of the road and enjoyed a close-up view of the mountain range. There were beautiful plants and cacti all over the place. That night we stayed in the home of the Registrar for the University of Arizona, David Butler and his wife Jeri. He later became president of the Arizona Baptist Convention.

The next morning we drove by the Davis-Monthan Airfield where planes, even helicopters are kept for their parts. They are shrink-wrapped! We heard on the radio as we headed for California one was being flown there but crashed a few miles away. We drove through a portion of western Saguaro National Park. There was a western town there where several movies had been filmed.

Just northwest of Los Angeles where Highway 101 leaves the coastline is the town of Solvang. Anderson's Animal Farm is there. Some of them have been used in movies. Back in the 70s Marcia, Bill, Kellye and I enjoyed that. On down the road Kellye showed Marcia where a deer had bit her finger!

The area around Sebastian, CA is settled by those of German descent. We sang at a church there two different times, the first time being in the main sanctuary. The second time there was a wedding in it so we met in another room with a fireplace and sliding glass doors. About fifty senior adults were there.

About halfway through the concert, a HUGE white goat came and stood like a statue by the glass door listening to us sing. Afterwards we said, "Tell us about that goat!" Here's the true story:

A man in the community owned it, but it often got out of the fence and would eat up the neighbor's gardens, flowers, etc. He had really become a nuisance. The church sanctuary had been flooded because berries, nuts, and any kind of trash would clog up the drainage pipe that went under the building! A man came up with an idea to solve both problems. The church bought the goat and built a high secure fence around it so that solved the neighbors' problem. The goat ate all the stuff that had been clogging up the drain so the church didn't flood any more. Everyone was happy. The punch line, "We refer to him as the Holy Goat!"

We sang somewhere in California and I cannot remember the name of the city or church. We spent the night with a couple whose son worked for WORD, Benson's competitor. As we went to leave the next morning he took us around to the side of the house to show us a tree. On one limb it bore apricots; on another it grew peaches, and on a third it had almonds! He had grafted those limbs into the trunk many years before.

Sutter Creek, CA is located SE of Sacramento and is an interesting area. We did a concert at a small church there and were sent afterward to a Bed and Breakfast. We've stayed in a lot of them across the USA. The room we were in still had the Assessor's scales hanging from a beam in the ceiling. The next morning our breakfast was hung on our door in a plastic bag. Gold had once been found all over that part of the state. A historic sign on the side of the road said the largest gold nugget ever found was discovered in that area.

Camas, Washington is on the Columbia River gorge across from Portland, OR. There is a huge Crown-Zellerbach mill there that makes everything from paper to cardboard boxes to lumber. At one time they owned what was once called Tremont Lumber Company in Winnfield (Joyce) and our friend Roy Jones worked there. A church up the mountain from Camas, called Lacamas Heights (pastor was Bro. Layton Rogers who had us sing at two other churches in later years) was the location of our only concert in that state. We fell in love with "the great Northwest." Years later Layton died visiting their son who lived in Germany.

We did concerts two different times at a church in Florrisant, MO, a northwest suburb of St Louis not too far from the Lindberg Airport. We were singing away and I realized Marcia's voice was giving her trouble. It so happened that I was to sing an upcoming verse. Right behind us was a door to the hall and she knew a water fountain was there. She stepped out, got a drink and came back in to join me on the chorus!

We met Art Creamer in Dothan, AL when we did a concert at his church. He was pianist and a great one, too. He had a recording studio in his home with the latest technology. This was in 1988. People attending our concerts had begun to ask if we had cassettes for sale. So, we decided to make an album. At the time we were doing a revival in Hartford, a town just west of Dothan.

We sang some of our songs and I also did three instrumental medleys. I made all the arrangements. I'd lay down the piano track then tell Art I wanted to add the bass part...he'd punch a button, and when I played the keyboard it sounded just like a bass. It was amazing to me! I added organ, electric piano, strings, etc. I even had a harp and a sax on a song or two. I would tell people Boots Randolph dropped by and insisted on playing on one of my song! NOT! I got the Circle City Boys from Dothan to do backup on my song, "One More Hill, One More Valley." I thought it turned out great. I also compiled an 8-1/2x11 song folio to sell along with it. They sold well and soon we made a second album at Art's studio.

Our close friend, Donna Hilley (President and CEO of SONY-ATV on Nashville's Music Row) told us we could use their facilities, so we did. Naturally I put "Recorded at SONY Studios in Nashville, TN," along with the engineer's name on the product. We made four albums there switching to CDs. Also on our merchandise table we carried other books Benson had published – the New Songs of Inspiration series, my solo piano books, also my piano/organ duet books, etc. Those sales helped us cover traveling expenses. Very few churches would pay expenses, but God always provided our needs. We simply asked for a "love offering."

In August we did an 8-day parish-wide revival in the Many, (MAN-e) LA High School football stadium. It was estimated some 700 people attended each night. We had a great choir directed by Randy Stone, R. O. and Angie Stone's middle son. He and his wife Kala sang special music as did Marcia and I. I played piano and the evangelist was Bro. Chuck Raley. His sweet wife was named Sally. We men wore suits and ties and we became soaked five minutes after we got there! It was so hot and muggy. Bro.Chuck had Miss Louisiana come one night and give her testimony. One night bad weather forced us into the school gym and it was hot in there!

Joe and Rita DeBose owned the *Country Boy Restaurant.* They served the best fried chicken and fried fish! They insisted we all come by AFTER the services to eat. Oh, it was so good. I'd eat chicken one night and fish the next! We just couldn't decide which one was the best. At the end of the meeting, they informed us that their contribution was the FREE food they had served us. That was so nice, and since then we have gone by many times to see them and, of course, enjoy a meal. We have taken several people by also. It's on US-171 South.

Each day of the revival the team would meet with some other folks at one of the participating churches in the area. We got to know a lot of fine people. My sister Gertrude and her husband Dan came almost every night since their 160 acre ranch was just a few miles north at Pelican, LA. We stayed at Hodges Gardens Motel which was several miles south on US-171. (Those gardens are beautiful, by the way). One night Randy and Chuck were late getting from the restaurant back to the motel. We asked them what delayed them and they raved about a highway patrolman giving them a ticket. They carried us high then admitted it was all a joke. We were driving on I-10 one time and the Raleys met us at a Stuckey's near their home in the FL panhandle.

WHERE'S THE...*FIRE?*

Metro police chief (at the time) Joe Casey invited Bro. Bob Mowrey to ride with him one night and he got a first-hand education. He was shocked at what went on in Nashville after darkness fell. On a Sunday morning sometime after that he had the chief come speak to our church. He gave some startling crime statistics. He also presented Bro. Bob with an honorary badge!

There is a permanent burning ban in Metro Nashville. Apparently Bro. Bob was not aware of this. One day he had raked up a pile of leaves in their yard and he proceeded to set them on fire, creating quite a smoke. They live perhaps four miles east of us as the crow flies, over some high hills. The fire truck arrived and put them out. Shortly after hearing about that I penned a little four verse poem in about ten minutes while waiting for Marcia to get ready for supper and prayer meeting. It went like this:

Well, I was drivin' around the other day when I spied a fire truck comin' my way, and he wadn't lettin' no grass grow under his tires. I took in after him, you see, but I wondered where he's a-takin' me and most of all I wondered, "Where's the fire?"

With me close behind we rounded a curve, right then I nearly lost my nerve; why the whole neighborhood was filled with awful smoke! And I remembered with a shock my pastor's house is in that block, and a lump in my throat just about made me choke.

Sure 'nough we stopped in front o' his house, there stood Bro. Bob as meek as a mouse; you could tell he was hot 'cause he'd done rolled up his sleeves. To his surprise and embarrassment the firemen grabbed their hose and went to sprayin' water on his burnin' leaves.

An irate neighbor had turned him in and you bet there was some made firemen, but Bro. Bob's honorary badge saved the hour! Then he made me promise not to say what'd really happened there that day if anybody asked me, "Where's the fire?"

You will remember the TV commercial where the little old lady in a fast food place asks "Where's the beef?"

One Sunday morning Bro. Bob said he was getting ready for church when he pulled the top drawer in a chest of drawers out too far. It fell on his big toe and broke it! He wore a slipper on that foot until it healed. He was preaching away one Sunday and when he made a point he stomped *that* foot then flinched it hurt so bad. I composed an appropriate poem, "Ode to a Broken Toe." He kept it under the glass on his desk for years.

SOME DEAR FRIENDS

Joanne Wilson (husband Don) had us come down to Hillcrest Baptist church in Cantonement, FL, a suburb of Pensacola for a senior adult program. We stayed in the home of the lady whose mother owned "Gatorland" in the Orlando area. There must have been a hundred senior adults present and we had a great time. She had me autograph something for her sister Joyce Bates who lived in Jacksonville.

Not long after that Joyce (husband Bob) had us at their church for a concert and we stayed in their beautiful home in Jacksonville. The next morning the four of us met our longtime friend Lee Turner for breakfast.

Lee and Diane Turner are very creative people, especially when it comes to writing lyrics and composing music. Longtime ASCAP members (like me), they have many compositions and works to their credit. Benson printed their children's musical "They All Sang Jesus." They wrote the song "Glory, Hallelujah, Jubilee" that was sung by Billy Graham's crusade choirs. George Beverly Shea recorded "Who Moved?" Lee can play any style of piano imaginable from ragtime to classical. He is such a crowd favorite. Sometimes he shares info on other music people (going back a hundred years even) that adds to the enjoyment of his concerts.

Because of his keyboard ability Lee moved his family to Nashville where he hoped to "break into" the studio musician field. Alas, 10% of the union members do 90% of the vocal and instrumental work and although he got some sessions it was not enough. They lived for two years in the house owned by Mr. and Mrs. C. E. Francis where Bobby Welch and his family lived, and the same place she gave us in August 1976!

Lee and Diane had three sons, all grown now. For many years he was Minister of Music at San Jose Baptist church in Jacksonville. They moved back "home." They have been by here to see us and the changes we have made on the house. Google him and learn more about them and their products.

BILL AND RENEE

Bill spent four years in south Florida. After his job with the FL Game and Fish Commission he taught science at the Okeechobee High School then was on the Indian River Community College lab staff. When Kellye's second son Joey was born in a Ft Pierce hospital, Bill put on his white lab coat and wrapped a stethoscope around his neck. He walked briskly down the hallway as nurses said, "Good evening, Doctor," and saw Joey before we did!

He decided to move back to Nashville and pursue a Master's degree. Renee, his childhood sweetheart was divorced (from an abusive husband) with two sweet little girls – Bethany age 7 and Lindsey age 4. They renewed their friendship and eventually were married in the old auditorium at Park Avenue church. A huge crowd came to the wedding. It was on Dec. 28, 1990. Christmas trees with clear lights circled around the back of the stage. Ray and Kay Newbill did the decorations – they also had done them for Kellye's wedding earlier. Marcia and I had written a song titled, "In God's Special Time." Since I had written one for Kellye's wedding, they should have expected that. But with their backs to the audience as it was sung you could tell that Renee was emotional. Bill also exchanged vows with the girls and gave them three-bead necklaces signifying "I Love You." They lit the unity candle and all four stood facing the audience as the song "We'll build a Household of Faith" was played. Later he adopted them and their last name was changed to Mercer.

Marcia and I had an apartment built in the 29x24 garage we had added onto the split-level house in 1977 and we moved in there. We let Bill, Renee and the girls have the "main part" of the house. Courtney was born in 1992 and Hailey was born in 1994. We enjoyed our local grandchildren and frequently visited those in down south Florida as well.

Bill taught 7th and 8th grade Earth and Life Sciences at Ewing Park Middle School, the one he had attended when we lived on Masonwood Drive! At a staff meeting before school teachers were being introduced. When the name Bill Mercer was announced, he said two women teachers looked at each other and said, "That name sounds familiar!" He was also defensive football coach. One year the team was not scored on until the championship game when he had the third string playing. They won the Metro Nashville Middle School football championship three years in a row. He also was head wrestling coach for several years and won Metro championships in that sport as well. He taught at Ewing Park for eighteen years! During the summers he worked as a Ranger at Opryland Theme Park and enjoyed that. Now for many years he has worked security at Gaylord Opryland Hotel complex, including the General Jackson showboat.

ANOTHER WESTERN TOUR

In the early 90s we were on a western tour and did a concert at the Redwood Valley Community Church. It is located in northern California. Just south of there is Ukiah where Jim Jones "got his start," eventually leading his congregation to their deaths by drinking poisoned cool-aid, remember that? We spent that night with a family who lived on ten acres of vineyards. Their house was built in a wide "V" shape. Next morning I heard a tractor and looked out to see him working away.

We did two concerts a few years apart at Central Baptist Church in Alameda, California. The second time we got there early and drove on up to the north end of the island. We sat and watched a cargo ship being unloaded at an Oakland dock. We could barely see the San Francisco skyline to the west across the bay. During the concert when I play the intro to "Son-stroke" the top notes on the piano did not play! Leroy Abernathy of Canton, GA taught me that downward arpeggio, the only one I do. I just have a mental block in running <u>down</u> the keyboard. I know...I should have practiced my finger exercises, but I hated them! I do play in octaves with both hands, but I copied that style from Rudy Atwood.

We also went two times to Gateway Baptist Church in Roswell, NM. I believe it came out of First Baptist and the first Sunday they had 700 in attendance! Gateway made an impact on the city. They later decided to start a church school. The day we were there they baptized about twenty new converts after the service. We enjoyed driving through Cloudcroft, NM, elevation around 9,000 feet. Earl and his family would drive out there for many years on vacation. The highway descends sharply into the plain below but from a turnout you can view the remains of a "switchback" on an old railroad! White Sands National Monument is unbelievably beautiful. Also the Great Sand Dunes of southern Colorado are something to see and try to walk on! We've been to both areas a number of times.

Near Stockton, CA we did a concert and drove by large fruit groves along the highway. At the church I said they looked like peaches but the trees were too big. One man said to me, "They're almonds…till we pick 'em then they're amons". I asked what he meant and he said, "When we shake the trees, it shakes the 'l' out of 'em!" I had been "had!" They all laughed.

We did music for the 25th anniversary of a big church in Garland, TX. The sanctuary was being remodeled so we met in the activities building. The organist was a small man, nick-named "Killer." The choir was good. I had them singing Lee and Dianne Turner's song "Glory, Hallelujah, Jubilee!" They wanted to do choreography to the lyrics: "Well, He picked me up…turned me 'round…Set my feet on higher ground," etc. I talked them out of it…I hadn't received the "love offering" yet!

We did music in two revivals at the SAME TIME! The regular nightly one was at Southside Baptist Church located in McComb, MS, where Bro. David Milligan was pastor. He went on the South Korea mission trip with us. Each morning at 10:30 Monday through Wednesday, we did a senior adult "revival" ten miles down I-55 at Magnolia Baptist, just north of the Louisiana state line. I had product display tables at both locations.

On our way one night to Southside, a couple invited us to stop by their house for coffee and cake. I ate the cake but drank water! Bro. David had become ill and missed the service the night before. The lady met us at the door and said something like, "I'm sure glad you're not home in bed with the pastor." What she meant to say was "***like*** the pastor." She was totally embarrassed! We're friends on Facebook.

THE KING FAMILY

A few miles northeast of Natchez, MS on old US-61 is the little town of Fayette. Bro. Eddie King was pastor of the Baptist church there and invited us to do the music in a revival. He told us there were 65 white people in town, along with 2,500 black people! He had thirty in his choir! He and his wife Edna had five children and "The King Family" often sang in the area churches. We met them when they visited a church in Meadville where we were in revival. Bro. Jack Evans (wife, Diane, the daughter of Mary and Don Taylor at Park Avenue) was pastor there. Our dear friend Mary passed away in 2012.

We just fell in love with Eddie and Edna. He had a head of white hair and a big smile on his face. We stayed in their home many times and ate at their table. He was a hunter and always had deer sausage, or turkey, as well as vegetables out of his garden. He shared with the neighbors around him. Edna made jam or jelly from his fruit trees and bushes. I remember us all sitting on their back porch dipping butter beans from a #3 washtub of water and shelling them. The parsonage was a white board house that set right behind the red brick church on a side street.

Down in the half basement garage (you couldn't park a car there!) he had turkey beards stuck up in a line all around the walls about head-high. He made some kind of a deal where he shot lots of deer and their hides would be shipped up north to a manufacturing company to make gloves, slippers and caps. He gave me some. He was a piano technician, not just a tuner. He said you could back up a pickup to his garage and dump out the hundreds of pieces of a piano in a pile and he would assemble it!

The neighbor east of Eddie on down the hill was a black man whose last name was Queen! He got unable to mow his yard so Eddie did it for him. The man said, "Lawd, der's a King a-mowin' da Queen's yard!" One time the four of us got in Eddie's big old Cadillac and went down to the Walmart in Natchez. Marcia and Edna went their way and Eddie and I went ours. In a few minutes he sidled up to me and said softly, "That woman over there (nodding) just keeps on lookin' at me." Well, in a few minutes she walked up to him and said, "Are you a preacher?" Quick as a flash Eddie answered seriously, "Uh, no ma'am, I've just been sick a long time!"

Benny Still preached a revival at the church one time. We were having choir practice before the service. I introduced myself to three young men. One said, "I'm Dallas, this is my brother Houston and my other brother Houston!" Remember the Bob Newhart TV show? Bro. Eddie led the choir into the loft as the service began, just smiling and walking backwards, right off the end of the row. It didn't faze him at all. This church had a 7 a.m. morning service then people could go on to work. I reckon twenty people came. After the music I sat down on the front row with Marcia and Bro. Eddie. Benny started his devotional and before he read the scripture the three of us laid our heads over and began snoring! Benny and everyone broke up!

There was a little shack across from the courthouse that made the best hamburgers! I wish I could recall it because it was a catchy name. We used to look forward to eating one when we were in town. Bro. Eddie's gone now but Edna phoned us the other day and we talked a long time, mostly about all these memories. Thanks, God.

COAST TO COAST

Many years we would travel coast to coast and border to border, going upwards of 30,000 miles in our car or van. We went in all 50 states numerous times and sang in 37 of them.

First Baptist Church in Blountstown, FL was another place we enjoyed going. We did the music in two revivals there. After the first one ended the pastor told us that he enjoyed having us. He said in one revival he dismissed the music man and got another one to finish. We were glad he approved of us! This pastor read his text from the Greek New Testament. In a second floor room in the church he had an unbelievable electric train and town laid out. He had over 50 locomotives! We had a 7 a.m. service after which we crossed a street to the activities building for a good breakfast and then people would go to their jobs.

Our friend Jimmy Kearse lives there and we have been friends for many years. We did revivals where he was song leader. He has a beautiful voice. He used to have a TV show in California. He has produced albums for southern universities. He told us about an open-air meeting he attended one night and was called up to sing special music. He bounded up on the stage, approached the mike and drew in a big breath to start singing. A big bug flew down his throat! In vain he tried to clear his throat to sing. He leapt off the platform and ran for his car. He drove down the highway with his head out the window, gagging. He said he could feel that sucker trying to come back up…but it was too late for the bug and too late to go back to the service!

We stayed in a motel out on SR-20 across from the airport. I called it Blountstown International…we didn't see a plane the whole time we were there! I worked on arranging music on an instrumental book during the day and also wrote the song "Don't be grounded when the Rapture Comes." After church we would drive over to Bristol to get something to eat, but it was on the Eastern Time side of the Apalachicola River. That created a problem some nights but the manager welcomed us.

In Bristol there is a grocery store named "Hoggly-Woggly." I asked why "Piggly-Wiggly" didn't sue them. I was told Hoggly-Woggly was FIRST in business.

DR. CARLTON C. BUCK

Dr. Carlton C. Buck was an interesting man. He was a pastor in the Christian Church (Disciples of Christ) denomination and he was also a lyricist. He wrote the words to "I Believe in Miracles," John W. Peterson wrote the music. He wrote the words to "The Sweetest Hallelujah," Henry Slaughter wrote the music. He wrote the words to "When God Speaks," I'm not sure who wrote the music. He and his wife lived in Eugene, OR up the hill a couple of blocks from the University of Oregon football stadium. We spent a week in their home and could hear the fans cheering and see the glow from the lights on Saturday night!

During that week we were to do a concert at a church in Oakridge, OR that Dr. Buck had arranged for us. They went with us. We ate at a café in town when we got there. He asked the waitress if she could give us directions to the church and she said, "Yeah, go down to the second light and hang a left; it'll be in the next block." Dr. Buck thought that was the funniest thing he'd ever heard and kept saying, "Hang a left!" whether I need to or not.

We sang Sunday morning in the Christian Church where Dr. Buck was the minister and another church in Springfield that night. They are twin cities separated by the beautiful Willamette River that continues north through Portland and empties into the Columbia River Gorge. On Monday morning we left their house, driving I-5 north to Portland, then heading to the Pacific on US-30, the first transcontinental highway.

Ft. Clatsop was an interesting historical place to visit. We drove down Highway 101 along the Oregon coast passing countless state parks. Wednesday afternoon we took the highway back to their house in Eugene to do a concert that night. On Thursday morning we went back that road to the coast again and drove along it across the California state line to Crescent City. There is a motel there that is constructed from ONE Redwood tree! We also drove the Avenue of the Giants, a two-lane road through a tall redwood forest. We took US-199 through the Siskiyou Mountains of SW Oregon to the city of Grants Pass.

There is a very unusual cemetery there that we drove through. [One area had a **light in each grave**! An Israelite, that is; it was a Jewish cemetery. *Sorry.*] We drove I-5 North back to Eugene for another weekend in the area. We sang in a church where our friends Lawrence Crook and his wife were members. He had a most beautiful tenor voice and I asked him to sing my song "If I Could Sing a Thousand Melodies"...written in Bb but he sung it four steps higher in Eb. After our concert I told the congregation that when we got home to Nashville I was going back to a Vanderbilt Hospital voice doctor. He suspected I had nodules on my vocal chords. The pastor called several names and they came to me, laid their hands on me and prayed. When I went to Dr. Ossoff, he could find NO trace of nodules. Prayer is powerful!

Dr. Buck's sister lived in Pasa Robles, CA and he arranged for us to do a concert in her church. The last name was Franklin. I must tell you about that experience. They farmed about 800 acres of barley and lived about 30 miles inland from the Pacific and Hwy-101 south of Big Sur country {that was a scenic drive}. He had built his own fishing boat and went to the ocean every now and then. That night Mrs. Franklin fired up the big popcorn machine they had bought when the movie theatre in town closed. Marcia loves popcorn and we ate and ate! The next morning when we got up they had a fire going in a free-standing wood heater and this was in August.

He was a big game hunter and had a huge elk head mounted on a wall. Its rack was an inch from the ceiling and the bottom of the neck was just a few inches above the floor. Also on the wall was a deer head and a big mountain goat, his chest and head appearing as if he'd thrust himself through the wall. Mr. Franklin said that was as far as he let that goat come in his house! After breakfast he took us in his pickup on a tour of the place. They had a vegetable garden and a flower garden. They also had a fruit orchard. He pointed out where different children lived...they'd had eight. He circled back around to their 5-acre lake, the driveway running across the center.

He told us that Chevron drilled for oil several years before and hit HOT water instead! He got them to cap it off and in a few days he and his bulldozer had scooped out a place for the pond. He built a smaller area and they put a "fountain head" on the pipe and turned it on again. He had his own natural outdoor hot tub. I asked him how often he got in it. In my mind I see him now with his back to us, standing there in his overalls and without turning around he drawled, "Oh, about...once...a DAY!" We thought he was going to say a week, month or even year!

We bid them farewell and on our way east toward I-5, we passed through a big oilfield. We also stopped at the memorial where actor James Dean was killed in a car wreck.

Marcia and I were in a Santa Rosa, CA Baptist church a couple of times. We did a Friday night concert and then a Saturday morning choir clinic! Afterward they had refreshments in the dining hall. They said, "You have got to try this soup." I took a spoonful and...it tasted like peanut butter. That's what it was! It was a veggie soup with a dollop of peanut butter in it. I love them both but want them separate, please!

SCARY PELICAN NIGHTS

We were doing some dates in northwest Louisiana and spent a couple of nights at my sister Gertrude's house in Pelican, LA. She and Dan were off on a trip somewhere. They lived on 160 acres and we loved to visit them. Often my brothers Earl and Ronnie would come when we were there.

The first night we arrived in time to catch the 10:00 news from a Shreveport TV station after which we began to get ready for bed. Marcia was back in the master bedroom bathroom and I yelled to her that I needed to use it. She replied, "There are two other bathrooms in this house, go to one of them!" Why hadn't I thought of that? Later when I walked in our bedroom, to my horror I saw a snake about a foot long wiggling across the floor! I grabbed my house shoe and proceeded to pound him with it, making a great deal of noise. From way down on the other end of the house Marcia yells, "What ARE you doing?"

I didn't know what to say and a few seconds went by. She yelled again and I said, "I don't know how to tell you this but I just killed a snake in our bedroom!" Out of the bathroom she came then! We looked up snakes in their encyclopedia and concluded it was a "bull" snake. Neither was about to touch it, so Marcia went in their utility room to get a folded newspaper out of a waste basket. Trash and dust fell from it and we both jumped back! I took a broom and eventually got the snake on the paper, concluding it was dead and into the trash he went. During the night when we had to use the bathroom we turned the light on first!

Well, the next night we had another concert and it was storming. On the drive back to their house trees were down and utility workers were everywhere along with police car flashing blue lights. Still we got home in time for the 10:00 news again. We were sitting in their big living room watching TV, a recliner between us. All at once Marcia screamed and like the cat in the cartoons my claws went to the ceiling and I was looking down!

Before we left that night for the concert a phone call came for the man who was there tending to their cattle. I opened the sliding glass door at the side of their family room and yelled to him to come to the phone. But we had to leave immediately. They were keeping Cinnamon, their son Frank's big dog and they had two of their own. Apparently when the man went back outside he didn't completely close the door and Cinnamon had wedged her snout in enough to push it open and come in – the dogs were very afraid of lightning and thunder. Unbeknown to us she came up behind Marcia and stuck her cold wet nose to her left elbow. After the snake episode the night before she became unglued and me along with her!

I got up, scolding Cinnamon as we both headed for that sliding glass door. I noticed she hesitated in the family room and looked over toward a big free-standing wood heater. Crouched behind it were the other two dogs! It was like Cinnamon said "if I have to get out, they do too!" Ah, life on the road with the Mercers!

ADDITIONAL STORIES

In the early 90s we did a revival at First Baptist in Bedford, IN. We stayed in the home of Frank and Doris Hampton. They were Okeechobee "snowbirds" and we always looked forward to a lot of fellowship during the winter while we were down there. One day they took us to see the Bedford cemetery which is so unusual it was featured on a national TV morning show once. Naturally many of the headstones are made from the Indiana limestone. One in particular that I remember was like a carpenter's workbench. There was a bent nail in one of the legs! Another had a child's shoes on it...and all was chiseled out of limestone! Both Frank and Doris passed away within weeks of each other several years ago.

Another time in that area, we stayed in the home of Dale and Marilyn Robinson in Oolitic. They took us out to a limestone quarry just west of town. The owner said stone had been taken from that tract of land since 1928, I believe.

The workers used a 15-foot "chainsaw" about 3 or 4 inches wide to cut down into the rock and run perhaps a hundred feet in length and eight feet wide. Airbags were stuffed in the crack and slowly inflated. That gigantic piece of rock would begin leaning outward ever so slightly and eventually it would fall on its side. Workers would find "veins" in it and take the saw again and cut it into huge pieces of stone. One would be set on the flatbed trailer over the back axles and another over the tractor (truck) back axles. They would be hauled to the processing plant in Bedford. Each piece would weigh at least 25 tons.

At the plant diamond-tipped saws would cut those big pieces into different lengths and depths of smooth building stone. If a rough outside finish was desired, the stone ran upright along a belt and some kind of object would hit it, flaking off some of the surface. Many government buildings, local, state and national are made from Indiana limestone. Also houses and churches are built using it also.

A few years later we went back to Bedford First Baptist for a concert. Passing a public building not far from the church we saw trucks and big spotlights and people all around. We learned when we got to church they were going to film a Bobby Knight TV commercial!

One Saturday afternoon Bill was over "on our side of the house" watching a movie "The Thin Red Line" starring Nick Nolte, John Travolta and George Clooney! I was in my Music Room. Bill yelled, "Get in here, Dad, they're singing one of your songs!" I said, "Yeah, sure!" but I went where he was and could not believe my ears. A bunch of natives were trottin' down a jungle path singing one of MY songs! It don't git no better 'n that! "What a Glad Reunion Day" was the song. I notified Benson and their lawyers got in touch with the producers at Twentieth Century Fox in California and a (good) settlement was reached. Praise the Lord! The movie is about three hours long, full of violence and bad language. Bill and Renee later gave us the DVD.

TOWN & COUNTRY MUSIC CLINICS

For ten years we were on staff for the Mississippi Baptist Town and Country Music Clinics. The state was divided into nine districts, the ninth being along the Gulf coast. I believe they were started by a Mr. Hall, then Danny Jones did one with us and the rest of them were under the direction of Jimmy McCaleb, retired from the Air Force. His book, "Church Music R. F. D." was a great help to the music minister in churches all over the south.

We would be at one place Thursday night and Friday morning, then drive somewhere else in that district and do the same thing Friday night and Saturday morning. One was held in a small town church running less than 150 in Sunday School, the other was done at a rural church. They were held in the month of August and it was "Mississippi HOT." Jimmy finally said, "Mo, let's quit wearing ties and coats. We need to identify with the people!" What I needed was an air-conditioned shirt, too. Usually we did two weeks each year, but sometimes we would do three! In the ten years we worked in them I figured we had gone into 44 churches with the T&C Music Clinic.

We had so much fun. That Jimmy is quiet, subtle, AND a riot! We met a lot of wonderful Christian folks that loved to sing. Jimmy would open up with a rousing, upbeat song, then read a verse of Scripture and have a prayer. I would take over for about 25 minutes, going quickly through some of my Benson choir books and octavos. Classes on various musical topics followed that. A few times I taught piano techniques. There were several different ones on staff, largely depending on the district we were in. After the classes, Jimmy would have them sing through some Lifeway music publications.

One week we were in Lucedale in the extreme SE part of the state. Because of the casinos along the Gulf coast we couldn't get motel rooms, so we had to drive US-98 all the way to Mobile, AL. Bill Herman was on staff for that one and he, Jimmy, Marcia and I had a late meal at a Denny's. He told about a trip he'd made to Russia with a group. He was put in a home where there was a teenage daughter who understood and spoke some English. She told him, "Sorry, no hot water." Bill said that was alright, he had taken showers in cold water before. Alas, he was thinking "Mississippi cold water."

He was a large man, probably 250 pounds. He stepped into the small tub and finally got the curtain around him. He reached up and turned on the water. He said he had a sudden drastic intake of breath that almost busted his lungs. There must have been a glacier within a quarter mile of the house! He said it was like an "out of body" experience. He could see his lifeless body crumpled in the tub. The Russian couple rushed in and the wife exclaimed, "Look, Vladimir! American lay dead in tub!" We were choking on our food and other patrons were getting concerned about the three of us.

Jimmy phones us every now and then. He called to wish us a merry 2012 Christmas. Said he was 88! God bless him – he's one of a kind.

EATING A...*TREE?*

Sometime in the 90s Earl and Betty brought Gertrude and Dan down to the condo to visit for a few days. It was in the winter, but we're in south Florida, remember! We drove around the area some, showed them the lake and the ranches, etc. We mostly sat around and talked. For supper one night I was going to add some swamp cabbage to the menu. A lady had given us two "trunks." Before a cabbage palm gets too big, the trunk is cut off... 'course that tree is never quite the same.

The outer part is chopped off with a big knife or machete down to the "heart," and then the heart is cut up in smaller pieces and boiled like cabbage. I figured it would be a treat for our "guests." I was on the concrete patio area inside the privacy fence hacking the heart into smaller pieces. Earl asked me, "Well, what does it taste like?" I said, "A tree!" It can be bought in cans in most grocery stores under the name "Heart of Palm."

LOIS AND LEE CAMMON

At First Baptist in Okeechobee Wayne Clark handed out church bulletins at one of the entrances. He called them "scorecards!" I remember after services one Sunday a couple came by the piano on their way out and introduced themselves as Lois and Lee Cammon. We were close friends from then on! In fact, we made Lee our Equitable Insurance agent. They leased winter housing in several places over the years. We took BJ and Joey fishing off their dock a time or two. It was fun to throw small fish over to a big crane and watch it slowing going down its long neck.

Their permanent home is Olney, IL, home of the white squirrels and they are everywhere. Over the years we stayed upstairs in their home many times. We did about three revivals at their First Baptist church. One time Ned and Mary Esther Kemper were invited there. I had volunteered to till up a spot near Lee's house so he could plant about five tomato plants. He'd borrowed a tiller from his neighbor. Well, the thing wouldn't crank. I was inwardly about to rejoice when Ned said, "Here's the problem," and fixed it. I did the tilling.

On one visit something broke in the tank of the commode upstairs, but Marcia and I fixed it and told Lee about it. [That year we repaired commodes in three homes]. The next time we went to their house Lee had a sign on the commode seat that said, "Be careful: you know how you are with the plumbing."

We were sitting at their breakfast nook one night playing cards when the phone rang. It was their daughter in California (the other daughter and family lived just west of Olney and their two sons were Equitable Insurance agents in St. Louis). We told them both to go and talk as long as they wished. While they were gone Marcia dealt the cards again and gave Lee a fabulous hand. They came back talking about the phone call, and when it came time for Lee to bid he looked at his hand and couldn't hide his joy! Finally we laughed and told them what had been done. From then on they would tell people, "You'd better watch Marcia and Elmo, especially when *they* deal the cards!"

Lee's cousin lived about 20 miles north up SR-130. Her husband had constructed a big pond on their land nearly 50 feet deep at the earthen dam. We went up there to fish sometimes and had lots of fun. We left the fish we had caught with them – maybe that was our "admission fee." The Cammon's house had a full basement and Lee would sit down there to watch Cardinals baseball. But he muted TV and listened to Jack Buck call the game on the radio! I remember when Lee went to his 50th high school reunion, and I thought he was OLD! We attended MY 50th back in 2000!!

One afternoon Lee and Lois took us down to the extreme southwest corner of Indiana to a quaint village named New Harmony. A big church is there with no roof on it. There is a hedge maze that I would not dare enter. There are unique shops and a nice hotel. Deer are all over the place. We crossed the beautiful Wabash River. When Marcia and I put on the senior adult variety show at Okeechobee FBC, Lee had the part of Liberace. Lois sewed lace on his shirt sleeves and he put on a show as the music played. Lee passed away several years ago and we attended the funeral in Olney. Their fifteen grandchildren sang "Take Me Out to the Ballgame" at the close of the service. When they finished one kid said, "Go, Cubs!" We all laughed.

Close friends of theirs and ours, E. A. and Hope Smith, live in a beautiful country setting just east of Olney and south of US-50. We have been in their home there and also in Okeechobee many times to enjoy a meal and play card games.

Years ago the new US-50 Bridge over the Wabash River was dedicated and named after the actor Red Skelton because he was from Vincennes. I heard that he said, "I think it is so appropriate that the bridge is built at this spot, because this is where I learned to swim…after I got of the toe sack!"

MORE MISSISSIPPI STORIES

We were at a church one time in Mississippi. The pastor had led a man to Christ who had been involved in witchcraft… he may have been a wizard. The pastor was told that retaliation would be forthcoming. After a Halloween night someone asked him, "What was going on at your house last night?" The pastor said, "What do you mean? My wife and I were home by ourselves." The man said, "Why, there were torches all around your house. How could you not have seen them? I thought y'all were having a big party." The pastor knew the angels of God had protected them that night. I don't believe anything ever happened afterward either.

[A side note: This pastor grew up in our hometown and often helped his Daddy deliver milk – back in those days they did that, and we didn't even lock our houses. Since we were both at work they would put the milk in our refrigerator! So, in a service at his church one time I told that and looked at him and said, "Oh! So that's what happened to my lemon pie! You thought I left it for you!" And everyone laughed. At the time he was in Kentwood, LA where the drink "10-K" is bottled. A big pure water spring is located there.]

We did a Sunday morning concert in McComb, MS one time then had to be in Hodge, LA for a night concert. It would be at least a 4 hour drive so we declined lunch with the pastor. We had been to this church before. So we went to Burger King, ordered and then Marcia went to a booth.

When I brought the tray over to set it down, I guess I tilted it a little too much and that big cup of soft drink poured onto Marcia's lap. *I was in the doghouse again.* She went to our van, got dry clothes and changed in the restroom (not the best in the west). As it turned out, we had to go through Winnfield and we had just enough time to go by her parents' house where she put on more suitable clothes. We got to the church in time and had a great service.

RAY WALKER

As you probably know, Ray Walker was the bass singer with the Jordanaires for many years. He had also been the song leader at the Madison TN Church of Christ which has 10,000 members. I've been told that Pat Boone's brother led singing there at one time, too. My song "Each Step I Take," is in the Church of Christ hymnal as well as many other denominational hymnals, ***except Lifeway!***

A couple of times Ray came out to our house and sat on the piano bench by me as I arranged a song for him. We were playing cards at Charlsie Matthews' house in the summer of 2012 and Ray phoned that he had some papers for her to sign (on behalf of her deceased husband Neal). She told him to come on over. While he was there we all enjoyed talking with him. He spoke at Neal's funeral also.

OUR NOVA SCOTIA TRIP

In the fall of 1997 Johnnie and Bart went with us on dates in North Carolina and New York. We went through New England into New Brunswick, passing the little town where Ann Murray was raised. In Nova Scotia we went to Halifax and the famous old lighthouse on the beach. It is the only lighthouse that has a (seasonal) post office located in its base! Remember when that big jetliner crashed several years ago? The victims that were recovered were brought to that rocky shore by the lighthouse.

We drove over to Cape Breton Island and around the Cabot Trail... such a beautiful scenic drive along the Atlantic Ocean. We crossed the brand new bridge to Prince Edward Island and saw the setting (house) for "Ann of Green Gables." Also, twice we have ridden the ferry between New York and Vermont. We had friends we met here at the National Quartet Convention that live in Derby, VT, which is within sight of Canada, and we went by to visit them.

BUNGE'S BUNGALOW

Another couple we met in Okeechobee during the winter was Gulia and Philip Bunge. They live north of Nashville, Indiana, which is a lot like Gatlinburg was 50 years ago. We would visit each other for food, fun and card games. And don't forget the Indiana Hoosiers basketball games! In February 2012 when the Lord sold our villa for us in three days (!) they came and helped us load the big 26' rental truck.

Guylia served on the American Baptist Board the same time our friend Lee Cammon did so they knew each other. Robin, the Bunge's married daughter was president of the Indiana American Baptist Women in 2012. She always wears (different) cute little hats...I call her "The Hat." Marcia and I sang at their national convention twice, in Indianapolis and Nashville. Several years ago Guylia got us about seven concerts in central Indiana and we spent ten days/nights in "Bunge's Bungalow" located a hundred yards on down Route 45 from their house.

What a neat place it was. We honestly felt at home the minute we walked in. It had a carport and you could go in the back door from a narrow deck that overlooked the lower backyard and a creek that was headed for Lemon Lake. There was a full basement. Upstairs was the kitchen and living room, a nice bedroom and bath and even a smaller bedroom. We were there in the winter and it came three snows. It was so pretty.

Either Guylia or Philip, sometimes both of them, would go with us to the concerts. We enjoyed going to their church as well. We met so many new folks during those days. We drove over the big double-wide covered bridge just east of Nashville into Brown County Park. The deer were everywhere. We saw a herd of "Oreo" cows. Reda Larson (she and Red own several dairies around Okeechobee, FL) told us the brand name and of course, I can't remember it. They are black on each end with a big white band around their mid-section.

Just East of Mitchell, IN is Spring Mill State Park. There is a tribute to Virgil "Gus" Grissom, one of the three astronauts who perished in that launch pad fire since he was from the area. Also a replica of a pioneer village is there, complete with school/church, blacksmith, general store, grist mill with big operating wheel, etc. Our friends Roland and Patsy Gaines live in Mitchell and had us in their church two different times. We always looked forward to being together in Okeechobee for the winter months.

MORE 90s EXPERIENCES

In south Knoxville, TN is Mt. Olive Baptist Church. It is very old and there are graves and headstones all around it. We were invited there for a Sunday, doing special music in the two morning services, then a full concert that night. As the (male) pianist played a beautiful offertory, a young woman came up on the platform and stood facing the congregation. A school for mentally-challenged persons was nearby and several attended the church. They would do a program once a year and apparently that came to her mind.

The pastor got up from his platform chair and asked her what she was doing. He told us this at lunch that day. She said, "I'm going to sing." He said he could tell her to sit back down or let her sing, so he did. We could see the minister of music (a lady) who had gone to the choir loft to sit, with bowed head in her hands. When the offertory was finished, the pianist swung around and was preparing to "get outta Dodge" when the pastor said, "Mary (not her real name) wants to sing, will you play for her?" The pastor asked for all to hear, "What are you going to sing?" and she replied, "How Great Thou Art."

Friends, what if she did get the lyrics to the verse mixed up... when she hit that chorus and lifted her eyes and voice... "Then sings my soul, my Savior God to Thee..." we lost it! We were to sing next. We went up to the piano but I managed to tell the people to give us a minute. You could hear sniffles all over that auditorium. What a blessing was given to us that day!

Over the years we must have sung in ten or more churches in the Knoxville, TN area. One Sunday night after a service, several of us went to Wendy's. My old friend Beecher Mize (fantastic organist and also a songwriter for Benson, "To be with God") introduced me to a minister of music from a neighboring church before we sat down. "I'd like you to meet Elmo Mercer… we've had him at our church today." A lady sitting at a table right by where I was standing looked up and said, "No, you ain't!" Startled, I said, "Yes, I am." I had to show my driver's license to prove it was me! She was familiar with my varied arrangements.

When Jerry Clower was starting his story-telling career along with some preaching, Bro. Bob had him at Park Avenue for the entire morning service. The people we stayed with in Liberty, MS (the first time we were there, big MS State fans) were close friends with Jerry. His wife called and they opened their electronic gates so Marcia and I could drive through. As we slowly drove around the circular driveway I held the video camera still. Marcia made a snapshot. Our friend Buddy McElroy was music minister at Liberty FBC one time we were there. He would be on staff with us for the MS Baptist Town and Country music clinics sometimes.

One Sunday we were heading west on Hwy 24 from McComb to Liberty. We topped a hill (and there are a lot on that 2-lane asphalt road) and surprised a dozen buzzards partaking of fresh armadillo road kill for breakfast. One circled the wrong way and shattered my rearview mirror, splattering on my window glass! Yuck! I told Marcia we could open our program with "I'm All Shook Up," because we really were!

Steve Jeffers, Kellye's brother-in-law at the time got us some dates around Kansas City while he attended Midwestern Baptist Theological Seminary. We sang at Northgate (the "Seminary church"), Pleasant Valley, Liberty and Faucet, a few miles north of the metro area, all located in Missouri. In Liberty we went in the first bank that Jesse James robbed. One window and the flooring were there when the robbery took place. Did you know that Jesse's father founded a college to train preachers?

A year or so after that we did some dates around St. Joseph, MO, just north of Kansas City. One was undoubtedly a "family" church, it appeared everyone was related! About 25 stood upfront and sang for quite a while after which we sang for thirty minutes. A man preached and then they observed communion. The bread and the "wine" were brought at the same time to each person.

Rankin, IL is about a hundred miles south of Chicago and near the Indiana state line. Gene and Elsie Hofbauer live there and had us in their church three times over about a fifteen year period. We met them in Okeechobee and became instant friends. They attended Treasure Island Baptist instead of First Baptist. We always loved going to visit them in Illinois. Gene and his brother farmed hundreds of acres of corn and soy beans. We drove by a storage place in Rankin, big as a football field with a long steel roof slanted from the center. That place was filled with shelled corn up to the roof. Next to that – outside – was the overflow, a mountain of shelled corn. Gene assured us that the corn (most of it) was usable and that the goffers, rats and snakes would not get into the food chain!

They took us up north a few miles to a company that grew white popcorn. A big ball of a mixture of the white corn and molasses or chocolate was really delicious. The first time we were there we drove about 20 miles north to a truck stop for a great Sunday buffet. The road was a single paved lane between rows of corn that must have been nine feet tall. When you met a vehicle you would slow down and move to the right, but kept the left tires on the pavement!

Tennessee is West, Central and East, and so it is called the "three states of Tennessee." The state flag has three stars in a triangle on it. Once we were at a church in west Tennessee and spent Saturday night with some folks who lived in an earth house. Windows (or just glass) went all across the front but the main part of the house is underground. It got down to 32 degrees that night but they had used their dryer that afternoon and the house was cozy!

Sunday afternoon we walked out to a pasture where they had exotic animals and fowl. A black and white turkey jumped up on the gate post by Marcia and just began "talking" with her. After a while Marcia looked at me and said, "I just realized I am carrying on a conversation with a turkey!" I thought to myself, well you've been talking to me for decades.

We attended a Church of God meeting (out of Anderson, IN – the denomination that the Gaithers and Doug Oldham belong to) on a Saturday night. We sang some and went over some of my choral books. That night we stayed with the pastor of the Germantown, OH Church of God as we were doing a concert there Sunday morning. While we were eating breakfast the phone rang. It was a lady in Dayton who had been at the service the night before. She wanted to talk to me.

She said she knew we planned to drive home Sunday afternoon, but would we please consider coming to her church Sunday afternoon at 5 p.m. We agreed to, and the pastor showed us how to take some "back roads" up about twenty miles or so to the church. It was a Christian Missionary and Alliance church. There were 34 in the choir and 22 in the audience! What a blessing it was to us and we still drove back to Nashville, arriving about midnight. (Thank the Lord for interstates!)

In Kentucky some Baptist churches honor their musicians – pianists, organists, ministers of music. We were invited to two such occasions. The first was at a restaurant overlooking beautiful Lake Cumberland near the city of Somerset. The second was at Central Baptist Church in Winchester.. We sang some then we all played a funny game or two. One was patterned after the TV show "Name That Tune," that was current at that time. A man who was said to be the most eligible bachelor in the church, looked at a lady and said, "Joyce, I can name that tune in…64 beats." We roared. That would be the entire song!

A couple of years before we had been on our way to a weekend at High Lawn Baptist Church in Huntington, WV. (We were there twice over the years and also sang at Eastside Baptist Church. We were to have a Saturday night choir practice so we left Friday, planning to spend the night out along the way. Elizabethtown, KY is where we ate lunch then we left I-65 and drove the scenic Blue Grass Parkway to Lexington and then headed east on I-64. We decided to stop for the night and ate at a Shoney's. In our motel room we watched a great TV program then discovered it was on public television. After we went to bed Marcia said, "Mo, where are we?" "I'm not sure, is it Westminster?" Marcia suggested Westchester. I got up and looked in our road atlas to find out where we were spending the night! It was at Winchester.

We did music in a revival at First Baptist in Chattahoochee, in the Florida panhandle. The evangelist was Dr. Howard Aultman. Our motel was directly across US-90 from a facility for the insane, plus there are three prisons in the area. But the town is beautiful in the springtime with dogwood and redbud trees lining the streets; also a lot of the trees had wisteria vines/flowers all in them. Bro. Gene Strickland was the pastor. He phoned me Sunday morning to tell me the evangelist did not show up at the motel. He said he just called his home number in Columbia, MS and **He answered!**

He thought the revival was the NEXT week. Well, Gene preached that morning; a visiting missionary spoke that night and on Monday the evangelist arrived. He said he reckoned the Lord was punishing him, that he drove in heavy rain all the way! That's the first time we ever did a revival with three different speakers! But a few years after that we did one in Warner Robins, GA with a different speaker each night.

Anyway, during the Chattahoochee revival we went to Sneads, FL to a nursing home to do a program. On Monday night after church we were at the pastor's house and I sang the first song I ever wrote (at 13 years of age) "I'm so LONESOME IN MY SADDLE since my horse died." Dr. Aultman had me sing it and then he talked a while with the folks. He said he didn't look back to the past – why, he couldn't even remember that horse's name but he pressed onward making his life count for God while resting in the saddle of God's grace. He had their attention! He was close to their age, plus his wife had been in a nursing home.

The second revival we did there, the evangelist was Bro. Chuck Raley, who had preached the eight day revival at the Many, LA football stadium. Bro. Gene took us back to the same nursing home in Sneads. Bro. Chuck tried to speak but the folks talked or slept and finally he turned to me and said, "Just play some old hymns for them," and I did.

Central Mississippi, around Indianola, Isola and Belzoni, is catfish country. Some ponds are much larger than football fields but only 3 to 4 feet deep. We've been in several churches in that area. We did music in two revivals at Isola and were there for a Town and Country music clinic. Marsha DePriest (husband Tommy is a crop dusting pilot) was music minister there at the time. We stayed in a house across the street from the church that they owned. Those folks loved to sing. The little town is surrounded by cotton and soy bean fields along with the catfish ponds. A mill manufacturing the catfish feed is near there. The feed is designed to float on top of the water so the catfish will come off the bottom to get it! Some days for lunch we would drive a mile or so to a café run by black folks.

I'm talking turnip greens, blackeyed peas, boiled okra, fried flat bread and catfish. The owner has since passed away and the place closed down.

They took us on a tour of a catfish processing plant. It was interesting. We had to wear light plastic "gowns" and hair coverings. I had to wear a mask covering my beard (I had no hair!). Special compartment trucks would bring fish in from the farms. A big net would draw them to a corner and the fish were gathered and brought to the plant. They would be tested somehow and sometimes the farmer would have to return that load to the pond to make a correction in feed or whatever. Then they would take them back again. We were told that twenty-five minutes after they were unloaded, they came out as frozen pieces packed in pasteboard boxes for shipping across the nation!

The evangelist in a revival at one Mississippi Baptist Church was a turkey hunter. He had the camouflaged clothes, face covering, caller, etc. I mean he was serious! He had gone a day or two with no luck at all. One day he was sitting in a concealed place using his caller and still saw no turkeys. He gave himself another five minutes. He was about to leave when a big turkey with a long beard came strutting into view. He got him! Later the taxidermist told him, "This is not a prize, it is a trophy."

Our dear friend for decades, Ralph Young, had us in three churches. [Remember I told you earlier about him leading the singing in a revival at my home church when I was the teenage pianist and he urged me to pursue an evangelistic career.] When he was at Moss Point, MS, in the heart of casino country, he had us do music in a revival. We stayed in a motel and while I was talking with the evangelist in his room, Ralph told Marcia he put us in this motel because someone had been breaking into rooms at the one he usually used. She forgot to tell me that.

Sometime during the night we heard a sound of glass breaking *inside our room!* I quickly sat up in the bed and Marcia asked, "What was that?" I got up and went to the light switch by the door. The "hangy-down" light over a little round table lit for a split second and went out. I turned the light on the dresser on and we began to look around. I looked up under the shade of the light hanging down and saw the bulb was missing – only the filament was left. We looked around on the floor and up under the air conditioning unit we found the bulb. For some reason it had separated and fallen, hitting the table top. I don't know why it didn't shatter.

The evangelist had been a famous wrestler who went by the name of "Nature Boy No. 2". He was likeable and a great preacher, but there was no response at invitation time. Sometimes during the services CB radios would come in on the sound system. Sometimes the lights would flicker and even go out. It was apparent that Satan didn't want revival to occur. On Thursday night the evangelist gave his testimony (the meeting ran for eight days) and revival "broke out." Praise the Lord.

The ladies of the church prepared huge meals on the second floor of the educational building, and we ate both after the morning and night services! Wow! One day Ralph took us to

Montana's in Gulfport for lunch. The buffet was unbelievable! I was near the evangelist when some man recognized him and exclaimed, "Hey, I've seen you wrestle here at the coliseum!" That made his day. He said that had been twenty years before.

He would always forget to turn on his mike when he got up to preach – the switch was attached on his belt. Someone would go toward him and he'd say, "Oh, I thought you were trying to kiss me!" Well, Marcia told Ralph later, "Tomorrow I'll go up and kiss his cheek if you'll give me a dollar." She did and that preacher freaked out. Marcia walked over to Ralph and stuck out her hand and said, "Give me my dollar." It turned out to be such a great revival that before we left, Ralph said, "Let's do this again next year!" We did, but it was not as great.

On a western tour, we were to sing at a church in Rock Springs, WY at 7 p.m. We were heading up there from Salt Lake City dates and I thought we had plenty of time. The mountains are especially beautiful in NE Utah. We drove out a forestry (or county) road and were soon enveloped in the wonders of God's creation. The way the road turned I thought we were going back to the highway north. Suddenly the road became almost impassable. By the time we got back to the paved road, we realized we were running short of time. We sped through the scenic Flaming Gorge area (been there before) and barely got to the church in time! In southern Nebraska we did a concert at the town of York, west of Lincoln and just north of I-80. We enjoyed being in that church and community. We stayed with a couple in their beautiful home. Traveling on westward near Kearney is the famous Great Platte River Road Archway Monument – it is something to see.

We were to be music guests at North Jacksonville Baptist Church and were staying in a hotel in the area. The lights went out but we quickly noticed that power was on in other places. An announcement was heard out in the hallway for all guests to come to the lobby! Kinda scary for me – Marcia didn't seem to worry about it. As I opened the door that request was cancelled. We never knew what it was all about.

Jimmy McCaleb always had Marcia and me on the Mississippi Town and Country Music Clinics staff. He used numerous others in that ten year period usually depending on what part of the state we were in. Irene Martin taught piano/organ sometimes. A lady named Lola Autry usually did that, however. We met her for the first time on the Thursday night when it began. Friday morning when she came in the front of the church I started singing, "Whatever Lola wants...Lola gets!" She was a remarkable person.

Raised in Memphis to become a concert pianist, God altered her path to marry a north Mississippi Baptist preacher somewhat older than she. He was pastor of about four little country churches and they traveled in a T-model or some such vehicle. One Sunday night they were heading home and it had been pouring rain most of the day. She had gone to sleep when suddenly she jumped and yelled, "Stop the car!" He did, scared half to death and asked her why. She said there was danger ahead. He got out in the rain and mud walking around the front of the car when his footing gave way and he grabbed onto the exposed headlight. He discovered the wooden bridge over a creek had been washed out! In later years she wrote her story and it was printed in Guidepost magazine. She had articles in several magazines. Her husband also wrote articles that were printed in Readers Digest, Field and Stream, etc.

We would visit her when we got anywhere near Hickory Flat in northern Mississippi. She lived on 80 acres that her deceased husband had owned and called it Whippoorwill Valley. We ate at her table, slept in her guest room several times. She was a piano teacher with students coming to her there; she was an artist and the house was filled with beautiful paintings. She was also a photographer especially at weddings. Also she had gone on numerous mission trips to other countries. One time at her house I stepped out the back door onto her deck and a wasp hit me right between the eyes!

After the big 1995 ice storm that even reached down in northern Mississippi we visited her and she drove us out to check on an elderly couple. We made our way along the dirt road with pine sapplings bent or broken all over the place. Another time she took us to her son Lanny's house to see where their pageant at Christmas was performed with the help of others. I think they called it "Christmas on the Lake." She also stopped by a hill and found rocks that you could break open and in the center was a reddish powder. When mixed with some water it made "war paint" for Indians. She told of going with others and grappling in the Tippan River (it flows into the Tallahatchie).

You reach underwater near the bank and grab unsuspecting catfish! You might come up with a moccasin every now and then! Hey, I'll pass on that sport!

In a revival at her church (her husband is buried in that cemetery) we stayed at the pastor's house about a hundred yards up the road. He and his wife took us to "our" room...but there was no bed in it. They had watched our reaction, then reached up and pulled it down from the wall! Our room was the second door on the left in the hallway. One night I had gone to bed before Marcia and already dropped off to sleep. She came in the room and was about to crack up. I said, "What's happened?"

She said, "I came out of the bathroom and it was so dark I had to feel my way along the wall. I found a doorknob and opened it. The pastor was in his robe sitting at his desk!" I scolded, "Aw, Marcia, you know where this room is!" Whoa! She threw the book she'd been reading over on an old church pew in our room, got in bed...and I believe she was a little peeved at me.

The next morning we were to go to Lola's and she met us at the door. In our conversation Marcia looked at me to say something then with a flip of her hand said, "Oh, I'm not talking to YOU this morning!" Lola clapped her hands and said, "Are y'all havin' an argument? My husband and I used to argue over the silliest things – like whether to use a comma or a semi-colon, stuff like that." Lola passed away several years ago, in her late 80s I would assume. She was a tremendous lady who loved and served people, and definitely loved and served her Lord. We will never forget her.

MORE EXPERIENCES

Marcia and I did a weekend at a small south Louisiana church. It poured down rain. They were having septic tank problems and mud was everywhere. Saturday night before choir practice we had some kind of seafood gumbo for supper. I didn't dare ask what was in it. When I started choir practice I saw immediately I could not use my choral books. There were about fifteen in the choir including a child or two. The pastor thought he was singing tenor. I ran out to the van and got my "Best of Gospel Hymnal," and had them to sing "Each Step I Take." I had the choir sing the first verse, I changed keys and sang the second then we all did the third verse inviting the congregation to join in on the last chorus. They were proud of themselves and I was, too.

The pastor and his wife's eighteen year-old-daughter had been killed five years before by a drunk driver and that's all the mother would talk about. It was so sad. Monday morning the pastor cooked three pans of biscuits and made gravy for breakfast. We bid them farewell and headed north.

Copperhill, TN and McCaysville, GA share the state line running down the middle of a street. The minister of music at a church there told us if we would get down there early enough on Saturday he would take us rafting down the Hiawassee River. We did and Kellye went with us. A dam upstream is opened at a certain time to let water rush out, raising the level somewhat. It was fun. We stopped along the way and had sandwiches. Later on the guy fell over backwards off the raft but we grabbed him by his legs and pulled him back in. He was acting as helmsman. It happened a second time! There were no falls over two or three feet.

Before we had traveled the ten miles to where we would get out of the river and be taken back to the rental place a TERRIFIC electrical storm came up. As soon as the lightning flashed it would hit right close to us. You could feel the hair rising on your forearms and neck. We saw the men on the bank waving and yelling for us to hurry up. Kellye screamed, "Paddle, paddle!" Then another strike would hit and she'd jump in Marcia's lap! We were scared speechless...or something like that!

Remember when Mrs. C. E. Francis gave us the split level house and basically fifty acres of land, she said, "Maybe it will make you some money someday?" In 1994 I answered the phone at home and a man introduced himself, said he was in Atlanta and would like to come up to talk with us about putting a cell phone tower on our land. We had seen them along highways but not given it much thought. I started declining when he told me, "Well, Mr. Mercer, if we don't put it on your land we'll put it on your neighbor's land, and you'll have regrets every time you see it. I'm talking about (amount not stated) over the 25 year contract period. I said, "Can you be here by noon tomorrow?" We signed the contract.

A road was constructed up to the top of our ridge and in places it has a 37 degree incline, they told me. The tall, 3 legged free-standing steel tower was erected in three days. It pays monthly. Thank you, God. In 1999, GOD gave us a <u>second</u>

tower and it pays annually. These towers helped us take our ministry where we felt the Lord wanted us to go – to the small town or rural church. We went on a "love offering" basis and rarely received any money for expenses. We made friends all over the USA and have stayed in touch with many of them by phone, e-mail or going by to visit. {We would love to have a third one but God would surely know I was greedy, right?}

In north Georgia in the Blairsville area, we did a mini-concert at a country church then our friend Bro. Gene Strickland brought the message. It was their home-coming and a great meal followed. A couple from Baker, FL, Jewel and Marvis Carr drove all the way up to be with us. Marvis used to play guitar and sing special music in their church and we've been there in revival also. That day after the meal at church Gene and Marcia drove us through the mountainous area to the quaint town of Helen, GA, similar to Gatlinburg. Traffic was terrible, however.

That night the concert at a different church further north was interesting. The pastor invited singers from the congregation to come on up and sing a while. There must have been forty people including some children. They had a live band to accompany them. We enjoyed that for almost thirty minutes! Then they had us do our concert and we thought that was it. But the pastor called on a young man to preach for them. He would suck in breath between every sentence, but we enjoyed that also. I was just hoping they wouldn't bring out any snakes! (Remember Wendy Bagwell's story). We weren't allowed to put our merchandise out in the church but were told to open the trunk of our car and we sold over a hundred dollars' worth! That same thing happened to us at a church near the intersection of I-40 and I-75 west of Knoxville, and we went there two times!

Marcia's sister Johnnie and her husband Bartlett have traveled with us on our various trips for many years. We've been in 49 states together and Marcia and I have been to Hawaii twice. They were with us on our first cruise on Carnival to the Bahamas. It was fun. On the way back the Captain turned the ship toward Cape Canaveral and the launched shuttle went right over us. We had stayed up till 1:30 a.m. to see it. The second cruise was the "Alaska Inland Passage" and we went from Vancouver, BC to Seward, Alaska. We were fascinated with the ports we stopped at – Ketchikan, Sitka, Juneau and Seward. We were bused from there to Anchorage where we immediately boarded an Alaskan Airlines plane back to Seattle. If we stayed at the same hotel the night we returned, we could park our van in a fenced lot for free, so that's what we did! At the airport we piled our 17 bags on a cart and Bart started to push it, but it suddenly veered to the left. He tried a couple more times and it did the same thing. We all ganged up on it, got down the elevator and out to our van!

That cruise was part of a five weeks trip we did together out west. We visited their brother Bernard in San Diego (retired after 27 years as an air traffic controller in the Navy, a Vietnam vet); then we headed up to Seattle seeing scenic sights along the way. This was in May and June. We went in eleven national parks and in every one of them some of the roads were still blocked with snow and ice!

In Ecru, MS we did a revival and the evangelist played a steel guitar. We had lots of good music during those services. We stayed in the home of a couple who owned a furniture manufacturing company. He took us on a tour. The lumber came in one end and the finished shrink-wrapped product was loaded on trucks at the other end. He had about 200 employees. That was interesting.

I guess we've been to Gatlinburg and Pigeon Forge each month of the year. The trails and roads are just awesome anytime. Once we were there and they were having an antique car show. On another trip a mini-van inched its way down the main street with its sliding rear doors open and the radio cranked up HIGH. It felt like your belly button was rubbing your backbone! We enjoy going to Cade's Cove and always look for bear on that long one-way scenic drive. There is a unique miniature golf place as you come into Gatlinburg. We played a round. I had the highest score and thought I'd won…so much for my golf game!

A unique jewelry shop was adjacent to our motel there and we engaged the owner, Tonya in conversation. We discovered she was a sister to "Big Tiny Little" who sometimes played a honkytonk piano on the Lawrence TV show.

One time we rented a chalet on the road up to Ober-Gatlinburg ski area. Kellye and her three children flew up and Bill and his family came also. Naturally the boys and girls were having a good time but they got too boisterous for Kellye. She said, "No more running!" After a while we heard little Joey crying.

Kellye asked what was wrong and he said, "I was run-...I mean I was walking fast and..." We love to walk the streets and go in an occasional shop. I was fascinated with the sock-making machine and the candy-making machine. Many times we have also enjoyed Pigeon Forge. Kellye took the kids to a "kid-die-park." BJ and Joey wanted to ride the ferris wheel and the operator told them when they wanted to get off just holler. Joey got sick pretty soon and BJ started yelling, "Somebody's sick! Somebody's sick!"

Just south of Shreveport down US-71 is the little town of Coushatta, LA, pronounced Kuh-shat-uh. It is an Indian name. [In fact there is a settlement of Coushatta Indians in extreme SE Texas]. Located about a mile east of the Red River it is surrounded by farms and ranches. One Mother's Day we were at the First Baptist Church. The pastor was trying to determine the oldest mother in the congregation. There were three ladies still standing, seemingly unconcerned as he said, "83, 84, 85." Then he said, "I'm embarrassed to ask you ladies your age." His five-year-old son sitting on the front pew with his coloring book, swinging his legs said, "Don't ask 'em their weight, Dad!" The congregation laughed.

One Sunday afternoon we did a 3 p.m. concert at a church in Jackson, MS. After we began, it seemed like heavy burden descended on us. I began forgetting my chords, we messed up lyrics and our voices gave us trouble. I felt compelled to stop, tell the congregation and pray. I told them and said frankly that I felt Satan was opposing us. After I prayed we had a great concert and time of fellowship with the people afterward.

We have had so many wonderful experiences with God's people across the USA. God is so good!

"APRIL FOOL"

We did music in a revival where Dr. Joe Whitt was the evangelist. He invited us to his church a year or so later...First Baptist in Hamilton, AL. We got there Saturday and stayed in a motel. We got to church early Sunday and went directly to his office.

We sat there and talked until it was about time for the morning worship to begin. Joe looked great in his white suit and shoes. He was shorter than me. I said, "Uh, Joe, before we go out I feel like I ought to share this with you. Uh...well, when we get back to Nashville, we're seeing a lawyer. We're gettin' a divorce, Joe. I hope this won't affect our serving in this meeting."

Joe looked at us and said, "Well, you know I've come to love you both and I guess you'll do what you think is best." I looked down and smiled, put my arm around his shoulders and hugged him up to my right side and said, "Joe, April Fool!" (It WAS April Fool Day).

He looked at me, thought a minute then said, "I'll git chee!" And I guess he did, in a way whether he realized it or not. About a year later we went to a small town in the same area where he was interim pastor. We hadn't been there long when I asked the pianist, "Where's Bro. Joe?"

"Oh, he's not here anymore!" The church had a new pastor and I believe this was his first Sunday. We went back to our merchandise table after the service and some folks bought CDs and songbooks. The organist and pianist from the Methodist Church rushed in as we were packing our stuff and bought some instrumental books. No one offered to take us to lunch. We were to be at another church in NE Mississippi that night, so we ate at a fast food place and left.

Later I found out the new pastor had told the pianist HE would take us out. He did not. I'm afraid he got off on the wrong foot with that piano-playin' woman.

ANOTHER MERCER FAMILY

I believe it was in the late 90s that we did music in a revival where Bro. Garland McKee was evangelist. This was at a big country church south of Meridian. He was originally from Mississippi, yet his only two pastorates were at Istrouma Baptist in Baton Rouge, LA and First Baptist in Pearland (Houston), TX. The Minister of Music at Pearland was Sonny Steed. He came to WHACHAMACALLIT and had us to come for a weekend.

Garland became quite famous by imitating black people and telling hilarious stories. He made records, CDs and DVDs. One was titled "Laughin' with 'Em." He was in demand as an after dinner speaker and a lot of them were in black churches! Garland was a great witness and soul winner. Every day, he said, he would witness to some person. One afternoon of the revival he and his wife June asked Marcia and me to go up to Meridian with them. He parked the car and when we got out he saw a man rolling a 2-wheeler filled with cases of beer. He whistled him down and witnessed to him.

June and Garland stayed in the home of a senior adult couple. Marcia and I stayed in the home of a family named MERCER. Their two-story house sat in a wooded area that was beautifully landscaped. He was minister of music at the church. His first name was Ronnie – I have a brother named Ronnie. They showed us pictures of their granddaughters. They had a granddaughter named Beth! We said, "Hey, we do, too!" They showed us one named Lindsey and we had a Lindsey also. We could not believe it when they showed us a third one named Hailey because we had one, too. We had three grandchildren with the same first and last names! And one of their daughter-in-laws was expecting! We told them they had to name him or her, Courtney! What a coincidence that was!

Every night after the service folks would go into their Fellowship Hall and have refreshments then Garland would tell some of his "black" stories. A speech therapist told him when he talked that way it was more "authentic" than his natural speech! They retired to live in Clinton, MS, just west of Jackson. Not far away from them our friends Jimmy McCaleb (MS T&C Music Clinics) and wife Ashley have a home.

CARD PLAYING

One winter night in Okeechobee, we had fourteen people over to the condo to eat home-made soup, cornbread, salad and dessert - then play card games. We had two card tables set up in the living room, plus six sat at the dining table. Bob and Louise Vierling, dear friends from Seymour, IN, sat at a card table for a while and played with Kayla, Kellye's young daughter, and BJ, Kellye's older son. Kayla played some card and BJ said, "Kayla, why didn't you play that one a while go?" She said, "I had to follow suit!" Louise talked about that for a long time. All three of Kellye's kids were playing card games before they started kindergarten...and they would occasionally beat us! BJ and Joey, 16 months apart, could really shuffle the deck, too. I hasten to mention that they also knew Bible songs and scriptures plus a lot of useful and helpful knowledge!

Bob and Louise had very *creative* talent. They made several clocks from cypress tree "knees" of all sizes. They made stained glass shades for lamps. Their big project was to make the window in the balcony (front) of First Baptist in Okeechobee. When their home church, First Christian in Seymour built a big new sanctuary, they made a LARGE stained glass window flanking the entrance.

Kellye's three kids, when they were smaller, would come to the condo almost every Friday night to stay with us. That's when we taught them how to play card games. In one game where you had to bid, we had only four cards in our hands and BJ bid three! All of us looked at him and he just grinned and said, "I know what I'm doing." And he did. He must have had the Ace, King and Queen of trumps! That has been his saying ever since... "I know what I'm doing!"

Have you ever played "Dirty Uno?" Don't! It gets aggravating and can go on for hours. One night after a concert over near Sebring on US 27 (there's an international race track there) we went by some friends' house (from Indiana) located in a citrus grove. After refreshments we started playing cards and someone wanted to play Dirty Uno. Marcia and I were tired and we were some fifty miles away from our beds! Suddenly, Marcia turned over a glass of tea in a guy's lap *(well of course it was an accident!)* and that ended the game!

SC SA CHOIR FESTIVAL

I got a call from a man with the South Carolina Baptist Convention. He wanted me to "adjudicate" the senior adult choirs at their state convention meeting in Myrtle Beach that year. I told him I didn't even know what that word meant. He said I was to listen to each choir sing and then talk privately to them in the choir loft about their performance. There were only six choirs there. It was NOT a contest and there would be no winner. Most of them were very good. But as I sat and listened to them I was praying, "Lord, give me something quick to talk about!"

There were 3600 people present and we met in HALF of the new civic center the city was building. That night I had 600 in my choir! They gathered in chairs down in front of me as I sat at the piano on the platform. We had a great time. Marcia was asked to say a few words and she very seldom speaks even during our concerts. But she got to the pulpit and must have talked for 15 minutes! (I was right proud of her!)

The man who had been their Director was retiring and he brought on a young man in his twenties. Marcia and I thought that was a bit unusual. But in five minutes that guy had those people hanging onto every word! One thing he did was to have us not talk while we rubbed our palms together. It sounded like rain on the roof! When we rubbed harder it sounded like a downpour! The outgoing Director then stood on his head on the platform and waved goodbye to everyone!

DISAPPEARING CARDS

Sometimes two nights a week Marcia and Elizabeth (partners) and Lyndal and Donna (partners) would play rook games at Donna's big house. They bought this huge 3-floor house with a full basement. It was built in 1904 by a sea captain. Entering the large foyer through double stained glass doors you saw a wide stairway to the second floor with white bannisters up it and also around the second floor like on a steamboat. It had a front porch with many stairs leading to it from the east and west sides. Porches were also on the second and third floors. Some women friends of Donna's would even live there temporarily. Their youngest daughter, Whitney lived on the top floor. They completely refurbished the entire house. I think it had seven bedrooms and bath rooms.

One Halloween Donna and Rayford had another engagement and asked Marcia and me to come to their house and give out treats. Some of the children would look inside, wide-eyed at the beauty. One said, "This must be a mansion!" Another asked, "Do you live here?" They had added a pool and done lots of landscaping over the huge lawn. Her sister was married on the lawn and I played a keyboard for it. The bell ringers from Park Avenue played and a string quartet was there also.

Donna would occasionally host a big Republican affair at their house. One time former President George H. W. Bush and Barbara came. Afterward, someone gave Donna two love birds in a cage. She would put a cloth over the cage at night so the "girls" could continue to play ROOK. Donna named them George and Barbara! One night Marcia happened to notice the cage was empty and asked Donna about them. Donna said, "Aw, somebody left the back door open and a cat got in and ate them." Marcia exclaimed, "Ate George and Barbara?!"

Senator Oren Hatch from Utah composed a song that was sung at the second inauguration of George Bush. Donna (SONY) acquired it, so he came to Nashville to spend the day at the SONY offices on Music Row West (next to ASCAP). He spent the night at Donna & Rayford's house. After that she referred to the bed room he was in as "The Hatch bed room!" Sometime later we were talking about the song and before I knew it she phoned him and had me talk to him! I told him I thought that song was a "born standard."

After choir practice one Wednesday night they went to Donna's to play Rook. But Lyndal (the organist) had to stay a while at church. They were sitting at the table and heard the back door open and close, thinking Lyndal had arrived. It was not her and they wondered about the incident. Prior to that the house had been a nursing home and it was over one hundred years old.

One night they were playing cards and Lyndal asked who was staying upstairs? Looking perplexed Donna said, "Why, nobody that I know of!" Lyndal said, "Oooohh! I think I just saw a man walk up those stairs!" It was a rather narrow staircase near the back of the house, actually in a dining room. Donna said she had found shoe prints on a newly-vacuumed carpet before, and talked about other unexplainable situations that had occurred in the past…

Marcia and I and a couple more friends were over at their house, all six of us playing a card game at a wooden dining table. At the end of a hand Marcia slid her five cards down the table to be shuffled. They disappeared! I thought they had gone through the crack between a panel (leaf?) and the table itself, so I bent over to get them off the floor. They were NOT on the floor! We all got a little uneasy. What was going on? Rayford and I pulled at each end of the table, and those five cards were just lying in a stack on the thin steel support under the table top! That was unbelievable and kinda spooky.

Donna and Rayford always hosted big parties on Memorial Day, July 4th, Labor Day, (all outside around the pool, with oodles of food, desserts and canned drinks). She also had parties at Thanksgiving and Christmas. Sometime fifty people would be there or come and go. Some of them were "stars", too. At Christmas her house was always so beautifully decorated both in and outside. One Christmas she had a young woman in the foyer playing a harp. There were gas fireplaces all over the house. A pool table and piano were in the library.

Donna was to attend an NMPA (National Music Publishers Association) meeting in Maui, Hawaii. Rayford was going with her and she invited Marcia and me to go along. We spent one night going and two nights coming back at a Beverly Hills Hotel. One time the elevator door opened and there stood *Richard Chamberlain* on his way to the pool on the roof of the fourth floor! We thoroughly enjoyed the time in Hawaii, staying at a fabulous hotel right on the beach. We flew to Honolulu one day and toured that island. The Japanese came from Japan and sitting by us at dinner one night we talked with one; and he said he was a graduate of Belmont University in Nashville! What a coincidence.

When Donna got sick, Marcia and I accompanied her and Rayford (along with Barbara, her caregiver) to Mayo Clinic in Rochester, MN. We flew up on Kenny Chesney's jet and back on Ronnie Dunn's jet. Rayford later sold that big house and bought one on the east side of Brentwood. A couple of years later the old house caught fire and did a lot of damage to the 2nd and 3rd floors. It was repaired.

When Donna passed away we were in another state. Our schedule prevented us from being at the funeral.

THE LATE 90s

A Mr. Evans in Shawnee Mission, Kansas (SW Kansas City) invited us to do a concert in his church. It was a Christian Church (Disciples of Christ) and they use musical instruments. They had two morning services and observe Communion each

Sunday. I was at the piano playing softly. The pastor came to Marcia first holding a whole loaf of baked bread on a plate and a small cup of "wine." Taken aback, she asked him what she was to do. He quietly said to break off a small piece of the bread and dip it in the cup and swallow it.

The second service began before Marcia had a chance to ask if she should partake in it as well. She did any way. The man brought the bread to me and I wouldn't stop playing to break off a piece, so he later brought me a wafer!

Johnnie and Bart were with us one time in northern Indiana when we passed grape vineyards. They were being harvested. We stopped the van to watch and the man yelled for us to pick what we wanted! We did, and ate as we continued our trip.

Years before when Bill and Kellye were young we drove through the Notre Dame campus. There was a lake there and from a distance it looked to us like there were penguins everywhere along the shore. We got closer and discovered they were nuns!

In Virginia we did a couple of dates on one trip along I-81. The first was at Woodstock and a few years later we were invited back. While there I was invited to a radio station up in Winchester to be on a radio program. The DJ played gospel songs and we would talk between them. I had a great time.

The second concert was at a church in Stuarts Draft, VA. Steve and Jennifer Hall do the music and his Dad is the pastor. They are on the Bible Truth Music Board and I see them annually at our meetings. Their work titled "This is My America...Under God" is widely used, and was published by Bible Truth Music.

Through the thirty years we were "on the road," we appeared on both radio and TV many times in many places across the nation. I remember one time we did an hour TV show with the host...this was in Michigan. The manager came in and said, "Please, would you do another hour show for us while you are here with us?" We did, and didn't have lunch till 4 p.m. A friend told me later that the shows were played several times on that station for a year or two afterward.

THE TRIPP FAMILY

We met Bea Tripp largely because of my piano/organ duet books. She was organist at Green Pine Baptist Church in Knightdale, North Carolina, an eastern suburb of Raleigh. She and her husband Kenneth were anesthetists at a hospital there. Bea was from Sweden and they met in England. We love to hear her talk. She maintains dual citizenship and went back annually to visit. Her Mother would also come to America, and they came to visit us three or four times, attending both Park Avenue and Scottsboro churches.

At our house one day Marcia asked her Mother why she didn't move to the USA. In broken English she said she loved this country but placing her hand on her heart she said, "Sweden is my home." I believe she lived to be one hundred before passing away. Kenneth was a drag racer and had many trophies and pictures to prove it. Their daughter Katrina played violin, and the first time we were at Green Pine Baptist I had her to play "The Way That He Loves" for offertory with her mother and me. Their son, Ken, Jr. is a dentist. Both are married now with children.

Remnants of a hurricane came through Knightdale a few years ago and a large oak tree in their front yard fell on the house. The trunk came right down where a window was. Bea was at work and Katrina had gone to bed. Kenneth could not get her bedroom door to open. When he was finally able to get to her she was pinned in bed but not crushed! Rescuers had to cut off the legs of the bed so it would drop down to where they could pull her out. She had only a few scratches! Her testimony of the incident filled the top half of a page in the Raleigh newspaper a day or so after. She gave God the glory for protecting her.

On our last trip to Bea's church, the associate pastor suddenly passed away while we were driving there. It was decided the evening service would be canceled so we said we'd just drive back home, perhaps 500 miles. Bea said, "Do not deny me the joy of feeding you lunch as I had planned to do!" She fixed three skillets of fried chicken and all that goes with it and we chowed down. We left at 3 p.m. EDT, passing through the Smoky Mountains on I-40 and still got home around midnight CDT.

TWO HEART ATTACKS

In 1996 I was cutting firewood with my chainsaw when I began having chest pains' They were severe enough that I put the saw, gas and oil in the wheelbarrow and headed to the house fifty yards away. I sat down and later felt better. Five days later we packed up to go to our Okeechobee, FL condo. We stopped by Smyrna, GA for her Uncle Leslie and Aunt Bea's 50th wedding anniversary at the new community center. I was to play some old WWII pop songs. Many of their friends were there, along with their son and daughter and their families. Bill and his family came from Nashville. Kellye flew up and the plan was for us to drive back down to Okeechobee after the event.

Here came those chest pains again after I finished playing the old songs. I was sitting by Johnnie's husband Bart in chairs around the wall and he was talking away to me. I wasn't hearing a word. Kellye walked up to me and said, "Daddy, what is wrong with you? You're white as a sheet and *profusing sweatly!*" I guess she was scared. They insisted I go to the hospital but that would not have been good for their celebration and I had gotten over them a few days before. Besides it would have been inconvenient to all for me to be put in an Atlanta-area hospital. After a while the three of us said goodbye and started the nine hour trip south.

Kellye drove as I slumped in the second row bucket seat of our '93 GMC van. When we got to the Florida Turnpike I said I felt better enough to drive so I did to the Yeehaw Junction exit where we got off. It had started to rain and Marcia said she would drive the 33 miles down US-441 South to Okeechobee. We got home just after midnight. Next morning after sleeping a bit late, we unloaded the van. That was always a job. Bill and Kellye had made me promise I would have a doctor check me out.

Tuesday we drove over to Martin County Hospital in Port St. Lucie on the coast. I was trailing Marcia as she approached the desk and told the lady, "My husband is having some chest pains." The lady hit a button, the swinging doors flew open and a gurney appeared. I was whisked behind the curtains. Forty minutes later a young doctor came to us (he looked like Jack Tripper on "Three's Company") and said, "Mr. Mercer, your tests reveal you've had a heart attack in the last week." I wanted to yell, "Aw come on, Jack!"

I was kept overnight then sent by ambulance to Palm Beach Gardens Hospital. I was lying there looking at my heart monitor machine when the green line went FLAT! I buzzed for the nurse and she said it had malfunctioned, that if that had really happened I wouldn't have seen the line or called her! I was moved to another room and the technician discovered THAT monitor was bad. He yelled out to Marcia (in the hall with Kellye, and it was around midnight) "Mrs. Mercer, would you get him outta here, he's ruining all our machines!" This was in an "overflow" room. The third floor was nothing but heart patients and it was full! I was assigned my own private nurse...hmmm? Sounds good to me! Come to find out she was black and nine and a half months pregnant!

Anyhow, I was there a couple of days while they ran an arteriogram. Now that was something. I was not unconscious but they had given me something to make me not really care what was going on!

I heard one doctor say to the other one, "Uh oh! Do you see that?" I knew that was not what I wanted to hear. Come to find out when they were removing the catheter (or whatever) it nicked a place which began to bleed. They left the port in my groin area in case they had to go back in quickly. I lay flat of my back for 54 hours with my right leg strapped down! The nurse asked later if I wanted a bedpan. I said, "No, thanks. I can see the headline now: ***'Famous composer found dead on bed pan in Florida Hospital!'***" I was released and we enjoyed the winter months in Okeechobee.

BUT in 2005 my local cardiologist told me I needed a triple bypass. Friends, that knocked the props out from under me. It took me awhile to get over that episode. He keeps a check on me annually and apparently I'm doing alright. Thank you, God.

ASCAP HONORS ME

It came as a total surprise to me. In April 1997 Donna Hilley (SONY) and Connie Bradley (ASCAP) – they are located next to each other on Music Row West – decided to honor me as a 40-year member of the American Society of Composers, Authors and Publishers. (Remember I was inducted in 1957). It was to be done at the ASCAP Dove Awards in their building. Kellye even flew up from south Florida. Bill and Renee were also in attendance and we all sat at a big round table right by the stage.

I got to see a lot of friends I had not seen in several years and we were having a great time of fellowship when Connie went to the mike. She said ASCAP wanted to honor one of its 40 year members. He had composed many gospel songs, recorded by many artists, etc. I still didn't have a clue, but when she said "...back in 1981 he made a missions trip to South Korea," I looked at Marcia and she smiled. Connie called me to the stage to accept and say a few words. Oh, my! I have no idea what I said. That was a night I will never forget.

A FAMILY VACATION

Kellye and her family flew into the Philadelphia, PA airport and we spent the night in Wilmington, Delaware. In Manhattan we went up the Empire State Building, rode the ferry out to the Statue of Liberty, then came back to south Central Park and Times Square. We drove through the New England states then went on up to Toronto, Canada. We ate at Hard Rock Café in the Skydome where the Expos played. We took the elevator up the CN Tower. It is 1200 feet up to the observation deck (4 football fields). A portion of the flooring is thick glass and people were bending over looking down. I strode between some and said, "Excuse me, please" and walked across it like it was wood. On a trip there later with Johnnie and Bart she lay down on her back on the glass and a picture was made looking down.

We re-entered the US at Port Huron, MI after coming through a curving 2-lane, 2-way traffic tunnel! We drove in downtown Detroit and headed west to Grand Rapids. There is a fish ladder there by a spillway on the Grand River that is interesting to see. Just east of there is the town of Ada, where the headquarters of the Amway Corporation is located.

Near Ada is a covered bridge over the Thornapple River and the area is so scenic. When we got back to our '93 GMC Safari my key broke off in the ignition! Kellye's husband Bruce owned an auto repair and tire store but he could not get the key out so we could use Marcia's key. I called AAA and we were towed to some town to a GMC dealer where it was repaired in two hours. The others had stayed at the covered bridge park.

We went through Holland, MI and down to a town called Michigan City, IN. Just west of there is Mt. Baldy, a huge pile of sand at the southeast end of Lake Michigan. It is moving to the south about 4 inches per year! In Chicago we drove along Lakeshore Drive then went up the Sears (then) Tower. What a view that was, being over 100 stories. We were there hardly an hour but parking cost $16!

Back in Philadelphia we went to Independence Hall, the Liberty Bell, the Mint and the grave of Benjamin Franklin. By it on the brick wall was a bronze plaque listing all his marvelous inventions. Kellye and family flew back to south Florida. What a good time together we had on that trip!

"BIG DOG"

Several years ago, after having the new waterline installed in our front yard, there was a low spot where it came under the driveway. Bill shoveled some dirt in the back of our Ford F-250 4WD (301 Cummins engine) pickup truck. [It was a "big dog." In fact, I taught it to "roll over."] The next day I went out to drive around and spread it in that low place. I didn't put on the seatbelt…I wasn't getting off my own property! I wish I had. When I turned onto the road up to the cell phone towers on our ridge behind the house, the right tire went off into the ditch and I was slung over toward the passenger door! I reached my left foot for the brake and hit the gas instead. It ran along the left bank of the road over some big poke sallet bushes at about a 45% angle for about 20 yards then leaned over on its right side!

I was sitting with my back against the passenger door with both legs sticking straight up on the seat near the steering wheel! I thought, "Well…I've had a wreck. What will Marcia think?" I blew the horn but was about 50 yards from the house and I'm sure Marcia was watching TV. What could she have done anyhow! It was hot and about 10:30 in the morning. The driver window was down and somehow I managed to climb UP and out although the metal was SO hot on my palms. I had emptied the dirt alright but not where I had meant to! I called AAA and a wrecker came out. The guy said, "I reckon you know this is not a parking place!" Later he said, "Don't ask to borrow my pickup, man. I ain't loanin' it to YOU!" He was a riot. We put 26,000 miles on that truck in *24 years!* I told Bill we were going to wear it out. I sold it for $1,200, dents and all.

OUR HIGH SCHOOL REUNIONS

I graduated from Winnfield High School in May 1950. We were the first class to go twelve years instead of eleven! There were 65 in it and I tied Gloria McDaniel (a preacher's daughter) for tenth place. [Gertrude was valedictorian of her class and Earl was salutatorian of his class]. My class went 25 years before having a reunion! Some were already grandparents, some had passed away. A former graduate and teacher Sara Jackson Shell started a general WHS reunion. Her husband Dennis – a twin to Denton, used to come in the bank and say, "Hello, Welmo," since I went by W. Elmo Mercer. The reunion has grown tremendously with usually 350+ in attendance. It is held the fourth weekend in June at the Winn Parish Forest Festival grounds on US-34 south of downtown. A newsletter is mailed out three times a year. I am somewhat amazed at how old and fat some of my classmates have become. After several decades Sarah gave up her duties and it took a committee to take her place!

My 50th was in 2000. We had been having the reunions at the new high school's cafeteria and outgrew that, so ours was held in the fellowship hall of the First Methodist Church on West Main Street, for that one year only. I played piano and led them in some of the pop tunes of the 40s. Jim Bob Key sang several Broadway hit songs and a classical one or two. He had just returned from a trip where he sang for the Pope in Rome! After that Jerre McBride did a great power point program that was enjoyed by all. What memories we have.

We always have a Friday night meeting with great food and fellowship. Some folks come from hundreds of miles away... Bernard (Marcia's brother) lived in San Diego; the first reunion he attended was his 50th! On Saturday morning at 10:00 a "coffee" is held, no charge for it. Saturday night is the banquet and the class celebrating their 50th is responsible for the program. Several of our former teachers attend as well. We all look forward to this each year. The 2013 class built a replica of Eula's Tiger Inn. It was across the side street from the high school and students could buy cokes, food, etc. She ran it for over 30 years!

A CANADA VACATION

Well, Y2K came and went without too many ill effects. We experienced the turn of the year, the decade, the century and the millennium. WOW! We have finally used the supplies we had stocked up.

Johnnie and Bart went with us on a trip to the northwest USA, and on up into Alberta and British Columbia, Canada. In Cardston, AB is the largest Mormon Temple outside of Salt Lake City. It sits gleaming white on a hill. In Calgary we visited where the Olympics were held. To me it was frightening and intimidating to be on top of the ski jump looking down! I don't know how they can do that. We praised the Lord for elevators.

In Edmonton, we dropped our luggage out the motel window to the van below! We discovered I had parked right below our room window. The first floor was half underground so instead of carrying all our belongings a hundred yards, we dropped them from our window and Bart and I packed the van. I reckon some people thought we were trying to leave without paying the bill. That's where I bought my WEM t-shirt...only that stood for West Edmonton Mall.

The highway west to Jasper is so scenic. But the Icefields Parkway from Jasper south to Banff was literally indescribable. Glaciers were everywhere as well as beautiful lakes and forests. We even came upon a huge porcupine lumbering along the roadway. Posts on the walkways indicated how fast the glaciers are melting. In Banff we rode the tram up a mountain for a breath-taking view of the vicinity. We saw up close several elk as they swam the river, climbing up the bank right by the highway bridge.

It was in this area that we drove a scenic road out to a beautiful lake. The water was a glacier bluish-green. Heavy snow and ice was everywhere but the roads were clear. Coming from a vista we walked carefully "with our claws out." I was ahead and when I looked down I saw a handrail sticking up from the ground an inch or so, showing how deep the snow was on the steps! I made it down and told the others to look for that and to use extra caution. I started the video camera rolling. Marcia and Johnnie made it alright, but both of Bart's feet left the ground at the same time. For a split second he was suspended in air flat of his back and that's the way he landed! Thank the Lord that nothing was hurt except his pride.

We went by Wells Gray Provincial Park to see lots of waterfalls, deep canyons and sharp peaks. On the return trip we had to wait 20 minutes or so while a crane lifted a tree and other rubbish from the upper side of a bridge over a roaring river. East of Kamloops we traveled a beautiful area where sheds were built OVER the highway so that avalanches or landslides would not block it. We spent a second night in Golden.

We love Montana. Twice we have gone by the Little Big Horn to see where Gen. Custer made his last stand. We have dear friends who live near Troy in the extreme northwest corner near Idaho and Canada. Her name is Carolyn Hudlet. She and her husband Herb were building a retreat when he passed away. The family kept working till it was finished. There are about twenty log cabins and a 2-story building for classrooms and meals. When we were there a fly fishing clinic was in progress. Regardless of who comes, Bonnie, her daughter says they always have Bible study and prayer-time after breakfast.

We met Carolyn because she had used my instrumental books for years. She called the family to her house; we had a meal then a great time of fellowship. One year the snow reached to the gutters. She got so tired of seeing nothing but white at the windows she taped beautiful landscape scenes on them! I believe she is 80+ and still enjoys water skiing and traveling.

South of their place is a park preserving absolutely huge cedar trees and further down the road north of Missoula is a big game preserve. One time we were driving through it and a black bear cub seemed to be watching for someone to drive by. He ran up in front of us and climbed up a pine tree trunk a few feet, then leaned back looking at us while we made its picture. There are many buffalo there as well as deer, elk and other animals. East of Great Falls, there are numerous rapids and falls on the Missouri River. A couple of miles on down there is a large spring that makes what is claimed to be the "shortest river in the world." It runs perhaps 50 yards and empties in the Missouri. A fish hatchery is there also.

THE SINGING NEWS ARTICLE

In the January 2001 edition of "The Singing News" is Roy Pauley's column *"IN MY OPINION."* It was titled "The Great Songwriters." He listed ten writers and a song they had written. They were:

LeeRoy Abernathy – "Who Could Ask for More?"

Ken Apple – "He's no Longer a Stranger to Me"

Albert Brumley – "If We Never Meet Again"

Bill & Gloria Gaither – "It is Finished"

Stuart Hamblen – "He Bought my Soul at Calvary"

Mosie Lister – "His Hand in Mine"

Elmo Mercer – "Till There Was Jesus"

Joe Roper – "A Sinner's Plea"

J. D. Sumner – "I Can Feel the Touch of His Hand"

It was certainly nice to be included on Roy's list of composers. Remember, that was "In HIS Opinion"!

ABIGAIL GRACE MERCER

We call her Abby. In Hebrew the name **Abigail** means *Source of Delight.* She has been that alright from Day One. Her day-old baby picture is perfect. She was born in the north tower at Baptist Hospital here in Nashville on December 12, 2000. Her mother was Beth, Renee's oldest daughter. Beth was shot and killed April 27, 2005 after a drug deal turned robbery. Abby was just four and a half years old. She calls Bill and Renee Daddy and Mama. Marcia is "Nana" and I am "Papa"...to all our grandchildren.

She has always lived in our big house with all of us. Bill and Renee live in the original split-level part; Marcia and I made our apartment in the big garage we added on after we moved out here. We've added another bedroom along with a wood burning fireplace. Kellye moved back home from Florida in late 2011 and refurbished two rooms and a bath upstairs. We have all our family together again!

Abby is a very bright and talented girl. She makes good grades in school. Like all the other granddaughters she went the first four years to Gower Elementary on Old Hickory Boulevard about two miles from where we live. She is presently attending H. G. Hill Middle School, located next to Hillwood High where she will go next. Courtney and Hailey graduated from Hillwood and are a senior and sophomore at UT-Chattanooga in autumn 2013.

When Abby was big enough to sit on a swing seat we would go out to the playground several times a day. I would teach her songs like "Jesus Loves Me," "Jesus Loves the Little Children," "One, Two, Three the Devil's After Me," etc. She especially liked "How Much is that Doggie in the Window?" One day I was swinging her and an 18-wheeler down on I-40 (650 feet to our east) began "jake braking," making a terrible noise. Alarmed she asked, "What is that?" I explained it to her and said I wish the police would make them stop doing that. (Even some small towns, especially out west have signs forbidding it). The next day we were out there and heard it again. She looked at me and said, "Police ought to make 'em stop doin' that!" BTW, our land borders I-40 for over 2,500 feet, from the pond to the ridge where the cell towers are.

I would teach her the alphabet, and that little song helped. I taught her numbers and even the meaning of humidity. We would talk about lots of subjects: trees, animals and the sky. She can spot jet passenger planes long before I can. She loved to play on the slide and swing from the monkey bars. She would do all kinds of bounces on the trampoline. In the summer of 2012 we bought yet another pool – this one is 18 feet in diameter and 52 inches deep, above ground. She loves it.

Abby loves all kinds of books, like Dr. Seuss and any Disney book (Lion King, etc.) are favorites. She learned to read before starting kindergarten and retains a lot of what she reads. She loves to work puzzles, play card games and dominoes (she always wins). She can also play a game called "Three to Thirteen" and is very good. She has a talent to compose stories and she can draw anything, inserting lots of cute items I would never have imagined. She and Kellye enjoy walking together and tending to Kellye's two big dogs.

Her dog is named Payton and her cat is named Bella. Her future is bright indeed if she will study hard, listen and learn. She professed faith in Christ, was baptized and is a member of Scottsboro First Baptist Church. It's nice having her "next door" in the same house, as we get to visit often.

EARL'S FUNERAL

In 1983 Earl had triple bypass surgery in a Houston hospital. He was later diagnosed with Hepatitis C. Blood was not analyzed as closely back then, I'm told. He lived for nineteen more years. Fluid would frequently have to be drawn from his abdomen. While he was hospitalized in St. Francis Hospital in Monroe, Marcia and I visited him. Betty, David and Rachel were by his side when in a hospital bed at home by the den's sliding glass doors he died. I think I've told you about that bird clock in their dinette area that scared me one night when it sounded off. They told me the clock "went off" and he smiled…and took his last breath! This was two days after his 77th birthday in 2002. Betty died five years later on the SAME day…September 9th.

Earl had his funeral planned and told me in their hallway one night NOT to play "Precious Memories" or "Life's Railway to Heaven." He typed out a statement, sealed the envelope and gave it to the Funeral Home director. He was to give it to Betty at his death and she was to give it to their pastor to open and read at the funeral service. His long-time friend Clarence Powell got up to speak and looked at me and said, "Elmo, I must tell you when I met you I was disappointed." I looked shocked and he continued, "Why, the way Earl talked about you I just knew you had to be nine feet tall and you weren't!" Earl told me to sing my song "I Do Not Ask" which was one of his favorites. Their son David sang, as did his grandson Jeremy.

Then their pastor told the audience about Earl's envelope and said, as he tore it open, "Let's see what Bro. Earl has to say to us." Earl talked about his love for Betty, their son David and their daughter Rachel. Then he said, "As pastor I always have the last word in a service and I see no reason to change now. You know, when you eat a nut, the shell is left. So it is today, all you see here is the shell...the NUT has gone!" Everyone laughed. He was buried by Betty's parents at Spearsville northwest of Monroe. Five years later Betty joined them. They used to drive up there to eat at a GREAT fish place. Our mutual friend, James Miller now pastors the church there and had Marcia and I come do a concert. We walked across the road to eat Sunday lunch at that fish place.

Each year when Marcia and I go to her family reunions (Fletcher and Boyd) and our high school reunions we stop by Monroe to see Rachel. Usually Clarence Powell and his wife Leatha will join us at "Charlie's Catfish" on Louisville Avenue. We always look forward to the meal and fellowship.

LITTLE LEAGUE WORLD SERIES

Marcia and Johnnie's brother Bernard retired from the Navy after 27 years and stayed in San Diego. He started volunteering in Little League baseball as an umpire. Soon he became head of umpires in District 32. He worked his way up through district and regional playoffs and eventually earned a place as umpire at the Little League World Series in South Williamsport, PA. This was in the summer of 2005.

Johnnie and Bart, Marcia and I drove up there, although we arrived about half-way through the tournament. We had a marvelous time and encourage you to attend if you can. Admission is FREE. We had to miss the championship game because we had to drive down congested state highway 15 to Harrisburg for a Sunday night concert. Later we were invited back by the same pianist, but she was at a different church in the city. We met her parents who taught at a seminar that Earl and Betty had attended several years before!

MINNEAPOLIS ADVENTURE

Marcia and I were passing through Minneapolis, MN one day and wanted to go to Minnehaha Falls Park. The 53-foot falls was noisy and beautiful. The beautiful Longfellow house is on the grounds. There is a statue of Hiawatha carrying Minnehaha in his arms. We wanted to see it and make a snapshot of it but by the time we found it darkness had fallen.

A young man on a bicycle asked if he could help us. He wore a backpack and was eating some pizza. We later wondered if he might have been homeless. He said he would be glad to show us where the statue was. He laid his bike down and started down a darkened pathway. I followed, somewhat apprehensive of what could happen, and Marcia stayed back even further. I hoped he wouldn't mug me. He showed me the statue and I made the picture, which didn't come out.

When we got back to where Marcia was he asked me, "Will you pray for me?" I said I would and asked him his name. He looked at Marcia and asked if she would pray for him, and we realized he meant *right then.* The three of us held hands and I prayed for him. Perhaps I missed a chance to win him to Christ, I don't know. Of course we never saw him again but have often thought of him.

We enjoyed going to the huge Mall of America in the southern part of Minneapolis on a previous trip when Johnnie and Bart were with us. It is unbelievable. It even has a roller coaster inside it! There are perhaps five or six levels to it. I mentioned earlier that we have been to the big Edmonton, Alberta, Canada mall, and it is even bigger. I read an article the other day about the huge malls of the world, and Mall of America did not even make the top ten!

NOW WHY DID I SAY THAT?

Kellye and her family flew out to Denver in 2005 when we were spending three weeks in that log cabin at Allenspark, CO. The elevation there is 8500 feet, a thousand feet higher than

Estes Park, the eastern entrance to Rocky Mountain National Park. We took them to Colorado Springs and rode the cog railway up Pikes Peak.

On the way back up I-25, our '99 Olds Silhouette had problems. I managed to pull into a well-lit Rest Area about ten miles south of Castle Rock. Kellye's husband Bruce discovered the belt had not only broken but had bent the tension arm. I phoned AAA and they sent a tow truck from Castle Rock. When he drove up and got out I said, "Hi, we're from Texas." WHY DID I SAY SOMETHING STUPID LIKE THAT? I looked behind me where Kellye and the three kids stood under a light and said, "Why did I say THAT?" They were already hysterical!

A car rental company at the Denver airport said they could not send a car that distance. We couldn't have all gotten in one car anyhow. We finally talked the tow truck driver into letting us ride with him or we would have been stranded overnight at the Rest Area and it was cold! He got the van on the carrier, then Marcia, BJ, Joey and Kayla climbed up and got inside. They were told to "lay low". Bruce, Kellye and I rode in the cab with the driver.

We had a time getting BJ into the van. He said, "Mom, this is not right. You've always told us that God would take care of us." Kellye said, "He has! Now get in!" We spent the night in a motel one block from a NAPA store. The next morning Bruce bought what was needed and fixed it and we were on our way again. We made a trip over Snowy Range Pass on SR-130 west of Laramie, WY then spent the night in the cabin. The next morning we drove through Estes Park, then through Big Thompson canyon to the "Dam" Store and on to the Denver airport. It is a very modern structure.

We never were able to make extended vacation trips with Bill and his family.

At Fort Hood, TX I made another stupid statement! Kellye's younger son Joey (Army Lieutenant, 1st Cav) had just returned from Afghanistan and we were there to greet him. We ate on base and after I paid and picked up my tray I told the girl at the register (nodding at Joey) that my grandson was in the group that just returned from Vietnam today. I took a couple of steps, looked back at her and said, "Did I say *Vietnam*?" She smiled and said yes. I said I mean Afghanistan and she said, "I knew you did!" Egads! I used to think I'd be alright…but I'm not too sure anymore!

Let me expand on this story. All three of Kellye's kids graduated from UCF (Central FL) in Orlando, second only to Arizona State in enrollment. Joey passed all tests to enter the Air Force. When the first call was made he was not on the list. It had been three years since he got his degree but he had not found a job in his field. He had become a certified soccer referee (volleyball and basketball also) and continued to Valet park cars at an Orlando hospital.

So he joined the Army! He did basic training at Ft. Benning, GA then stayed there for officer's training and was put in the

Signal Corp as a 2nd Lieutenant. He went to Ft. Gordon in Augusta, GA and from there he went to Ft. Hood, TX. He knew he would be deployed to Afghanistan. BJ (Bruce II) and Allison Weber were to be married March 10, 2012 and naturally BJ wanted Joey as his best man. We prayed that would happen. Thursday before the Saturday wedding Joey got the call on his cell phone that Sunday night at 11 pm he and others would fly out of Ft Hood! God answered our prayers, plus He brought him back safely.

We were all at Ft. Hood when he returned including his Dad Bruce and grandmother Catherine Jeffers. We have seen such occasions on TV many times but we were *involved this time!* There were 323 men in formation and people filled the stands. After a chaplain's prayer, the CO made a short statement to the troops – a job well done, welcome home, etc." and then he counted, "Three, two, one…CHARGE!" Bedlam broke loose!

BJ had made a big sign, "Welcome Home, Joe Cool". That's what we called him – remember those camel billboards? They finally found each other and pointed to Marcia and me in the stands. We had a great couple of days together. Joey is supposed to be at Ft. Hood for at least two years, except in October 2013 he is due for another deployment. I told him I hoped it wasn't Syria, Iran or North Korea!

COLLEEN COBLE

I encourage you to read fiction books written by Colleen Coble. I e-mailed her one day after reading her *Rock Harbor* series to say how much I enjoyed it. I told her I was the retired music editor for Benson and had written "Each Step I Take," and "The Way that He Loves." In a couple of hours her reply came saying the first solo she sang in church was "The Way that He Loves".

She and Dave, her husband, were passing through Nashville on their way to Atlanta. We met at the Santa Fe restaurant near Opryland Hotel. Traveling with them was Diann Hunt (also a well-known writer) and her husband.

Later Colleen had me pre-read her new book, "Fire Dancer," and asked me to write an endorsement. I did and it appears in the front of the book along with others. I was honored to have that privilege.

TWO PREACHER FRIENDS

We met Bro. Hiram Lemay after we'd lived in Nashville a short while in the early 60s. He was pastor of Grace Baptist Church in east Nashville. He had us there for a banquet one night. As I got toward the end of my song "The Sweet Days of Yore" Hiram began shouting! It had touched him somehow.

Through the years we have kept in touch as God led and blessed. In 1977 Hiram preached a revival with his son Mark leading the music. I played the piano. Mark at the time was in the landscaping business. I bought six Southern White Pine trees about five feet tall and set them out in our front yard here in Thousand Oaks Estates.

I should never have put one so close to our house. It was over two feet in diameter when in August 2010 a tornado (or some kind of strong, swirling winds) popped it off about halfway up. The top fell on our den and bedroom knocking down the chimney. Several trees were blown down on the steep hill immediately behind our house also. We were on a mid-Atlantic tour with Kellye and her son Joey who had already enlisted in the Army. State Farm Insurance had the two-foot diameter trunk cut down before we got back home. Had I been in bed it would have killed me. The front of the house had to be rebuilt as well as the chimney and a new fire box installed. New carpet had to be put down in both the den and bedroom because of broken glass. We had to move EVERYTHING out of those rooms! We had passageways through our apartment and before it was completed we left for Colorado! It was depressing and frustrating. Anyhow, in 2012 Hiram published his autobiography and we enjoyed reading it so much.

When we would be at our condo in Okeechobee for the winter months, Bro. Marshall Phillips and his wife Dorsey were frequent visitors. In fact, one year he was interim pastor at FBC. They are from Kentucky. He puts on an excellent and entertaining program. He plays guitar and sings some funny songs. He is a master storyteller and a lot of them are true. Sometimes he will cause you to laugh uncontrollably and other times you get caught up in events that occurred during their 14 years as missionaries in Kenya and Tanzania, East Africa. He speaks Swahili fluently.

In 2012 Marshall published a book about their lives and how God blessed and led them all the way. I took renewed interest in finishing my own autobiography after reading theirs. I had actually started it in 1996! You are almost finished reading it now. Thanks.

ANTHONY BURGER

Anthony has quite a background, but one thing is certain: he took his God-given talent and used it for His glory. We met him when he did his first (of three through the years) concert at FBC Okeechobee. We later enjoyed him at the first 3-day taping of Homecoming Friends at Bill Gaither's studio in Alexandria, IN. His second concert in Okeechobee was right before Christmas and he featured the season's songs, both pop and sacred. As you know he sometimes plays with excellent sound tracks.

The third concert was about three weeks before his sudden death on a cruise ship. I was told as he ended Dottie Rambo's song "We Shall Behold Him," HE DID!!! What a way to go! His body was brought by helicopter to an Okeechobee funeral home for preparation to be shipped home.

Before the concert began as Marcia and I entered a door into the back area just off the sanctuary where his merchandise table was set up, we could see him standing with his back to us. Several folks were gathered around. I said to one as I winked my eye, "What's the big deal anyhow about hearing this guy play a piano?" He looked around, shouted my name and gave us a hug.

Marcia and I sat in the balcony overlooking where he would sit and play the grand piano. His daughter sang a couple of songs beautifully and then Anthony began his program. After concluding the first piece he took the mike and approached the front of the platform and said, "I'm kinda nervous tonight. Somebody told me Elmo Mercer is here...where are you, Elmo?" I said, "I'm right up here in the balcony where I can watch your hands!" Anthony looked at the congregation and said, "Now I'm really nervous!" We all laughed.

Afterwards we had our picture made standing by the piano. He said, "Hey, this could be on the cover of our new duet album!" We both knew he was joking and laughed. Oh, how Anthony is missed by us all!

WEDDING ANNIVERSARIES

Bill and Kellye totally surprised us with a 45th anniversary. It was Donna Hilley's "job" to keep us occupied so she took us out to Hillwood Country Club for a while, for our anniversary! We had been invited over to their house. When we started to leave the HCC she said, "Oh, I almost forgot. I need to run by the church just a minute, do you mind?" We got there and as she started inside she stopped and said, "Y'all come on in, this could take a little while."

When we went through the double glass doors off "Pigeon Alley" and turned right into Temple Bible Class a host of people shouted "Surprise!" I mean "snowbirds" were everywhere as well as local friends and church members. It really was a surprise and we all just had a wonderful time of fellowship.

Then Bill and Kellye and our grandchildren DID have a 50th anniversary for us at Park Avenue (again). Several of those "snowbird" friends had passed away in those five years. Johnnie and Bart came, as they have the same wedding date but are four years behind us. {Marcia and Johnnie told their brother Bernard he needed to get married on October 2nd also. But an extensive background check was made on Keiko Uno, the Japanese woman he married. Her father was some kind of assistant to the Emperor and was killed right before the end of WWII. They could not meet the Oct. 2nd date.}

We made several large montages of pictures of Marcia and me from birth on up to the present. We included Bill and Kellye and their families, and even some of Johnnie and Bart, explaining our dates were the same. We were presented with all kinds of gifts.

I SWALLOWED A VOLCANO

One Friday morning in 2006 I woke up at 4 a.m. and thought I had swallowed a volcano! No medication helped. Finally at noon Marcia insisted I go to the Baptist Hospital ER. It was determined to be a gall bladder attack. I had never had any trouble before. {Marcia had about seven over a period of time. Once while we were in Okeechobee for the winter she had a bad one and Kellye set her up for an operation at Raulerson Hospital}.

Saturday afternoon the doctors were going to send me home and I said, "I'm not going anywhere. I'm still hurting!" Finally on Sunday afternoon they operated and the dadgum gall bladder had gangrene on it! It was starting to affect my pancreas, too! My room overlooked a famous donut place and I could just taste 'em!

A week later we were to go on two dates in Sturgis, MA in the north Boston area. Marcia insisted we get a motel and STAY THERE, driving to those two dates. We found a very nice "Mom and Pop" motel a couple of miles from the beach in Saco, Maine. After resting a day or two, we went sight-seeing around the Yorks area, including Kennebunkport (the Bush home), and also a JFK museum.

The first concert was at a Salvation Army Rehab Center which we did with mixed emotions. We met with the director and his wife (both Majors in the SA) in their office beforehand. We shared with them the tragedy of our granddaughter Beth. They insisted we relate that incident in the concert that night. There were about 100 men (most of them young, too) and 20 girls in the audience as we talked about Beth. Since then we tell that in many of our concerts, especially when there were children and youth present, warning them of the consequences of drug involvement. I remember after a South Carolina concert a lady came to me and said her grandson had committed suicide as a result of drugs. {People down through the years have told me how my song "Each Step I Take" has been a blessing to them. One lady said it was sung at her 12-year-old son's funeral – he had been killed while riding his bicycle.} Renee's second daughter Lindsey also became drug-dependent for a while but has successfully completed rehabilitation.

Another day we attempted to drive up Mt. Washington in New Hampshire but could not because of clouds. That was the third time we had not been able to go up! The other concert in that area was at a Nazarene Church (also in Sturgis) the following Sunday night, where Bro. Steve Pelechowicz was pastor. {He and his wife Sandy now live in Maine}. Afterward the concert we drove through the costly tunnel **under** the city of Boston to a motel on Cape Cod. The next day we drove up to the north end of the Cape. We headed south by-passing New York City. You know, there is beautiful scenery everywhere in these United States, and I'm glad Marcia and I have been privileged to see and experience much of it. I say again – God is so good.

MARTHA & TOM BRITT

Martha Britt was pianist at Hillcrest Baptist church east of Jackson, TN. She was familiar with my piano collections and called to see if Marcia and I would come do a concert. We went for a weekend, had a Saturday choir practice and great services that Sunday. We met her husband Tom Britt, News Director at the local Jackson TV station. Marty Phillips is the music director and his sister Jan Acuff is organist. Everyone was so friendly to us, and soon we were back again. The pastor Jerry Welch wanted us to move down there!

Tragically one morning as Martha and Tom were on their morning walk, they were hit by a car that left the scene. Martha was killed and Tom badly injured. The driver was later apprehended. I was honored to play and sing at Martha's funeral at Second Baptist church in Jackson. Tom was wheeled in on a hospital gurney.

A new grand piano was purchased for Hillcrest in her memory. I was privileged to play for its dedication.

WOLF CREEK PASS, CO

Johnnie and Bart were with us on a western trip when we spent the night at Wolf Creek Pass, CO. It was a nice 2-story motel. We were at 10,850 feet in the San Juan Mountains on US-160 between South Fork and Pagosa Springs. The office sign said that it closed at 10 p.m. We had all gone to bed except Bart when he came in and told us the commode was not flushing properly at all and that he was going to the office to get a plunger. He had removed his hearing aids so he could not hear Johnnie tell him the office was closed. He just waved and said, "I'll be right back," and went out the door.

In about ten minutes he came back in, not with a simple plunger, but with a plumber's "snake." He started cranking the apparatus, his elbows ricocheting off the walls. We were afraid he was disturbing any number of rooms around us. Finally Johnnie got up, went in and tapped his shoulder and signaled for him to STOP. He smiled and said, "I've just about got it." But after a few more noisy minutes Johnnie went in again. She told us she crossed her arms (like an umpire giving a "safe" signal) and said, "ENOUGH!"

Bart took the "snake" back to wherever he got it and returned to the room. It was now near midnight. He tried to slide the chain back on the door for perhaps five minutes. Marcia and I (in bed) were about to bust out laughing. Enter Johnnie again. She sat up in their bed and said loudly so he might hear, "What in the (bleep) is going on?" We didn't know if she was serious or being funny, but we exploded anyway.

During the night when we went to the bathroom (BP pills, you know) there was a sign Bart had printed saying we could use the commode but NOT to attempt to flush it! The next morning Bart, who always got up before the rest of us went to the office and got a key to another room so we could use the bathroom. It was at the opposite end of the building! Now picture this – we're walking, as fast as we could with our legs crossed, in anticipation of finding a commode that worked! For several years we did not talk about this around Bart…he had done his best. Now he will laugh about the incident that occurred at Wolf Creek Pass that night!

I believe I've mentioned that Johnnie and Bart have traveled with us on a lot of our trips.

THE DAVID JOHNSON SINGERS

David Johnson lived in Jackson, TN and started a 40-voice chorale aptly named "The David Johnson Singers." Some traveled quite a distance to practice and to perform. They made *beautiful music.* And they looked sharp in their evening gowns and tuxedos.

Our good friend, (Judge) Tommy Moore from Dresden sang in the group. He invited us down for a concert at "The Ned" in Jackson: named after Gov. Ned McWherter. It was a total surprise to me when David said to the audience the next song was titled "The Way that He Loves," written by Elmo Mercer and he was present. He said, "Come on up, Elmo and direct your song." Tommy's wife Carol was sitting by Marcia, but she was busy trying to revive me. I made it up on the stage. I quietly told the singers, "Hey, guys, I do NOT direct music. So just sing it like you practiced it, ok?" After the intro I gave the downbeat as professionally as I knew how. I felt like a bird with a broken wing, but I was in hog heaven, too! That night lives long in my memory.

THE DRIP AT LUNCH

One rainy day, Marcia, Donna Hilley, Connie Bradley, and Patsy Bruce (she and husband Ed Bruce wrote "Mamas, Don't Let your Babies grow up to be Cowboys,") went down to Christiana to eat lunch at Miller's store. It is located on US-231 between Murfreesboro and Shelbyville, the Tennessee walking horse town.

Every now and then a drop of water would fall from the ceiling onto Connie's plate! The others noticed it and said, "Connie! Move down this way." She replied, "It ain't botherin' me!" and continued to eat. Her husband, Jerry Bradley was Owen Bradley's son and head of Acuff-Rose Publishing Company, later bought by SONY. He asked me to map out a western trip for them one time.

Later, Patsy had Marcia and me down at her church for a Sunday afternoon concert. Fernvale Community Church at Leeper's Fork, TN was built in the late 1800s. A tornado destroyed it in the late 1990s but it has been rebuilt. The area is beautiful and is close to the Natchez Trace, a scenic drive (no trucks) from Nashville down to Natchez, MS.

A SURPRISE MEETING

For many years Don Marsh was Director of Publications at the Benson Company. He also wrote some well-known songs and orchestrated countless albums. He and his family visited us down on the Francis farm one Saturday in the mid-70s. Jim Van Hook followed Don in that position for a two years at our MetroCenter location. He left in November 1980 to found Brentwood Music.

It may have been twenty years later that Marcia and I went out to Opryland theme park to watch the fireworks show one night. We found the perfect spot for a good view as other people walked up. It was already dark. I tried to move a bench and a man stepped over to help.

He said to me, "You're Elmo Mercer, aren't you?" I said I was and he continued, "I'm Don Marsh. We used to work together at Benson. *I recognized your voice.*" Does that mean he wouldn't have known me otherwise? I HAD quit wearing my hairpiece, had grown a full beard and put on a few pounds, however!

THE EAGLE

Donna Hilley would sometimes invite Marcia to go with her to our NFL Titans' football games. At one game the man was there with his eagle that circles during the National Anthem and lands on his outstretched arm. Marcia and Donna said it was an awesome sight and experience.

Donna would call us to come over to their house and the four of us would go in their van to Gaylord Arena (now Bridgestone) to watch our NHL Predators play ice hockey.

ST. SIMONS ISLAND

In the 90s J. D. Davis was Youth Director at Park Avenue Baptist. Everyone loved him and his wife Ashley. He wrote a play called "Lucifer's Lies" that was really great. Our people performed it many nights, and buses would bring folks from surrounding churches. I encouraged him to get it published.

Later as pastor at Frederica Baptist Church on St. Simons Island (east of Brunswick, GA), he had us do music in a revival and Bro. Bob Mowrey to preach. We drove down together. The choir was great and we had a great meeting. One night we had a "low country boil," of shrimp, potatoes, corn on the cob, etc.

There was a causeway going out to Sea Island and we drove around it some. At the time privacy gates were under construction. I'm told the state of Georgia was paid for having paved the streets and it became a private gated community. It is also said to be the fourth richest zip code in the United States!

A few years after that J. D. and Ashley moved to Sparta, TN First Baptist Church. This is on the Cumberland Plateau and is surrounded by waterfalls. We had been there in revival before and J. D. invited us for another. We experienced a great revival.

THE MYSTERY DOG

I'll call him Herbert. He did yard work in Oak Lake Villas in Okeechobee where our condo was located. He drove an old Nissan pickup in which he had somehow installed a recliner for the driver's seat. I'd be out walking in the morning and see him coming toward me. He'd manage to poke his head out the window and say, "Hey! You know the Bible…what does it mean by…?" I witnessed to him often.

One morning as I passed a side road going to the condos behind the ones on the main street I heard loud talking and then hollering. Our eyes met about the same time and Herbert came huffing toward me. His eyes were big, he was sweating, his hair was disheveled and I could tell he was NOT a happy camper. He didn't stop till he was right in my face. Motioning with his hands he yelled, "If you don't keep your (bleep) dog outta my (bleep) yard I'm gonna kick his (bleep)!" We didn't even have a dog!

I said, "Herbert, it ain't MY dog; quit hollerin' at me!" He wilted. To be on the safe side a little black and white dog took off for more friendly neighborhoods. I then noticed another neighbor, I'll call him Henry (a deacon at First Baptist) standing between his and Herbert's house and he was just a-laughing! I went on home. That afternoon our doorbell rang and there stood Henry with a jar of pickles and a note that said, "Pickles for you from Henry and Sue!" Then he confessed that he had told Herbert the dog belonged to me!

The next day or so Herbert and I met up and I told him about Henry bringing us the pickles. Herbert said, "A (bleep) jar o' pickles ain't no (bleep) peace offerin'!" The First Baptist Church revival was held soon afterward and I told Herbert about it and invited him to come. He told me Monday that he wanted to come Sunday night but couldn't. He was there Monday night and I was glad to see him sitting in the back. Dr. Ron Herrod from east Tennessee was the evangelist. At the invitation time he asked everyone to bow their heads and close their eyes. Even I did as I kept playing softly. When he asked us to look up there stood ol' Herbert in the midst of several children. On Wednesday he came to me at church and said, "Where's that preacher? I want to see if he can help me to stop cussin'!" I believe he really got saved.

Kellye saw Jack Coker's daughter-in-law a few days later and told her, "Your dog almost got my Daddy in trouble the other day." She said, "Why, Kellye, we haven't lived over there in almost two years!" Do you reckon that little dog could have been an "angel in disguise," sent to lead Herbert to salvation?!

A VERY BRIEF SWIM

I told you earlier about doing two revivals at Isola, MS Baptist Church. Marcia DePriest was the minister of music. They moved down west of Carrolton into an old two story house they'd bought and refurbished. She had us at McCarley Baptist Church for two revivals also. The first one we stayed in the home of a man who was a contractor. He and his wife had a beautiful home, with a pool and pool house that we stayed in. Down in a pasture he had built a big lake. At church one night a busload of folks from the Isola church came and it was so good to see them.

We said our thanks and goodbyes on Wednesday night to the couple we stayed with. Marcia and I decided to sleep late the next morning and then drive on back to Nashville. I got up and told Marcia I was going to take a quick dip in that pool. Well, it's a good thing I got in at the shallow end, because when I pushed off into the deeper part, I SANK! Like an anvil! I mean, I admit I'd put on a few more pounds but that was ridiculous! The second revival there we stayed with Marsha and Tommy and really felt at home there with them.

BRIDGITT & DON DRYDEN

During our almost thirty years of spending the winters down in Okeechobee, FL we were privileged to meet a dedicated couple, Bridgitt and Don Dryden. They are missionaries with BIMI and have served faithfully in Haiti between 35 and 40 years!

They raised their family there and their son will one day be taking over.

The work is often assailed by those who will do anything to disrupt their ministry. Sometimes outright lies are told about them and/or church members. There is a lot of "voodoo" practiced there. The government is unsteady. The Drydens established a school that is training local men to start churches and pastor them. Occasionally groups of people from the U. S. (and especially First Baptist of Okeechobee) will go there for a week or two to help perform various jobs. The terrible earthquake was devastating to everyone. It occurred perhaps 150 miles south of their location.

More than once Marcia and I have enjoyed fellowship with Bridgitt and Don when they happened to be in Okeechobee (and the U. S.) for a few days. We've met them at Pizza Hut and talked for 2 or 3 hours. Please pray for this couple and their ministry there.

A KEY AND A PROTESTER

One Sunday at Park Avenue, Bro. Orgeron (the new pastor) invited a black preacher to speak in the morning service. His wife was to do the special music. Another black lady came over to me as we played the prelude and said, "Sister (so and so) is going to sing 'My Heavenly Father watches over me.'"

The time came and I played a beautiful intro in D flat. This lady starts out, "O Lord, my God…" and it hit me! O Lord, my God, I am a minor third HIGHER than "How Great Thou Art." She never found the melody. In fact I think she was on an alto part (good thinking). I tried to softly discover what key she was in. Once I thought I had it but she veered off another way. I began to slide off the bench UNDER the piano. After the service a lady told Marcia I had done the impossible...I had played between the cracks!

Our deacons were selected this way – a sheet of paper listed the names of men 21 years and older. You were to circle the names of those you wanted as deasons, up to a certain number. Some were shown to be already "on the board." I think they served one, two and three year terms, so the "personnel" was changing every year to some extent.

One man on the list was known to be "gay." Apparently his wife knew it and she made a sign of protest, tacked it on a stick and paraded up and down the sidewalk in front of our church during services. This went on awhile and she either gave up or the church put a stop to it.

A NEW YORK CITY JAM

On one of our trips to the northeast we decided to see as many MLB and NFL stadiums as we could. I don't recall the total but we saw a lot of them. We were leaving the Bronx after seeing the old Yankee Stadium when I discovered too late I was in the wrong lane approaching a toll gate. Big trucks would not let me change lanes so I approached the gate that prevented my passing through. At that time it cost $4.50 to cross a bridge or go through a tunnel.

I was in the "Easy Pass" lane, and of course we didn't have one. What can I do? We were approaching a condition next to "panic." I hit the button and my driver window went down and I lamely said, "Help!" A uniformed man – could he have been my Guardian Angel? – appeared and said to give him $4.50. Marcia is bouncing off her side of the van and he bent over and said, "Just be cool, lady." She gave me a five dollar bill and I said to just keep the change, but by all means to raise that gate in front of me. We got out of there!

On a trip to New England we did a weekend at Diamond Springs Baptist Church in Virginia Beach, VA. The pastor's daughter buys guitar picks and makes earrings with the words "Pick Jesus" on them. After the Sunday night service we went to a fast food place for food and fellowship. Marcia mentioned that our old camera (used film) needed to be replaced with the new digital kind. The pastor began showing Marcia how his worked, what to punch and stuff like that. He asked if she thought she understood and she said she thought that she did. He handed it across the table and said, "We're going to upgrade and we want you to have this one!" We used it on many of our trips.

PAUL FERRIN

We met Paul Ferrin in the early 60s after I went to work at Benson. For over 50 years now he and his wife Marjorie have faithfully served the Lord in various ways through their music ministry. They have traveled in many countries as well. In 1963 Paul made a beautiful choral arrangement of my song "Oh What a Price!"

In recent years they have been traveling the nation doing Old Time Gospel Hymn Sing. Marjorie plays beautifully on the organ and Paul is an outstanding concert pianist. Aren't you thankful that people like that use their God-given talent to glorify our wonderful Lord! They live in Colorado Springs and usually do one of those programs there each year. Paul invited us to attend one of them and we did with our friends Charles and Diane Roberts who live on 35 acres near Ft. Lupton north of Denver. It was held at the big beautiful Radiant Assembly of God church just east of I-25 in Colorado Springs. Paul and I had an idea.....

Their daughter sang two beautiful solos then Marjorie and Paul did a mini-concert. After that they started the hymn singing – great old songs we've known and sung through the years. After a while he said, "Do any of you remember this old song?" and Marjorie moved into the right key and he started singing the chorus of "Each Step I Take." The audience of some 2500 began singing. I was thrilled to listen.

Then he said, "Is there anyone here who remembers how the verse goes?" I hesitated but a moment then put up my hand. He stepped down and came to me with his cordless mike and said, "Alright sir, sing it for us." My mind went blank I was so excited! It was like the Lord said, "Come on, man! Remember the title!" Whew! I started singing the verse and Paul had the congregation sing the chorus again.

Then he said, "Sir, how is it that you recall this song so well?" I spoke into the mike, "Well, I'm Elmo Mercer and I wrote that song!" You could hear a loud intake of breath then the crowd burst into applause as they stood to their feet! What a memory! I am so grateful to Paul and Marjorie for doing that for us. Afterward we drove a couple of hours back up to the Roberts' home and stayed overnight with them. God is good!

SCOTTSBORO CHURCH

After leaving Park Avenue Baptist Church, Marcia and I visited many churches in Nashville. We even visited Vine Street Christian Church on Harding Road (historic) and actually got our best "reception" there. Several years before we did a concert at a senior adult meeting there. We attended one church near us several times. Before a service one Sunday morning a man greeted us and said his wife was the pianist. Every time she saw me in the congregation she just went to pieces! Well, we didn't want that to happen again and didn't go back.

We visited the First Baptist Church in the Scottsboro community. It is a country church, on Old Hickory Boulevard just north of Hwy 12 going to Ashland City. Our former PABC pastor Bro. Bob Mowrey is pastor there, actually since April of 2001, now the second longest pastorate in his ministry! He just could not retire. For two years he was interim pastor at

FBC Cookeville, TN; also for two years he was interim at FBC Sparta, TN. Out of about 185 churches in the Nashville Baptist Association, Scottsboro church consistently ranks somewhere around 10th place in the number of persons saved and baptized. The criteria is only five in one year! Many churches don't even make the list! How sad.

We have morning and night services on Sunday, supper and prayer meeting on Wednesday night, with various other activities during the week. We have a spring and a fall revival. Sometimes chairs have to be put in the aisles and the overflow crowd sits in the fellowship hall and watches closed circuit television. There is an active senior adult ministry called JOY (Just Older Youth); monthly meetings for women and for men. In the first week of June 2013 the church celebrated its 58th anniversary. A few years ago a tent was erected and after a great meal together, Dr. Bobby Welch brought an inspiring message.

The church needed someone to play piano (keyboard), so we attended there while I filled that need. Finally we moved our membership and enjoy the fellowship so much. Our motto is "Love Meets You at the Door" and it truly does. The membership is made up of all ages. One night at prayer meeting there were 136 present and 51 of them were children and youth, meeting separately. George Osment, his family and other helpers do a superb job preparing the meals for Wednesday night and on other occasions. Herschel Temple visits hospitals and shut-ins daily. There are many faithful members who perform needed jobs in the church – I will not attempt to name them.

On fifth Sunday nights we have a "singing extravaganza" that everyone enjoys. Our Sunday school attendance is from about 100 to 120. There is a lot of talent in the church, and not just in music. A new church directory was printed in the fall of 2012. A bunch of us usually go to Cracker Barrel on Charlotte Pike after church on Sunday night and many times softly sing "The Lord's Prayer" as our blessing on the food. It has become expected, actually. Some people from other churches sometimes join in with us.

God is at work in Scottsboro First Baptist Church.

THE DENVER AREA

We met CHARLES AND DIANE ROBERTS when they lived in Longmont, north of Boulder, CO. Johnnie and Bart were traveling with us and we spent the night in the Roberts' spacious basement. After our concert at East Boulder Baptist Church where they attended, Marcia and I felt we had done poorly because of allergies and the high elevation, and we admitted that as we walked to the van in the parking lot. Johnnie looked at Marcia and said, "You know, that's about the worst I ever heard you do!" Have mercy! Her own sister said that out loud! Bart wears a hearing aid and I'm sure he turns it off when we start sing, he's heard us so many times!

The Roberts had two boys and two girls, and now have a host of grandchildren, too. They took us through the only Celestial Seasonings tea factory and it is located in an area near the "Diagonal" highway 119. Flavors not selling well are discontinued and about five new ones are introduced each year. The tour was so interesting. They obtain tea leaves from all over the world. We came to a big steel door like to a garage. The guide told us the peppermint flavoring had to be kept there or it would permeate all the other flavors! He raised the door and invited us to step inside. I took two steps and the pungent smell almost knocked me down! It was fascinating to watch the entire operation. We ate lunch in their restaurant and bought several boxes of tea. We have taken other people there several times. The tour is free.

A mile or so on down the road is the only "Leaning Tree" greeting card company. We toured that also and it was very interesting, both outside and inside. That was the last time we saw Charles. He passed away suddenly right after that particular time. What an interesting and brilliant man he was! Diane continues to be a producer at Channel 3 in Longmont and we make a point to spend time with her when we're out that way. There is so much to see in the Boulder area and always to the west is the imposing Front Range of the Rocky Mountains. Boulder, like Denver, has an extensive park system to enjoy. Our CDs were pressed by **Tapes Again**, a company in Boulder. They have since relocated to Lafayette, LA. I recommend them.

Diane and Charles bought 35 acres on a sloping hill just north of Ft. Lupton north of Denver. They had us come sing at the First Baptist Church there a couple of times. After a few years they started attending a big church in Brighton, northeast of Denver where they became extremely active. We did a concert there as well.

Their daughter Kim, her husband Len and family live on the acreage and have a couple of horses. The prairie dogs are getting closer to their land and could pose a hazard for the horses with all the holes they dig. Jacob had to have several heart surgeries but is a robust youngster. His little sister is Jessica. A few years ago we were all eating dinner at a restaurant and Jacob, sitting across from me said, "Elmo?" I said, "Yes, Jacob." He said, "I love you!" In the fall of 2010 when we were out there and they met us at a quaint hotel for lunch overlooking the Estes valley. It snowed, covered the ground then melted off while we were there!

We sang at a church just north of 104th Street in Denver, Colorado. The first time Dean and Brenda Eades were with us. They played the dulcimers. The flagman we had met on Guanella Pass (near Georgetown, CO), Jamie Bent drove up from Bailey. We've kept in touch – in fact he and his daughter Ayla have visited us here in Nashville. They live in California now. On Mother's Day 2013 he called to wish Marcia a happy Mother's Day! Anyhow, Diane Roberts came to that Denver church also and we all had wonderful fellowship. The next year we were invited back and we enjoyed being there so much. Not long after we were there, the 72-year-old man who played the organ suddenly passed away. Then the lady who played the keyboard became seriously ill and spent many days in the hospital. By the way, we've not been invited back again....?

Allenspark is a little community at 8500 feet in the Front Range, sixteen miles south of Estes Park. There is no gas station or grocery store. Several quaint gift shops are there along with the US post office, a horse lot and a community church built out of logs. Marcia, Kellye and I have sung there. There is a little café a couple of hundred yards down the mountain that serves excellent breakfasts and lunches. Another very exclusive restaurant is nearby. I'm told that people fly in from other states to feast on their $120 entrees! Across the highway from it is a natural spring where the sign says you can "fill up your jug for a quarter!"

Just up the road from that big spring is a log cabin named Greenbrook that Marcia and I rented for three weeks in September 2005. It came about a ten inch snow. One morning I was in the living room and Marcia was still in the bedroom. Suddenly it sounded like an elephant fell on the roof and Marcia yelled, "What are you doing?" It was a big glob of snow that feel off an evergreen tree – they are so pretty with snow on them.

It was providential that we found this particular place. I went online and found Pinebrook Vacation Rentals, Sandy Nelson, proprietor. She manages about twenty in that general area – some for hunters, some for folks like us, and some are quite elegant. Sandy came over to meet us the next day after we arrived. We visited for perhaps two hours and she said, "If I cook supper, would you come over some night?" We did and not only enjoyed supper, but spent time around her piano then played a card game or two. The main floor of her house has a loft. Underneath is a full basement – two bedrooms with a bath in between then kitchen and den in a long room. She rents it out and it is named "The Refuge." Verandas are at each level.

It is just southeast of Mt. Meeker (looks like an Indian lying on his back) near the southeast corner of Rocky Mountain NP.

Marcia and I then had her over for home-made soup and cornbread. Sandy was raised in Minneapolis and had never eaten cornbread! We have become very close since then, united in Christian fellowship. Johnnie and Bart have been with us several times. Johnnie and Marcia refer to Sandy as their "little sister." One time Dean and Brenda Eades were with us when we stayed there while on a western tour together. Sandy had a little dog named Muffin that passed away a couple of years ago and a palomino horse named Blaze. One day we went in "The Egg and I" restaurant in Estes Park for a late lunch and there sat Sandy. We were to get to "The Refuge" the next afternoon. That is where we stay now – to be with Sandy.

I believe the first time we went to Colorado was 1969, Bill and Kellye were with us and we went on up to Yellowstone National Park in NW Wyoming. I fell in love with Colorado. I think during the Millennium I'm going to ask the Lord for 160 acres of green pastures with a stream running through it and a view of the snow covered Rocky Mountains. I believe I could enjoy that setting for a thousand years!

One Sunday after the service at the little log Community Church, several of us seniors drove down near Raymond to Peaceful Valley Resort to eat lunch. What great fellowship we had! There was snow and ice everywhere and as we were pulling away from the parking space one of the ladies stuck her leg out pretending to "thumb a ride." I put the window down and yelled, "Show me some skin!" She reached and pulled up her panst leg and I said, "I said SKIN, not support hose!" A couple of other times we drove up to Estes Park and ate at a nice restaurant on the River Walk by the Big Thompson River. Kellye, Marcia and I were at Sandy's place in late October 2012 and got snowed in for two days. The three of us sang special music at the church. Snow and big 5 foot icicles were everywhere. The church was filled that day. We went to Peaceful Valley.

West of Denver off SR-72 is the Moffat railroad tunnel under the Continental Divide. It is seven miles long and was completed in 1928. The day we were there it was COLD. Bart mentioned that he went through it on a troop train during WWII. It is said that the builders started on each side of the mountain drilling out the tunnel and met perfectly in the middle! That was an amazing accomplishment back then.

Just south of that is Central City and Black Hawk, historic mining towns in the 1800s. The poem "The Face on the Bar Room Floor" comes from Central City, if you've read about that. There are still lots of old mines and tailings all over the area, but it is mostly casinos now. We have eaten lunch at the Red Dolly many times. They have a $5.95 complete prime rib dinner. It started out a few years ago at $3.95. We go in, manage to make our way through the smoke and bell ringing, climb the stairs, eat and pay at the table then walk out!

If you're ever out there, you must drive the "Oh, my Gawd!" road from Idaho Springs (on I-70) up to Central City. You may have to get a local to tell you how to find it. We've done it twice. Do NOT drive DOWN it!

Colorado Springs area is so interesting and beautiful. You have Seven Falls, Garden of the Gods, Cliff Dwellings, Cave of the Winds, North Pole where you can drive up Pikes Peak if you want to...we didn't! Twice Johnnie and Bart were with us and we could not ride the cog railway because of snowfall.

Just west is the historic town of Cripple Creek. Our family visited it in the early 70s. The historic part is still there but a lot of casinos are nearby. My friend Jeff Jeffrey's father was town marshal there for six years when Jeff was young. Jeff and I worked at Benson together for many years. He was music director at Beech Cumberland Presbyterian church for several years, located between Goodlettsville and Hendersonville. It is on the National Historic Places list. Marcia and I have sung there a couple of times. He had an excellent 50+ voice choir and they loved my music! On our last visit Jeff presented me with a plaque of appreciation. Jeff had me to arrange the music for a July 4th celebration at Goodlettsville several years ago. He talked me into emceeing a concert by John England and the Western Swingers at a school there. What a night that was! Those guys are great.

THE "500 YEAR FLOOD"

The house Mrs. Francis gave us in August 1976 sits on a hillside at the end of Forrest Valley Drive. Believe me we never worried about being flooded...until May 1st and 2nd 2010. But the water came from the steep hill BEHIND us. We and all of Middle Tennessee got 30 hours of heavy rain! Even interstates had several feet of water over them in places. Property was destroyed. Even downtown Nashville flooded up to Fifth Ave North almost to the steps of the Ryman Auditorium!

Our usual seven card players were gathered at Charlsie Matthews' house in Brentwood that Saturday. We became concerned when Marcia and Bill Woodard noticed the sidewalk in back of her house disappeared. Bill and I decided we should move our vehicles around on the street in front of her house. We kept playing our game. After a while we looked out the front windows and the front lawn was under water! The decision was made for us to head for the hills!

Bill and I made several trips across the lawn to the vehicles that we moved (again) to a neighbor's driveway. The water was now just below our knees and we had to slide our feet along or the current would cause us to fall. I came back to the front steps to escort another person out but as I took a step backward I stepped in a much lower place and fell flat on my behind! Oh, well, I was wet already anyhow! I saw a long black snake curling along the surface near the vehicles but I didn't mention it! We got two blocks from Charlsie's house and I realized I'd left my glasses on her table. I made another trip and could tell the water was much higher.

Eventually it got up into Charlsie's house! Her daughter and son rushed over and retrieved memorabilia from the walls of the den. Her late husband Neal sang with the Jordanaires, made their arrangements and even played guitar every now and then. So they had plenty of pictures with famous people like Elvis and others they had backed up. It took almost a year for her house to be refurbished where she could move back in it.

Next morning was Sunday but forget about going to church. Bill and I got our industrial brooms and tried to sweep the water away from the back of our house. It was coming down off the steep hill, deep enough that 2x4s and other items were floating in the current! It went under the crawl space beneath "their" kitchen/living room and got into their den on the lowest level of the house. It even came in the front of our apartment that had been the double garage we added on to the split-level house in 1977. Our insurance paid for our losses. We are so thankful for that. This was referred to by the media as the "500 year flood!"

Many years ago the Opryland Theme Park was flooded and levies were rebuilt to 422 feet above sea level. But in 2010 the Opryland Hotel complex flooded with the level reaching 437.25 feet! Portions were under 15 feet of water. The stage of the Opry House had four feet of water over it. The nearby Opry Mills shopping mall had water to the roofline and it took over a year to be re-opened. Now about a 15 foot concrete wall is being constructed around the Opry House and the Hotel. Our son Bill has been on their security force there for many years and enjoys his work.

THE WAL-MART EXPERIENCE

I think it was in December 2010 that Marcia began having problems with another "trigger" finger. It would curl up and not straighten back out like it should. When she would force it, it would snap and hurt. We were grocery shopping at "our" Wal-Mart four miles east of our house.

Suddenly, a brightly-dressed black woman sashayed down the aisle toward us with outstretched arms proclaiming, "Merrrr-ry Christmaaas!" We were somewhat taken back and she said, "Well, it is, isn't it?" We agreed. She asked about Marcia's finger. The woman laid her hand on Marcia's on the buggy handle and said, "Let's pray." We heard shoppers going by us as she prayed.

Marcia thanked her and then said, "Have you ever heard the song 'Each Step I Take'?" She said NO and I fainted! No, just kidding. About that time, we assumed he was her husband, a man came around the corner into our aisle, leaning forward on the buggy's handle. She asked him. He said, "Sure, it's in E flat," and he moved his fingers like he was playing! I knew I had found a new friend! They couldn't believe I had written it when I was nineteen.

Here's the punch line: Marcia's finger never gave her any more problems! Do you think she was an angel in disguise?

On the other hand, it is amazing how people always come to talk with Marcia about their life's problems. A lady asked her one day, "Do you know where the stewed toma…" and not finishing the question looked at Marcia and moaned, "My husband left me last week!" her arms going around Marcia's neck. I mean, now look at that face…would you buy a used car from her? Yet, over and over again, people we don't even know will start talking and end up telling her their life stories.

THE NEWBILL FAMILY

We met Kay and Ray Newbill at Park Avenue Baptist church where they were very active members. We made Ray our auto and home insurance agent. They did the decorations for both Kellye and Bill's weddings at PABC. One summer they visited us at our Okeechobee, FL condo.

During their marriage they had over twenty foster children in their home. One night we were part of several friends they had over for supper and afterwards we sat around talking. Then Bill got to telling some of his experiences growing up, and at MTSU that we didn't even know about! We all laughed. Next day at church Ray told Marcia that at first he was quite upset. Then he realized our relationship was such that we could talk and laugh about it. He said he hoped to create such a relationship with all his "kids."

Kay asked me to sing a couple of songs at Ray's funeral at a Hendersonville church in 2011 and our mutual friend Ethel

Lunn accompanied me on the piano. After he sold his business they had moved there. It was good to see several of "their" kids there. We're glad the Lord brought our families together.

BRO. BOB AND PEGGY

Where do I begin to talk about these two dear friends? I've already mentioned them several times previously. We have been friends for decades. They've lived in their present house for over forty-two years. It has a big sloping front yard, but behind the house it rises sharply.

One day Bro. Bob lost his footing and somehow ended up setting down on his ankle, breaking it! It took some time for him to get over that. Meanwhile he preached from a wheelchair. It just occurred to me – I did not think to compose a poem about that incident!

Marcia and I were returning from Texas about two years after that. In the Little Rock, AR area Marcia called Peggy's cell phone number. She answered and said, "I can't talk right now, Marcia, I just broke my leg!" Marcia yelled, "**WHAT?**" I almost ran off the interstate! Peggy had just fallen in the SAME place Bro. Bob did and broken her leg! PTL! She had her phone with her. A plate and 27 screws were required during surgery. We told them to stay away from that part of their yard from now on!

We've known these two since the early 60s and are thankful God brought us together in service to Him.

IN MEMORY OF PERRY BAGGS

Perry grew up in Park Avenue Baptist church, was saved and baptized there. Later as an adult for about twenty years he traveled worldwide as the drummer for ***Jason and the Scorchers***, a Nashville country punk rock band. We saw them on Conan's late night show once. His bad health forced him to leave the band. He came back to Park Avenue and played drums in our church band for a while.

One Sunday after a service an elderly friend of ours, Mrs. Gerry Minnigh asked Marcia to introduce her to Perry. She told him he reminded her so much of her grandson. That was the beginning of a wonderful friendship between the two – they were good for each other. But before long, Gerry passed away. Perry told Marcia and me we were all he had left. That was sad.

Around 2009 Perry came to Scottsboro First Baptist Church where Bro. Bob Mowrey was pastor and I was leading the music from the keyboard. Since Robert Graves was playing drums, I invited Perry to play the electric bass, he played just about any instrument! Beth Cyrus was the organist. She also plays the violin. Her husband Andrew Cyrus – his dad is a first cousin of Billy Ray, plays piano and saxophone. They sing specials in our services. We often play from "The Best of Country-Western Hymnal," and "The Best of Gospel Hymnal," books that I compiled for the Benson Company years ago.

One Wednesday night in 2012 Perry did not come to church supper or prayer meeting. Katrina Cornwell, a close friend of his became concerned as did many of us. When a knock at his door went unanswered the police were called. {Perry had to go to Vanderbilt Hospital three times a week for dialysis and he was also a severe diabetic}. Upon entering his house they found Perry dead.

It was as though the Shepherd had gone out once more and found the sheep that had gone astray. Perry's back home now. Katrina arranged a memorial service held at Scottsboro. The church was packed and there were many music people who attended, including Jason and the band.

LADDERS ARE NOT "MY THING"

In the spring of 2009 I was cleaning out the gutters around our apartment. Usually I did that while sitting on the roof. This time I used an extension ladder, only I guess I should have extended it another rung! I was up high enough so my arms could sweep pine straw off the roof when the ladder slipped off the gutter and down to the brick wall. I just went over backward. I'm not sure if I passed out or not, but I remember laying there on the pine straw and grass and moving around some checking myself out, so to speak.

I got up and went in the house and told Marcia then got a drink, washed off my hands and went back outside. I had only a few more feet to go and the job would be completed. I'm up there again when Marcia comes around the house and announces, "I'm going to lay down some "ground" rules, so listen up!"

I ended up in Baptist Hospital ER. The doctor came in after some tests and said, "Well, I've got good news and bad news. The good news is your aorta is ok. The bad news is you broke your back!" I said, "WHAT?" A vertebrae was cracked and I had to wear a tight brace for a few weeks. I was cleared to make the trip to Austin, TX for Kellye's older son BJ's Master's Degree graduation at the University of Texas. I could not drive. We called and her younger son Joey changed his flight plan to come to Nashville and drive us. We picked him up at the airport around noon, passed our place on I-40 and spent that night in Texarkana, TX. I made the trip alright, PTL.

Perhaps a year later...can you believe this? I was climbing up the same ladder at the BACK of the house, which is by our front door. That doesn't make much sense, does it? I put my right foot on the roof but when I pushed off with my left foot the ladder slipped (not again?). My forehead hit the roof and as I started going down. I remembered the ground was concrete! I grabbed out with my left hand and caught the gutter and bent it somewhat. My feet fell through the rungs of the ladder. I was somewhat shook up but managed to call Marcia.

I believe she had seen the whole episode and came out the door just dying laughing. I hung on till she got control of herself and then she pushed a foot back onto a rung and I was able to climb down. Whatever I was going to do on the roof that day did NOT get done. But in May 2013 I climbed up on our apartment roof and cleaned out the gutters. Guess I'll never learn, huh?

IN MEMORY OF BERNARD FLETCHER

In September 2012 Marcia got a phone call from Leonard, her nephew. He said Bernard was in ICU in San Diego's Naval Hospital.

Kellye, Marcia and I took off for Houston to pick up Johnnie and go to San Diego. Before we got to her house Marcia got a cell phone call that Bernard had passed away. We left Houston (Katy) the next day and spent the night in El Paso. The next night we got to our hotel in the Mira Mesa part of San Diego. We had traveled some 2200 miles in three days. We stayed there three days and his two sons had the visitation on Monday for our benefit. The funeral was not until Friday. We got to meet and talk with many of his friends and learned a lot about his life there. Several told us he taught them how to umpire. They said "beneath his gruff exterior was a heart of gold." The week before, he had carried fresh flowers to his wife's grave as he had done for well over twenty years. We all miss him so much.

He was buried next to his wife, who had preceded him in 1988 as the result of a house fire. He had been retired only about ten days. She had attempted to put it out herself but passed away about two months afterward. Each week he would carry fresh flowers to her grave in that huge cemetery.

As with all our departed loved ones, we have "precious memories." I'm sure everyone does.

OKLAHOMA CITY BOMBING

Marcia and I have been to the Memorial in OK City three times as of November 2012. We went with Dean and Brenda Eades (Dulcimer couple from Seneca, SC) and with Marcia's sister Johnnie and husband Bart. The third time Kellye was with us on our return trip from visiting Sandy Nelson in Allenspark, CO. This was in Oct/Nov of 2012. We saw many different animals and birds on this trip. The Continental Divide was <u>white</u> and so beautiful. God is the master Creator!

Michael Harris worked in the Benson Art Department for several years. He drew a large caricature of me playing the piano...the keys flopping up, one foot in the air, hairpiece and mustache emphasized – it is hilarious. In 2011 several of us former Benson employees had a reunion, made possible by the efforts of Sue Buchanan. Paul Johnson, a well-known music composer and arranger came; also John III, his wife Jane; Peggy, Bob Benson's widow, Peggy and many others I will not attempt to name. In fact, we have had two such reunions and it's good to see each other.

Anyhow, Mike who lives in Lawton, OK now told us that he and a friend happened to be three blocks away from the federal building when the truck bomb exploded that day. It knocked their car side-ways a foot or so and they thought they had been hit by another vehicle.

By the way, while I was at Benson, an album was released of several of my songs, sung by different artists; also a 9x12 folio was printed. On the front Bob McConnell drew a picture of me. I asked him why he didn't give me more hair and he said he thought he was pressing his luck as it was! I liked to keep folks guessing… sometimes I had a mustache, sometimes a goatee, sometimes clean shaven, but once I started wearing the hair-piece I kept doing it for about ten years. When I became a grandpa in 1983 I tossed it in the corner. Then when I stepped through the door to the piano at PABC without it, I felt like I was stark naked! A lady told me that night after the service, "There was a man playing the piano this morning but he couldn't play nearly as good as you!"

I've always enjoyed playing parts, pretending to be something I'm not, in other words. When I was in the fifth grade, I won a $25 war savings bond for being Little Black Sambo. In my senior play in high school I was a cop. I borrowed the Army uniform and cap from Jim Russell and later worked with him at the bank.

At various churches, I have played different parts in plays: Floyd Cramer; TV program host; live host of a variety show; a wise old shepherd at Christmas. I have always been a "ham"… guess that's where Bill gets it.

SOUTHEAST KANSAS

My sister's younger daughter, Beverly and husband Walter Keener, convinced Gertrude and Dan to leave their dream home on the 160-acre farm south of Shreveport to move up near them in southeast Kansas. They both live in an earth house... glass is across the front and the rest is underground. They have a garden between them. The little town is Oswego. The terrible tornado to hit Joplin, MO went right over their area.

Walter is a bi-vocational pastor and got us dates in Chetopa down near the Oklahoma state line, also at Independence where he was interim pastor. We also sang at Gertrude and Dan's church in Oswego. We enjoyed our time with them. Both are in their eighties. Kellye, Marcia and I visited them in October 2012 on our way to Colorado.

In 2005 while staying at the log cabin for three weeks a bear came by and tore up a bird feeder. I sat up the next night by the window with our camera to get his picture if he came by again. About midnight Marcia woke me up and told me to come to bed! In 2012 another bear came by Sandy Nelson's house where we were staying at the "Refuge" and utterly destroyed a bird feeder! We witnessed two buck deer butt heads and horns near Rocky Mountain YMCA at Estes Park. We saw elk, moose, buffalo, big horn sheep and llamas but didn't see a bear!

I encourage you all to see the huge cross at Groom, TX east of Amarillo – the Palo Duro canyon just east of I-27 south of

Amarillo, and the Memorial at Oklahoma City. Although we are technically "off the road" we still travel a lot doing some church dates during the week, mostly for senior adults. We love to visit family and friends all over the country.

THE TRICKY GARAGE DOOR

Remember we play cards about once a month at Charlsie Matthews' house in Brentwood. In April 2013 she had a doctor's appointment and Marcia went by to pick her up. She was sitting in our van when Marcia set the alarm then ran out of the garage. But the door went back up. Charlsie said there was a laser beam a few inches off the floor. Marcia tried it again and jumped crunched over to keep from hitting her head on the door as it came down. Didn't work! I think she tried about five times and Charlsie is breaking up watching it all. Finally Marcia dashed to the door, stopped then quickly stepped high with each foot over the beam with her head bowed, too. Success! If that had been video-taped and put on youTube it would have gone viral!

SLAPPED AT WAFFLE HOUSE

In March 2013 I met Bro. Bob and Herschel Temple for breakfast at the Waffle House on Charlotte Pike across from Cracker Barrel where many of our Scottsboro folks go after Sunday night services. We were to attend a funeral that morning. Bro. Bob sat across from Herschel and me.

When our orders were brought Bro. Bob said, "Ma'am I need cream for my coffee, please." She said, "Sure, darlin'." Later Herschel told her he needed more syrup and she said, "Comin' up, sweetheart." I happened to notice she had not brought my glass of milk and told her. She brought it and said, "Here you go, buddy!"

There's something wrong with that picture! But wait till you read the next one!

THE BURGER KING RUB

The Sunday after Easter the Fletcher (Marcia's maiden name) family reunion is held and has been for decades. It is held now at the old home place near Verda, LA where her first cousin lives. Not many attend any more. Marcia and I left Nashville and my cell phone rang. It was my brother Ronnie asking us to run by their place in Crossett, AR. We had not seen him and Janice in quite a while. [We did and had a great visit]. But Marcia also planned to go to Burkes Outlet in Batesville, MS.

We decided to grab lunch "to go" at the Burger King nearby. I could eat my Whopper meal while she went in and shopped. I had gone out and got in our van when I heard an old man saying over and over again, "I'm gonna pass out!" He and his wife, I assumed, were parked right next to us to my right. I looked and saw Marcia coming toward us. She asked if they needed help. The lady said they had driven from St. Louis and he had a bad cramp. Meantime he was carryin' on, "I'm gonna pass out!" Their sliding door was open and he was leaning back on the seat.

Well, Marcia began rubbing his calf (!) and he yelled, "Further up!" She moved just above the knee and he said it again! She said to him, "Mister, I'll have you know I don't go around parking lots rubbing men's legs!" I was crackin' up sitting under the wheel. Marcia later fussed at me for not getting out to help. I told her there was already three people standing between our vans – there was no room for another person. He stomped his foot a few times, grabbed his cane and started for BK. I got out then to help him get over a wide curb in front of where we had parked which separated parking from the drive-through traffic. I got him inside but he refused to sit down! We noticed he was wearing a pin that said "He is Risen." I didn't introduce myself.

Marcia and I got outta there. I ate in the van as planned and after 20 minutes or so I saw Marcia approach the checkout. I cranked up and pulled in front of the exit door. After waiting a long time I got out and stood for a while. Finally Marcia came out and we drove on down I-55 to US-82 where we turned west toward Ronnie's house. I asked what took her so long at the checkout. She said the charge card machine "pen" would not let her write her name. The clerk said to use her finger. WHAT? Even the fingernail didn't work. They said to just make an "X" and somehow she did.

I exclaimed, "That's great, Marcia! Now if the FBI tries to trace you after rubbin' that ol' guy's leg, the trail will go cold because you signed with an 'X'." Don't you think? But that's still not the end of the story. We used that charge card not only twice in MS but also in LA. When she tried to use it in TX it was blocked! She phoned the company and they had stopped it believing someone had taken our card and was on a trip west! She got it straightened out and thanked them for their vigilance. That had happened to us before because we stayed on the road so much.

IN CLOSING…

I know I will think of a lot more memories that I forgot to include in this book after it has gone to press. I may have repeated a story or two – I just sat at the computer and typed it all, then tried to sort it out in a chronological order. I've enjoyed this project, started in 1996 when I typed about 130 pages. In the last year or so I decided to complete the project in case someone wanted to read it.

I tell folks I've told "might near ever'thing!" The rest is between me and God.

On February 15, 2014, I'll turn 82. As John W. Peterson's song says, "Jesus Led Me All The Way." Only thing is, sometimes I failed to SEEK and DO His will for my life and always messed up big time. The Bible tells us that God loves and chastens His children. Well then, I have assurance I belong to Him! You see, our relationship cannot be altered…I am His and He is mine! My wonderful Lord Jesus not only loves me and forgives me but He sends grace that is sufficient for my need! "Trusting Jesus, that is all."

Hey, I'm on a roll…I can't stop now! ***Thanks, God.***

"N E G L E C T"

(By W. Elmo Mercer)

I stood and viewed the old home place and wondered how it came
To such a shameful, run-down state: sure someone was to blame!
The roof was sagging helplessly, the chimney tottered so;
The old rail fence was half torn down, the well was mighty low.
Out in the field the weeds were high and all the trees were bare;
And then I ceased to wonder why – Neglect was everywhere!

I stood and viewed a human life bent low with care and shame;
How dark, I thought, must be his way and sin alone the blame!
No witness now was he at all by word of mouth or deed;
Yet day by day he lived right on in spite of his great need.
Some folks at church had things to do and so they passed him by,
It seemed Neglect stepped closer still to wait for him to die!

I stood and viewed another life o'er-flowing with God's love;
It seemed to me his face reflected sunshine from above!
And quick was he to testify of God's redeeming grace,
How Jesus came and on the cross took ev'ry sinner's place.
'Twas not Neglect on someone's part that helped him find the way,
But a faithful Christian – one who shared the gospel day by day.

ABOUT THE AUTHOR

Elmo and his wife Marcia live on fifty acres west of Nashville, Tennessee, along with their son and daughter. Now in his 80s he claims he is too young to be this old! He has no plans to slow down his daily routine as he enjoys being with family and friends while using his talent at his local church.

He would love to hear from you –

E-mail: elmomercer@aol.com
Web site: www.welmomercermusic.com
and on Facebook

This book is available directly from him, or Amazon.com, or your local Christian bookstore.